YOU DECIDE!
2006
Current Debates in American Politics

JOHN T. ROURKE

University of Connecticut

PEARSON
Longman

New York   Boston   San Francisco
London   Toronto   Sydney   Tokyo   Singapore   Madrid
Mexico City   Munich   Paris   Cape Town   Hong Kong   Montreal

Executive Editor: Eric Stano
Senior Marketing Manager: Elizabeth Fogarty
Production Cordinator: Virginia Riker
Project Coordination and Electronic Page Makeup: Lorraine Patsco
Cover Design Manager: John Callahan
Cover Illustration/Photo: Cover image courtesy of Getty Images, Inc.
Manufacturing Buyer: Roy L. Pickering, Jr.

Cover Printer: Courier Corporation

Library of Congress Cataloging-in-Publication Data
Library of Congress Control Number: 2005936241

Visit us at www.ablongman.com

ISBN 0-321-41108-0

345678910–CRS–08 07 06

CONTENTS

Ethnic Foreign Policy Lobbying: All-American Traditions

ADVOCATE: Yossi Shain, Aaron and Cecile Goldman Visiting Professor,
Georgetown University; Professor of Political Science, Tel Aviv
University

SOURCE: "For Ethnic Americans, The Old Country Calls," *Foreign Service
Journal*, October 2000

Also suitable for chapters on Political Culture, Foreign Policy

---

HILLARY CLINTON AND THE 2008 PRESIDENTIAL ELECTION:
THE DEMOCRATS' BEST BET *OR* A PROBLEMATIC CANDIDATE?

**Hillary Clinton and the 2008 Presidential Election: The Democrats'
Best Bet**

ADVOCATE: Carl Cannon, White House correspondent for the *National Journal*

SOURCE: "She Can Win the White House," *Washington Monthly.* July/August
2005

Hillary Clinton and the 2008 Presidential Election: A Problematic Candidate

ADVOCATE: Amy Sullivan, editor, *Washington Monthly*

SOURCE: "Not So Fast," *Washington Monthly*, July/August 2005

Also suitable for chapters on Elections

THE ELECTORAL COLLEGE:
ABOLISH *OR* PRESERVE?

The Electoral College: Abolish

ADVOCATE: Becky Cain, President, League of Women Voters

SOURCE: Testimony during hearings on "Proposals for Electoral College Reform:
H.J. Res. 28 and H.J. Res. 43" before the U.S. House of
Representatives Committee on the Judiciary, Subcommittee on the
Constitution, September 4, 1997

The Electoral College: Preserve

ADVOCATE: Judith A. Best, Professor of Political Science, State University of New
York at Cortland

SOURCE: Testimony during hearings on "Proposals for Electoral College Reform:
H.J. Res. 28 and H.J. Res. 43" before the U.S. House of
Representatives Committee on the Judiciary, Subcommittee on the
Constitution, September 4, 1997

Also suitable for chapters on Presidency, Federalism

11. CONGRESS 138

CONGRESSIONAL TERM LIMITS:
PROMOTING CHOICE *OR* RESTRICTING CHOICE?

Congressional Term Limits: Promoting Choice

ADVOCATE: Paul Jacob, Executive Director, U.S. Term Limits

SOURCE: Testimony during hearings on "Limiting Terms of Office for Members of the U.S. Senate and U.S. House of Representatives," U.S. House of Representatives, Committee on the Judiciary, Subcommittee on the Constitution, January 22, 1997

Congressional Term Limits: Restricting Choice

ADVOCATE: John R. Hibbing, Professor of Political Science, University of Nebraska

SOURCE: Testimony during hearings on "Limiting Terms of Office for Members of the U.S. Senate and U.S. House of Representatives," U.S. House of Representatives, Committee on the Judiciary, Subcommittee on the Constitution, January 22, 1997

Also suitable for chapters on Elections

12. PRESIDENCY 150

QUALIFIED TO BE PRESIDENT:
NATURAL-BORN CITIZENS ONLY *OR* ALL CITIZENS?

Qualified to Be President: Natural-Born Citizens Only

ADVOCATE: Matthew Spalding, Director, Center of American Studies, The Heritage Foundation

SOURCE: Testimony during hearings on "Maximizing Voter Choice: Opening the Presidency to Naturalized Americans," before the U.S. Senate Judiciary Committee, October 5, 2004

Qualified to Be President: All Citizens

ADVOCATE: John Yinger, Professor of Economics and Public Administration, The Maxwell School, Syracuse University

SOURCE: Testimony during hearings on "Maximizing Voter Choice: Opening the Presidency to Naturalized Americans," before the U.S. Senate Judiciary Committee, October 5, 2004

Also suitable for chapters on Civil Liberties, Political Culture, Elections

13. BUREAUCRACY 164

THE DEPARTMENT OF EDUCATION AND TITLE IX:
CHAMPION OF EQUALITY *OR* OVERZEALOUS CRUSADER?

The Department of Education and Title IX: Champion of Equality

ADVOCATE: Judith Sweet, Vice-President for Championships and Senior Women
Administrator, National Collegiate Athletic Association

SOURCE: U.S. Department of Education, Secretary's Commission on
Opportunity in Athletics, Hearings, August 27, 2002

The Department of Education and Title IX: Overzealous Crusader

ADVOCATE: Amanda Ross-Edwards, Visiting Professor of Political Science, Fairfield
University

SOURCE: "The Department of Education and Title IX: Flawed Interpretation
and Implementation," an essay written especially for this volume,
October 2003

Also suitable for chapters on Civil Rights, Education Policy

16. ECONOMIC POLICY   206

CONSTITUTIONALLY REQUIRE A BALANCED BUDGET: FISCAL SANITY *OR* IRRESPONSIBILITY?

Constitutionally Require a Balanced Budget: Fiscal Sanity

ADVOCATE: William Beach, Director, Center for Data Analysis, Heritage Foundation

SOURCE: Testimony during hearings on the "Balanced Budget Amendment" before the U.S. House of Representatives Committee on the Judiciary, Subcommittee on the Constitution, March 6, 2003

Constitutionally Require a Balanced Budget: Fiscal Irresponsibility

ADVOCATE: Richard Kogan, Senior Fellow, Center on Budget and Policy Priorities

SOURCE: Testimony during hearings on the "Balanced Budget Amendment" before the U.S. House of Representatives Committee on the Judiciary, Subcommittee on the Constitution, March 6, 2003

Also suitable for chapters on Constitution, Congress, Economic Policy

17. CRIMINAL JUSTICE POLICY   218

THE DEATH PENALTY: RACIALLY BIASED *OR* JUSTICE SERVED?

Racially Biased

ADVOCATE: Julian Bond, Professor of History, University of Virginia and Distinguished Professor-in-Residence, American University

SOURCE: Testimony during hearings on "Race and the Federal Death Penalty," before the U.S. Senate Committee on the Judiciary, Subcommittee on Constitution, Federalism, and Property Rights, June 13, 2001

Justice Served

ADVOCATE: Andrew G. McBride, former U.S. Associate Deputy Attorney General

SOURCE: Testimony during hearings on "Race and the Federal Death Penalty," before the U.S. Senate Committee on the Judiciary, Subcommittee On Constitution, Federalism, and Property Rights, June 13, 2001

Also suitable for chapters on Civil Rights

18. EDUCATION POLICY   230

AFFIRMATIVE ACTION ADMISSIONS: PROMOTING EQUALITY *OR* UNFAIR ADVANTAGE?

Promoting Equality

ADVOCATES: 41 College Students and 3 Student Coalitions

SOURCE: Amicus Curiae brief to the United States Supreme Court in *Grutter v. Bolligner* (2003)

EXTENDED CONTENTS

WEB ISSUES

The following topics are available on the Web at:
http://www.ablongman.com/YouDecide/

Regulating the Campaign Finance Activity of Nonprofit Organizations: Oppressive Restriction

ADVOCATES: 415 civil rights, environmental, civil liberties, women's rights, public health, social welfare, religious, consumer, senior, and social service organizations

SOURCE: "Comments and Request to Testify Concerning Notice of Proposed Rulemaking on Political Committee Status, e-mail letter to the Federal Elections Commission, April 5, 2004

Suitable for chapters on Bureaucracy, Civil Liberties, Elections, Interest Groups

---

26. TORTURING TERRORISTS

SOMETIMES JUSTIFIED *OR* ALWAYS ABHORRENT?

Torturing Terrorists: Sometimes Justified

ADVOCATE: Robert G Kennedy, Professor of Management, University of St. Thomas

SOURCE: "Can Interrogatory Torture Be Morally Legitimate?" paper presented at the Joint Services Conference On Professional Ethics, U.S. Air Force Academy, January 2003

Torturing Terrorists: Always Abhorrent

ADVOCATE: Lisa Hajjar, Professor of Sociology, Law and Society Program, University of California–Santa Barbara

SOURCE: "Torture and the Future," *Middle East Report Online*, May 2004

Suitable for chapters on Civil Liberties, Criminal Justice, National Security Policy

PREFACE

To the Students

This book is founded on two firm convictions. The first is that each of you who reads this book is profoundly affected by politics, probably in more ways than you know. The second "truth" is that it is important that everyone be attentive to and active in politics.

POLITICS AFFECTS YOU

The outcome of many of the 20 debates in this printed volume and the 6 supplemental debates on the Web will impact your life directly. If you play college sports, for example, the controversy over Title IX in **Debate 13** has and will help determine what teams and athletic scholarship support are available at your school. Similarly, the issue of affirmative action in **Debate 18** may influence your admission to graduate school, if that is the course you take. More generally, **Debate 16** over whether there should be a balanced budget amendment to the U.S. Constitution will play a role in what taxes you pay and what services you receive from the government. Such an amendment might, for example, reduce the availability of Pell Grants and other financial support for college students. It is also college-age students who are most likely to be sent to and to die in wars. There has not been a military draft since the Vietnam War era, and U.S. casualties in wars have been relatively few since then. But in that war, 61% of the more than the 58,000 Americans killed were between the ages of 17 and 21. Now, after many years, there is renewed talk about a draft, in part because the U.S. military is having trouble meeting its recruitment goals amid its ongoing involvement in Iraq, featured in **Debate 19**.

Freedom of religion is one of Americans' most cherished rights and is protected by the First Amendment. But the application of the First Amendment is something of a double-edged sword. There is widespread agreement that people should have the right to whatever religious belief they may hold. What is controversial and presented in **Debate 4** is whether the courts have taken the language in the First Amendment barring the support of religion by the government too far and are frustrating the ability of those who wish to express their religious beliefs publicly in such settings as school assemblies.

PAY ATTENTION TO THE POLICY PROCESS

Process may seem less interesting than policy to many people, but you do not have to study politics very long to learn that *who* decides something very often determines *what* the policy will be. Process does not always determine which policy is adopted, but plays a large role. Therefore, there are a number of debates in this volume whose outcome does not directly affect a specific policy, but which could have a profound impact on the policy process. For example **Debate 2** on Federalism may seem abstract, but one of the cases on which the debate turns involved whether or not California could legalize the use for medical reasons marijuana grown and distributed entirely within the state. Washington opposed the California measure and claimed that it could regulate the drug under the interstate commerce clause, and the Supreme Court had to decide the issue in a case about the division of power between the Washington, D.C. and the state governments in the federal system. **Debate 22** also addresses federalism, and one advocate proposes to diminish the traditional power of the states to determine marriage law by amending the Constitution to bar marriages between homosexuals.

Policy is also a reflection, in part, of who serves, and Debates 9, 10, 11, and 12 all focus on that issue. The Democrats have now lost two presidential elections in a row and are a minority in both Houses of Congress, and **Debate 9** takes up whether the Democrats have the best chance of reversing their losing streak by making Senator Hillary Rodham Clinton (D-NY) their presidential nominee in 2008. If the Electoral College had been earlier abolished, which is the topic of **Debate 10**, then Al Gore, not George Bush, would have won the presidency in 2000. Both advocates in **Debate 11** argue they want to give you more choice as to who will represent you in Congress. One advocate says the way to do that is to limit the term of federal legislators so that there will be a regular turnover. The other advocate replies that doing so will limit your ability to be represented for many terms by an effective legislator whom you support. **Debate 12** explores who can serve in the country's highest office, the presidency. Arnold Schwarzenegger may have been elected as governor of California, and Jennifer M. Granholm may be the governor of Michigan, but as foreign-born citizens both are constitutionally barred from becoming president. Should that barrier be eliminated? **Debate 23** takes up changing to a proportional representation system of elections. If adopted that would loosen, if not break, the seeming strangle-hold that the Republicans and Democrats have on who gets elected. Indeed, such a change might end the tradition of the United States being a two-party system.

YOU CAN AND SHOULD AFFECT POLITICS

The second thing that this volume preaches is that you can and should take part in politics. One prerequisite for good participation is good information. Much of that comes through the new media, and, focusing on a instance in which one reporter was sent to jail in 2005 for refusing to disclose a confidential source to a grand jury, **Debate 7** asks whether journalists should be able to shield sources even in a criminal case.

Armed with knowledge, you should strive to become involved in the policy process. Anti-terrorist legislation is the subject of **Debate 24.** Many critics think that the Patriot Act, which was enacted soon after the 9-11 terror attacks, threatens the freedoms of Americans. Others reply that such fears are overblown and that the minor restrictions in the bills help keep Americans safer from terrorism. The debate here rests on whether the Patriot Act should be renewed in 2005 as required in the initial law. Whatever your view, your liberties and life are involved, and you can become active in defeating or promoting the necessary renewal of Patriot Act or, depending on its fate, the law's eventual reinstatement or repeal.

Other debates may influence your ability to be active. Some people criticize those Americans who feel a strong tie to the land of their heritage and who favor U.S. policies that favor that land. Whether doing so is misplaced allegiance or an all-American tradition is taken up in **Debate 8** on ethnic lobbying. Another line of criticism is leveled at those who take it upon themselves to volunteer to supplement the government efforts to cut down on the flow of illegal immigrants into the United States. The advocates in **Debate 6** differ on whether such volunteers are laudable patriots or dangerous vigilantes. A closely related topic is the larger question of immigration. **Debate 5** features one advocate who argues that the relatively high rate of legal immigration supplemented by the inflow of illegal immigrants is threatening to dilute American culture or "who we are." A second advocate dismisses this view point as an unfounded fear.

Debate 25 about campaign finance reform also addresses participation. Those who argue that there should be strict limits on how much people and organizations can spend to support or oppose a candidate for office claim that the impact of money on politics makes a mockery of the idea that all citizens should have an equal say. Opponents rejoin that the proposed restriction violates their freedom of speech. Perhaps more than any other issue, Debate 21 relates to the idea that would most radically change participation in this country. That is instituting direct democracy by allowing the people as a whole to makes law directly through processes called initiatives and referendums.

STATE AND LOCAL GOVERNMENTS ARE IMPORTANT TOO

The federal government is just one of the more that 80,000 different governments in the United States. Each of the state and local governments has the power to pass laws, establish regulations, and tax and spend. For example, state and local governments now spend over $2 trillion a year. One power exercised by state and local is eminent domain, the ability to take property from private individuals for public use. Relating to an instance where property was taken by New London, Connecticut, and turned over to private developers, Debate 15 takes up the issue of what "public use" means and how far eminent domain should go. Debate 20 focuses on another locality, New Orleans. Rebuilding it after Hurricane Katrina ravaged it in 2005 will cost an estimated $200 billion. Some believe that should be done; others argue that it is both a waste of money and inviting future damage and death to rebuild a city that lies below sea level and is threatened by surrounding bodies of water.

THERE ARE OFTEN MORE THAN TWO SIDES TO A QUESTION

Often public policy questions are put in terms of "pro and con," "favor or oppose," or some other such stark choice. This approach is sometimes called a Manichean approach, a reference to Manicheanism, a religion founded by the Persian prophet Mani (c. 216–276). It taught "dualism," the idea the universe is divided into opposite, struggling, and equally powerful realities, light (good) and darkness (evil).

The view here is that many policy issues are more a matter of degree, and the opinion of people is better represented as a place along a range of possibilities rather than an up or down Manichean choice. Numerous debates herein are like that. For example, surveys of the American people over abortion, the subject of Debate 3, find that only a small minority of people is staunchly pro-choice or pro-life. The majority have a nuanced view that, on the one hand, supports women being able to terminate their pregnancies but that, on the other hand, reflects reservations based on timing and circumstances. Opinion is also something like that about the death penalty, the focus of Debate 17. A large majority of Americans favor it, but surveys also show that people are troubled by a range of possible injustices such as the relationship of wealth to the ability to mount a top-notch defense, the ability to execute people for crimes committed while a juvenile, and claims of racial injustice.

Yet another emotional topic on which most people are unwilling to give a categorical yes or no answer is whether it is justified to torture terrorists. One advocate argues that doing so is always abhorrent, but another advocate contends that torture is sometimes justified. In light of the recent controversy over the Bush Administration's refusal to classify captured terrorists as prisoners of war and its willingness to tolerate more forceful interrogations, the issue of torture is not an abstract question but a real policy debate.

MANY ISSUES HAVE MULTIPLE ASPECTS

Often political issues are sort of like Matryoshkas, the Russian nested dolls in which each comes apart many times, each time revealing an ever-smaller doll inside. **Debate 1** is about "the right to bear arms." At its most specific, the issue is whether individuals have such a right. But deciding that involves larger question of how to decide what those who wrote the Second Amendment meant. That matter, in turn, takes us to an even larger debate about whether we should follow the literal intent of those who wrote constitutional language, most of which is more than two centuries old, or apply the language of the Constitution within the context of the 21st century. In much the same way, **Debate 14** features the use by the minority party in the Senate of filibusters (the practice of unlimited speeches on a topic) to block the president's judicial nominees. The topic has some specific and historical aspects, such what the phrase "advice and consent" of the Senate means. There are also specific constitutional controversies over whether a filibuster is permissible as a way for a minority of senators to block the judicial nominees of the president. Because the maneuver is usually based on the nominee's ideology (such as his or her stance on abortion), Debate 14 additionally includes the degree to which ideology and partisan politics should play a role in the confirmation or rejection of judges by the Senate. A larger and related question is whether filibusters used to block the majority will on legislation and other matters before the Senate are acceptable constitutionally or democratically.

The discussion in **Debate 5** over whether English should be make the national language is also multifaceted. The language issue is just part of a larger question abut what being an American means. The idea of the "melting pot" is not attractive to everyone because, to them, melting into the culture means giving up their own and adopting the largely European-based culture that has so far defined Americans.

SOME CONCLUDING THOUGHTS

The points with which we began are important enough to reiterate. Whether you care about politics or not, it affects you every day in many ways. As the legendary heavyweight boxer Joe Louis put it after knocking out Billy Conn, a more agile but less powerful opponent, in their 1941 championship fight, "You can run, but you can't hide."

Simply paying attention is a good start, but action is even better. Everyone should be politically active, at least to the level of voting. Doing so is in your self-interest because decisions made by the federal, state, and local governments in the U.S. political system provide each of us with both tangible benefits (such as roads and schools) and intangible benefits (such as civil liberties and security). Also, for good or ill, the government takes things away from each of us (such as taxes) and restricts our actions (such as speed limits). It is also the case in politics, as the old saying goes, that the squeaky wheels get the grease. Those who participate actively are more likely to be influential. Those who do not, and young adults are by far the age group least likely to even vote, are cosigned to grumbling impotently on the sideline.

As an absolute last thought (really!), let me encourage you to contact me with questions or comments. My e-mail address is john.rourke@uconn.edu. Compliments are always great, but if you disagree with anything I have written or my choice of topics and reading or have a suggestion for the next edition, let me know.

To the Faculty

Having plied the podium, so to speak, for three decades, I have some well-formed ideas of what a good reader should do. It is from that perspective that I have organized this reader to work for the students who read it and the faculty members who adopt it for use in their classes. Below are what I look for in a reader and how I have constructed this one to meet those standards.

PROVOKE CLASS DISCUSSION

The classes I have enjoyed the most over the years have been the ones that have been the liveliest, with students participating enthusiastically in a give-and-take among themselves and with me. Many of the debates herein have been selected to engender such participation in your classes by focusing on hot-button topics that provoke heated debate even among those who are not heavily involved in politics and who do not have a lot of background on the topic. The very first topic, gun laws, in Debate 1, is just such a subject. More than once I have had students get into spirited exchanges over the "right to bear arms," so I thought it would be a great debate to open the volume. Just a few of the other hot-button topics are abortion (Debate 3), the level of immigration (Debate 5), the impact of Title IX on college athletics (Debate 13), and the death penalty (Debate 17). I hope they rev up your classes as much as they have energized mine.

Another point about class discussion that I point out in the Preface section "To the Students" is that while the debate titles imply two sides, many policy topics are not a Manichean choice between yes and no. Instead, I have tried to include many issues on which opinion ranges along a scale. From that perspective, I often urge students to try to formulate a policy that can gain majority support if not a consensus. You will also find that many of the issues herein are multifaceted, and I try to point that out to the students. For instance, the debate about gun control is more than about weapons, it is also about how we interpret and apply the Constitution.

BE CURRENT

An important factor in engaging the students is being current. Debating Franklin Roosevelt's court-packing scheme has importance, but it is not as likely to interest students as the acceptability of the Senate Democrats' current practice of sometimes filibustering President Bush's judicial nominees. Therefore, I vigorously update each edition. Even though *You Decide* appears annually, half of the topics in *You Decide 2006* are new from *You Decide 2005*. Additionally, some of the readings in the carry-over debates are new.

PROVIDE A GOOD RAGE OF TOPICS

I always look for a reader that "covers the waterfront," and have tried to put together this reader to do that. There are numerous debates on specific policy issues and others on process. All the major institutions are covered in one or more debates, and there are also debates touching on such "input" elements as parties, campaigns, interest groups, and the media. The primary focus of the reader is on the national government, but federalism also receives attention in Debates 2 and 20. State- and local-government issues are taken up in Debate 15 on eminent domain and Debate 20 regarding the future of New Orleans. I have also included several debates at the intersection of domestic and foreign affairs, including Debate 8 (the acceptability of ethnic groups of Americans lobbying the U.S. government for policies favoring the country of their heritage), Debate 18 (the U.S. presence in Iraq) and Debate 24 (anti-terrorist legislation).

My sense of a good range of topics also has meant balancing hot-button topics with others that, while they will draw less of an emotional response, are important to debate because they give insight about how the system works and might work differently. For example, Debate 2 relates to the hot-button topic of gay marriage, but its more basic point is federalism. Hopefully the debate will get students to think of the federal system, which my experience tells me they mostly take as an unchanging given. Another example is the idea presented in Debate 23 of going from a single-member, plurality electoral system to a proportional representation system.

GIVE THE STUDENTS SOME BACKGROUND FOR THE READING

Readers that work well provide the students with some background material that is located just before the reading. This debate volume follows that scheme. There is a two-page introduction to each debate that establishes the context of the debate. As part of this setup, each introduction provides the students with several "points to ponder" as they read the debates.

Moreover, the introductions do more than just address the topic per se. Instead they try to connect it to the chapter of the text for which it is designed. For example, the introduction to Debate 14, on the tensions between President Bush and the Senate Democrats over judicial nominations, begins with the power of the judiciary in the American system and how that makes judicial appointments such a high-stakes issue.

PROVIDE FOLLOW-UP POSSIBILITIES

One of the rewards of our profession is seeing students get excited about a field that intrigues us, and the reader provides a "continuing debate" section after each of the two readings. This section has three parts. **What Is New** provides an update of what has occurred since the date(s) of the two articles. **Where to Find More** points students to places to explore the topic further. I have particularly emphasized resources that can be accessed on the Internet on the theory that students are more likely to pursue a topic if they can do so via computer than by walking to the library. Needless to say, I think libraries are great and students should have to use them, so there are also numerous references to books and academic journals. Finally, the continuing debate section has a **What More to Do** part. This segment presents topics for discussion, suggests projects (like finding out how well your school is doing by Title IX standards), and advises how to get active on a topic.

FIT WITH THE COURSE

I favor readers that fit the course I am teaching. I prefer a book with readings that supplement all or most of the major topics on my syllabus and that also allows me to spread the reading out so that is evenly distributed throughout the semester. To that end, this book is organized to parallel the outline of the major introduction to American politics texts in use today. For those who favor the foundations-politics-institutions-policy approach, the table of contents of this volume should match almost exactly with their text and syllabus. For those who use a foundations-institutions-politics-policy scheme, a little, but not much, adjustment will synchronize the debates herein with your plans. Moreover to help with that, I have labeled each debate in the table of contents with the syllabus topic that fits with the debate. Additionally, for the 20 debates in the printed edition, I have indicated alternative syllabus topic for each, and I have also made suggestions about how each of the six debates on the Web might fit with various text chapters and syllabus topics.

FLEXIBILITY

While there is a fair amount of similarity in the organization of the major introduction to American politics texts, I suspect that the syllabi of faculty members are a good deal more individualistic. With that in mind, I have provided flexibility in the reader. First, there are 20 debates in the printed edition, each which is related to a topic, but each of which has suggestions in the table of contents for alternative assignment. Then there are 6 additional readings on the Longman Web site associated with *You Decide!* Each of these also has multiple uses and my suggestions about how to work each one into your syllabus. Thus, you can use all 26 debates or many fewer; you can substitute some on the Web for some in the printed edition; you can follow the order in the book fairly closely with most texts or you can rearrange the order at will. As the Burger King slogan goes, "Have It Your Way!"

As a final note, let me solicit your feedback. Every text and reader that anticipates future editions should be a work in progress. *You Decide* certainly is. Of course I will be pleased to hear about the things you like, but I and the next edition of the text will surely benefit more from hearing how I could have done better and what topics (and/or readings) would be good in the next edition. Thanks!

JOHN T. ROURKE

CONSTITUTION

GUNS, SAFETY, AND THE CONSTITUTION'S MEANING:
Individual Right *or* Subject to Regulation?

INDIVIDUAL RIGHT

ADVOCATE: Joyce Malcolm, Professor, Department of History, Bentley
College and Senior Fellow, MIT Security Studies Program

SOURCE: "Infringement," *Common Place*, July 2002

SUBJECT TO REGULATION

ADVOCATE: Daniel A. Farber, Henry J. Fletcher Professor of Law and
Associate Dean of Faculty and Research, University of Minnesota

SOURCE: "Disarmed by Time: The Second Amendment and the Failure of
Originalism," *Chicago-Kent Law Review*, 2000

In the early days of World War II, British Prime Minister Winston S. Churchill
famously described the Soviet Union as a "riddle wrapped in a mystery inside an
enigma." Had he been commenting on the current debate in the United States over
gun control, Churchill might have used the same words to describe it.

The riddle, so to speak, is the meaning of the words of the Second Amendment
to the U.S. Constitution: "A well regulated Militia, being necessary to the security of
a free State, the right of the people to keep and bear Arms, shall not be infringed."
Ask yourself, for example, Does "people" mean individuals, or does it refer to the collective citizenry, as in "We the people"?

The mystery is what, if anything, the framers of the U.S. Constitution and the
Bill of Rights intended the amendment to accomplish. Scholars disagree mightily
about this issue.

The enigma is whether the lawmakers of the late 1700s would argue that 21st
century Americans should be bound by the literal meaning of words written more
than 200 years ago, or should interpret them in the light of modern circumstances.

We might look to the courts to unravel these issues, but they have not been crys-
tal clear. Generally, they have upheld the authority of government to regulate the
ownership of weapons, but the Supreme Court has never ruled directly on the essence
of the Second Amendment. To date, the most important case has been *United States
v. Miller* (1939), in which the Supreme Court upheld a provision of the National
Firearms Act (1934) requiring registration of sawed-off shotguns. The majority opinion held that "in the absence of any evidence…that possession [of a sawed-off] shot-
gun…has some reasonable relationship to…a well-regulated militia, we cannot say
that the Second Amendment guarantees the right to keep and bear such an instru-
ment." Notice that the opinion neither denies nor affirms a right to bear arms. It only
rules that sawed-off shotguns are not protected, leaving it unclear if other weapons
might be.

Most recently, gun control opponents were buoyed by the decision of the Fifth U.S. Circuit Court of Appeals in *United States v. Emerson* (2001). The majority opinion construed the word "people" in the Second Amendment to mean individuals, and said that the clause, "necessary to a well regulated militia," served merely to explain why individuals had the right to keep and bear arms. Still, it was a mixed case, because the judges also upheld the specific federal law that barred Timothy Emerson from owning a firearm based on his history of domestic violence. When the Supreme Court declined to hear Emerson's appeal, as it does in most cases, the major constitutional issues were left largely unresolved. In essence, no Supreme Court decision, including *Miller*, has definitively ruled either that there is an unrestricted right of individuals to keep and bear arms or that government has the unchecked authority to regulate, or even abolish, gun ownership and use.

What would you decide? Considering weapons is one way to start thinking about these policy and constitutional issues. There can be no doubt that weapons have changed. Flintlock pistols and rifles were the personal firearms when the amendment was written in 1789. Today's weapons have much faster firing rates and higher muzzle velocities and, therefore, vastly greater killing power than did their forerunners.

The presence and role of weapons in America is another piece of the puzzle. The latest data indicate that approximately 4.9 million firearms (including 1.7 million handguns) are manufactured or imported for the domestic U.S. market annually. In all, there are about 200 million privately and legally owned firearms in the United States, about 30% of which are handguns. Between 40% and 50% of all households have a legal gun. The uncertain but significant number of illegal weapons adds to these totals.

As for the yearly use of firearms, most are either never fired or are used for target shooting or hunting. But statistics also indicate that 29,477 people died in the United States in 2001 as a result of a gunshot. Most (57%) were suicides. Of the remaining gunshot deaths, 38% were homicides, 3% were accidents, and about 1% each was for unknown causes or by "legal intervention" of law enforcement officers. Left unclear in the government data is what percentage of the "homicides" was committed by individuals exercising their lawful right of self-defense.

POINTS TO PONDER

➤ The most specific debate is about gun control policy and whether widespread gun ownership provides greater or less safety. Given your views on this issue, would you vote for a bill in Congress to ban the manufacture, importation, sale, and possession of all handguns?

➤ At a second level, the debate is about the specifics of the Second Amendment and the intent of those who drafted and ratified it. What do the two advocates claim that those who wrote the language of the Second Amendment intended it to mean?

➤ The third, most general, and most important dispute is over whether the Constitution is a fixed document whose meaning should be derived by "strict construction" of its words and the original intention of those wrote it, or whether the Constitution is a "living document" that it should be interpreted in light of modern realities. What is your view? Should we be bound in the first decade of the 21st century by what people meant in the last decade of the 19th century when the Second Amendment was added to the Constitution?

Guns, Safety, and the Constitution's Meaning: Individual Right

JOYCE MALCOLM

In April 1995, I joined three other scholars testifying before the U.S. House Judiciary Committee's Subcommittee on Crime about our research into the meaning of the Second Amendment. As we gave evidence that the Second Amendment guaranteed an individual right to be armed and why the Founders believed it essential, the Republican members of the committee listened politely and with interest. Every Democrat on the committee, however, turned upon us with outrage and disdain. I felt startled and dismayed. The meaning of the amendment, at least for these representatives, seemed less a matter of evidence than of party politics. Sitting opposite us, arguing against an individual right, Dennis Henigan, general counsel for Handgun Control, Inc., presented the committee with a full-page advertisement from the *New York Times* signed by scores of scholars denying that a right to be armed existed. At this juncture one of my co-panelists, Daniel Polsby, then a professor at Northwestern School of Law, pointed out that one signer, a colleague of his, was no expert on constitutional law, let alone the Second Amendment, and that to his knowledge none of the other signers had ever conducted research into the issue. For the scholars who put their names to that testimonial, the conviction that there was no individual right to be armed was an article of faith. The attitudes of both the politicians and the scholars are regrettable. We are all the losers when constitutional interpretation becomes so politicized that otherwise reasonable people are neither willing to accept, nor interested in historical truth.

Political wrangles over the limits of constitutional guarantees are common, proper, and even necessary. The battle over the Second Amendment, however, is being waged at a more basic level, the very meaning of the amendment. This too is understandable where there is doubt about the Framers' intent. But once evidence of that intent is clear, as it now is, further argument, even in the service of a worthy political agenda, is reprehensible. It becomes an attempt to revise the Constitution by misreading, rather than amending it, a precedent that puts all our rights at risk. The argument over the Second Amendment has now reached that stage. But first, some background.

Two important points should be kept in mind as we briefly review this history. First, the debate over the meaning of the Second Amendment is surprisingly recent. Second, many of those who question or disparage the right do so because they believe that guns, in and of themselves, cause crime. Until the end of the nineteenth century, few Americans doubted their right to be armed. The Founders believed privately owned weapons were necessary to protect the three great and primary rights, "personal security, personal liberty, and private property." An armed people could protect themselves and their neighbors against crime and their liberties against tyranny. [James] Madison and his colleagues converted their English right to "have Armes for their defence Suitable to their Condition, and as allowed by Law," into a broader protection that took no account of status and forbade "infringement." "As civil rulers, not having their duty to the people duly before them, may attempt to tyrannize," the *Philadelphia Federal Gazette* explained when the proposed amendment was first publicized, "and as the military forces which must be occasionally raised to defend our country, might pervert their power to the injury of their fellow citizens, the people are confirmed...in their right to keep and bear their private arms." In the 1820s William Rawle, who had been offered the post of attorney general by George Washington, found, "No clause in the constitution could by any rule of construction be conceived to give Congress a power to disarm the people. Such a flagitious attempt could only be made under some general pretense by a state legislature. But if in any blind pursuit of inordinate power, either should attempt it, this amendment may be appealed to as a restraint on both." Supreme Court Justice Joseph Story, writing in 1840, agreed that the right of the people to keep and bear arms had "justly been considered, as the palladium of the liberties of a republic." And after the Civil War, the charge Southern whites were depriving blacks of their right to be armed was instrumental in convincing Congress to pass the Fourteenth Amendment.

Then politics intervened. Early in the twentieth century when American whites, fearful of blacks in the South and the millions of foreign immigrants in the North, wanted to restrict access to firearms, alternative reading of the amendment gained credence. In the absence of serious scholarship, constructions that reduced or eliminated the individual right to be armed seemed plausible, especially in light of the awkward construction of the Second Amendment and the sparse congressional debates during its drafting, both of which relied upon common understandings of the value of a society of armed individuals

that had faded over time. These new interpretations emphasized the dependent clause referring to the militia, to the neglect of the main clause's guarantee to the people. The theory developed that the Second Amendment was merely intended to enhance state control over state militia; that it embodied a "collective right" for members of a "well-regulated" militia—today's National Guard—to be armed, not a personal right for members of a militia of the whole people, let alone for any individual. Even when an individual right was conceded, the amendment was proclaimed a useless anachronism. After all, twentieth-century Americans had the police to protect them while armed individuals would be helpless against a government bent on oppression.

Beset by fears and armed with alternative readings of the Second Amendment, restrictive gun legislation followed. In 1911 New York State passed the Sullivan Law that made it a felony to carry a concealed weapon without a license, or to own or purchase a handgun without obtaining a certificate. Discriminatory laws in the South kept blacks disarmed. The first federal gun legislation, the National Firearms Act of 1934, introduced controls on automatic weapons, sawed-off rifles and shotguns, and silencers, weapons popular with gangsters. It was more than thirty years before rising crime-rates, urban riots, and three political assassinations again led to demands for stricter federal firearms legislation. The resulting Gun Control Act of 1968 limited mail-order sales, the purchase of firearms by felons, and the importation of military weapons. Professor Robert Cottrol [historian and legal scholar] finds this statute "something of a watershed" for, since its passage, the debate over gun control and the right to be armed have become "semi-permanent features" of late twentieth century American life. And "semi-permanent" the debate remains as we enter the twenty-first century.

The argument over the Second Amendment became and remains intense and highly political because the stakes are so great. Americans suffer from a high rate of armed crime that many insist is caused, or made worse, by easy access to firearms. Eliminate these, the thinking goes, and streets will be safer. Thousands of federal, state, and local firearms regulations adorn statute books, but a Second Amendment guarantee of the right to be armed blocks the dramatic reduction or banning of firearms that gun-control groups seek. There is a deep desire on their part to believe no individual right exists. On the other side, the traditional belief that guns protect the innocent and deter offenders is even more widely accepted. Studies show the majority of Americans have always believed the Constitution guarantees them a right to be armed. Approximately half of America's households have at least one gun, an estimated arsenal of some 200–240 million weapons, kept for sport and, more crucially, for personal protection. Every new threat to regulate weapons provokes thousands of additional purchases.

Both sides seek a safer nation. But whether one believes guns cause crime or prevent it, the Second Amendment figures in political solution at every level. National elections turn on a candidate's position on the right to be armed. A small Illinois town bans handguns completely; a small Georgia town requires a gun in every home. The state of Vermont, with no gun restrictions at all, boasts the lowest crime rate in the nation. In the name of public safety, the cities of New York, Chicago, Boston, and Washington, D.C., impose ever tighter gun restrictions. In the name of public safety, thirty-three states—some two thirds—now allow every law-abiding citizen to carry a concealed weapon. Is an individual right to be armed an anachronism? Not in their opinion. Other states are considering this option.

In this clash of strategies, political gestures and competing claims abound. The Clinton administration allocated millions of dollars for gun buy-back programs, knowing a Justice Department study found this approach ineffective. Flushed with the success of lawsuits against tobacco companies, public officials in thirty-one municipalities sued gun manufacturers claiming millions in damages for gun crimes. In response, twenty-six states passed legislation forbidding such suits. Philanthropic foundations finance research that favors gun control, some even establishing whole institutes for "the prevention of violence." Notwithstanding plummeting rates of gun homicides, leading medical journals publish articles that proclaim guns a health emergency. They print seriously flawed research that purports to demonstrate that the presence of a firearm transforms peaceful citizens into killers, although studies of police records show the great majority of murderers are individuals with a long history of violence.

Nor has the popular press been shy in broadcasting its preferences. For seventy-seven consecutive days in the fall of 1989, the *Washington Post* published editorials calling for stricter gun controls. This was something of a record, but it is indicative of a national media in which three-quarters of the newspapers and most of the periodical press have advocated severe curbs on gun ownership and have denied a right to be armed exists. The press is entitled to its opinions, but unfortunately this bias has often affected and distorted news coverage. Every gun accident or shooting, every study that supports gun restrictions, is intensively reported, while defensive uses of firearms are downplayed along with scholarly investigations that tabulate these or that call into question the notion that legally owned firearms increase violent crime.

As a result, much conventional wisdom about the use and abuse of guns is simply wrong. Such reporting, for example, gives the impression that gun accidents involving young children are common and increasing when, in fact, they are happily rare and declining. The same is true of gun violence in schools. Do guns cause violence? In the thirty-year period from 1968 through 1997 as the stock of civilian firearms rose by 262%, fatal gun accidents dropped by 68.9%. Numerous surveys have shown that far more lives are saved than lost by privately owned guns. And John Lott's meticulous study of the impact of statutes permitting citizens to carry concealed weapons found them of value in reducing armed crime. Yet, convinced advocates are unwilling to examine the evidence of the constitutional protection or studies that contradict their view of the danger of private gun use.

All this has taken its toll. Alone among the articles comprising the Bill of Rights, the Second Amendment has, in recent years, come very near to being eliminated from the Constitution, not through the prescribed process of amendment, but through interpretations that reduced it to a meaningless anachronism. The low point came in 1975 when a committee of the American Bar Association was so befuddled by competing interpretations that members concluded, "It is doubtful that the Founding Fathers had any intent in mind with regard to the meaning of this Amendment." Leading textbooks on constitutional law, such as that by Lawrence Tribe, had literally relegated the Second Amendment to a footnote. Yet the American people remained convinced of their right to be armed despite textbooks and newspaper advertisements to the contrary.

Now scholarship has come to the rescue. The past twenty-five years have witnessed a growing number of studies of the Second Amendment, and these have found overwhelming evidence that it was meant to guarantee an individual right to be armed. In 1997, Supreme Court Justice Clarence Thomas in *Printz v. United States,* noting that the Court "has not had recent occasion to consider the nature of the substantive right safeguarded by the Second Amendment," hoped, "Perhaps, at some future date, this Court will have the opportunity to determine whether Justice Story was correct when he wrote that the right to bear arms 'has justly been considered, as the palladium of the liberties of a republic.'" Thomas added, "[A]n impressive array of historical evidence, a growing body of scholarly commentary indicates that the 'right to keep and bear arms' is, as the Amendment's text suggests, a personal right." Such evidence includes the individual right to be armed inherited from England; Madison's intent to list the right to be armed with other individual rights, rather than in the article dealing with the militia; his reference to his proposed rights as "guards for private rights"; the Senate's rejection of an amendment to tack the phrase "for the common defense" to the "right of the people to keep and bear arms"; and numerous contemporary comments. By contrast, no contemporary evidence has been found that only a collective right for members of a militia was intended. The evidence has convinced our leading constitutional scholars, among them Lawrence Tribe, Akhil Amar, and Leonard Levy, that the Second Amendment protects an individual right. In March 1999, Judge Sam Cummings of the Fifth Circuit [of the U.S. Court of Appeals], in the case of *United States v. Timothy Joe Emerson,* found a federal statute violated an individual's Second Amendment rights. The Fifth Circuit Court of Appeals, in a meticulously researched opinion, agreed that the Second Amendment protected an individual right to keep arms. As the [state] Court of Appeals in Ohio pointed out when, in April 2002, it found Ohio's prohibition against carrying a concealed weapon unconstitutional, "We are not a country where power is maintained by people with guns over people without guns."

Since the evidence clearly shows an individual right was intended, we should now move on to discuss the prudent limits of that right. Yet that discussion can't take place because denials of that right continue along with ever more tenuous theories to refute it, claims that the phrase "bear arms" was used exclusively in a military context; that the amendment resulted from a conspiracy between Northern and Southern states to control slaves; and that since the phrase "the right of the people to keep and bear arms" is set off by a comma it can be eliminated. But in early American discourse, as today, "bear arms" often meant simply carrying a weapon; there is no direct evidence of any conspiracy; and the elimination of every phrase set off by commas would play havoc with constitutional interpretation. [Historian] Michael Bellesiles claimed to have evidence there were few guns in early America, Americans were uninterested in owning them, and therefore no individual right to be armed could have been intended. However, his results seriously underestimate numbers of weapons and distort the attitudes toward them. Other scholars looking through some of the same evidence have found widespread ownership of guns.

Why does debate over original intent continue? Lawrence Tribe, who concluded there is an individual right after considering the new evidence, points to the "true poignancy," "the inescapable tension, for many people on both sides of this policy divide, between the reading of the Second Amendment that would advance the policies they favor and the reading of the Second Amendment to which intellectual honesty, and their own theories of constitutional interpretation, would drive them if they could bring themselves to set their policy convictions aside." The time has come for those who deny an individual right exists to set policy convictions aside in favor of intellectual honesty—and a more productive discussion.

Guns, Safety, and the Constitution's Meaning: Subject to Regulation

Daniel A. Farber

INTRODUCTION

[The prevailing] wisdom [is that] the Second Amendment is little more than a footnote to Militia Clauses of the Constitution, themselves virtually irrelevant to today's military. But this conventional view has been challenged by revisionist scholars [who] contend that the framers had a far more sweeping vision of the right "to keep and bear Arms." In their view, the Constitution protects the individual's right to own guns for self-defense, hunting, and resistance to tyranny. These scholars find no room for uncertainty about the historical meaning of constitutional language. "The Second Amendment," we are told by one scholar, "is thus not mysterious. Nor is it equivocal. Least of all is it opaque." The meaning of the "right to bear arms," says another, "seems no longer open to dispute," and "an intellectually viable response…has yet to be made."

The revisionists' confidence about the original understanding is the foundation for their reinterpretation of the Second Amendment. Yet, the appropriate role of original intent in constitutional law has been debated for the past two decades. That debate should, if nothing else, caution against this sense of certainty about the implications of historical materials for present-day constitutional issues such as gun control….

Reading the historical record on the right to bear arms turns out to be a difficult exercise, full of perplexities. And even if we had a definitive answer that turned out to favor the revisionists, the claim that original

intent should always trump contemporary legislative decisions is itself problematic….

Thus, history cannot provide the kind of unshakable foundation for gun rights. that some scholars have sought. Indeed, there is something profoundly amiss about the notion that the Constitution's meaning today should be settled first and foremost by a trip to the archives. The effort to apply this notion to an issue as contemporary and hotly contested as gun control only serves to underline the fundamental peculiarity of the originalist approach to constitutional law.

Given the deep flaws in originalism, its continuing appeal may seem mysterious. For its more sophisticated adherents, it may appeal as a value-neutral method of decision and as a solution to the counter-majoritarian difficulty—perhaps a solution they would admit to be flawed, yet better than the alternatives. These arguments are ultimately unsatisfactory.

For less sophisticated adherents, however, originalism may have another, more visceral appeal. It harkens back to an earlier, purer age, when today's petty political concerns and squalid politicians were replaced with great statesmen devoted to high principle. This implicit appeal to a nobler, more heroic past may have particular resonance in the context of the Second Amendment, where it brings to mind visions of minutemen and frontier lawmen valiantly defending justice and freedom with their guns. These mythic versions of the past, however, can only obscure the all-too-real issues facing our society today. Being inspired by myth is healthy; being ruled by it is unsafe.

[There are] doubts [about] whether originalism provides a workable methodology for judges in deciding Second Amendment cases. Originalism requires them to make difficult historical judgments with little training in doing so; it gives no guidance about how concretely or abstractly to define the original understanding or about how to distinguish the framers' understanding of the text from their expectations about its implementation; and it leaves open the difficult problem of when to relinquish original understandings in favor of precedent or tradition. Furthermore, as practiced today, originalism may not even correspond with the methods used by the framers themselves to understand the text. Consequently, the so-called "original understanding" may not reflect the understanding of the original framers of how the provision would be applied under new circumstances. In short, with the best will in the world, judges who practice originalism will find themselves in vast disagreement over the meaning of the Second Amendment. Thus, if originalism is intended to constrain judges, it is a failure.

But even apart from these difficulties of implementation, the question remains whether we would want to implement originalism even if we could. The Second Amendment is a good illustration of why we should not want to be bound by the original understanding. Originalists claim that only originalism can reconcile judicial review with majority rule and make the Supreme Court something other than a super-legislature. But in reality, the Justices do not need to give up their bar memberships and join the American Historical Society in order to do their jobs properly. The conventional methods of constitutional law are completely legitimate and adequate to the task at hand. Originalism's

greatest failing—in contrast to the conventional process of Common-law decision—is its inability to confront historical change. We should reject the originalist's invitation to ignore all of the history that has transpired since 1790 when we interpret the Constitution.

The Second Amendment once again provides an apt illustration of the defects of originalism. If the original understanding is to constrain judicial discretion, it must be possible to ascertain that understanding in a reasonably indisputable way. But, it is not even possible to give a clear-cut definition of what constitutes the original "understanding," as opposed to the original "expectation" or the original "applications" associated with a constitutional provision. And having cleared that hurdle, formidable difficulties confront the originalist judge, including a historical record that combines enormous volume with frustrating holes in key places, a complex intellectual and social context, and a host of interpretative disputes. If we do not trust judges to correctly interpret and apply their own precedents—a skill which they were supposedly taught in law school and have practiced throughout their professional lives—it is hard to see why we should trust them to interpret and apply a mass of eighteenth-century archival documents.

FIDELITY AND CHANGE

Originalism is an effort to fix of the Constitution once and for all at its birth. But there is an opposing view, one most eloquently expressed by Justice [Oliver Wendell] Holmes:

> [W]hen we are dealing with words that also are a constituent act, like the Constitution of the United States, we must realize that they have called into life a being the development of which could not have been foreseen completely by the most gifted of its begetters. It

was enough for them to realize or to hope that they had created an organism; it has taken a century and has cost their successors much sweat and blood to prove that they created a nation. The case before us must be considered in the light of our whole experience and not in that of what was said a hundred years ago.

The Second Amendment is among the provisions of the Constitution that seem most to call out for Holmes's approach—for the historical changes relating to the right to bear arms have been far-reaching indeed.

Some of those changes relate directly to the two subjects of the Second Amendment: firearms and and the militia. There is first of all the disappearance of the kind of militia contemplated by the framers. As [legal scholar] Akhil Amar explains, perhaps with some regret:

> [T]he legal and social structure on which the amendment is built no longer exists. The Founders' juries—grand, petit, and civil—are still around today, but the Founders' militia is not. America is not Switzerland. Voters no longer muster for militia practice in the town square.

Another relevant change is the development of professional police departments, which limit the need for individuals and groups to engage in self-help. Because these changes, unanticipated by the framers, undermined the asserted original purpose of the Second Amendment, its application today becomes problematic.

Apart from these changes relating directly to the Second Amendment's subject matter, broad changes in the constitutional landscape are also relevant. One watershed is the Civil War, which undermines the insurrectionist argument that armed revolt is a constitutionally sanctioned check on federal power....

Perhaps there may be those who reject the validity of the decision at Appomattox even today. What cannot be disputed as a lesson of the Civil War, however, is that insurrection is not an acceptable practical check on the federal government. Quite apart from the question of whether insurgents could defeat a modern army, the Civil War suggests that the costs of exercising this option would simply be unbearable: if a similar percentage of the current population died during such an insurgency today, we would be talking about five million deaths. Brave talk about insurrection is one thing; "paying the butcher's bill" is quite another. Perhaps the framers can be forgiven for failing to appreciate this reality; it is harder to excuse similar romanticism today.

The Civil War also transformed our concept of the relationship between the state and federal government. The Second Amendment, at least if revisionist scholars are to be believed, was based on the threat a powerful national government posed to liberty. But one effect of the Civil War was to cement the federal government's role as a guarantor of liberty. Since the time of the Fourteenth Amendment, rather than state and local communities being seen as bulwarks of freedom against the federal leviathan, the federal government has been pressed into service to defend liberty. The Fourteenth Amendment arose in part out of a sense of the obligation of the federal government to protect the rights of its citizens, by force if necessary, whether the threat came from a foreign nation or a state or local government.

Thus, rather than entrusting liberty to the "locals," the Fourteenth Amendment calls into play federal judicial and legislative power to ensure that the states respect individual rights. This realignment of the federal government as friend rather than threat to liberty underlies much of our modern Supreme Court jurisprudence and a plethora of twentieth-century civil rights legislation. This fundamental reassessment of the relationship between federal power and liberty would make independent state and local militias as much a threat to liberty as a protector.

If the insurrectionist argument is at odds with the lessons of the Civil War, the self-defense argument for constitutional protection clashes with the modern regulatory state. It is a commonplace that the New Deal [beginning in 1933] was a "watershed" in the development of the regulatory state, enough so to lead one prominent theorist to build a whole theory of constitutional interpretation around this shift. But the New Deal was only the beginning. In the 1960s and 1970s came a new wave of legislation covering matters such as consumer protection, discrimination law, and the environment. As a result, we live in a world where citizens routinely rely on the federal government rather than self-help to protect them against a host of threats.

Today, we expect federal protection against everything from potentially dangerous traces of pesticides in our foods to unwanted sexual overtures in the workplace. In this context, the notion that the government cannot protect us from the dangers of firearms seems like an odd relic of an earlier laissez-faire period. Indeed, it seems peculiar at best to say that the government can constitutionally protect us from one kind of hostile environment—coworkers displaying lewd pictures—but not from a more dramatic kind of hostile environment—neighbors carrying Uzis.

The point here is not that the Second Amendment is an anachronistic text that ought to be ignored, or that its interpretation should necessarily be narrowed in light of these later developments. It is not even that these later developments are fun-

damentally correct. What is wrong with originalism is that it seeks to block judges from even considering these later developments, which on their face seem so clearly relevant to the legitimacy of federal gun control efforts. But try as they may, it seems unlikely that judges can avoid being influenced by these realities.

CONCLUSION

What do we learn about originalism from the Second Amendment debate? What do we learn about the Second Amendment from the originalism debate?

One set of lessons relates to constitutional interpretation. The Second Amendment shows how the standard academic criticisms of originalism are not just academic quibbles: they identify real and troubling flaws. The debate about the Second Amendment vividly illustrates critical problems with originalism:

- The historical record concerning the right to bear arms is difficult for non-historians such as judges to evaluate, requiring a high level of historical expertise to evaluate the credibility and import of the evidence.

- Originalism might not accurately reflect the way in which contemporary readers understood the document; in particular, it may underestimate their willingness to contemplate limiting the "right to bear arms" clause in light of the purpose clause.

- The original understanding of the Second Amendment can be defined at different levels of generality, and the interpretation will depend on the choice of level as well as on how we distinguish the original "understanding" from mere original "expectations."

- Originalism, to be a realistic option, must acknowledge stare decisis, yet it does not provide us with clear guidance about whether the current Second Amendment case law should stand.

- Although originalism claims simply to be enforcing the will of "We the People," the Second Amendment shows how originalism can undermine majority rule.
- Because of the difficulties judges would face in basing their decisions on purely historical grounds, originalism would not eliminate the role of personal values in judging.
- Originalism forces us to ignore the ways our world has changed since the eighteenth century: the Civil War and its aftermath have cut the ground away from the notion of insurrection as a protection of liberty against federal power; and the New Deal and *its* aftermath have created a world in which we customarily turn to the regulatory state rather than to self-help to protect ourselves from threats.

It would, in short, be a serious mistake for judges to use originalism as their recipe for interpreting the Second Amendment or other ambiguous constitutional language. The fact that the arguments against this approach are familiar does not make them any less damaging.

At a more fundamental level, however, the lesson is not simply that originalists are wrong about how judges should read the Constitution. More importantly, they are wrong about the nature of the Constitution itself. In general, disputed constitutional provisions cannot simply be applied on the basis of whatever examples were discussed at the time, and so it is natural for originalists to attempt, instead, to reconstruct the theories underlying those provisions. This effort to theorize constitutional provisions is quite evident with the Second Amendment originalists we have discussed, but it is equally clear in the efforts of other originalists to find in the original understanding some unified theory of executive power or of federalism. But to look for an underlying theory is to misconceive the nature of the constitutional enterprise. Unlike physics, law does not lend itself to a "standard model" or a grand unified theory.

While the framers were indeed "concerned with such fundamental questions as the nature of representation and executive power," they were also engaged in "a cumulative process of bargaining and compromise in which a rigid adherence to principle yielded to the pragmatic tests of reaching agreement and building coalitions." In short, they were doing their best to create a viable set of democratic institutions, a task that required the utmost attention to both principle and pragmatism. Their task was not to agree on a theory but to create the basis for a working democracy. We hardly do justice to the spirit of their undertaking if we treat the resulting document as *their* Constitution alone rather than being ours as well. The last thing they would want would be for us to be ruled by false certainties about their intentions. Unfortunately, that is an invitation we have received all too often with respect to the Second Amendment.

THE CONTINUING DEBATE:
Guns, Safety, and the Constitution's Meaning

What Is New

Advocates and opponents of gun control have both had victories in recent years. Advocates were heartened by several court cases in 2004. The Supreme Court in effect upheld a restrictive California gun law by refusing to hear a challenge to it, and a Federal District Court rejected a suit brought by the National Rifle Association challenging the constitutionality of a Washington, D.C. municipal law limiting gun ownership. But also in 2004, Congress let lapse a 10-year-old ban that barred weapons from having muzzle-flash suppressors, large capacity ammunition magazines, and other characteristics commonly associated with military assault weapons. Anti–gun control forces won a further victory in 2005 when Congress enacted legislation barring most civil suits against most firearms makers for the use of their products in crimes and other instances where victims were killed or wounded.

Where to Find More

For data, laws, and related information on firearms go to the U.S. Bureau of Alcohol, Tobacco and Firearms Web site http://www.atf.treas.gov/pub/#Firearms. The most recent data on firearms deaths in the United States is available from the U.S. Public Health Service's Centers for Disease Control Web site at: http://www.cdc.gov/nchs/fastats/homicide.htm.

For policy advocacy, turn to the Web sites of two of the major opposing interest groups. The anti–gun control forces are represented by the National Rifle Association's Web site at http://www.nra.org. For the opposing view, the URL http://www.bradycampaign.org/ will take you to the Website of the pro–gun control Brady Campaign to Prevent Violence (named after James Brady, a former White House press secretary who was shot in the head and disabled during the assassination attempt on President Ronald Reagan on March 30, 1981). For a rebuke of both camps, read John Casteen, "Ditching the Rubric on Gun Control," *Virginia Quarterly Review* (Fall 2004).

Scholarly legal arguments in favor of a strict constructionist reading of the Second Amendment include Eugene Volokh, "The Amazing Vanishing Second Amendment," *New York University Law Review* (1998). Taking the opposite view is David C. Williams, *The Mythic Meanings of the Second Amendment* (Yale University Press, 2003).

What More to Do

One constant suggestion for this and every debate in this book is to get involved no matter which side you are on. The issue is important, and you can make a difference if you try. Also keep the larger constitutional questions in your mind as you read other debates in this book. Like this debate, some will involve questions about the meaning of words or phrases, such as "due process of law" in the Fourteenth Amendment. Other debates will also include the ongoing dispute over strict construction versus contemporary interpretation of the Constitution by the courts. Perhaps before any of this, though, think about and discuss with others the policy and constitutional issues presented in this debate. Then, as this book's title urges, You Decide!

FEDERALISM

FEDERAL REGULATION OF MEDICAL MARIJUANA:
Appropriate National Power *or* Usurpation of State Authority?

APPROPRIATE NATIONAL POWER

ADVOCATE: John Paul Stevens III, Associate Justice, U.S. Supreme Court
SOURCE: Opinion in *Gonzales v. Raich*, June 6, 2005

USURPATION OF STATE AUTHORITY

ADVOCATE: Sandra Day O'Connor, Associate Justice, U.S. Supreme Court
SOURCE: Opinion in *Gonzales v. Raich*, June 6, 2005

Students are commonly taught that one way the delegates to the Constitutional Convention of 1787 in Philadelphia sought to safeguard democracy was by creating a federal system that divides powers between the central government and the states. The true story is more complex than that, but James Madison, the "father of the Constitution," did argue in the *Federalist Papers* (No. 45), "The powers delegated by the proposed Constitution to the Federal Government, are few and defined. Those which are to remain in the State Governments are numerous and indefinite."

Whatever anyone thought or intended, the Constitution is very imprecise about the boundaries between the authority of Washington and that of the state capitals. As a result, the division of powers has been the subject of legal, political, and even physical struggle ever since. It has not, however, been an even contest. Since 1789 authority has generally flowed away from the states and toward the central government.

One reason for this shift is the congressional use and judicial view of the Constitution's interstate commerce clause. Located in Article I, section 8, it gives Congress the authority "to regulate commerce…among the several states." For many years, the Supreme Court usually rejected attempts by Congress to use the interstate commerce clause to assert national control over an area traditionally within the realm of the states. But beginning in the 1930s, the court became more willing to allow the expansion of federal power under the interstate commerce clause. During the 1960s and beyond, the Supreme Court also usually upheld federal civil rights laws' use of the commerce clause to attack discrimination. In *Heart of Atlanta Motel v. United States* (1964), the Supreme Court upheld federal action against the motel's restaurant, Ollie's Barbecue, which only served white people. The court ruled that even though Ollie's only served local people, it was subject to federal regulation because some of the food it served originated outside of Georgia. Scholar Richard S. Randall (*American Constitutional Development*, 2002) has termed such use of the interstate commerce clause a constitutional "revolution" that "transformed the commerce power into an almost unlimited federal grant" of authority.

Something of a counter-revolution occurred, however. The Supreme Court under Chief Justice William Rehnquist (1986–2005) made several decisions rejecting federal laws enacted under the logic of the commerce clause. This counter-trend brings us to the debate here. Throughout most of history, there was limited federal power to regulate drugs because many of them are produced, distributed, and used locally, and thus fell within the purview of the states.

This changed in 1970 when Congress issued a "finding" that drugs travel in and impacted interstate commerce and enacted the Controlled Substances Act (CSA). It regulated the production, distribution, and possession of five classes of "controlled substances." Of these all those listed in Schedule 1, including 42 opiates, 22 opium derivatives, and 17 hallucinogenic substances (including marijuana) were banned outright.

The specific debate here involves federal authority to regulate "medical marijuana." Many physicians believe that marijuana can be medically useful, especially in easing pain and other side effects of cancer. Based on this belief, a 1996 referendum (see Debate 21) in California approved the "Compassionate Use Act" permitting the use of marijuana on a doctor's recommendation. Patients could either grow their own or obtain the drug from a "caregiver" (grower) within the state. Ten other states enacted similar laws. In 2002, federal agents seized medical marijuana being used by several Californians, including Angel Raich, who was using marijuana to treat brain tumor symptoms. Raich sued the U.S. Attorney General. The District Court found against Raich, but the Ninth Circuit of the Court of Appeals ruled that locally gown and used marijuana was not involved in commerce and, therefore, federal regulation was unconstitutional. The Bush administration appealed to the Supreme Court, which brings us to the readings by Justices John Paul Stevens and Sandra Day O'Connor presenting their perpectives about whether or not regulation represented an abuse of federal authority by overextending the meaning of the interstate commerce clause.

POINTS TO PONDER

➤ Separate your views on the main point of this debate, federal authority, and the second point, medical marijuana. You can, for instance, believe that on the constitutional level, the growth of federal authority is positive and also believe that on the policy level, medical marijuana should be legal.

➤ As you read, think about how well Madison's portrayal of the federal government's powers as "few and defined" and those of the states as "numerous and indefinite" corresponds to federalism's current reality. Is the change or lack of change positive or regrettable?

➤ Not too far below the surface of some critics' position on federalism is the view that it is an outdated system. The argument is that the United States has become a single country economically and socially and, therefore, should also be a unified politically. The defenders of federalism argue that it still, as it did in 1789, protects freedom, promotes diversity, and permits policy experimentation. What do you think? Does federalism make sense any more?

Federal Regulation of Medical Marijuana: Appropriate National Power

John Paul Stevens, III

California is one of at least nine states that authorize the use of marijuana for medicinal purposes. The question presented in this case is whether the power vested in Congress by Article I, §8, of the Constitution "[t]o make all Laws which shall be necessary and proper for carrying into Execution" its authority to "regulate Commerce with foreign Nations, and among the several States" includes the power to prohibit the local cultivation and use of marijuana in compliance with California law.

I

California has been a pioneer in the regulation of marijuana. In 1913, California was one of the first states to prohibit the sale and possession of marijuana, and at the end of the century, California became the first state to authorize limited use of the drug for medicinal purposes. In 1996, California voters passed Proposition 215, now codified as the Compassionate Use Act of 1996. The proposition was designed to ensure that "seriously ill" residents of the state have access to marijuana for medical purposes, and to encourage federal and state governments to take steps towards ensuring the safe and affordable distribution of the drug to patients in need. The act creates an exemption from criminal prosecution for physicians, as well as for patients and primary caregivers who possess or cultivate marijuana for medicinal purposes with the recommendation or approval of a physician. A "primary caregiver" is a person who has consistently assumed responsibility for the housing, health, or safety of the patient.

Respondents [those charged with violating the law] Angel Raich and Diane Monson are California residents who suffer from a variety of serious medical conditions and have sought to avail themselves of medical marijuana pursuant to the terms of the Compassionate Use Act. They are being treated by licensed, board-certified family practitioners, who have concluded, after prescribing a host of conventional medicines to treat respondents' conditions and to alleviate their associated symptoms, that marijuana is the only drug available that provides effective treatment. Both women have been using marijuana as a medication for several years pursuant to their doctors' recommendation, and both rely heavily on cannabis to function on a daily basis. Indeed, Raich's physician believes that forgoing cannabis treatments would certainly cause Raich excruciating pain and could very well prove fatal.

Respondent Monson cultivates her own marijuana, and ingests the drug in a variety of ways including smoking and using a vaporizer. Respondent Raich, by contrast, is unable to cultivate her own, and thus relies on two caregivers, litigating as "John Does," to provide her with locally grown marijuana at no charge. These caregivers also process the cannabis into hashish or keif, and Raich herself processes some of the marijuana into oils, balms, and foods for consumption.

On August 15, 2002, county deputy sheriffs and agents from the federal Drug Enforcement Administration (DEA) came to Monson's home. After a thorough investigation, the county officials concluded that her use of marijuana was entirely lawful as a matter of California law. Nevertheless, after a 3-hour standoff, the federal agents seized and destroyed all six of her cannabis plants.

Respondents thereafter brought this action against the Attorney General of the United States and the head of the DEA seeking injunctive and declaratory relief prohibiting the enforcement of the federal Controlled Substances Act (CSA) to the extent it prevents them from possessing, obtaining, or manufacturing cannabis for their personal medical use. In their complaint and supporting affidavits, Raich and Monson described the severity of their afflictions, their repeatedly futile attempts to obtain relief with conventional medications, and the opinions of their doctors concerning their need to use marijuana. Respondents claimed that enforcing the CSA against them would violate the Commerce Clause, the Due Process Clause of the Fifth Amendment, the Ninth and Tenth Amendments of the Constitution, and the doctrine of medical necessity.

The District Court denied respondents' motion for a preliminary injunction [in 2003]. Although the court found that the federal enforcement interests "wane[d]" when compared to the harm that California residents would suffer if denied access to medically necessary marijuana, it concluded that respondents could not demonstrate a likelihood of success on the merits of their legal claims.

A divided panel of the Court of Appeals for the Ninth Circuit [later in 2003] reversed and ordered the District Court to enter a preliminary injunction [to block federal action]. The [appellate] court found that respondents had "demonstrated a strong likelihood of success on their claim that, as applied to them, the CSA is an unconstitutional exercise of Congress' Commerce Clause authority." The Court of Appeals distinguished prior Circuit cases upholding the CSA in the face of Commerce Clause challenges by focusing on what it deemed to be the "*separate and distinct class of activities*" at issue in this case: "the intrastate, noncommercial cultivation and possession of cannabis for personal medical purposes as recommended by a patient's physician pursuant to valid California state law." The court found the latter class of activities "different in kind from drug trafficking" because interposing a physician's recommendation raises different health and safety concerns, and because "this limited use is clearly distinct from the broader illicit drug market— as well as any broader commercial market for medicinal marijuana—insofar as the medicinal marijuana at issue in this case is not intended for, nor does it enter, the stream of commerce."

…[This] case is made difficult by respondents' strong arguments that they will suffer irreparable harm because, despite a congressional finding to the contrary, marijuana does have valid therapeutic purposes. [A congressional finding is a statement within a law of what Congress believes is a fact related to the purpose of the law.] The question before us, however, is not whether it is wise to enforce the statute in these circumstances; rather, it is whether Congress' power to regulate interstate markets for medicinal substances encompasses the portions of those markets that are supplied with drugs produced and consumed locally. Well-settled law controls our answer. The CSA is a valid exercise of federal power, even as applied to the troubling facts of this case.

II

Shortly after taking office in 1969, President Nixon declared a national "war on drugs." As the first campaign of that war, Congress set out to enact legislation that would consolidate various drug laws on the books into a comprehensive statute, provide meaningful regulation over legitimate sources of drugs to prevent diversion into illegal channels, and strengthen law enforcement tools against the traffic in illicit drugs. That effort culminated in the passage of the Comprehensive Drug Abuse Prevention and Control Act of 1970.

This was not, however, Congress' first attempt to regulate the national market in drugs. Rather, as early as 1906 Congress enacted federal legislation imposing labeling regulations on medications and prohibiting the manufacture or shipment of any adulterated or misbranded drug traveling in interstate commerce. Aside from these labeling restrictions, most domestic drug regulations prior to 1970 generally came in the guise of revenue laws, with the Department of the Treasury serving as the federal government's primary enforcer. For example, the primary drug control law, before being repealed by the passage of the CSA, was the Harrison Narcotics Act of 1914. The Harrison Act sought to exert control over the possession and sale of narcotics, specifically cocaine and opiates, by requiring producers, distributors, and purchasers to register with the federal government, by assessing taxes against parties so registered, and by regulating the issuance of prescriptions.

Marijuana itself was not significantly regulated by the federal government until 1937 when accounts of marijuana's addictive qualities and physiological effects, paired with dissatisfaction with enforcement efforts at state and local levels, prompted Congress to pass the Marihuana Tax Act…(repealed 1970). Like the Harrison Act, the Marihuana Tax Act did not outlaw the possession or sale of marijuana outright. Rather, it imposed registration and reporting requirements for all individuals importing, producing, selling, or dealing in marijuana, and required the payment of annual taxes in addition to transfer taxes whenever the drug changed hands. Moreover, doctors wishing to prescribe marijuana for medical purposes were required to comply with rather burdensome administrative requirements. Noncompliance exposed traffickers to severe federal penalties, whereas compliance would often subject them to prosecution under state law. Thus, while the Marihuana Tax Act did not declare the drug illegal *per se*, the onerous administrative requirements, the prohibitively expensive taxes, and the risks attendant on compliance practically curtailed the marijuana trade.

Then in 1970, after declaration of the national "war on drugs," federal drug policy underwent a significant transformation. A number of noteworthy events precipitated this policy shift. First, in *Leary* v. *United States,* (1969), this Court held certain provisions of the Marihuana Tax Act and other narcotics legislation unconstitutional. Second, at the end of his term, President Johnson fundamentally reorganized the federal drug control agencies. The Bureau of Narcotics, then housed in the Department of Treasury, merged with the Bureau of Drug Abuse Control, then housed in the Department of Health, Education, and Welfare (HEW), to create the Bureau of Narcotics and Dangerous Drugs, currently housed in the Department of Justice. Finally, prompted by a perceived need to consolidate the growing number of piecemeal drug laws and to enhance federal drug enforcement powers, Congress enacted the Comprehensive Drug Abuse Prevention and Control Act.

Title II of that Act, the CSA, repealed most of the earlier antidrug laws in favor of a comprehensive regime to combat the international and interstate traffic in illicit drugs. The main objectives of the CSA were to conquer drug abuse and to control the legitimate and illegitimate traffic in controlled substances. Congress was particularly concerned with the need to prevent the diversion of drugs from legitimate to illicit channels.

To effectuate these goals, Congress devised a closed regulatory system making it unlawful to manufacture, distribute, dispense, or possess any controlled substance except in a manner authorized by the CSA. The CSA categorizes all controlled substances into five schedules. The drugs are grouped together based on their accepted medical uses, the potential for abuse, and their psychological and physical effects on the body. Each schedule is associated with a distinct set of controls regarding the manufacture, distribution, and use of the substances listed therein. The CSA and its implementing regulations set forth strict requirements regarding registration, labeling and packaging, production quotas, drug security, and recordkeeping.

In enacting the CSA, Congress classified marijuana as a Schedule I drug. This preliminary classification was based, in part, on the recommendation of the Assistant Secretary of HEW "that marihuana be retained within schedule I at least until the completion of certain studies now underway." Schedule I drugs are categorized [by the law] as such because of their high potential for abuse, lack of any accepted medical use, and absence of any accepted safety for use in medically supervised treatment. These three factors, in varying gradations, are also used to categorize drugs in the other four schedules. For example, Schedule II substances also have a high potential for abuse which may lead to severe psychological or physical dependence, but unlike Schedule I drugs, they have a currently accepted medical use. By classifying marijuana as a Schedule I drug, as opposed to listing it on a lesser schedule, the manufacture, distribution, or possession of marijuana became a criminal offense, with the sole exception being use of the drug as part of a Food and Drug Administration preapproved research study.

The CSA provides for the periodic updating of schedules and delegates authority to the Attorney General, after consultation with the Secretary of Health and Human Services, to add, remove, or transfer substances to, from, or between schedules. Despite considerable efforts to reschedule marijuana, it remains a Schedule I drug.

III

Respondents in this case do not dispute that passage of the CSA, as part of the Comprehensive Drug Abuse Prevention and Control Act, was well within Congress' commerce power. Nor do they contend that any provision or section of the CSA amounts to an unconstitutional exercise of congressional authority. Rather, respondents' challenge is actually quite limited; they argue that the CSA's categorical prohibition of the manufacture and possession of marijuana as applied to the intrastate manufacture and possession of marijuana for medical purposes pursuant to California law exceeds Congress' authority under the Commerce Clause.

In assessing the validity of congressional regulation, none of our Commerce Clause cases can be viewed in isolation....Our understanding of the reach of the Commerce Clause, as well as Congress' assertion of authority [under the cause] has evolved over time. The Commerce Clause emerged as the Framers' response to the central problem giving rise to the Constitution itself: the absence of any federal commerce power under the Articles of Confederation. For the first century of our history, the primary use of the Clause was to preclude the kind of discriminatory state legislation [against the products of other states] that had once been permissible. Then, in response to rapid industrial development and an increasingly interdependent national economy, Congress "ushered in a new era of federal regulation under the commerce power," beginning with the enactment of the Interstate Commerce Act in 1887.

Cases decided during that "new era," which now spans more than a century, have identified three general categories of regulation in which Congress is authorized to engage under its commerce power. First, Congress can regulate the channels of interstate commerce. Second, Congress has authority to regulate and protect the instrumentalities of interstate commerce, and persons or things in interstate commerce. Third, Congress has the power to regulate activities that substantially affect interstate commerce. Only the third category is implicated in the case at hand.

Our case law firmly establishes Congress' power to regulate purely local activities that are part of an economic "class of activities" that have a substantial effect on interstate commerce....We [the justices] have never required Congress to legislate with scientific exactitude. When Congress decides that the "'total incidence'" of a practice poses a threat to a national market, it may regulate the entire class. In this vein, we have reiterated [in an earlier case] that when "a general regulatory statute bears a substantial relation to commerce, the [importance or lack of importance of the] character of individual instances arising under that statute is of no consequence."

...Thus establishes that Congress can regulate purely intrastate activity that is not itself "commercial," in that it is not produced for sale, if it concludes that failure to regulate that class of activity would undercut the regulation of the interstate market in that commodity....

[In] this case...respondents are cultivating, for home consumption, a fungible commodity for which there is an established, albeit illegal, interstate market. ...[and] a primary purpose of the CSA is to control the supply and demand of controlled substances in both lawful and unlawful drug markets....[Therefore], Congress had a rational basis for concluding that leaving home-consumed marijuana outside federal control would similarly affect price and market conditions.

More concretely,...[a] concern making it appropriate to include marijuana grown for home consumption in the CSA is the likelihood that the high demand in the interstate market will draw such marijuana into that market....The diversion of home-grown marijuana tends to frustrate the federal interest in eliminating commercial transactions in the interstate market in their entirety. In both cases, the regulation is squarely within Congress' commerce power because production of the commodity meant for home consumption, [including] marijuana, has a substantial effect on supply and demand in the national market for that commodity....

Findings in the introductory sections of the CSA explain why Congress deemed it appropriate to encompass local activities within the scope of the CSA. The submissions of the parties and the numerous *amici* [supporting arguments submitted to the court by interested parties or "friends"] all seem to agree that...a national and international market for marijuana [exists]. ...Respondents nonetheless insist that the CSA cannot be constitutionally applied to their activities because Congress did not make a specific finding that the intrastate cultivation and possession of marijuana for medical purposes based on the recommendation of a physician would substantially affect the larger interstate marijuana market. Be that as it may, we have never required Congress to make particularized findings in order to legislate, absent a special concern such as the protection of free speech. While congressional findings are certainly helpful in reviewing the substance of a congressional statutory scheme, particularly when the connection to commerce is not self-evident, and while we will consider congressional findings in our analysis when they are available, the absence of particularized findings does not call into question Congress' authority to legislate.

In assessing the scope of Congress' authority under the Commerce Clause, we stress that the task before us is a modest one. We need not determine whether respondents' activities, taken in the aggregate, substantially affect interstate commerce in fact, but only whether a "rational basis" exists for so concluding. Given the enforcement difficulties that attend distinguishing between marijuana cultivated locally and marijuana grown elsewhere, and concerns about diversion into illicit channels, we have no difficulty concluding that Congress had a rational basis for believing that failure to regulate the intrastate manufacture and possession of marijuana would leave a gaping hole in the CSA. Thus…, Congress was acting well within its authority to "make all Laws which shall be necessary and proper" to "regulate Commerce…among the several States." That the regulation ensnares some purely intrastate activity is of no moment. As we have done many times before, we refuse to excise individual components of that larger scheme.

IV

…The activities regulated by the CSA are quintessentially economic. "Economics" [according to a dictionary] refers to "the production, distribution, and consumption of commodities." The CSA is a statute that regulates the production, distribution, and consumption of commodities for which there is an established, and lucrative, interstate market. Prohibiting the intrastate possession or manufacture of an article of commerce is a rational (and commonly utilized) means of regulating commerce in that

product. Such prohibitions include specific decisions requiring that a drug be withdrawn from the market as a result of the failure to comply with regulatory requirements as well as decisions excluding Schedule I drugs entirely from the market. Because the CSA is a statute that directly regulates economic, commercial activity, our opinion in *Morrison* casts no doubt on its constitutionality.

The Court of Appeals was able to conclude otherwise only by isolating a "separate and distinct" class of activities that it held to be beyond the reach of federal power, defined as "the intrastate, noncommercial cultivation, possession and use of marijuana for personal medical purposes on the advice of a physician and in accordance with state law." The court characterized this class as "different in kind from drug trafficking." The differences between the members of a class so defined and the principal traffickers in Schedule I substances might be sufficient to justify a policy decision exempting the narrower class from the coverage of the CSA. The question, however, is whether Congress' contrary policy judgment, *i.e.*, its decision to include this narrower "class of activities" within the larger regulatory scheme, was constitutionally deficient. We have no difficulty concluding that Congress acted rationally in determining that none of the characteristics making up the purported class, whether viewed individually or in the aggregate, compelled an exemption from the CSA; rather, the subdivided class of activities defined by the Court of Appeals was an essential part of the larger regulatory scheme.

First, the fact that marijuana is used "for personal medical purposes on the advice of a physician" cannot itself serve as a distinguishing factor. The CSA designates marijuana as contraband for *any* purpose; in fact, by characterizing marijuana as a Schedule I drug, Congress expressly found that the drug has no acceptable medical uses. Moreover, the CSA is a comprehensive regulatory regime specifically designed to regulate which controlled substances can be utilized for medicinal purposes, and in what manner. Indeed, most of the substances classified in the CSA "have a useful and legitimate medical purpose." Thus, even if respondents are correct that marijuana does have accepted medical uses and thus should be redesignated as a lesser schedule drug, the CSA would still impose controls beyond what is required by California law. The CSA requires manufacturers, physicians, pharmacies, and other handlers of controlled substances to comply with statutory and regulatory provisions mandating registration with the DEA, compliance with specific production quotas, security controls to guard against diversion, recordkeeping and reporting obligations, and prescription requirements. Furthermore, the dispensing of new drugs, even when doctors approve their use, must await federal approval. Accordingly, the mere fact that marijuana—like virtually every other controlled substance regulated by the CSA—is used for medicinal purposes cannot possibly serve to distinguish it from the core activities regulated by the CSA.

More fundamentally, if [it is true, as has been contended,] the personal cultivation, possession, and use of marijuana for medicinal purposes is beyond the "outer limits" of Congress' Commerce Clause authority, it must also be true that such personal use of marijuana (or any other homegrown drug) for recreational purposes is also beyond those "outer limits," whether or not a state elects to authorize or even regulate such use....One need not have a degree in economics to understand why a nationwide exemption for the vast quantity of marijuana (or other drugs) locally cultivated for personal use (which presumably would include use by friends, neighbors, and fam-

ily members) may have a substantial impact on the interstate market for this extraordinarily popular substance. The congressional judgment that an exemption for such a significant segment of the total market would undermine the orderly enforcement of the entire regulatory scheme is entitled to a strong presumption of validity. Indeed, that judgment is not only rational, but "visible to the naked eye" under any common-sense appraisal of the probable consequences of such an open-ended exemption.

Second, limiting the activity to marijuana possession and cultivation "in accordance with state law" cannot serve to place respondents' activities beyond congressional reach. The Supremacy Clause [in the U.S. Constitution] unambiguously provides that if there is any conflict between federal and state law, federal law shall prevail. It is beyond peradventure that federal power over commerce [prevails]...Just as state acquiescence to federal regulation cannot expand the bounds of the Commerce Clause, so too state action cannot circumscribe Congress' plenary commerce power.

Respondents acknowledge this proposition, but nonetheless contend that their activities were not "an essential part of a larger regulatory scheme" because they had been "isolated by the State of California, and [are] policed by the State of California," and thus remain "entirely separated from the market." The notion that California law has surgically excised a discrete activity that is hermetically sealed off from the larger interstate marijuana market is a dubious proposition, and, more importantly, one that Congress could have rationally rejected.

Indeed, that the California exemptions will have a significant impact on both the supply and demand sides of the market for marijuana is...is readily apparent. The exemption for physicians provides them with an economic incentive to grant their patients permission to use the drug. In contrast to most prescriptions for legal drugs, which limit the dosage and duration of the usage, under California law the doctor's permission to recommend marijuana use is open-ended. The authority to grant permission whenever the doctor determines that a patient is afflicted [according to the California law] with "any other illness for which marijuana provides relief" is broad enough to allow even the most scrupulous doctor to conclude that some recreational uses would be therapeutic. And our cases have taught us that there are some unscrupulous physicians who overprescribe when it is sufficiently profitable to do so.

The exemption for cultivation by patients and caregivers can only increase the supply of marijuana in the California market. The likelihood that all such production will promptly terminate when patients recover or will precisely match the patients' medical needs during their convalescence seems remote; whereas the danger that excesses will satisfy some of the admittedly enormous demand for recreational use seems obvious. Moreover, that the national and international narcotics trade has thrived in the face of vigorous criminal enforcement efforts suggests that no small number of unscrupulous people will make use of the California exemptions to serve their commercial ends whenever it is feasible to do so. Taking into account the fact that California is only one of at least nine states to have authorized the medical use of marijuana, Congress could have rationally concluded that the aggregate impact on the national market of all the transactions exempted from federal supervision is unquestionably substantial....

V

We...do note...the presence of...[an] avenue of relief....[The CSA] authorizes procedures for the reclassification of Schedule I drugs. But perhaps even more important than these legal avenues is the democratic process, in which the voices of voters allied with these respondents may one day be heard in the halls of Congress. Under the present state of the law, however, the judgment of the Court of Appeals must be vacated.

Federal Regulation of Medical Marijuana: Usurpation of State Authority

SANDRA DAY O'CONNOR

We enforce the "outer limits" of Congress' Commerce Clause authority not for their own sake, but to protect historic spheres of state sovereignty from excessive federal encroachment and thereby to maintain the distribution of power fundamental to our federalist system of government. One of federalism's chief virtues, of course, is that it promotes innovation by allowing for the possibility that [according to the often quoted words of Justice Louis D. Brandeis in 1932], "a single courageous State may, if its citizens choose, serve as a laboratory; and try novel social and economic experiments without risk to the rest of the country."

This case exemplifies the role of states as laboratories. The states' core police powers have always included authority to define criminal law and to protect the health, safety, and welfare of their citizens. Exercising those powers, California (by ballot initiative and then by legislative codification) has come to its own conclusion about the difficult and sensitive question of whether marijuana should be available to relieve severe pain and suffering. Today [in the decision written by Justice John Paul Stevens, III] the Court sanctions an application of the federal Controlled Substances Act that extinguishes that experiment, without any proof that the personal cultivation, possession, and use of marijuana for medicinal purposes, if economic activity in the first place, has a substantial effect on interstate commerce and is therefore an appropriate subject of federal regulation. In so doing, the Court announces a rule that gives Congress a perverse incentive to legislate broadly pursuant to the Commerce

Clause—nestling questionable assertions of its authority into comprehensive regulatory schemes—rather than with precision....

I

What is the relevant conduct subject to Commerce Clause analysis in this case? The Court takes its cues from Congress, applying the above considerations to the activity regulated by the Controlled Substances Act (CSA) in general. The Court's decision rests on two facts about the CSA: (1) Congress chose to enact a single statute providing a comprehensive prohibition on the production, distribution, and possession of all controlled substances, and (2) Congress did not distinguish between various forms of intrastate non-commercial cultivation, possession, and use of marijuana. Today's decision suggests that the federal regulation of local activity is immune to Commerce Clause challenge because Congress chose to act with an ambitious, all-encompassing statute, rather than piecemeal. In my view, allowing Congress to set the terms of the constitutional debate in this way, i.e., by packaging regulation of local activity in broader schemes, is tantamount to removing meaningful limits on the Commerce Clause.

The Court, [in the opinion written by Justice Stevens, argues that]...the CSA is "a lengthy and detailed statute creating a comprehensive framework for regulating the production, distribution, and possession of five classes of 'controlled substances.'" Thus, according to the Court,...the local activity that the CSA targets (in this case cultivation and possession of marijuana for personal medicinal use) cannot be separated from the general drug control scheme of which it is a part.

Today's decision allows Congress to regulate intrastate activity without check, so long as there is some implication by legislative design that regulating intrastate activity is essential (and the Court appears to equate "essential" with "necessary") to the interstate regulatory scheme....The Court appears to reason that the placement of local activity in a comprehensive scheme confirms that it is essential to that scheme....Furthermore, today's decision suggests we would readily sustain a congressional decision to attach the regulation of intrastate activity to a pre-existing comprehensive (or even not-so-comprehensive) scheme. If so, the Court invites increased federal regulation of local activity even if, as it suggests, Congress would not enact a *new* interstate scheme exclusively for the sake of reaching intrastate activity.

I cannot agree...[with the constitutionality of] such evasive or overbroad legislative strategies or that the constitutionality of federal regulation depends on superficial and formalistic distinctions. Likewise I did not understand our discussion of the role of courts in enforcing outer limits of the Commerce Clause for the sake of maintaining the federalist balance our Constitution requires as a signal to Congress to enact legislation that is more extensive and more intrusive into the domain of state power. If the Court always defers to Congress as it does today, little may be left to the notion of enumerated powers.

The hard work for courts, then, is to identify objective markers for confining the analysis in Commerce Clause cases. Here, respondents challenge the constitutionality of the CSA as applied to them and those similarly situated. I agree with the Court that we must look beyond respondents' own activities. Otherwise, individual litigants could always exempt themselves from Commerce Clause regulation merely by pointing to the obvious—that their personal activities do not have a substantial effect on interstate commerce. The task is to identify a mode of analysis that allows Congress to regulate more than nothing (by declining to reduce each case to its litigants) and less than everything (by declining to let Congress set the terms of analysis). The analysis may not be the same in every case, for it depends on the regulatory scheme at issue and the federalism concerns implicated.

A number of objective markers are available to confine the scope of constitutional review here. Both federal and state legislation—including the CSA itself, the California Compassionate Use Act, and other state medical marijuana legislation—recognize that medical and nonmedical (*i.e.*, recreational) uses of drugs are realistically distinct and can be segregated, and regulate them differently. Respondents challenge only the application of the CSA to medicinal use of marijuana. Moreover, because fundamental structural concerns about dual sovereignty [federal and state independent authority] animate our Commerce Clause cases, it is relevant that this case involves the interplay of federal and state regulation in areas of criminal law and social policy, where [according to earlier court decisions,] "States lay claim by right of history and expertise"...[Moreover, as found by the Court in another case,] "State autonomy is a relevant factor in assessing the means by which Congress exercises its powers" under the Commerce Clause. California, like other states, has drawn on its reserved powers to distinguish the regulation of medicinal marijuana. To ascertain whether Congress' encroachment is constitutionally justified in this case, then, I would focus here on the personal cultivation, possession, and use of marijuana for medicinal purposes.

Having thus defined the relevant conduct, we must determine whether, under our precedents, the conduct is economic and, in the aggregate, substantially affects interstate commerce. Even if intrastate cultivation and possession of marijuana for one's own medicinal use can properly be characterized as economic, and I question whether it can, it has not been shown that such activity substantially affects interstate commerce. Similarly, it is neither self-evident nor demonstrated that regulating such activity is necessary to the interstate drug control scheme.

The Court's definition of economic activity is breathtaking. It defines as economic any activity involving the production, distribution, and consumption of commodities. And it appears to reason that when an interstate market for a commodity exists, regulating the intrastate manufacture or possession of that commodity is constitutional either because that intrastate activity is itself economic, or because regulating it is a rational part of regulating its market. Putting to one side the problem endemic to the Court's opinion—the shift in focus from the activity at issue in this case to the entirety of what the CSA regulates. The Court's definition of economic activity for purposes of Commerce Clause jurisprudence threatens to sweep all of productive human activity into federal regulatory reach.

The Court uses a dictionary definition of economics to skirt the real problem of drawing a meaningful line between "what is national and what is local." It will not do to say that Congress may regulate noncommercial activity simply because it may have an effect on the demand for commercial goods, or because the noncommercial endeavor can, in some sense, substitute for commercial activity. Most commercial goods or services have some sort of privately producible analogue. Home care substi-

tutes for daycare. Charades games substitute for movie tickets. Backyard or windowsill gardening substitutes for going to the supermarket. To draw the line wherever private activity affects the demand for market goods is to draw no line at all, and to declare everything economic. We have already rejected the result that would follow—a federal police power.

In [earlier cases], we suggested that economic activity usually relates directly to commercial activity. The homegrown cultivation and personal possession and use of marijuana for medicinal purposes has no apparent commercial character. Everyone agrees that the marijuana at issue in this case was never in the stream of commerce, and neither were the supplies for growing it. (Marijuana is highly unusual among the substances subject to the CSA in that it can be cultivated without any materials that have traveled in interstate commerce.) Possession is not itself commercial activity. And respondents have not come into possession by means of any commercial transaction; they have simply grown, in their own homes, marijuana for their own use, without acquiring, buying, selling, or bartering a thing of value....

Even assuming that economic activity is at issue in this case, the [federal] government has made no showing in fact that the possession and use of homegrown marijuana for medical purposes, in California or elsewhere, has a substantial effect on interstate commerce. Similarly, the [federal] government has not shown that regulating such activity is necessary to an interstate regulatory scheme. Whatever the specific theory of "substantial effects" at issue (*i.e.*, whether the activity substantially affects interstate commerce, whether its regulation is necessary to an interstate regulatory scheme, or both), a concern for dual sovereignty requires that Congress' excursion into the traditional domain of states be justified.

That is why characterizing this as a case about the Necessary and Proper Clause does not change the analysis significantly. Congress must exercise its authority under the Necessary and Proper Clause in a manner consistent with basic constitutional principles. Congress cannot use its authority under the Clause to contravene the principle of state sovereignty embodied in the Tenth Amendment. Likewise, that authority must be used in a manner consistent with the notion of enumerated powers—a structural principle that is as much part of the Constitution as the Tenth Amendment's explicit textual command. Accordingly, something more than mere assertion is required when Congress purports to have power over local activity whose connection to an intrastate market is not self-evident. Otherwise, the Necessary and Proper Clause will always be a back door for unconstitutional federal regulation.

There is simply no evidence that homegrown medicinal marijuana users constitute, in the aggregate, a sizable enough class to have a discernible, let alone substantial, impact on the national illicit drug market—or otherwise to threaten the CSA regime. Explicit evidence is helpful when substantial effect is not "visible to the naked eye." And here, in part because common sense suggests that medical marijuana users may be limited in number and that California's Compassionate Use Act and similar state legislation may well isolate activities relating to medicinal marijuana from the illicit market, the effect of those activities on interstate drug traffic is not self-evidently substantial....

The Court [in Justice Steven's opinion] refers to a series of declarations in the introduction to the CSA saying that (1) local distribution and possession of controlled substances causes "swelling" in interstate traffic; (2) local production and distribution cannot be distinguished from interstate production and distribution; (3) federal control over intrastate incidents "is essential to effective control" over interstate drug trafficking....[These clauses] amount to nothing more than a legislative insistence that the regulation of controlled substances must be absolute. They are asserted without any supporting evidence—descriptive, statistical, or otherwise....

In particular, the CSA's introductory declarations are too vague and unspecific to demonstrate that the federal statutory scheme will be undermined if Congress cannot exert power over individuals like respondents. The declarations are not even specific to marijuana. (Facts about substantial effects may be developed in litigation to compensate for the inadequacy of Congress' findings; in part because this case comes to us from the grant of a preliminary injunction, there has been no such development.) Because here California, like other states, has carved out a limited class of activity for distinct regulation, the inadequacy of the CSA's findings is especially glaring. The California Compassionate Use Act exempts from other state drug laws patients and their caregivers "who posses[s] or cultivat[e] marijuana for the *personal* medical purposes of the patient upon the written or oral recommendation of a physician" to treat a list of serious medical conditions. The Act specifies that it should not be construed to supersede legislation prohibiting persons from engaging in acts dangerous to others, or to condone the diversion of marijuana for nonmedical purposes. To promote the Act's operation and to facilitate law enforcement, California recently enacted an identification card system for qualified patients. We generally assume states enforce their laws and have no reason to think otherwise here.

The [federal] government has not overcome empirical doubt that the number of Californians engaged in personal cultivation, possession, and use of medical marijuana, or the amount of marijuana they produce, is enough to threaten the federal regime. Nor has it shown that Compassionate Use Act marijuana users have been or are realistically likely to be responsible for the drug's seeping into the market in a significant way. The [federal] government does cite one estimate that there were over 100,000 Compassionate Use Act users in California in 2004, but does not explain, in terms of proportions, what their presence means for the national illicit drug market. [A study by the U.S.] General Accounting Office, Marijuana: Early Experience with Four States' Laws That Allow Use for Medical Purposes" (2002) [found that] in four California counties before the identification card system was enacted, voluntarily registered medical marijuana patients were less than 0.5 percent of the population; in Alaska, Hawaii, and Oregon, statewide medical marijuana registrants represented less than 0.05 percent of the states' populations. It also provides anecdotal evidence about the CSA's enforcement. The Court also offers some arguments about the effect of the Compassionate Use Act on the national market. It says that the California statute might be vulnerable to exploitation by unscrupulous physicians, that Compassionate Use Act patients may overproduce, and that the history of the narcotics trade shows the difficulty of cordoning off any drug use from the rest of the market. These arguments are plausible; if borne out in fact they could justify prosecuting Compassionate Use Act patients under the federal CSA. But, without substantiation, they add little to the CSA's conclusory statements about diversion, essentiality, and market effect. Piling assertion upon assertion does not, in my view, satisfy the substantiality test.

III

We would do well to recall how [in *Federalist* No. 45] James Madison, the father of the Constitution, described our system of joint sovereignty to the people of New York: "The powers delegated by the proposed constitution to the federal government are few and defined. Those which are to remain in the state governments are numerous and indefinite.…The powers reserved to the several states will extend to all the objects which, in the ordinary course of affairs, concern the lives, liberties, and properties of the people, and the internal order, improvement, and prosperity of the state."

Relying on Congress' abstract assertions, the Court has endorsed making it a federal crime to grow small amounts of marijuana in one's own home for one's own medicinal use. This overreaching stifles an express choice by some states, concerned for the lives and liberties of their people, to regulate medical marijuana differently. If I were a California citizen, I would not have voted for the medical marijuana ballot initiative; if I were a California legislator I would not have supported the Compassionate Use Act. But whatever the wisdom of California's experiment with medical marijuana, the federalism principles that have driven our Commerce Clause cases require that room for experiment be protected in this case. For these reasons I dissent.

THE CONTINUING DEBATE:
Federal Regulation of Medical Marijuana

What Is New

One June 6, 2005, the Supreme Court handed down its decision in *Gonzales v. Raich*. By a 6 to 3 vote, the court reversed the ruling of the Court of Appeals and held that the federal government could regulate marijuana under the interstate commerce clause. The decision applies to California and, by extension, to all other states permitting the use of medical marijuana. In one of the last cases over which he presided before his death in September, Chief Justice Rehnquist, who had often sided with the states, did so again and dissented along with Justice O'Connor and Justice Clarence Thomas. On the day of the decision, John P. Walters, President George Bush's director of national drug control policy, proclaimed, "Today's decision marks the end of medical marijuana as a political issue." Walters was almost certainly wrong. With the states barred from legalizing the use of medical marijuana, the focus of those who favor doing so will shift to Congress. Indeed, just before the decision, Barney Frank (D-MA) and 36 cosponsors introduced the States' Rights to Medical Marijuana Act (H.R. 2870) in the U.S. House of Representatives.

Where to Find More

For an entertaining view of the history of non-medical drug control, read "The History of the Non-Medical Use of Drugs in the United States" a speech to the California Judges Association 1995 annual conference at www.druglibrary.org/schaffer/History/whiteb1.htm. An authoritative review, "Workshop of the Medical Utility of Marijuana," sponsored by the National Institute for Health is available at www.nih.gov/news/medmarijuana/MedicalMarijuana.htm. Also worthwhile is Lawrence O. Gostin, "Medical Marijuana, American Federalism, and the Supreme Court," *JAMA: Journal of the American Medical Association* (2005). For the views of a group favoring the use of medical marijuana, go to the Web site of the Medical Marijuana Project at www.mpp.org/medicine.html. The view of an anti-use organization, the U.S. Drug Enforcement Administration, in its report, "Exposing the Myth of Smoked Medical Marijuana: The Facts" is at www.usdoj.gov/dea/ongoing/marijuana.html.

What More to Do

Analyze the positions of those in your class on this subject by dividing them into four groups according to each person's view of whether or not the expansive view of the commerce clause is acceptable or not and whether or not medical marijuana should be legalized. How many people have a constitutional position and a policy position that, in this case, are at odds with one another? Another project is to pick a different policy area that you think should not be subject to federal law under your concept of how federalism should work. Spend a little time finding out if there are federal laws governing that policy area. A group or an entire class can do this project together, with each person taking a different policy area.

3 | CIVIL RIGHTS

EVALUATING THE "RIGHT TO AN ABORTION" DECISION IN *ROE V. WADE*:
Positive Impact *or* Negative Impact?

POSITIVE IMPACT

ADVOCATE: R. Alta Charo, Professor of Law and Bioethics; Associate Dean for Research and Faculty Development, University of Wisconsin Law School

SOURCE: Testimony during hearings on "The Consequences of *Roe v. Wade* and *Doe v. Bolton*," U.S. Senate Committee on the Judiciary, Subcommittee on the Constitution, Civil Rights and Property Rights June 23, 2005

NEGATIVE IMPACT

ADVOCATE: Teresa Collett, Professor of Law, University of St. Thomas School of Law, Minneapolis, Minnesota

SOURCE: Testimony during hearings on "The Consequences of *Roe v. Wade* and *Doe v. Bolton*," U.S. Senate Committee on the Judiciary, Subcommittee on the Constitution, Civil Rights and Property Rights June 23, 2005

January 22, 1973, was a pivotal day in one of the most contentious legal and social debates in U.S. history. On that date the U.S. Supreme Court handed down its decision in *Roe v. Wade*. By a 7–2 vote, the justices, in effect, invalidated state restrictions on the ability of women to medically abort their pregnancies. At that time, four states permitted abortion "on demand" (for any reason), 15 allowed abortions if continuing the pregnancy endangered a woman's health, and 31 banned abortions unless the woman's life was endangered.

The court based its decision on a "right to privacy." In the majority opinion, Justice Harry Blackmun conceded, "the Constitution does not explicitly mention any right of privacy." Nevertheless, he continued, "The Constitution recognizes that rights exist beyond those specified in that document…this right of privacy…is broad enough to encompass a woman's decision whether or not to terminate her pregnancy."

Supporters of *Roe v. Wade* often claim it secured the right of women to have to an abortion and to control their bodies. However, Blackmun said otherwise. In his words, "Some argue that the woman's right is absolute and that she is entitled to terminate her pregnancy at whatever time, in whatever way, and for whatever reason she alone chooses. With this we [justices] do not agree." Blackmun continued, "The privacy right…cannot be said to be absolute," and he indicated, "It is not clear to us [the justices] that the claim…that one has an unlimited right to do with one's body as one pleases bears a close relationship to the right of privacy."

Thus, instead of unrestricted right, the court outlined a limited right with different standards for each trimester of a normal pregnancy. In Blackmun's words, during the first trimester, "the abortion decision…must be left to the medical judgment of the pregnant woman's attending physician." Abortion could only be regulated during the second trimester in "ways that are reasonably related to maternal health." And during the third trimester, a state "may, if it chooses, regulate, and even proscribe, abortion except where it is necessary…for the preservation of the life or health of the mother."

The Court's decision changed the law, but the debate continues. Indeed, it is hard for many of those who differ on abortion to discuss the subject calmly. They do not even agree on what the fundamental issue is. Abortion rights advocates view the issue as about a woman's right to choose and thus label themselves "pro-choice." Foes of abortion say they are "pro-life" based on their view that human life begins at conception—or at least much sooner than the beginning of the third trimester.

Since *Roe v. Wade*, those oppose abortions altogether or who want to limit them have made numerous attempts to overturn the decision by amending the Constitution. They have also sought to pass state or federal laws that regulate abortion within the parameters set down by the Supreme Court in *Roe v. Wade* and subsequent court decisions.

As the readings that follow by R. Alta Charo and Teresa Collett demonstrate, passions about the abortion issue have not abated in the more than 30 years since the *Roe v. Wade* decision. During the 108th Congress (2003–2005) alone, dozens of bills related to abortion were introduced in the House and Senate. For example, in 2003 congress enacted a ban on an abortion procedure termed "intact dilation and extraction" (D&X), also commonly called "partial-birth abortions" by anti-abortion advocates.

Public opinion is has been very divided on abortion since *Roe v. Wade* in 1973. Soon after that decision, one poll found 47% in favor of the ruling, 44% opposed, and 9% unsure. A poll taken in 2005 just a month before the congressional hearings from which the readings that follow were drawn revealed similar opinion, with, on average, 48% of respondents saying they were "pro-choice," 44% being "pro-life," and 10% unsure.

POINTS TO PONDER

➤ The *Roe v. Wade* decision generally allows states to bar abortions during the third trimester of pregnancy because the fetus is considered "viable," that is, it could survive outside the womb. Are "viability" and "life" synonymous?

➤ If advances in medicine make it possible for fetuses to usually become viable earlier and earlier into pregnancy, would you favor generally banning abortions earlier to meet the existing viability time?

➤ In addition to abortion, Justice Blackmun's declaration in the *Roe v. Wade* decision that people to not have an unlimited right to do whatever they want with their body affects issues like suicide, assisted or not. Do you agree with the court on this matter?

Evaluating the "Right to an Abortion" Decision in *Roe v. Wade*: Positive Impact

R. Alta Charo

Roe v. Wade's broad vision of the right to privacy is our constitutional bulwark against legislation mandating a Chinese-style one-child policy; governmental eugenics policies that penalize parents who choose to have a child with disabilities; state prohibitions on home-schooling our children; forcible intubation of competent but terminally ill patients; and the issuance of a state-approved list of permissible forms of sexual intercourse between husband and wife. If we reject the core holding of *Roe v. Wade* that some activities are too intimate and some family matters too personal to be the subject of governmental intrusion, then we also reject any significant limit on the power of the government to dictate not only our personal morality but also the way we choose to live, to marry, and to raise our children.

Roe v. Wade is at the core of American jurisprudence, and its multiple strands of reasoning concerning marital privacy, medical privacy, bodily autonomy, psychological liberty, and gender equality are all connected to myriad other cases concerning the rights of parents to rear their children, the right to marry, the right use contraception, the right to have children, and the right to refuse unwanted medical treatment. Overturning *Roe* would unravel far more than the right to terminate a pregnancy, and many Americans who have never felt they had a personal stake in the abortion debate would suddenly find their own interests threatened, whether it was the elderly seeking to control their medical treatment, the infertile seeking to use IVF to have a child, the woman seeking to make a decision about genetic testing, the couple heeding public health messages to use a condom to reduce the risk of contracting AIDS or other sexually transmitted diseases, or the unmarried man who, with his partner, is trying to avoid becoming a father before he is ready to support a family. As a legal matter, the right of the government to regulate, or even prohibit, reproductive choices depends both on whether they are considered an exercise of especially protected personal liberties and whether their absence has a sufficiently disparate impact on women's lives that it amounts to a denial of equal protection of the law.

Various aspects of reproductive privacy rights have been articulated in a number of landmark cases in the U.S. Supreme Court. The earliest case limited the right of the government to order involuntary sterilization. In the 1960s and 1970s, the Court issued other landmark rulings that protected access to contraceptives and abortion services, declaring that the "decision whether or not to beget or bear a child is at the very heart of this cluster of constitutionally protected choices" and that "if the right of privacy means anything, it is the right of the individual…to be free of unwarranted governmental intrusion into matters so fundamentally affecting a person as the decision to bear or beget a child."

The earliest cases, such as those concerning forced sterilization, were grounded in a traditional, common-law concern about bodily integrity, but the later cases incorporated concerns about marital privacy and psychological autonomy. For example, a right to contraception for men—for whom conception is a psychological and potentially economic burden, but not a physical one—implicitly endorsed a theory of reproductive liberty that went beyond mere bodily integrity and included a more general right to set the course of one's future. This is a notion of reproductive liberty that embraces a variety of activities that have no physical implications but are at the core of the right to self-determination, for example the right to marry, the right to rear one's children in the manner of one's choosing, or the right to use medical services to predict one's risk of having offspring with devastating diseases.

Subsequent abortion decisions have recognized the scope and implications of this expansive notion of personal liberty. Where psychological autonomy was raised, as in Justice Sandra Day O'Connor's statement that "at the heart of liberty is the right to define one's own concept of existence, of meaning, of the universe, and of the mystery of human life," it was ravaged by some of her colleagues, as when Justice [Antonin] Scalia wrote that this "collection of adjectives...can be applied to many forms of conduct that this Court has held are not entitled to constitutional protection...(for example) homosexual sodomy, polygamy, adult incest and suicide, all of which are equally 'intimate' and 'deeply personal' decisions involving 'personal autonomy and bodily integrity,' and all of which can constitutionally be proscribed because it is our unquestionable constitutional tradition that they are proscribable." Left unsaid in Justice Scalia's dissent, however, is an equally strong historical tradition of banning contraception and interracial marriage, which would once again be an option for individual states should personal and psycho-

logical liberty no longer be constitutionally protected.

These comments by Scalia did presage a series of doctrinal struggles within the Supreme Court, and subsequent abortion cases have emphasized instead gender equality or bodily autonomy. Similarly, cases concerning control over the manner of one's death backed away from expanding upon *Roe v. Wade*'s vision of personal liberty. But by the same token, the Court has steadfastly upheld the right to refuse unwanted medical treatment as consistent with the right to privacy and bodily autonomy enunciated in *Roe*. Overturn *Roe* and one risks losing the constitutional grounds with which to challenge a state law that forces hospitals to inflict painful and even futile medical interventions on competent, protesting patients.

Thus, the implications of overturning *Roe v. Wade* are difficult to predict but certainly go beyond the narrow question of abortion. Much depends upon how the court would choose to identify the key justifications for the right to privacy deployed in *Roe* and which they would now propose to overturn.

If the court reverses *Roe v. Wade* and limits the right to privacy to intimate marital relations, then technologies such as artificial insemination and in vitro fertilization that often use a third party may not be protected, because they represent a departure from the purest form of marital privacy. Perhaps even more alarmingly, the longstanding right of unmarried persons to obtain contraceptives would be undermined, as would the right of unmarried persons to be free of coercive state efforts to prevent them from bearing children, for example, through forced sterilization or exorbitant tax penalties for having children outside marriage.

If it reverses *Roe v. Wade* and limits the right to privacy to preventing the government from casually interfering with the physical bodies and reproductive capabilities of its citizens, although there might still be protection from involuntary sterilization, there would be only a far weaker claim of any right to access medical services such as IVF that depend on extra-uterine maintenance or diagnosis of embryos. And again, perhaps more alarmingly, an interpretation narrowly focused on bodily autonomy would no longer support the more expansive notions of privacy and liberty that support parental discretion to choose the language of instruction for their children or to make other fundamental decisions about how to rear their children.

But however it chooses to reverse *Roe v. Wade*, it would be necessary to reject existing case law, which singles out human reproduction for the profound way in which it reflects individual choices, aspirations and self-identity. This is because neither marital intimacy nor bodily autonomy rights could explain the right of men to use a simple condom to avoid unintended pregnancy or the right of parents to freely choose whether or not to use genetic testing, that is, to freely choose whether to avoid or embrace the possibility of having a child with genetic disabilities. Rejecting the notion that our liberty rights encompass a right to control the path our lives would clear the way for a broad range of government intrusions into both reproductive decisions and other matters of personal life.

Of course, it is possible that the Court might overturn *Roe v. Wade* not by backing away from its principle of a fundamental right to privacy but rather by a claim that the fertilized egg and developing embryo have competing rights that outweigh even a fundamental right to privacy. One hears this point of view in the claim that the founding fathers listed "life, liberty, and the pursuit of happiness" in that order. But to accept this argument, however, the court would be forced to redefine the egg or embryo as a "person" for the purposes of the 14th Amendment; without that status, the interests imputed to the embryo could not outweigh the undisputed interests of an adult woman.

If the courts conclude that embryos are protected as persons by the 14th Amendment, it is not only the abortions that follow unprotected sex that could be outlawed. It is not only the abortions following failed contraceptive efforts that could be outlawed. It is also abortions following cases of rape and incest that could be outlawed, because the effect of ruling that embryos have the same rights as children is to rule that nothing short of a threat to a woman's life could justify their destruction.

And re-defining the egg or embryo as a 14th Amendment person, entitled to equal protection under the law, has implications that go far beyond the legality of abortion. Now viewed as legally equivalent to a live-born child, a parent would be required to provide nurture, to avoid undue risk, and to effect a rescue when the conceptus was in danger, just as a parent must do for a child. In practical terms, providing nurture and avoiding undue risk might well mean that women would lose the right to choose midwives over physicians, or to use herbal remedies and nutritional supplements rather than prescribed drugs during pregnancy. Indeed, they might even lose the right to treat their own illnesses, such as epilepsy or slow-growing cancer, if such treatments might destroy the embryo but foregoing the treatments would merely interfere with the health, but not the life, of the woman herself.

Even contraceptive techniques such as breast feeding and the rhythm method might be banned, as they not only reduce the odds of fertilization, but when fertilization nonetheless occurs, they reduce the chances that the fertilized egg will successfully implant in the uterine wall. This is precisely the reasoning by which many abortion opponents advocate a ban on birth control pills, IUDs and all other forms of hormonal contraception. Indeed, given that in most months a sexually active woman will lose a fertilized egg during her menstrual cycle, abandoning *Roe v. Wade* would mean, at least theoretically, that the government could prescribe the precise time of the month when sexual activity is permitted, in order to reduce the chances that a fertilized egg will fail to implant in the uterine wall. More realistically, a duty to rescue an embryo in danger could mean that women would be forced to have every IVF [n vitro fertilization] embryo they create put back in their bodies, even if additional embryos posed a threat to fetal and maternal health, and even if pregnancy attempts were likely futile.

Practical consequences such as these demonstrate not only the moral, ethical, and logistical challenges that await us if *Roe v. Wade* is overturned, but also the tremendous implications this would have for women's equality interests. A blanket principle that accords equal rights as between embryos and adults functions, in fact, to place virtually all responsibility and burden upon women. It is women who will be vulnerable to state mandated medical interventions. It is women whose edu-cations will be interrupted, with potentially lifelong consequences. It is women whose jobs and careers will be at risk, with all the economic losses that entails.

That men and women are biologically different is a physiological fact. For some, this suggests that it is women's lot to bear the cost of intimate relations. For others, however, and for the Supreme Court in many of its decisions that go far beyond *Roe v. Wade*, it means that it is the duty of the government to avoid adopting policies or announcing principles that forever place women at the service of the state rather than as the mistresses of their own lives.

Overall, *Roe v. Wade* represents the culmination of decades of constitutional law on the need to restrain over-zealous governmental intrusions on personal decisions concerning our families, our bodies, and our lives. In turn, it has formed the basis for yet more decades of constitutional law on the importance of maintaining a zone of personal liberty and privacy, in which individuals may flourish. In a century that will bring ever greater temptations and technological capabilities for governmental surveillance and control of its citizens, maintaining the integrity of this zone of personal liberty and privacy is more important than ever.

Evaluating the "Right to an Abortion" Decision in *Roe v. Wade*: Negative Impact

TERESA COLLETT

Contrary to the intention of [its] authors and proponents, *Roe v. Wade* [has] significantly undermined the well being of women and children in the United States, as well as seriously damaged the political fabric of American civil society. Due to the time constraints of the committee, my testimony today will just address the first issue. Throughout this country's history women have struggled to gain political, social, and economic equality. By 1972 however, the year before *Roe* [was] decided, women were making considerable strides towards achieving these goals. According to a 1972 report by the United States Census Bureau, "Women who had completed 4 years or more of college were as likely as men with the same education to be professional, technical, administrative, or managerial workers." In 1964 [Senator] Margaret Chase Smith [R-ME] became the first woman in our nation's history to be nominated for the presidency of the United States by a national political party. In 1967 Muriel Seibert became the first woman to own a seat on the New York Stock Exchange, and five short years later Juanita Kreps became the first woman director of that eminent institution. Women were making great progress in our society, and it is not by means of denying their capacity to conceive and bear children. Rather than furthering these achievements while accommodating the unique maternal capacity of women, *Roe* adopted the sterile "male model" of society effectively forcing women to conform to ideal of childlessness in order to gain equality.

It was no accident that the early feminists, such as Elizabeth Cady Stanton and Susan B. Anthony, opposed abortion. They saw it as a tool of oppression, manifesting men's domination and mistreatment. Elizabeth Cady Stanton wrote, "When we consider that women are treated as property, it is degrading to women that we should treat our children as property to be disposed of as we see fit." Susan B. Anthony was of the same opinion:

> "Guilty? Yes. No matter what the motive, love of ease, or a desire to save from suffering the unborn innocent, the woman is awfully guilty who commits the deed. It will burden her conscience in life, it will burden her soul in death; But oh, thrice guilty is he who drove her to the desperation which impelled her to the crime!"

In their newspaper devoted to women's equality, *The Revolution*, Matilda Joslyn Gage wrote "[This] subject lies deeper down in woman's wrongs than any other…I hesitate not to assert that most of [the responsibility for] this crime lies at the door of the male sex." So strongly did these women reject abortion that they put the solvency of their publication, *The Revolution*, at risk rather than accept advertisements from abortionists.

By their rejection of abortion, these women demanded something more meaningful (and more radical) than what the majority [of the justices in] the *Roe* [case]…ordered—they demanded equality as full women, not as chemically or surgically altered surrogates of men. The early feminists understood that abortion on demand, not motherhood, posed the real threat to women's rights. The early feminists recognized that abortion was the product, not of choice, but of pressure, particularly from the men in women's lives. The current regime of abortion which *Roe* instigated has not changed this sad fact. A 1998 study published by the Guttmacher Institute, a research affiliate of Planned Parenthood, indicates that relationship problems contributed to the decision to seek abortions by 51% of American women.

Underlying this general reason are such specific ones as that the partner threatened to abandon the woman if she gives birth, that the partner or the woman herself refuses to marry to legitimate the birth, that a break-up is imminent for reasons other than the pregnancy, that the pregnancy resulted from an extramarital relationship, that the husband or partner mistreated the woman because of her pregnancy, or that the husband or partner simply does not want the child. Sometimes women combined these reasons with not being able to afford a baby, suggesting the importance of having a partner who can offer both emotional and financial support. The simple fact is that today, as in the 19th century, for many women abortion is the man's solution for what he views as the "woman's problem." *Roe's* harmful effects on women have not been confined to the social realm. Medical science has shown that abortion damages women's physical and mental health as well. By aborting their pregnancies, women lose the health benefits that childbirth and its accompanying lactation bring, including reduced risk of breast, ovarian, and endometrial cancer.

One-third of all women in the U.S. will suffer from cancer in their lifetime.

Cancer is the second leading cause of death in the United States.

Breast cancer is the most common cancer diagnosed in women, and the second leading cause of cancer death in women. It is estimated that about 211,240 women in the United States will be diagnosed with invasive breast cancer in 2005, and about 40,410 women will die from the disease. One of the recognized risk factors for breast cancer is having no children or delaying childbearing until after the age of thirty.

In 1970 the World Health Organization published the results of an international study of breast cancer and reproductive experience involving 250,000 women from seven areas. The study established that women having their first child under age 18 have only about one-third the breast cancer risk of those whose first birth is delayed until age 35 or older. The researchers also noted that "data suggests an increased risk [of breast cancer] associated with abortion contrary to the reduction in risk associated with full-term births."

Childbirth also has a protective effect against ovarian cancer. Ovarian cancer is the seventh most common cancer, but ranks fourth as the cause of cancer death in women. It causes more deaths than any other cancer of the female reproductive system. The American Cancer Society estimates that there will be about 22,220 new cases of ovarian cancer in this country in 2005. About 16,210 women will die of the disease. While less common than breast cancer, it is more likely to be fatal. Childbirth reduces this risk.

Endometrial cancer is a cancer that develops from the inner lining of the uterus. In 2005, 40,880 new cases of endometrial cancer are expected to be diagnosed, and 7,310 women are expected to die from this cancer. Researchers have found that the process of childbirth results in the shedding of malignant or pre-malignant cells which lead to endometrial cancer. This protective effect increases with each birth.

In contrast, abortions render women thirty percent more likely to develop breast cancer and also increase the likelihood of developing cervical and ovarian cancer.

Abortion also creates numerous health hazards for subsequent pregnancies, including increasing the likelihood of death during childbirth. Furthermore, women who have had abortions experience varying degrees of emotional distress and are more likely to exhibit self-destructive behaviors, including suicide.

While it is often said that abortion is significantly safer than completing the pregnancy, the fact is we simply don't have the statistical information to know. Abortion providers have concede this fact in the published literature. Yet any attempts to remedy this critical lack of public health information are furiously fought by abortion-rights advocates.

Yet women are not the only ones harmed by the mentality reflected in the *Roe* [decision]. It is often said that the Court did not understand the physical development of the unborn at the case [was] heard. Yet I recently had occasion to go back and read the [legal] briefs presented to the *Roe* Court and was amazed by the amount of detail concerning the development of the unborn child, even in 1973. While there were no pictures as compelling as tiny Samuel Armas's hand apparently grasping the finger of the perinatal surgeon who was repairing his spine while Samuel was still in his mother's womb or those currently available from a 4-D ultrasound system, our common humanity was made clear by the Attorney General of Texas from the medical materials available, even at that time. The failure of the Court to engage this material in its opinion deeply troubles me.

Courts have traditionally recognized some rights in unborn children, and medical science continues to demonstrate with increasing veracity that even at the earliest stages of development, an unborn child is a human being. Even *Roe* recognized that the States have a compelling interest in protecting this human life. Nevertheless, this decision authorized expectant mothers to choose abortion over life, and since 1973, over thirty-nine million legal abortions have been performed in the United States. In this country alone, roughly 700 pregnancies per year continue after an initial abortion attempt, and children born after these failed attempts are likely to suffer from developmental abnormalities. Also, as previously noted, children conceived after an abortion and carried to term run a higher risk of prenatal complications.

Perhaps even more troubling is the mounting evidence that abortion has contributed to the reemergence of the idea of children as possessions. In 1972, one year before the *Roe v. Wade* decision, there were 2.05 reported abuse cases per 1,000 children, according to the U.S. Bureau of the Census. In April 2004 the U.S. Department of Health and Human Services reported 12.3 out of every 1,000 children were victims of abuse or neglect. In the six short years from 1986 to 1993 the total number of children endangered quadrupled. While many factors may have contributed to this increase, the attitude that we are free to dispose of human life that is "unwanted" certainly must be among them.

With the advent of in vitro fertilization, technology that only became available five years after *Roe v. Wade*, some would-be parents now dream of "custom-order" children resulting in today's debate regarding the morality of selecting the sex and other characteristics of a child. The parameters of this debate have expanded so far as to include those who defend the right of two deaf lesbians to intentionally create a deaf child.

All of these facts lead me to agree with a recent opinion of Judge Edith Jones of the United States Court of Appeals for the Fifth Circuit: Hard [science] and social science will of course progress even though the Supreme Court averts its eyes. It takes no expert prognosticator to know that research on women's mental and physical health following abortion will yield an eventual medical consensus, and neonatal science will push the frontiers of fetal "viability" ever closer to the date of conception. One may fervently hope that the Court will someday acknowledge such developments and re-evaluate *Roe* accordingly. Some of us think that day needs to be now.

THE CONTINUING DEBATE:
Evaluating the "Right to an Abortion" Decision in *Roe v. Wade*

What Is New

During 2004 and 2005, several U.S. District Courts and the Eighth Circuit of the U.S. Court of Appeals rejected the 2003 act banning D&X abortions as violating *Roe v. Wade* and other precedent. Many believe the case will ultimately wind up in the Supreme Court. Additionally, during its 2005–2006 term, the Supreme Count has agreed to decide *Ayotte v. Planned Parenthood*, a case in which the U.S. Court of Appeals struck down New Hampshire's parental notification law. Even more importantly, conservative John G. Roberts succeeded William Rehnquist as chief justice on the Supreme Court and President Bush is likely to nominate another conservative to succeed Sandra Day O'Connor. With the court narrowly divided on some abortion questions, the new justices could tip the balance in favor of the pro-life position.

As for public opinion, polls showed very mixed opinions. Some 60% said they thought the *Roe v. Wade* decision was a "good thing," but, as noted in the introduction, there was a nearly even split between those describing themselves as pro-choice and pro-life. Moreover 70% said abortion was "morally wrong" either always or sometimes. When asked about trimesters, 60% thought abortion should be legal in the first trimester, but only 26% supported in the second trimester, and a mere 12% favored it in the third trimester.

Where to Find More

The abortion debate in the United States dates back even beyond Connecticut's enactment of the first anti-abortion law in 1821. For a review of that debate, see Rosemary Nossiff, *Before Roe: Abortion Policy in the States* (Temple University Press, 2002). A study comparing abortion laws in 64 countries is Albin Eser and H. G. Koch, *Abortion and the Law: From International Comparison to Legal Policy* (Cambridge University Press, 2005).

Current information on the abortion debate and its politics can be found on the Web sites of those representing both points of view. That of the Center for Reproductive Rights, author of the first reading is at: http://www.crlp.org/. Representing the pro-life point of view is the National Right to Life Committee at http://www.nrlc.org/. A site that claims to be balanced and seems to strive for that can be found at: http://www.religioustolerance.org/abortion1.htm.

What More to Do

The greatest challenge is to try to reach an agreement on this emotionally charged issue. Certainly it will not be possible to reconcile everyone. There are ardent voices that see no middle ground between the right to choose and the right to life. But polls show that most Americans are less doctrinaire. A 2005 poll recorded 20% of its respondents thinking abortion should be legal in all cases, 37% saying legal in most cases, 24% arguing it should be illegal in most cases, 12% wanting abortion to be illegal in all cases, and 7% uncertain. Somewhere in that majority of 68% Americans who are in the "most cases" or "uncertain" middle there may be a place that takes into account fetal/infant viability, maternal health, and other factors and creates a policy that most Americans can accept. Can your class craft a statement of standards that would receive a majority vote in the class?

4 CIVIL LIBERTIES

CURRENT SEPARATION OF CHURCH AND STATE DOCTRINE:
Reasonable Balance *or* Suppressing Public Displays of Faith?

REASONABLE BALANCE

ADVOCATE: Melissa Rogers, Professor, Wake Forest University Divinity School

SOURCE: Testimony during hearings on "Beyond the Pledge of Allegiance: Hostility to Religious Expression in the Public Square," U.S. Senate Committee on the Judiciary June 8, 2004

SUPPRESSING PUBLIC DISPLAYS OF FAITH

ADVOCATE: Vincent Phillip Munoz, Professor of Political Science, North Carolina State University and Civitas Fellow of Religion and Public Life, American Enterprise Institute

SOURCE: Testimony during hearings on "Beyond the Pledge of Allegiance: Hostility to Religious Expression in the Public Square," U.S. Senate Committee on the Judiciary June 8, 2004

As with many political debates, the Constitution is an important starting point. The First Amendment requires that "Congress shall make no law respecting an establishment of religion [the establishment clause], or prohibiting the free exercise thereof [the freedom of religion clause]...."

This debate focuses on the establishment clause. What is clear about it is that the authors of the First Amendment were reacting against the British practice of establishing and supporting an "official" church, in that case the Church of England. It is equally certain that Congress meant the amendment to bar prohibiting any religion or religious belief. There the certainties end. For example, freedom of religion does not mean that the government cannot proscribe certain religious practices. Polygamy, animal sacrifice, and taking illegal drugs are just a few of the practices exercised in the name religion that have been barred by the government with subsequent court approval. More to the point of this particular debate, it is also unclear how far the establishment clause should go in barring various religious symbols and other expressions of religion in government-owned buildings and spaces and government-run activities.

Religion has always had a presence in government in the Untied States. The Great Seal of the United States, adopted in 1782 (and found on the back left of one-dollar bills) contains an "all seeing eye of Providence," which probably means God, especially given that it is framed in a triangle, thought to represent the Christian trinity. The Great Seal also contains the Latin phrase "annuit coeptis," which translates as "It/He (Providence/God) has favored our undertakings." Also, first adopted in 1964 and currently on all U.S. paper currency is the motto "In God We Trust." That phrase is also found in the fourth stanza of the Star Spangled Banner (written 1813; official adopted 1931), which concludes, "Then conquer we must, when our cause it is just, And this be our motto: "In God is our trust." Finally, in 1957 Congress added "under

God" after one nation" to the Pledge of Allegiance.

Government also has always, and continues to, support religion and to choose among religions in other ways. For example, the military employs chaplains for all the major religious faiths, but does not employ atheist counselors. There is also a level of choosing among religions in having chaplains for the major religions, but not for the minor ones. Each year the president lights an immense Christmas tree, although these days in a bow to restrictions on religious displays on public property the giant fir is call the "national tree" and is lighted as part of the "Pageant of Peace," which, of course, corresponds with the Christmas season.

Throughout most of U.S. history, displays of the Ten Commandment, Christmas trees, crèches or similar religious symbols on public property, prayers in public schools, and other now controversial topics were not high-profile issues. One indication of that is that prior to the 1940s the Supreme Court heard almost no cases related to religion because few federal laws touched on that subject. The flow of cases changed when in *Cantwell v. Connecticut* (1940) and *Everson v. Board of Education* (1947) the court ruled that the due process cause of the Fourteenth Amendment respectively made the free exercise of religion wording and establishment clause of the First Amendment applicable to the states, as well as federal government. During the ensuing years, as the following readings by Professors Melissa Rogers and Vincent Munoz detail, a significant number of cases involving practices at the state and local levels were brought before the federal courts and ultimately to the Supreme Court.

With regard to establishment clause cases, the Court struck down prayers and religious invocations in public schools, releasing children from regular curriculums to attend religious instruction, most religious displays on public property, and other explicit and implicit supports of religion by public officials. However, the Supreme Court has also allowed religious groups to meet in public buildings as long as there is no discrimination, has supported prayers opening legislative sessions, and having student groups fees go to student religious groups.

Writing in 1802 to a Baptist group in Connecticut, President Thomas Jefferson argued that the freedom of religion and establishment clauses of the First Amendment were meant to build "a wall of separation between church and state." In the first reading, Melissa Rogers contends that the courts have done an admirable job of doing that. Vincent Phillip Munoz disagrees in the second reading, arguing that the Supreme Court has gone too far, has become hostile to religion and restricted its role in public activities far more than warranted by the Constitution or wanted by the American people.

POINTS TO PONDER

➢ Expressing an absolutist position when writing the majority opinion in the Everson case, Justice Hugo Black argued that the wall between church and state "must be kept high and impregnable. We [should] not approve any breach." What would be the implications of adopting that no-compromise standard?

➢ Is there a difference, as some argue, between freedom *of* religion and freedom *from* religion?

➢ Compare Rogers' argument that government-sanctioned religious expressions are a "coercive influence" and the view of Munoz that tolerance should be a "a two-way street."

45

Current Separation of Church and State Doctrine: Reasonable Balance

Ms. Melissa Rogers

I. INTRODUCTION

I believe religion can and should play a vital role in American public life. The rights to free speech and the free exercise of religion are fundamental to American citizenship and human dignity. These rights allow religious people to live in fidelity to their faith and their nation, a treasure many in this world do not enjoy. The Constitution wisely recognizes that people cannot be expected to limit their religious expression to their homes or places of worship—faith informs many Americans' daily lives and decision-making on public as well as private matters. Indeed, our national dialogue would be impoverished and distorted if religion were to be excluded from the public square, and our work together as a nation would be less just, humble and kind. These rights have helped to create an American landscape in which religious freedom and religion are strong.

I also believe that the constitutional prohibition on governmental establishment of religion plays an equally important role in protecting religious freedom. The Establishment Clause of the First Amendment prohibits the government from promoting religion or sponsoring religious activities and exercises. This prohibition not only protects the right of all Americans to choose in matters of faith, it strengthens the American public square and religion in other ways. By insisting that the government stay neutral between religion and religion, it creates confidence among those of minority faiths that they will have equal rights as citizens. This safeguards our nation's stability amidst growing religious diversity. By securing governmental neu-

trality between religion and non-religion, the Establishment Clause builds solidarity among all Americans, regardless of their faith or lack thereof. By ensuring that religious, rather than governmental, authorities define religion and shape its course, the prohibition on governmental establishment of religion, no less than the rights to free exercise and free speech, protects religion's vitality and integrity.

In its decisions regarding religious expression in the public square, the U.S. Supreme Court has struck a wise balance by protecting the right of citizens and religious groups to promote their faith and prohibiting the government from doing so. When the Court has found certain religious expression to be unconstitutional, I believe the evidence demonstrates that it has been motivated by a desire to protect choices in matters of faith from government's coercive influence, not by hostility toward religion or religious expression.

Moreover, it has been my general experience that, on those occasions when other governmental bodies over-interpret the law prohibiting governmental establishment of religion, those misinterpretations are due to ignorance of or confusion about this complex area of law rather than to bad intent. I also should note that I have encountered situations in which governmental bodies under-interpret the Establishment Clause, which results in another kind of serious deprivation. Both kinds of violations should be viewed as matters that are equally troubling. Both kinds of violations should be swiftly rectified through education about and enforcement of the law.

I do not believe, therefore, that there is persistent or frequent governmental hostility toward religious expression in the public square. Indeed, it strikes me that religious freedom is something America usually gets remarkably right....

II. DO THE DECISIONS OF THE U.S. SUPREME COURT REFLECT HOSTILITY TO RELIGIOUS EXPRESSION IN THE PUBLIC SQUARE?

Do the decisions of the U.S. Supreme Court reflect hostility to religious expression in the public square? My answer to this question is "no" for at least two reasons. First, the Court has ruled in favor of protecting religious expression in public places many times. Second, when the Court has found that religious expression is unconstitutional because it constitutes governmental promotion or sponsorship of religion, its reasoning has not reflected or been rooted in hostility toward religious expression. The following two sections expand on these issues.

A. The Public Role Religion May Play Under the U.S. Constitution

The U.S. Supreme Court has said: "[T]here is a crucial difference between government speech endorsing religion, which the Establishment Clause [of the First Amendment] forbids, and private speech endorsing religion, which the Free Speech and Free Exercise Clauses [of the First Amendment] protect." This reference to "private speech" is not limited to speech "in private," of course, but describes religious expression attributable to private individuals and groups rather than to the government. Thus, under the First Amendment, the government has two principal responsibilities regarding religious expression: it must not endorse religion itself, but it must protect the right of citizens and religious groups to do so.

Using this reasoning, the Court has made it clear that there is a role for public religious expression on government property, in policymaking and politics. For example, while public school teachers cannot lead their classes in prayers or Bible readings, the Court's decisions leave room for public school students to say grace over their lunches and to read their Bibles at school. As the Court has said: "[N]othing in the Constitution...prohibits any public school student from voluntarily praying at any time, before, during or after the schoolday." It is widely agreed that these decisions also allow public school students many other opportunities to express and exercise their faith, including the right to "express their religious beliefs in the form of reports, homework and artwork" and to "distribute religious literature to their schoolmates, subject to those reasonable time, place and manner or other constitutionally acceptable restrictions imposed on the distribution of all non-school literature."

It also should be noted that, while these rulings prohibit public schools from engaging in devotional teaching of religion, they allow public schools to teach about religion in an academic way. As the Court said decades ago:

> [I]t might well be said that one's education is not complete without a study of comparative religion or the history of religion and its relationship to the advancement of civilization. It certainly may be said that the Bible is worthy of study for its literary and historic qualities. Nothing we have said here indicates that the study of the Bible or of religion, when presented objectively as part of a secular program of education, may not be [done] consistently with the First Amendment.

Comments such as these have opened the door to a movement to teach about religion in the public schools, a movement that has had added vigor since the attacks of September 11, 2001, when it became painfully clear that we cannot understand our world or our nation without understanding religion.

The Supreme Court also has generally embraced a broad equal access policy that essentially allows religious groups to express themselves on public property when a wide range of other non-governmental groups are permitted to do so. Not only has the Court required a state university to open its facilities to student-organized religious clubs when it made those facilities available to a wide range of other student clubs, it also has upheld a federal law that essentially applies this same policy to public secondary schools. Further, Supreme Court rulings have extended this general principal to community groups' after-hours use of public school property. The Court also has held that a cross sponsored by private citizens may be temporarily erected in a city park if other symbols also were permitted this access and it was otherwise clear that the displays were not endorsed by the government. In many ways, these public spaces represent the quintessential American public square, and it is particularly important that the Court has found that the government generally must welcome religious groups and expression here when it welcomes non-religious groups and expression.

As discussed in greater detail below, there are times when the Court has found that even religious expression by a citizen or private group can be so closely associated with the government that it is properly attributable to the state and thus unconstitutional, but this is not a hostile attempt to cleanse public property of religious speech. Rather, it is a careful effort to avoid governmental promotion or endorsement of religion.

Unlike France, for example, which is moving toward the adoption of a legal ban on the wearing of "conspicuous religious symbols" by students in its public schools, the key question in our country is to whom the speech is attributable, not where the speech takes place. This constitutional standard captures the common-sense truth that when a Muslim girl wears a headscarf to public school, it is abundantly clear that the headscarf is her religious expression, not that of the government. Thus, this standard protects the crucial right of individual and corporate religious expression while also guarding against the damaging impression that the state favors certain religions over others, or religion over non-religion.

The Supreme Court's decisions also preserve a public role for faith in the realm of politics and policymaking. Private citizens clearly have a constitutional right to comment on issues of public concern in religious terms, as do non-governmental organizations. The Court said in 1970: "Adherents of particular faiths and individual churches frequently take strong positions on public issues…Of course, churches as much as secular bodies and private citizens have that right." Moreover, religion may inform public policy, as long as religion is not the "preeminent" reason for the government's action and the action has a clear, bona fide non-religious purpose and primary effect.

Furthermore, the Constitution protects the right of all Americans to hold public office, regardless of their faith or lack thereof. More specifically, the Court has found that a state law disqualifying ministers from holding public office violated the Constitution. And, although the Court has not directly addressed this issue, many agree that the Constitution provides political candidates and public officials with a great deal of freedom to talk publicly about their religious convictions.

B. Where the U.S. Supreme Court Has Drawn the Line

Thus, the Supreme Court has protected religious expression in the public square on many occasions. But it is also true that the Court has sometimes found certain religious expression unconstitutional because it is properly attributable to the government rather than to private citizens and groups.

Do these rulings reflect hostility toward religious expression in the public square, or are they rooted in animus toward faith? The list that follows is a very brief and informal attempt to demonstrate some of the basic reasons why I answer these questions negatively. It describes some of the cases in which the Court found that the religious expression involved was unconstitutional, and discusses a few of the ways in which these rulings reflect benevolent motivations, rather than hostility to religion or religious speech.

◆ In its 1962 decision in *Engel v. Vitale*, the Court held unconstitutional a New York law that directed the principal of each school district to ensure that a state-written prayer was said aloud by each class at the beginning of every school day. The Court said:

> [W]e think that the constitutional prohibition against laws respecting an establishment of religion must at least mean that in this country it is no part of the business of government to compose official prayers for any group of the American people to recite as a part of a religious program carried on by government.

Furthermore, the Court noted:

> [The] first and most immediate purpose [of the Establishment Clause] rested on the belief that a union of government and religion tends to destroy government and to degrade religion....It has been argued that to apply the Constitution in

such a way as to prohibit state laws respecting an establishment of religious services in public schools is to indicate a hostility toward religion or toward prayer. Nothing, of course, could be more wrong.

This decision safeguards religious freedom and religion. If public school teachers lead their classes in prayer, it inevitably results in governmental favoritism for some faiths over others. The teacher must determine whose prayer to pray and which faiths will have more public prayer opportunities. In some school districts, for example, scores of religions are represented, which highlights the unwieldiness of this task. Even in places that are not as religious diverse, there are usually at least several different faiths represented, along with multiple theological interpretations of each of these faiths.

Furthermore, allowing public schools to engage in the explosive task of picking and choosing among prayers and sacred texts invites political divisiveness along religious lines. It also sends the message that public schools only belong to those who hold certain religious beliefs, rather than to all students and all who support these schools with their tax money.

And when the state is permitted to prescribe prayers, the state also is allowed to usurp the rights of parents to direct the religious upbringing of their children. More broadly, this permits the state to have a role in shaping religious expression, a prospect that should frighten all religious people, but especially those who support a more limited government.

Finally, it should be noted that school-sponsored prayer usually produces one of two bad results. Sometimes this practice results in prayers that are specific to a particular religious tradition and thus have the tendency to upset those outside the faith who are pressured to participate. At other times, this practice results in an effort to make public prayer please everyone. In these cases, worship of and dialogue with God is reduced to, as some have said, a "nice thought" that actually offends many people of faith.

◆ In its 1968 decision in *Epperson v. Arkansas*, the Court held unconstitutional an Arkansas law that prohibited the teaching in its public schools and universities of the theory of evolution. In its opinion, the Court stated:

> Government in our democracy, state and national, must be neutral in matters of religious theory, doctrine, and practice. It may not be hostile to any religion or to the advocacy of no-religion; and it may not aid, foster, or promote one religion or religious theory against another or even against the militant opposite. The First Amendment mandates governmental neutrality between religion and religion, and between religion and nonreligion.

The Court specifically noted that "study of religions and of the Bible from a literary and historic viewpoint, presented objectively as part of a secular program of education, need not collide with the First Amendment's prohibition, [but] the State may not adopt programs or practices in its public schools or colleges which 'aid or oppose' any religion." This reasoning conveys a respect for the neutral role of the state rather than hostility to religion.

◆ In its 1985 decision in *Wallace v. Jaffree*, the Court struck down an Alabama moment-of-silence statute. The Court's opinion did not indicate that all moments of silence laws were unconstitutional, but that this particular Alabama measure must be invalidated because it "was not motivated by any clearly secular purpose—indeed the statute had no secular purpose."

As Justice [Sandra Day] O'Connor has emphasized, requiring a law to manifest a secular purpose "is not a trivial matter"; instead, it "serves [the] important function" of "remind[ing] government that when it acts it should do so without endorsing a particular religious belief or practice that all citizens do not share." Consistent with this reasoning, other commentators have explained:

> [I]f government (a state legislature, say) makes a coercive political choice requiring or forbidding persons to do something, and if the only reason or reasons that can support the political choice are religious—if no plausible secular rationale supports the choice—then government has undeniably imposed religion on those persons whom the choice coerces. That is so whether or not the political choice compels persons to engage in what is conventionally understood as an act of religious worship.

Moreover, the other guidance the Court has offered regarding the requisite "nonreligious purpose" reveals that, while the balance the Court has struck is not perfect, it is fair-minded.

◆ In its 1989 decision in *Allegheny County v. ACLU*, the Court held that a crèche placed on the "Grand Staircase" of a county courthouse was unconstitutional because it constituted a government endorsement of religion. Given the centrality and importance of the Grand Staircase in the city building, the Court found that "[n]o viewer could reasonably think that [the crèche] occupied [its particular location there] without the support and approval of government."

The Court majority noted that dicta [comments] from its previous opinions spoke approvingly of the pledge of allegiance and the national motto. The Court observed that "there is an obvious distinction between crèche displays and references to God in the motto and the pledge[;] [h]owever history may affect the constitutionality of nonsectarian references to religion by the government, history cannot legitimate practices that demonstrate the government's allegiance to a particular sect or creed." The majority opinion concluded:

[O]nce the judgment has been made that a particular proclamation of Christian belief, when disseminated from a particular location on government property, has the effect of demonstrating the government's endorsement of Christian faith, then it necessarily follows that the practice must be enjoined to protect the constitutional rights of those citizens who follow some creed other than Christianity. It is thus incontrovertible that the Court's decision today, premised on the determination that the crèche display on the Grand Staircase demonstrates the county's endorsement of Christianity, does not represent a hostility or indifference to religion but, instead, the respect for religious diversity that the Constitution requires.

Further, in a later ruling, the Court made it clear that religious symbols can be displayed on public property if the setting is open to other privately sponsored symbols and if it is otherwise clear that the government is not endorsing religion.

◆ In its 1992 decision in *Lee v. Weisman*, the Court invalidated a public middle school's policy of including clergy-led prayer as part of the official school graduation ceremony. The Court found that "[t]he government involvement with religious activity in this case is pervasive, to the point of creating a state-sponsored and state-directed religious exercise in a public school," and that the state-sponsored ceremony was "in a fair and real sense obligatory [for the students]"…The Court also noted the "heightened concerns with protecting freedom of conscience from subtle coercive pressure in the elementary and secondary public schools." Writing for the Court majority, Justice Anthony Kennedy said:

The First Amendment's Religion Clauses mean that religious beliefs and religious expression are too precious to be either proscribed or prescribed by the [government]. The design of the Constitution is that preservation and transmission of religious beliefs and worship is a responsibility and a choice committed to [the non-governmental] sphere, which itself is promised freedom to pursue that mission.

Furthermore, the Court concluded:

Our society would be less than true to its heritage if it lacked abiding concern for the values of its young people, and we acknowledge the profound belief of adherents to many faiths that there must be a place in the student's life for precepts of a morality higher even than the law we today enforce. We express no hostility to those aspirations, nor would our oath permit us to do so. A relentless and all-pervasive attempt to exclude religion from every aspect of public life could itself become inconsistent with the Constitution. We recognize that, at graduation time and throughout the course of the educational process, there will be instances when religious values, religious practices, and religious persons will have some interaction with the public schools and their students. But these matters, often questions of accommodation of religion, are not before us. The sole question presented is whether a religious exercise may be conducted at a graduation ceremony in circumstances where, as we have found, young graduates who object are induced to conform. No holding by this Court suggests that a school can persuade or compel a student to participate in a religious exercise. That is being done here, and it is forbidden by the Establishment Clause of the First Amendment.

Thus, this case stands for the important proposition that the state cannot direct prayer and religious activities and coerce citizens, particularly students, to participate in such activities. This ruling helps to prevent the government from creating a union between church and state while it allows other graduation-related religious expression to occur on public property, such as a voluntarily attended, privately sponsored baccalaureate services that use school facilities.

◆ Finally, in *Santa Fe Independent School District v. Doe*, the Court held invalid a public school policy that established a student vote regarding "a brief invocation and/or message" to be delivered during the pre-game ceremonies of home varsity sporting events because "it establishe[d] an improper majoritarian election on religion, and unquestionably ha[d] the purpose and creates the perception of encouraging the delivery of prayer at a series of important school events. Before 1995, the student council chaplain delivered prayers over the public address system before each varsity home football game. This policy was later revised to include a school-sponsored election to designate one student to deliver the "brief invocation and/or message" at home games during a

particular football season. The Court found that the school's involvement in this process was substantial, and that, "[i]n this context[,] the members of the listening audience must perceive the pregame message as a public expression of the views of the majority of the student body delivered with the approval of the school administration." [The Court] also noted:

> The Religion Clauses of the First Amendment prevent the government from making any law respecting the establishment of religion or prohibiting the free exercise thereof. By no means do these commands impose a prohibition on all religious activity in our public schools. Indeed, the common purpose of the Religion Clauses "is to secure religious liberty." Thus, nothing in the Constitution as interpreted by this Court prohibits any public school student from voluntarily praying at any time before, during, or after the schoolday. But the religious liberty protected by the Constitution is abridged when the State affirmatively sponsors the particular religious practice of prayer.

Both the Court's rationales and its words, therefore, demonstrate that its decisions do not reflect hostility toward religious expression....

IV. CONCLUSION

Religion plays a vital role in public life, but religion's public role is not limitless, nor should it be. Rather than criticizing the constitutional prohibition on governmental promotion of religion, we should honor it for the way in which it guarantees equality for all, freedom of choice in religious matters, and basic autonomy for the religious sphere.

Current Separation of Church and State Doctrine: Suppressing Public Displays of Faith

Vincent Phillip Munoz

If I can communicate only one point in my testimony today it is this: The United States Supreme Court remains primarily responsible for the continued legal hostility toward religious expression in the public square. Stated simply, the Supreme Court has interpreted the Establishment Clause in a manner that encourages and sometimes demands hostility toward religion.

Two Establishment Clause doctrines, in particular, lead to hostility toward religion: The "endorsement" test and the "coercion" test.

The "endorsement" test, which was invented by Justice Sandra Day O'Connor in the 1984 case *Lynch v. Donnelly*, prohibits state actors from endorsing religion. It purportedly keeps government religiously neutral. In practice, however, "no endorsement" quickly becomes outright hostility, especially in the context of public schools. Under this rule, activities that a child might perceive to favor religion must be prohibited to avoid the appearance of governmental endorsement.

The quintessential example of how the "endorsement" test purges religion from public schools occurred in the 1985 case *Wallace v. Jaffree*. The Supreme Court used the test to strike down an Alabama law that directed the public school day to begin with a moment of silence for voluntary prayer or meditation. Justice [Sandra Day] O'Connor claimed that to set aside one minute for children to pray silently endorses religion, and thus, under her interpretation, violates the Constitution.

In 1989 the Supreme Court used the "endorsement" test to require the removal of a privately funded nativity scene in front of a courthouse in Allegheny County, Pennsylvania. Perhaps most notoriously, the 9th Circuit Court of Appeals employed the "endorsement" test to prohibit teacher-led recitations of the Pledge of Allegiance in public schools. The words "under God," the 9th Circuit explained, endorse a particular religious concept, namely monotheism.

The 9th Circuit's decision has come under heavy criticism, including criticism from the Senate. But the 9th Circuit only followed the example set by the Supreme Court. "Under God" endorses the civic faith Americans have adopted since the signing of the Declaration of Independence. But this expression, if we use Justice O'Connor's standard, violates the Constitution.

The second leading test used by the Supreme Court for Establishment Clause jurisprudence is the "coercion" test. Invented by Justice [Anthony M.] Kennedy in the 1992 case *Lee v. Weisman*, the "coercion" test sounds reasonable—no one believes that the state legitimately may coerce religious practice—but, as applied by the Court, it too drives religion out of the public square.

In *Lee v. Weisman*, the Court eliminated non-denominational invocations and benedictions at public school graduations. According to Justice Kennedy, to ask public school children to stand respectfully while others pray "psychologically coerces" religious practice. In 2000, the Court prohibited the Texas tradition of non-denominational prayer before high school football games, because, it said, some fans might feel like "outsiders." Thus interpreted, the "coercion" test secures "the right not to feel uncomfortable" because of others publicly expressing their religious beliefs.

It's common sense to say that the government may not force a student to pledge allegiance to the flag or to recite a prayer. It's something altogether different to say that because some feel like outsiders, others may not pray. Tolerance should be a two-way street.

Like the "endorsement" test, the logic of the "coercion" test calls for the curtailment of public expressions of religious sentiment. It's no coincidence that the 9th Circuit also cited Justice Kennedy's psychological coercion reasoning when it struck down the Pledge of Allegiance.

While the cases I have mentioned are significant in and of themselves, their impact extends far beyond the specific parties involved. What constitutes an impermissible "endorsement" or "psychological coercion" is inherently indistinct. The law's vagueness makes state acknowledgement of religious sentiment suspect. It enables special interest litigators, who are professionally hostile toward religion, to file lawsuits to challenge almost any state action that accommodates religion. The chilling effect of such litigation and the mere threat it is considerable.

Imagine yourself as a city council member or a high school principal: it's easier to remove the Ten Commandments from the public park or to silence the school valedictorian who wishes to speak about religious faith, than it is to undertake a costly legal battle against ACLU. Fearful local officials and public school administrators have the incentive to eliminate the public acknowledgement of religious sentiment in order to avoid costly litigation. In this way, the Supreme Court

has armed anti-religious activists to impose their vision of the secular state through legal threats and litigious intimidation. The result is not only "the naked public square," but the trampling of religious individuals' constitutional rights to religious free exercise and freedom of expression.

The Constitution's text prohibits laws respecting an establishment of religion or prohibiting the free exercise thereof. It says nothing about government "endorsement of religion." Justice O'Connor effectively has replaced the text and original meaning of the First Amendment with her own words and ideas. Justice Kennedy's "psychological coercion" test is also far off the mark. The Founders understood religious "coercion" to mean being fined or imprisoned on account of one's religion; not feeling uncomfortable when other people mention God.

The modern Court has lost sight of the fact that framers of the First Amendment meant to protect religious freedom, not to banish religion from the public square. The free exercise of religion is the primary end of the First Amendment; no-establishment is a means toward achieving that end.

By prohibiting religious establishment, the Founders sought to end practices like state officials appointing bishops, limiting public office to members of the established church, and the licensing and regulation of dissenting religious ministers. They did not mean to forbid the public acknowledgement of God or even non-sectarian endorsement of religion. They certainly did not intend to constitutionalize doctrines like the "endorsement" test and the "coercion" test. Until these doctrines are overturned, legal hostility to religion in the public square will continue.

THE CONTINUING DEBATE:
Current Separation of Church and State Doctrine

What Is New

The Supreme Court continues to demonstrate a careful, some might say inconsistent, view about the establishment clause. In *Van Orden v. Perry* (2005), the court allowed a monument to the Ten Commandments on the grounds of Texas' capitol building. The court found the monument to be a historical reflection of the country's tradition-al recognition of the importance of the Ten Commandments and argued, "Simply hav-ing religious content or promoting a message consistent with a religious doctrine does not run afoul of the establishment clause." However on the same day, the Supreme Court also ruled in *McCreary County v. ACLU* (2005) that displays of the Ten Com-mandments in Kentucky state court houses violated the establishment clause. In this case, the majority reasoned, "When the government acts with the ostensible and pre-dominant purpose of advancing religion, it violates...[the] central establishment clause." In another case almost sure to reach the Supreme Court, a U.S. District Court judge in California ruled the it was unconstitutional to have students in a public school recite the pledge of allegiance because it contained the phrase "under God."

Public opinion on the debate often varies depending of whether the question is abstract or applied. One 2005 poll found a majority (54%) of Americans saying the government harms people's right anytime it promotes religion. Yet when asked about the *Van Orden* and *McCreary* cases, 75% said the Supreme Court should allow the dis-plays of the Ten Commandments. And another 2005 poll found that 62% of Americans would favor a constitutional amendment permitting voluntary prayer in schools.

Where to Find More

One site of a group that believes in a wall between church and state is the "nonthe-ist" Freedom From Religion Foundation at www.ffrf.org/. Taking the opposite view is the Rutherford Institute at www.rutherford.org/issues/religious_freedom.asp. A com-prehensive view of the Supreme Courts role in the church-state issue is James Hitchcock, *The Supreme Court and Religion in American Life, Vol. 1 : The Odyssey of the Religion Clauses* (Princeton University Press, 2004). Looking at the current strains over what the establishment clause means is Noah Feldman, *Divided by God: America's Church-State Problem—and What We Should Do About It* (Farrar, Straus and Giroux, 2005). Information on the understanding before and at the time of the writing of the First Amendment language on religion can be found at a University of Chicago Web site, http://press-pubs.uchicago.edu/founders/tocs/amendI_religion.html.

What to More to Do

One way to try to approach this debate is to try to unravel the seemingly contradic-tory decisions of the Supreme Court in *Van Orden v. Perry* (2005) and *McCreary County v. ACLU.* You can read opinions of the justices in these cases and also find a good deal of supporting material at the site of the First Amendment Center at www.firstamendmentcenter.org/. Enter the name of the case in the search window. Once your views are clear, try jotting down some notes for a hypothetical essay, "How High Should Jefferson's Wall Between Church and State Be?"

5

AMERICAN PEOPLE/
POLITICAL CULTURE

IMMIGRATION AS A THREAT TO "WHO WE ARE":
Valid Concern *or* Unfounded Fear?

VALID CONCERN

ADVOCATE: John O'Sulllivan, Editor-in-chief of the *National Interest*

SOURCE: "Who We Are," *The American Conservative*, July 19, 2004

UNFOUNDED FEAR

ADVOCATE: Jim Sleeper, Lecturer in Political Science, Yale University

SOURCE: Review of Samuel Huntington's *Who Are We?: The Challenges to America's National Identity*, History News Network, May 3, 2004

The face of America is changing. A nation that was once overwhelmingly composed of European heritage whites is becoming more diverse ethnically and racially. Of the 4.6 million people in the United States in 1790, whites made up two-thirds of the population. The other third was divided about equally between black slaves, and American Indians, none of whom were citizens. Of the whites, 92% were Anglo Saxons, tracing their heritage to the British Isles.

The American population grew rapidly, reaching 281 million in 2000. Immigration has been a key factor. More than 60 million individuals have come to the United States since 1790. The greatest influx of came between 1870 and 1920. During that period, an average of 14% of the U.S. population was foreign born, and in some decades the inflow of immigrants equaled 10% of the U.S. population. Then immigration plunged, with only 500,000 newcomers admitted during the 1930s. It slowly recovered, but through the 1960s both the number of immigrants and their percentage of the population remained well below the rate during the late 1800s and early 1900s. Most immigrants came from Europe, and as late as the 1960s, more than 70% of immigrants were coming from Europe or European-heritage countries (primarily Canada). Reflecting that, the 1960 U.S. population was approximately 82% white, 11% black, 6% Hispanic, 0.5% Asian American, and 0.5% Native American. By 2000, according to the 2000 census, the U.S. population was 69% white, 12% African American, 13% Latino, 4% Asian American, and 1% Native American. This shift is expected to continue, with the Census Bureau estimating that in 2050, the U.S. population will be 52% white, 24% Latino, 15% African American, 9% Asian American, and 1% Native American. One reason for the change is different fertility rates, which is the average number of children a woman in her childbearing years will have. In 2000 the fertility rate was 2.0 for whites, 2.1 for African Americans, 2.5 for Native Americans, 2.3 for Asian Americans, and 2.9 for Hispanics.

Changes in immigration are a second factor accounting for growing diversity. First, immigration increased, nearly tripling for an annual 330,000 in the 1960s to 950,000 annually in the late 1990s. This number seems huge, but during the 1990s, total immigrants equaled only 3.6% of the population, a proportion much lower than some early decades, such as the 10.4% rate between 1900 and 1909. The recent growth of immigration has increased the percentage of the U.S. population that is foreign born to 10.4% in 2000, but that percentage is lower than it was at any time between 1860 and 1940.

A second change is that the flow of immigration now brings in a much greater percentage of people from Asia, Latin American, and Africa. In the late 1990s, Europeans were only 16% of newcomers, compared to 32% from Asia and 48% from Latin America and the Caribbean, and 4% from Africa. The significant shift in the geographic origin of immigrants occurred after Congress amended the immigration laws in 1965 to eliminate the quota system that favored immigration from Europe and replace it with a qualifications system based on job skills and other criteria. Another important factor relates to illegal immigration from Latin America, especially Mexico. Millions have arrived without documentation, and federal legislation in 1986 gave permanent residency to about 4 million of these individuals.

The increased rate of immigration and its increasingly non-European complexion have raised concerns in some quarters. One expression of that view is a book, *Who We Are: The Challenges to America's National Identity* (Simon & Schuster, 2004) written by political scientist Samuel P. Huntington, the Albert J. Weatherhead III University Professor at Harvard University and chairman of the Harvard Academy for International and Area Studies. An introductory review of the book in the *Washington Post* noted that, "Huntington has written a book that poses some of the most critical questions facing our nation" including, "How can a people already preoccupied with ethnic identity absorb and acculturate the millions of immigrants being driven to our shores by global economics?" and "How in the long run will America cohere if everyone feels they belong to a minority?" and the book "tackles these questions with passionate intensity." That effort has engendered other passionate commentary, some of it praising and some of it condemning Huntington, as the following two reviews of his book reveal.

POINTS TO PONDER

➤ John O'Sulllivan in the first article disparages critics who dismiss Huntington as a bigot and argue his work should have not been published. Do you agree that Huntington should be ignored or do you think his views should be read, analyzed, and debated?

➤ The traditional goal has been a cultural melting pot in which immigrants merged into existing American culture. Some people now advocate multiculturalism, the coexistence of more than one culture. What are the benefits and drawbacks of the melting pot and multicultural images?

Immigration as a Threat to "Who We Are": Valid Concern

JOHN O'SULLLIVAN

Samuel Huntington's book was notorious even before the page proofs were sent out to magazine editors for the pre-publication of extracts. Rumors had circulated for at least a year beforehand that the author of *The Clash of Civilizations* [1998] and other distinguished works of political theory was about to produce a book on immigration that was not wholly in favor of it. In fact, while *Who Are We?* deals in detail with current immigration to the U.S., the book as a whole is about the wider and more important topic of national identity. As we shall see, that is making it more controversial rather than less. Still, the first intimations of controversy were inspired by the astounding prospect of an anti-immigration book from one of the nation's most respected political scientists and a fully paid-up member of the American establishment. If Sam Huntington broke ranks, then elite support for high levels of immigration might fracture at the very moment that the Bush administration was proposing an open-borders policy. And that would be high politics as well as intellectual controversy.

Excitement rose higher when the first extract of *Who Are We?* was published [in an article "The Hispanic Challenge"] in *Foreign Policy* magazine [March/April, 2004]. This turned out, as suspected, to be devoted to immigration—and to a particularly contentious aspect of it.

In his book, Huntington argues that post-1965 immigration is very different from previous waves in two significant ways. In the first place, it consists of continuously high levels of immigration. Previous immigration was either low but continuous (e.g., from the Revolution to the 1840s) or a series of high peaks followed by low troughs (e.g., the second great wave of 1880–1920 followed by 40 years of low immigration under the restrictive quotas of the 1920s). Continuous high immigration tends to retard the assimilation of immigrants into the host community and to foster ethnic ghettoes that then accommodate semipermanent ethnic diasporas. All of these trends will be maximized if the immigration occurs in conditions of official bilingualism and multiculturalism rather than of Americanization. Immigrants will then be less likely to assimilate and more likely to retain ethnic identities and links with home.

The second difference is that the new immigration intake is much less diverse than the immigrants in earlier periods. In brief, one half of new legal immigrants come from Latin America—and 25 percent of them from a single national source, namely Mexico. Even in the absence of other factors, this would hinder assimilation. If immigrants speak several languages, they have a clear incentive to master the *lingua franca* that will help them to communicate both with each other and with the native-born. If they speak one language, however, they are more easily able to continue living in a linguistic enclave that is an overseas version of home, such as Miami, where it is the native-born who feel foreign.

That central difficulty in the case of Latinos in general is aggravated in the case of Mexicans by several other characteristics. Again in brief, Mexican Americans are especially numerous—25 percent and rising of the total of legal immigrants. Their numbers are further supplemented because they are the overwhelming majority of illegal immigrants. They come from a nation contiguous to the U.S. with a long and porous border. They are regionally concentrated in the Southwest (as were Cubans in Florida) so that they are more likely to concentrate themselves in linguistic enclaves. They seem likely to keep coming indefinitely—i.e., in the absence of strong official discouragement, the supply of Mexican arrivals is for practical purposes infinite. And finally Mexicans have a historical presence in the region—there are even some who cherish irredentist claims [to reincorporate the U.S. southwest Mexico] on what they call "Aztlan."

Making these and other points, Huntington concluded that there is a real possibility that the American Southwest might become in time another Quebec [a culturally and linguistically French dominant province of Canada]—namely, a region of the U.S. where the dominant language and culture would be Hispanic —in a Nuevo United States that would be a bilingual and bicultural society. And as Quebec and Belgium [divided between French-speaking Flemings and Dutch-speaking Waloons] demonstrate in different ways, bilingualism distorts and obstructs democratic governance.

It was, of course, this second "inflammatory" theme that *Foreign Policy* magazine made its front-page lead article. The editors of *Foreign Policy* cannot be wholly acquitted of coat-trailing here. They know that controversy sells and set out to have the maximum impact. Still, even they were probably surprised by all the results that followed—namely, an article that everyone talked about, superb advance

publicity for the book, and a string of insulting and threatening remarks about Huntington—"racist," "nativist," "xenophobe," and the rest—in newspaper columns and *FP*'s own letters section.

Three points emerge in retrospect from these early criticisms. First, almost all the replies simply ignored the vast wealth of social science, census, and polling data that the author laid out in support of his thesis. Huntington has been reproved by otherwise respectful critics for the sheer volume of survey evidence he deploys since it inevitably slows down the book's readability. But these spluttering and indignant responses justify its presence. They show that the weight of prejudice against his argument is such that he would have been destroyed if he had not armored himself in advance against it.

Some of the critics, however, promptly dealt with the difficulty that they could not refute what he *had* said by refuting things he *had not* said but would have said if he had been the unreconstructed bigot they desperately wanted to wallop. Several denounced him for relying on the "lazy Mexican stereotype." In fact, he had pointed out that Mexicans' propensity for hard work led *inter alia* [among other things] to the displacement and reduced incomes of low-paid native-born American workers. True, he had also quoted Mexican and Hispanic writers to the effect that Mexicans and Mexican-Americans were less inclined than Americans to believe that hard work was likely to lead to success—and that they were held back by that. Yet this argument is so different from the "lazy Mexican stereotype" that they could be confused only by minds already disabled by ideological fanaticism. It is worth noting, though, that falsely accusing others of relying on stereotypes is fast becoming stereotypical in itself.

Second, when his critics did seek to refute his array of evidence, they mostly got it wrong. Sometimes they got it wrong in respectably complicated ways. Writing in *Time* magazine, Michael Elliot produced polling data that showed Mexicans expressing admiration for the U.S. and sharply criticized Huntington for not taking this into account. But Huntington had not denied that many Mexicans were grateful for the opportunities given to them by the U.S. In a subtle examination of the full range of evidence, he had merely pointed out that such feelings were likely to be offset by a range of other influences over time—notably, that under multiculturalism they might assimilate not into Americanism but into a subordinate ethnic identity that was ambivalent at best towards the U.S. He also cited evidence to suggest that this was happening—indeed that the longer Mexicans lived in the U.S., the less they identified with America and American values, very unlike earlier generations of immigrants. Above all, as John Fonte has pointed out (both reviewing Huntington and responding to Elliot in *National Review*), on the key question of patriotic assimilation—i.e., do immigrants identify themselves primarily as Americans or prefer some other identity?—Huntington has the better of the argument. According to a Pew Hispanic Center study taken after Sept. 11—a date and event that had demonstrated the emptiness of Huntington's nativist anxieties according to Louis Menand in the *New Yorker*—55 percent of Americans of Mexican descent said that they considered themselves Mexican "first," 25 percent chose "Latino" or "Hispanic" as their primary identity, and only 18 percent chose "American." That is not conclusive proof of national disintegration, but it is worrying—not least because reluctance to embrace an American identity is not confined to Hispanic- or Mexican-Americans.

Fonte quotes a study of Muslims in Los Angeles showing that only 10 percent of such immigrants felt more allegiance to America than to a Muslim country. Elliot's citation of more optimistic statistics is not false, but it is partial and complacent.

Other critics got it wrong in simple and straightforward ways. Tamar Jacoby of the Manhattan Institute, who seems to have set herself up as a One-Woman Anti-Huntington Truth Squad, sending media organizations an offer to be interviewed in order to correct his errors, declares, "Huntington also mistakes what it means to assimilate. We as a nation have never asked immigrants to buy into the particulars of our culture, Anglo or otherwise." This confident assertion will astonish (in addition to the world) Norman Podhoretz who, in his autobiographical writings, has written powerfully of "the brutal bargain" whereby immigrants and their children surrendered their cultural identities and transformed themselves into imitation WASPs. It also overlooks the "Americanization" campaigns of both government and private industry, the English language proficiency test in citizenship examinations, and even the Battle of the Bulge, when G.I.s tested each other on such cultural particulars as the name of Betty Grable's husband in order to separate the Americans out from Otto Skorzeny's infiltrators.

The final resort of critics when faced with evidence they don't like—especially statements by irredentists claiming that the American Southwest is destined to return to Mexico—was either "well, they don't represent anyone" (even when the speaker was the spokesman for an irredentist organization) or "well, they don't really mean it." There is no answer to that. Nor is any answer needed.

But the third point is more worrying. An alarming number of critics, some apparently academics, denounced Huntington's arguments as "poisonous," "incendiary," "unabashed racism," and so forth in a highly intemperate fashion, while misquoting and misunderstanding his actual arguments. Professor Bruce E. Wright of California State at Fullerton remarked that the article was an affront not only to Hispanics and Catholics (a Catholic myself, I had failed to be affronted) but also to "those of us"—such *sang froid* [imperturbability]!—"whose identity is not so shallow as to be threatened by a massive invasion of others." The Rev. Edward Lopez of New York thought that Huntington was "threatened by diversity" and "frightened by the world around him." Patricia Seed of Rice University lamented "the arrogance of an East Coast Brahmin." There was the usual irrelevant blather about how earlier Huntingtons had measured skulls and dismissed the potential of now successful immigrant groups. And there was a theme running through almost all of these critiques—the America of Huntington's youth was being replaced by a better, more vibrant, and more just America, one of diversity and multiculturalism. To resist this evolution in defense of a past America was a sign of nostalgia at best, of wicked nativist racism at worst.

It is tempting to dismiss these denunciations as a cry for help. But they must be taken more seriously. After all, several letter-writers went to the lengths of arguing that Huntington's article should not have been published and that *Foreign Policy* should apologize for printing it. It seems reasonable to infer that people holding such views would not willingly allow such arguments to be expressed in their churches, schools, and colleges or treat fairly any student who submitted an essay advancing them. The later anonymous *Economist* reviewer, who was not uncritical of the book, was nonetheless upset by these outbursts that sought, in effect, to censor the rational expression of reasonable fears. They reflect a disturbing willingness to enforce an orthodoxy on dissenters and indicate a moral atmosphere that might best be described as "soft totalitarianism"—even when, or particularly when, the orthodoxy is a minority opinion and the majority has invariably rejected any clear expression of it.

The first effect of these attacks—and the controversy they generated—was to make people want to read the book. (At the National Airport [Washington, D.C.] bookshop where I bought it, I got their last copy a day after publication.) But the book they bought was very different from the article that had prompted them to buy it. It is about much more than immigration. It is a comprehensive analysis of the threats that are undermining America's common culture and sense of itself. As such, it analyses virtually every major skirmish in the cultural wars of the last 40 years. And it analyzes them from a distinctly conservative standpoint.

Huntington is, of course, very far from being a "movement conservative," or even a neoconservative, let alone a paleoconservative. He is a Democrat for starters, and he gave the *New York Times* interviewer a bad fit of cognitive dissonance by telling her that he opposed the war in Iraq and intended to vote for John Kerry. Yet almost 50 years ago, in an article in the *American Political Science Review*, he advanced what still remains the single best definition of conservatism: namely, that it is the set of ideas that men adopt in defense of their social and political institutions when they come under fundamental attack. Huntington believes that America's national identity and the social and political institutions and traditions that sustain it are under fundamental attack. His book is a conservative defense of them.

His starting point is that the American nation, as it developed from the colonial period to the 1960s, was built around certain core institutions, customs, and practices. To oversimplify brutally, these were the English language, dissenting Protestant Christianity, individualism and work ethic, and the political culture of the Founding Fathers with its emphasis on individual rights. Over time, later immigrants groups assimilated to the cultural core of "Anglo-Protestant Christianity" that evolved from these origins and assented to the American Creed that was its self-conscious political expression. They added spicy cultural contributions of their own, of course, but these did not fundamentally alter the national character. And by the late '50s, "Americans were one nation of individuals with equal political rights, who shared a primarily Anglo-Protestant core culture, and were dedicated to the liberal-democratic principles of the American creed."

In the course of outlining this national development, Huntington punctures several comforting national myths dear to both liberals and conservatives but false and sometimes destructive in their current implications. He points out, for instance, that the U.S. is not "a nation of immigrants." It is a nation that was founded by settlers—who are very different from immigrants in that they establish a new polity rather than arrive in an existing one—and that has been occupied since by the descendants of those settlers and of immigrants who came later but who assimilated into the American nation. Americans therefore are under no moral obligation to accept anyone who wishes to immigrate on the spurious grounds that everyone is essentially an immigrant. Americans own America, so to speak, and may admit or refuse entry to outsiders on whatever grounds they think fit.

Huntington similarly demolishes the notion that America is a "proposition nation" and that its national identity consists of adherence to the liberal principles of the American Creed of liberty and individual rights. The American Creed is certainly part of America's national identity—it is the distilled essence of America's culture—but it is too abstract and theoretical to provide a fulfilling patriotism on its own. Men sacrifice themselves for home and beauty, for the comradeship of battle, for loyalty to the flag, to ensure that experience of a free life is not lost to their children—they are very unlikely to sacrifice themselves for political ideas unless they also convey this range of loyalties.

Nor does the Creed sufficiently distinguish Americans from people in other countries. If belief in liberty and individual rights were sufficient to make one an American, half the people in the world could claim citizenship. And if the Creed is seriously taken to be the totality of American identity, then the way is open for a multiculturalism that treats the English language, U.S. history, and American cultural practices from baseball to hard work as simply one set of options in a cultural and ethnic smorgasbord—a smorgasbord, moreover, in which preference for traditional American beliefs and customs counts as discrimination. Of course, words and ideas take a goodly portion of their meaning from the surrounding culture—so that our current understanding of such concepts as liberty would be significantly altered if we were to interpret them in the light not of "Anglo-Protestantism" but of Hispanic, Confucian, or Islamic culture or even of continental Roman Law. Are such anxieties alarmist? Judge Robert Bork has recently pointed out that U.S. Supreme Court justices have been advocating that American courts take account of legal precedents from courts as remote as European Court and the Zimbabwe Supreme Court. It would be a curious irony if the Zimbabwe Supreme Court ended up exercising more legal influence in the U.S. than it does in [authoritarian President] Robert Mugabe's Zimbabwe. But if this is alarmism, it may perhaps be early-warning alarmism.

What has aroused most disquiet among otherwise receptive readers, however, is Huntington's claim that America's common culture to which later immigrants assimilated is one of "Anglo-Protestant conformity." Interestingly, this is one of his less controversial arguments among cultural historians, who have long acknowledged the role of dissenting British religious groups in the shaping of America. Recent major social and cultural histories, such as *Albion's Seed* by David Hackett Fischer, suggest that, if anything, this influence was even stronger than traditionally understood. It may soothe affronted Catholics to learn that this influence was not, strictly speaking, a matter of religious belief, but rather a set of social practices that encouraged freedom of belief in the first instance, and following on from that other sorts of freedom under a dispersed social and economic leadership. As the Anglo-American religious sociologist David Martin has observed of the modern revival of evangelical Protestantism in Latin America in *Tongues of Fire*, dissenting sects brought to the fore a hitherto "buried intelligentsia" that in turn took the leadership of their communities in non-religious roles. Plainly this had effects in strictly religious terms—*inter alia*, the establishment of a still flourishing "marketplace of religions" in the U.S., the conversion of the Catholic Church in America to Protestant notions of liberty, and the gradual adoption by Rome of these "Americanist" heresies. Most devout American Catholics today are Protestants in political theory. But the main effect in the colonial period and the early years of the Republic was to instill in Americans the habits of self-reliance and voluntary cooperation that so impressed [Alexis de] Tocqueville on his visit [in the 1830s, leading to his famous book, *Democracy in America*]. And the vital, successful political culture built on these foundations—Anglo-Protestantism, the American Creed, and the rest—was still clearly traceable to its early origins in the 1960s.

It was at this point, circa 1965—or just after the Civil Rights Act had finally brought black America fully within the ambit of the American political nation—that influential Americans set about systematically demolishing this impressive structure. Huntington lists the accomplishments of "the deconstructionists" in the following paragraph:

> The deconstructionists promoted programs to enhance the status and influence of subnational, racial, ethnic and cultural groups. They encouraged immigrants to maintain their birth country cultures, granted them legal privileges denied to native-born Americans, and denounced the idea of Americanization as un-American. They pushed the re-writing of history syllabi and textbooks so as to refer to the "peoples" of the United States in place of the single people of the Constitution. They urged supplementing or substituting for national history the history of subnational groups. They downgraded the centrality of English in American life and pushed bilingual education and linguistic diversity. They advocated legal recognition of group rights and racial preferences over the individual rights central to the American Creed. They justified their actions by theories of multiculturalism and the idea that

diversity rather than unity or community should be America's overriding value. The combined effect of these efforts was to promote the deconstruction of the American identity that had been gradually created over three centuries and the ascendance of subnational identities.

On every point listed here, Huntington examines in detail how these changes occurred and what their significance is to America's future. He pulls not a single punch. To take just one example, he makes clear that the replacement of individual rights by group rights amounts to a "counter-revolution" that reintroduced racial discrimination into American law and practice, implied that individuals are defined by blood, undermined equal justice and equal citizenship, and ultimately denied the existence of a common good. And by the time he has performed the same surgery on the challenge to the English language, the undermining of the common culture, the discrediting of assimilation, the erosion of American citizenship, and much else, he has in effect mounted a comprehensive attack on the main social policies of the last 40 years.

The scale and boldness of Huntington's assault appears to have unmanned reviewers of his book. It seems at times as if they can hardly believe that one author is taking on so many social pieties simultaneously. *Who Are We?* is a veritable abattoir [slaughterhouse] of sacred cows. And the reviewers reacted by looking nervously away, by failing to grasp the main point, and by taking refuge in minor and trivial critiques.

Thus, writing in *Foreign Affairs*, Alan Wolfe disputed Huntington's historical account thus:

> It is...incorrect to claim that American identity was shaped by dissenting Anglo-Protestantism.

Two of the churches prominent at the United States's founding were established rather than dissenting: the Church of England became the established church of Virginia under the Episcopal name, and Presbyterianism had been established in Scotland.

Really, this is the kind of thing that gives nit-picking a bad name.

Or here is Louis Menand in the *New Yorker*:

> ...it is absurd to say that [multiculturalism] is anti-Western. Its roots, as Charles Taylor and many other writers have shown, are in the classic texts of Western literature and philosophy.

Has Menand never heard of [Karl] Marx? The German social philosopher is undoubtedly a major figure in the Western tradition of literature and philosophy— few more so. Yet there is no doubt either that his major works are anti-Western. They seek to undermine Western society and to replace it with something fundamentally different—and from all the evidence of experiments in Marxism, something a great deal worse. If it finally succeeds in replacing America's traditional national identity, multiculturalism seems likely to be a great deal worse too.

Menand is nearer the mark when he observes that *Who Are We?* is a work of identity politics and that for Huntington "the chief reason—it could even be the only reason—for Americans to embrace their culture is that it is the culture that happens to be theirs." That is not strictly true. Both Huntington and Americans in general can give other good reasons for thinking their culture admirable—and Huntington does so at intervals throughout the book. Given that American culture, like Western culture in general, is a self-conscious culture of critique, it could hardly be otherwise. But to love something because it is familiar and one's own is, in fact, a perfectly respectable reason for loving it. Many good daughters love fathers who are thoroughly dislikeable by any objective standard—and the world is a better and more stable place for it. Huntington even quotes the Copenhagen School to the effect that people want "societal security" almost as much as they want "national security." In other words, they want a society "to persist in its essential character" and to sustain "within acceptable conditions for evolution, of traditional patterns of language, culture, association, and religious and national identity and custom." If these are all removed or destroyed, then anomie, despair, and disintegration tend to be among the consequences. Why should Americans not be protected against them?

The answer, as it emerges in this controversy, is twofold. The first reason is consequential: there are trade-offs. If some people are contented living in a society made in their own image, then others—namely, minorities of one kind or another—are likely to feel out of place. A sentimental reluctance to make minorities feel like outsiders, even if that means discomfiting the American majority, is one of the major factors driving the critical hostility to Huntington. Huntington himself has the courage to say straightforwardly that if people have minority opinions or minority tastes, then they will to that extent be outsiders—and cannot reasonably expect the majority to conceal or suppress its loyalties in order to make them feel at home. He makes this argument both in relation to atheists who want American Christians to surrender all public expression of their religion and in relation to immigrants who want society to be re-ordered to make the

English language and American institutions merely one set of cultural options. And he does so because, in the end, he thinks that solidarity—or "societal security"—is essential to the well-being of American society as a whole, including in time the well-being of the minorities.

If Huntington's argument is designed to prefer the interests of the American majority, however, why is it at bay rather than triumphant? Here the second sociological reason comes into play: America's elites—both the corporate elites of the Right and the academic elites of the Left—do not share the opinions and tastes of the American people. Both elites have been, in effect, "de-nationalized" by the processes of economic and cultural globalization. They are more likely to share the tastes and opinions of their counterparts in other countries than those of their own countrymen in provincial and small-town America. They regard patriotism and national feeling as atavistic emotions that retard both economic rationality (in the case of the Right) and cosmopolitan ideologies of "democratic humanism" (in the case of the Left). And they see America not as a nation like other nations, if more powerful, but as the embryo either of the global market or of a new "universal nation" without boundaries or restrictive citizenship. As a result, on a whole range of policy issues—racial preferences, bilingual education, military intervention abroad, open borders—the American people are firmly on one side and the American elites are on the other. This tends to produce cynicism about government and electoral abstention, punctuated by rebellious referendum initiatives such as Propositions 187 and 209 in which the voters briefly impose their will on the elites. Even then elitists in the courts frequently declare the people's victories to be unconstitutional.

This is an unstable situation, and the elites are well aware of the fact. Hence their usual reluctance to join debate on the kind of issues raised by Huntington's book. But the extremes of both elites—libertarians on the Right and multiculturalists on the Left—cannot restrain themselves. Their solution, as illustrated in the early reactions to Huntington's *Foreign Policy* piece, is to treat anyone who departs from the official orthodoxies on these matters as a heretic to be shamed, scarred, and effectively silenced. Huntington, fortunately, is too eminent to be crushed in that way.

So *Who Are We?* is worth ten divisions in the new American culture war about patriotism. It demystifies every radical argument employed to deconstruct the American nation and the customs, habits, and traditions that sustain it. Even more usefully, it demonstrates that some conservatives and neoconservatives are unwitting accomplices in this demolition. They are misled in this direction either because of their attachment to outworn ideological definitions of America—formulae that once served a useful role in smoothing assimilation but that now act as carriers for multiculturalism—or because they have the false patriotic belief that America is not a nation with its own character but the entire world in embryo and so capable of indefinite expansion. Above all, perhaps, by attracting the kind of denunciations that reveal a deep animus towards the United States in the attackers, Huntington's book has revealed that there is a substantial anti-American intelligentsia (and lumpen [mentally sluggish] intelligentsia) within the American nation committed to a sort of "counter-tribalism." These are the patriots of an America that does not exist—the America of multiculturalism, bilingualism, and diversity that, in President Clinton's words, "can live without a dominant European culture." They therefore hate the America that does exist as an obstacle to their dreams. And they tend to sympathize with attacks upon it—and to react against anyone who defends it.

In acting as a sort of lure to draw the various tribes of "counter-tribalists" from their academic and corporate lairs into the open, Huntington has performed an important intellectual service. After ...*Who Are We?* perhaps his next book should be *The Anatomy of Counter-Tribalism*.

Immigration as a Threat to "Who We Are": Unfounded Fear

Jim Sleeper

With the publication of this, his thirteen book, the magisterial, sometimes dyspeptic Harvard political scientist Samuel P. Huntington has once again indulged—nay, has stage managed—his inclination to administer jolts of counterintuitive, debate-changing Truth to distracted American elites. Once again, establishment players of many stripes are swooning in dismay at his dark revelations or girding up their loins to join him in another long, twilight battle for Western civilization. Once again, Huntington is arrestingly right about challenges facing liberal democracy that many liberals have been loath to acknowledge.

But never before has so big a part of his argument been so thunderously wrong and so cheaply sustained. Those who value his chastening realism about liberalism's dicey prospects will have to work hard to follow his most important insight in *Who We Are?*: that American cosmopolitans who would like to dispense with nations and multiculturalist zealots who would like to dismantle them have converged with American multinational profiteers to fray the fabric of liberal democracy, which only a renewed civic patriotism here at home can sustain. This argument, eminently worth arguing about, has already been overshadowed by another: about Huntington's ill-conceived, crotchety and (pardon the word) undocumented jeremiad against Latino immigration.

The distraction is the fault of Huntington the stage manager as much as of Huntington the thinker. In 1993, to prompt a national debate about themes that would figure in his 1996 book, "The Clash of Civilizations and the Remaking of World Order," he published a *Foreign Affairs* essay of virtually the same title highlighting his most important warning: The economic, ideological and nationalist rivalries that most global analysts and activists presumed were driving world affairs would soon be eclipsed by deep cultural and religious differences among civilizations. He foresaw the ferocity of our conflict with Islamicist terrorists and warned against the American unilateralism and moralism that have been brought to bear on it, widening the civilizational divide.

Huntington didn't clearly define these civilizations; he seemed unsure whether Latin America is a distinct civilization or is part of the West. Two months ago [in March 2004] he seemed to answer the latter question by heralding *Who We Are?* with an essay in *Foreign Policy*, this one called "The Hispanic Challenge." It has made the book a lightning rod for the least credible of his warnings: America's Latino immigration deluge, he claims, is so little like any earlier wave, so hostile or resistant to sharing the common American language, civic rites and virtues upon which our republican self-governance depends, that it constitutes "a major potential threat to the cultural and possibly political integrity of the United States." If this clash isn't civilizational, what is?

The problem is that, most likely, it isn't, and *Who We Are?* doesn't persuade this reader that most Latino immigration is a threat to liberal democracy. Two months ago, Huntington also published (in the conservative journal *National Interest*) a less-noted essay, "Dead Souls: The Denationalization of the American Elite," whose title and contents come from another, smaller section toward the end of the book. Contradicting his own claims that the Latino tidal wave is shifting the balance of American political culture against patriotism, he announces, "A major gap is growing in America between its increasingly denationalized [academic, corporate and cultural] elites and its 'Thank God for America' public." The latter, he reports, has remained consistently patriotic over time, even as the former "reject expressions of patriotism and explicitly define themselves as multinational....The CIA...can no longer count on the cooperation of American corporations...[which] view themselves as multinational and may think it not in their interests to help the U.S. government." And we're supposed to wring our hands instead about Mexican immigrants?

He opens *Who Are We?* by admitting he's too close to our crisis of American identity to address it only as a scholar; he's writing also as a patriot to defend a distinctive "Anglo-Protestant" political culture, which he believes is indispensable to republican self-governance here. Anyone of any race or ethnic background can join this "nonracial society composed of multiracial individuals," but only after having absorbed and adapted—or been absorbed into—the enduringly Anglo-Protestant idiom and ethos that most Americans of all colors and ethnicities do share but which, he says, most Latino immigrants resist.

But Huntington is disappointingly dull in evoking the Anglo-Protestant civic nationalism he wants to defend. These sections are as potted and derivative as an undistinguished term paper. "Eighty-five percent of Americans...cited their 'gov-ernmental, political institutions' as that aspect of their country of which they were the most proud, compared with 46 percent of Britons, 30 percent of Mexicans, 7 percent of Germans, and 3 percent of Italians. For Americans, ideology trumps territory." Endless recitations like this trump reader engagement.

Sometimes his flinty realism yields observations as arresting as they may be uncongenial: "America was created as a Protestant society just as and for some of the same reasons Pakistan and Israel were created as Muslim and Jewish societies in the twentieth century." This is classic Huntington—an understatement so true it makes us realize how much we have forgotten. (It also makes me wonder if he understands how much we have changed.) He chooses interestingly among familiar culinary metaphors for American civic identity, rejecting "melting pot" (too monolithic and suppressive of legitimate differences) and "tossed salad" (too diffuse) for a sturdy Anglo-Protestant "tomato soup," to which new arrivals contribute croutons and distinctive spices without changing its basic constitution.

Most new Americans have been glad to do this, but Huntington turns the holdouts' own words against them with a trademark sang-froid: Writers such as the black nationalist Harold Cruse declared that "America is a nation that lies to itself about who and what it is. It is a nation of minorities ruled by a minority of one—it thinks and acts as if it were a nation of white Anglo-Saxon Protestants." To which Huntington responds, Kabuki-like: "These critics are right." Then he says that Anglo-Protestant conformity, which absorbed people of many colors and faiths into a common identity that made possible the New Deal, the war against fascism and the rise of a new middle class, has "benefited them and the country."

Why doesn't it do so now? Here he sounds diversionary and at times testy. Pondering widespread adoption of the name "African American" over "black" in the 1980s, he writes, "Given the pervasive penchant of Americans to prefer single-syllable over multi-syllable names for almost everything, this high and growing popularity of a seven syllable, two-word name over a one-syllable, one-word name is intriguing and perhaps significant." As is Huntington's own preference for the eight-syllable "white Anglo-Saxon Protestant" over "WASP" to denote his own ethno-religious group.

He doesn't take black Americans seriously in this book, by whatever name. It was the black civil rights movement that made Huntington's Anglo conformism even possible for millions of nonwhites, and yet he takes no cues from that breakthrough and its subsequent breakdowns: The fabric of American civic trust has been nowhere more severely tried than in blacks' cultural, electoral, legal and public psycho-dramatic renderings of disaffection with white America.

Nor does Huntington examine such Latino responses to black disaffection as a 1992 editorial in San Diego's Mexican American newspaper *La Prensa* that declared Latinos the new "bridge between blacks, whites, Asians, and Latinos." Latinos, the editorial said, "will have to bring an end to class, color, and ethnic warfare. To succeed, they will have to do what the blacks failed to do: incorporate all into the human race and exclude no one."

If Huntington wants "a non-racial society composed of multiracial individuals," shouldn't he reach for those Latino immigrants whose notions of race are more fluid and ecumenical than those of most blacks and whites, locked together for so long in a brutal embrace? Mightn't they lead in renewing the quasi-ethnic bondings of an

American civic culture that, shorn of racist exclusions, could ask more of citizens than does the current ethnic pandering in commercialism and demagoguery?

There's no denying Huntington's observations about the uniqueness of the 2,000-mile-long border that (barely) separates Mexico's northern states from its former provinces in the United States, or that Mexican and other Latino immigrants' sheer numbers and concentration bring them linguistic and political hegemony, not only in southern Texas and California but also in Miami and parts of New York.

But he conflates demographic and political developments through intuition, stray anecdotes, newspaper stories and poll after vapid poll, whose findings are often contradictory: At times the gaps between Latinos and the rest of us in patriotism and perception are growing; at other times the American public—already 12.5 percent Latino, thanks to immigration that is 50 percent Latino—is maintaining its patriotism, defying cosmopolitan and capitalist elites. He can't have this both ways and describe a Latino "reconquista" of former Spanish territories in California, Texas and Florida that is "well underway."

Although he gives no evidence of having left a metaphorical armchair, Huntington sometimes writes as if he's just returned from a visit like the ones Henry James made to Eastern European Jewish immigrants on Manhattan's Lower East Side, where he concluded that the Yiddish-speaking "hard glitter of Israel" could never be truly American [see James' book, *American Scene*, 1907]. And Huntington glosses the tortuous reception of peasant, supposedly anti-republican, "papist" waves of Irish Catholics, and of Germans in the Midwest who long resisted efforts to impose English.

Not surprisingly, the public and private bureaucrats in our vast, national race industry are lambasting Huntington's claims. Some have noted quite rightly that American forces in Iraq are commanded by Army Lt. Gen. Ricardo Sanchez, who grew up in one of the dirt-poor, 98 percent-Latino counties in Texas that prompted Huntington's quasi-civilizational despair. But they and Huntington's Latino "nationalist" critics ignore his condemnation of American interventions abroad, such as the very war Sanchez is fighting. That skews debate about who we are as a nation. (It also misses the possibility that Huntington would be relieved if his pessimism about Latinos' becoming full Americans provoked enough of them to prove him wrong.) Keeping him busy answering charges of racism only spares him the trouble of having to own up to his book's anti-corporate arguments and implications.

For example, even as he angers multiculturalist activists by condemning the Ford Foundation's national "diversity" crusades—on the grounds that a country as diverse as ours should work overtime to deepen some common bonds—he also condemns Ford Motor Co., one of the corporations he tells us no longer describes itself as American and has non-Americans as top executives. The company, even more than the foundation, drives what he bemoans as the "deconstruction" of civic patriotism. That's a point worth developing, as are his criticisms of such enemies of civic trust as these companies' intrusive culture of consumer marketing and what he considers our government's faux-patriotic interventions abroad.

Huntington's condemnation of the latter, in which some honorable conservatives are now joining, is squarely in the tradition of his Harvard predecessors William James and Charles Eliot Norton, and of Andrew Carnegie and Carl Schurz, who opposed the Spanish-American War on republican grounds. And since he's writing about clashes between Mexican and American identities, why not examine Woodrow Wilson's disastrous, humiliating efforts to impose "democracy," Iraq-like, in Mexico in 1917?

Why doesn't he ponder the irony that George W. Bush and Jeb Bush, two of this country's most prominent "Anglo-Protestant" political leaders, accept the corporate defections from America and, in the former Spanish territories, including Texas, Florida and California, bear responsibility for immigration policies that Huntington would tighten and enrich with stronger civic socialization?

When the venerable black former U.S. Rep. Barbara Jordan of Texas chaired the U.S. Commission on Immigration Reform in 1995, she called for just such programs to induct immigrants more fully into American civic life. She noted that the word "Americanization" had "earned a bad reputation when it was stolen by racists and xenophobes in the 1920s....But it is our word and we are taking it back." Shouldn't Huntington join Jordan's successors against both facile multiculturalists and caste-forming, low-wage employers, instead of sniping at blacks and uttering dire prophecies about Latinos? This book and the way he has promoted it suggest he isn't up to the challenge.

THE CONTINUING DEBATE:
Immigration as a Threat to "Who We Are"

What Is New

The debate about Huntington's book and its off-shoot articles in such journals as *Foreign Policy* has remained torrid in intellectual and ideological circles and among those, such as Latinos, who were offended by his assertions. Although much of the general public may not have heard of Huntington's book, immigration, multiculturalism, and the other topics that it addresses are very much part of the national policy debate. For example, President Bush and congressional Democrats have proposed competing plans to allow illegal immigrants who have been in the country and working for an extended time to remain and, in the Democratic plan, gain resident status. There are also many related debates, such a periodic attempts in Congress to enact legislation designating English as the official U.S. language and a current debate in California about whether illegal aliens should be able to apply for driver's licenses. The general level of immigration is also at issue, with 49% of Americans wanting it decreased according to a 2004 poll, 33% thinking the current levels are about right, 14% wanting to increase them, and 4% unsure. As far as the "melting pot" versus the multicultural visions of American society, most Americans favor the melting pot. A 2003 poll found 60% of respondents saying immigrants should "blend in" to American culture, compared to 31% who thought newcomers should retain their own culture, 6% who favored doing both equally, and 3% who were unsure.

Where to Find More

Read Huntington's two articles derived from his book, "The Hispanic Challenge," *Foreign Policy* (March/April 2004) and "Dead Souls," *National Interest* (Spring 2004). For other reviews of Huntington's work, read Francis Fukuyama, "Identity Crisis," June 4, 2004, on the ezine *Slate* at http://slate.msn.com and John Fonte, "How to Make an American," American Enterprise Online, September 2004, at http://www.taemag.com/. An important source of information about matters such as the attitudes and language capabilities of Latinos, the largest group of immigrants, is the Pew Hispanic Center at http://www.pewhispanic.org/. Yet more data can be accessed by consulting "Race and Ethnicity in 2001: Attitudes, Perceptions and Experiences," a Washington Post/Kaiser/Harvard Survey Project report, September 2001, at http://www.kff.org/kaiserpolls/3143-index.cfm.

What More to Do

One thought is for your class to analyze Huntington's evidence for itself. Take the book and divide it up, looking for key arguments and the evidence that Huntington cites to support it. Then investigate the evidence using, but not limiting yourself to, the sources noted above in Where to Find More. Give each assertion a 1 if it proves right, 0.5 if the evidence is contradictory, and a zero if it proves wrong. A score of 0.5 or above favors Huntington's thesis; a score of below 0.5 means the professor may have flunked his analysis.

6 PUBLIC OPINION/PARTICIPATION

VOLUNTEER BORDER PATROL GROUPS:
Laudable Patriots *or* Dangerous Vigilantes?

LAUDABLE PATRIOTS

ADVOCATE: Chris Simcox, President of Minuteman Civil Defense Corps

SOURCE: Testimony during hearings on "Securing Our Borders: What We Have Learned From Government Initiatives and Citizen Patrols," U.S. House of Representatives Committee on Government Reform, May 12, 2005

DANGEROUS VIGILANTES

ADVOCATE: Asheesh Siddique, Editor, *The Princeton Progressive Review*, Princeton University

SOURCE: "The New Nativism," *Campus Progress News*, Spring 2005

Perhaps even more intense than feelings in Debate 5 about the level of immigration and the impact of immigrants are attitudes about the issues swirling around the millions of people who have come to the United States without going through established immigration procedures and the tens-of-thousands more who arrive each year. In 2000, the federal government estimated that between 7 million and 8 million such immigrants were in the United States and that between 400,000 and 500,00 new ones were arriving each year. These individuals are variously called unauthorized, undocumented, or illegal immigrants. Although they come from nearly everywhere, most of these immigrants are from Latin America, with, according to one study, 58% from Mexico and another 20% from Central America. Analysts estimate that about half of all undocumented immigrants have been in the country for a decade or more, and another quarter for five to ten years.

There are numerous issues related to unauthorized immigrants. These include such matters as whether or not they should be able to get driver's licenses and their access to social services. Another issue is whether attempt to round up and expel as many unauthorized immigrants as possible or to give them legal temporary or even permanent status. Generally, there has been little official interest in a mass expulsion program because of the sheer scope of trying to locate, detain, and repatriate unauthorized immigrants and because of the economic importance of undocumented workers to many powerful interest groups (especially fruit and vegetable growers, meatpackers, and other agribusiness groups). The status of many of these immigrants changed in 1986 when Congress enacted the Immigration Control and Reform Act, extending amnesty to many undocumented residents by granting permanent residency to an estimated 3.9 million of them who had been living continuously in the United States since January 1, 1982. The ICRA also included heavier fines for employers hiring unauthorized workers and others provisions meant to stem illegal immigration. But they have been spottily enforced, and the flow of unauthorized immigrants continues.

During the past five years or so, the status of unauthorized workers and their families has once again become a major political issue. One reason is the post-9/11 fear that some of those slipping into the United States might be terrorists. A second factor has been the cumulative increase in foreign-born residents, both legal and illegal, as discussed in Debate 5. Politics is a third factor. Democrats and Republicans are aware of the importance of the Latino vote, but they are also cognizant of the strong sentiment against illegal immigration by many people, especially in states along the U.S.-Mexico border. Among all Americans, a 2004 poll found that 69% of its respondents were "very" or "somewhat" concerned about undocumented immigrants. A fourth reason for the increased focus in undocumented immigration has been the inability of U.S. Border Patrol forces, despite increased personnel and equipment since 2001, to substantially stem the tide of unauthorized immigrants entering the United States. That is not because the Border Patrol has not tried. During 2004, it intercepted more than 1.1 million illegal immigrants trying to cross the southwest border alone. But many others gain entry and of those who are caught, many keep trying until they succeed. The president of the American Federation of Government Employees' National Border Patrol Council, estimates that the Border Patrol catches only between 25% and 33% of those trying to cross the border illegally. "We're just overwhelmed," he says. "We don't have enough people to keep up with the volume of traffic."

One response to the continuing flood tide of people entering the United States without permission has the formation of volunteer groups to patrol the border, particularly the frontier with Mexico, in support of the Border Patrol's mission or detaining and returning illegal immigrants. One such group was founded by Chris Simcox, owner and editor of the newspaper *Tombstone Tumbleweed*. He argues in the first reading that he and fellow volunteers are public-spirited citizens acting out of frustration after many years of seeing the federal government fail in its responsibility to secure U.S. borders. Taking a very different view in the second reading, Asheesh Siddique, a student at Princeton University, labels Simcox and his compatriots "right-wing activists allied with white supremacists" and accuses them of waging "a vigilante campaign of aggression against illegal Mexican migrants along the border."

POINTS TO PONDER

➤ What is the difference between patriotic groups laudably taking direct action and unsavory vigilante groups taking the law into their own hands? Were the 150 members of the American "Sons of Liberty" who, protesting what they saw as onerous British taxes on tea, boarded three ships in Boston in 1773 and dumped their cargo of tea into the harbor in the famous Boston Tea Party, patriots or vigilantes?

➤ Other than that they have entered the country without permission, what, if anything, about undocumented immigrants is worrisome?

➤ Does the fact that most illegal immigrants are from Latin American necessarily mean that those who want to halt the influx of undocumented people are racists?

Volunteer Border Patrol Groups: Laudable Patriots

CHRIS SIMCOX

Almost four years after the terrible terrorist attacks upon our country on September 11, 2001, citizens of the United States remain concerned about our national security, specifically our outrageously porous international border with Mexico. Those who live along the border-state region with Mexico have great concern for their personal safety as well as concern over the lack of border security.

Despite repeated warnings from citizens, local law enforcement and various public officials, our border remains intolerably porous and presents not only a threat to public safety but also a clear and present danger to the security of our nation. Millions of dollars have been thrown at the problem and new technology has been promised—some delivered, some conspicuously absent. Citizens who live with daily incursions of illegal aliens through our property and into the sparsely populated back country along the border realize one thing: the Department of Homeland security cannot effectively stop migrant workers, mothers carrying small children, vicious drug smugglers, known criminals and human smugglers from breaching our border security—we do not feel confident that our government is able to stop terrorist elements from entering our country with the intent of inflicting harm upon our citizens.

After years of writing letters, sending faxes, sending e-mails and making countless phone calls to elected officials pleading, begging and demanding redress of our grievances, frustration led us to but one conclusion—we must act and address the problem with a citizen movement. In

November of 2002, I began assembling a group of citizens to undertake the responsibility in assisting what we realized was a Border Patrol woefully undermanned and, as it stood, unable to provide for the safety of the citizens of our local community, Cochise County, Arizona.

We began with a small group of about 40 concerned citizens who knew the only way to bring attention to the problem was with bold statement combined with effective active participation, and so a neighborhood border watch movement was born. Working with retired and active law enforcement and military personnel, we formed Civil Homeland Defense—a group of citizens who worked within the law to assist law enforcement with battling an overwhelming flood of incursions by foreign nationals from around the world who daily breached our border security. Since the formation of the CHD, over 400 citizens from Arizona and other states have participated in spotting, locating and reporting people who entered our country illegally. Our citizen effort has led to the capture, by the proper authorities, of 4,609 individuals from 26 different countries including China, Brazil, Colombia, Haiti, Poland and, yes, even people from Russia. During the same period, volunteers of our modest citizen patrol group have provided life saving water and medical attention to save the lives of 158 men, women and children. From the beginning, our volunteers have worked seamlessly with field agents of the U.S. Border Patrol; agents in the field have always acted with courtesy and have shown appreciation for our assistance with a problem they are not able to control, given the support they receive from the Congress.

Supervisors and sector chiefs of the U.S. Border Patrol have been a different story. Despite a public service campaign asking for the help of citizens, they contradict themselves when it comes to the point of actually going beyond picking up a phone to report groups of people who have obviously entered our country illegally.

Video provided by Civil Homeland Defense and the Minuteman Project illustrates just how porous our border is. Each of the nearly 5,000 identified illegal entrants is presented in videotape evidence supplied to this committee. Not only have local citizens documented persons from other countries entering Cochise County, but we also present evidence of incursions by Mexican military personnel—sometimes found up to a mile inside the borders of the United States. During the month of April 2005, 876 citizens volunteered at least one 8-hour shift manning static observation posts along a 26-mile sector of Cochise County. The areas were chosen because of their repeated use by human smugglers to bring thousands of foreign nationals into our country illegally. We identified the most heavily traveled routes used by smugglers and we formed static observation posts spaced approximately one-quarter of a mile apart, to create an obvious presence that resulted in deterring anyone from entering the country in those areas. Sixty-three volunteers spent the entire 30-day period working multiple shifts to maintain a presence. On our "Naco line," an area east of Bisbee, Arizona, stretching towards Douglas, Arizona, an area notorious for up to 500 illegal crossings a day, we saw a drop to nearly zero during the 30-day mission.

On our "Huachuca line," an area 5-miles from the Mexican border at the base of the Huachuca Mountains, we witnessed a dramatic decrease in groups of illegal

aliens descending through canyons leading through neighborhoods south of Sierra Vista and the unincorporated area known as Hereford, Arizona.

During the month-long mission, volunteers of the Minuteman Project assisted Border Patrol with locating and apprehending 349 people entering the United States illegally. Also during the month of April, calls to Border Patrol from local residents led to more than 1,500 apprehensions that would not have been made had citizens not taken the initiative to report suspicious illegal activity in their neighborhoods. Border Patrol officials reported that apprehensions of illegal aliens in the Naco sector dropped 65% from the previous year during the same time period. During the month-long project, volunteer encounters with Border patrol field agents were nothing less than amicable and friendly. Agents were overtly appreciative and supportive of the assistance provided by citizens. Agents thanked the volunteers for bringing national attention to their plight and their frustration with being ignored by supervisors as well as the lack of support both in equipment and personnel by Congress, and expressed anger at comments made by the President of the United States, George W. Bush.

When volunteers of the Minuteman Project made calls for assistance to the Border Patrol they responded quickly and shared words of appreciation for the efforts of the volunteers. At no time did any field agent state concerns about citizens impeding their duties or getting in the way. At no time did field agents express frustration regarding the setting off of sensors.

The Minuteman Project was a phenomenal success due to the law abiding and conscientious efforts of many retired law enforcement and military veterans who gave their time and offered expertise in organizing, supervising and ensuring volunteers remained explicitly aware of the tactics outlined in our carefully written Standard Operating Procedures (S.O.Ps.). That S.O.P. format is included in the packet of information offered as testimony to this committee. The S.O.Ps. provided a framework that assured citizens' exemplary behavior and code of conduct during the month-long protest.

Our message is clear: Congress must move immediately to assign military reserves to the border to assist with controlling our border, or we the people will continue to organize, train and act to assist doing the job—right alongside our courageous Border Patrol agents. Our effort now continues in Cochise County, and will expand towards a much larger citizen volunteer group preparing for a month-long effort in all four southern border states in October 2005.

Each of our volunteers must submit to a criminal background check; they must be interviewed by recruitment personnel and must understand their participation hinges on their strict adherence to a policy of law-abiding engagement with those who willfully break the laws of our nation by entering our country illegally. We intend to share all intelligence information with the proper authorities and will work in ways that do not impede their operations.

We know our border is rife with hardened criminals who have no respect for human life. Volunteers are prepared for the consequences of violent encounters with criminals; we are prepared to defend our lives and our country with reasonable counter-force if necessary. Volunteers will abide strictly by the laws of the states in which they operate such patrols. Volunteers fully understand the weight of responsibility heaped upon their shoulders by the lack of attention to this problem by Congress and the President of the United States. It is your duty to immediately respond to our grievances and quickly act to supply pro-

fessional personnel who would bring an end to the necessity for ordinary citizens to band together to provide the services that are clearly delegated by the Constitution to the Federal Government.

Our plan is continue recruiting retired law enforcement personnel and we are actively recruiting military veterans, from WWII vets to veterans returning from the most recent war in Iraq—they are ready and willing to serve their country again by assisting with border security.

The success has led to an outpouring of support and volunteerism, skyrocketing to the point where organizers have been contacted by over 15,000 people wishing to volunteer for future operations.

We consider this a mandate from the citizens of the United States who are no longer demanding better border security—they are now willing to participate in securing the borders themselves. Our intentions are to follow the will of the people. The Minuteman Civil Defense Corps. is now undertaking the task of recruiting, training and deploying thousands of U.S. citizens to the four southern border states with Mexico. This effort will also continue to expand to northern border states with Canada.

We now consider the movement to be a revival of the Civil Defense movement of the World War II era. While our troops are fighting on foreign soil, while our Department of Homeland Security applies its resources and efforts to provide for our national security in other areas, we the people will take up the slack by developing civil defense volunteers to support the U.S. Border Patrol.

We consider this a no-compromise situation. Until the time that Congress appropriates sufficient funding and develops personnel levels to the numbers needed to effectively secure our borders, we the people will roll up our sleeves in the time-honored tradition and creed of a "cando" society, and we will assist until honorably relieved from duty by the government of the United States.

Only one scenario is possible in convincing citizens to return to our normal everyday lives: deployment of U.S. military reserves and/or assigning National Guard personnel, to augment a woefully understaffed Border patrol; only this will convince ordinary citizens to retire from this endeavor.

The tactics and logistics now seem obvious. Static observation posts are the only effective method of deterrence short of building a wall along the almost 2,000 mile border with Mexico. Elevated observation outposts spaced approximately one-half-mile apart and staffed with teams of two to four Border Patrol or military personnel are needed to deter drug and human smugglers from entering the country. It is all about creating an obvious presence that deters individuals from entering our country illegally.

We know that posse comitatus [an 1878 law prohibiting the use of the military for civilian law enforcement] cannot be used as an excuse for preventing the deployment of military reserves to assist with border security. President Theodore Roosevelt set aside the 60 foot right of way known as the international border road in 1907 explicitly for the purpose of using the military to protect the United States. We of course are not concerned about the military being used against citizens of the United States; we are asking for the military to augment Border Patrol to improve national security and to prevent people and illicit goods from entering the U.S. illegally.

U.S. military reserves and National Guard personnel could use the border for training exercises, creating a presence to deter illegal activity. Border Patrol could work as a secondary layer of protection and would pursue and apprehend people who breach the first line of defense. For the citizens who have worked the border, we know first hand this tactic works. While we watched the border during April, every illegal alien who chanced crossing the border in our area of operations was quickly apprehended by the proper authorities. Using advanced technology, ground sensors, cameras and UAVs [Unmanned Aerial Vehicles] are important in providing security; however, nothing is as effective as a physical presence of personnel on the border.

Volunteer Border Patrol Groups:
Dangerous Vigilantes

ASHEESH SIDDIQUE

The Arizona-Mexico border is one of the most arid parts of America, but also holds some of this country's most beautiful national landmarks. Deep canyons, along with ancient pueblos built as early as 700 AD, dot the land, making the region a prime tourist destination. Tall mountain ranges, swift rivers, jackrabbits, and coyotes create a natural environment like no other in the world.

But there's trouble in paradise.

Right-wing activists allied with white supremacists this past month to wage a vigilante campaign of aggression against illegal Mexican migrants along the border. Throughout April [2005], a coalition of anti-immigration activists calling themselves the Minuteman Project engaged in an effort to "peacefully observe" the border for signs of illegal immigration. The organizers of the effort, which came to a temporary end this past Sunday, claimed that their intentions are legal, benign, and free of racist motivations. "Our objective will be to spot these intruders and inform the U.S. Border Patrol of their location so that border patrol agents can intercept and detain them," read the project's web site. "We will NOT be confronting the illegal aliens or making citizens' arrests."

But the Project was not as innocent as it claimed to be. Many members of the National Alliance, the largest Neo-Nazi group in America, attended meetings of the vigilante group, and even distributed flyers to local residents on behalf of the Minutemen stating that "Non-Whites are turning America into a Third World slum." And even as the Minutemen claimed to be

acting to protect America, their actions directly violated basic human rights protections guaranteed to migrant workers under international treaties—irrespective of their status under U.S. immigration law (Part III, Article 10. Note: no distinction made in terms of legal status).

The rhetoric of the participating organizations' leadership also belied their true motivations. Glenn Spencer, one of America's leading anti-immigration activists and the founder of American Border Patrol, has argued that "Mexican culture is based on deceit" and "Chicanos and Mexicanos lie as a means of survival." Civil Homeland Defense's founder, Chris Simcox, has argued that Mexican immigrants "have no problem slitting your throat and taking your money or selling drugs to your kids or raping your daughters and they are evil people." Most of the funding for these groups has come from organizations with extremist connections, such as the Federation for American Immigration Reform—an organization that has ties to the racist Council of Conservative Citizens. And while the Minuteman Project has denied being a racist organization, James Gilchrist, its founder, recently defended white supremacists on Fox News' Hannity & Colmes.

Southeast Arizona has a long history of racially motivated violence against immigrants, but things had been fairly calm during the 1980s and 1990s. Tensions between the white population and Mexican migrants, however, flared up beginning in 1999 as groups like American Border Patrol, Ranch Rescue, the Minuteman Project, and Civil Homeland Defense began to organize campaigns of harassment and intimidation against these laborers.

These new efforts among conservatives have surged in the wake of 9/11, seeking to capitalize on the new climate of fear to push an anti-immigrant, jingoistic agenda that seeks to curtail due-process rights to non-citizens and impose federal restrictions on the types of documentation government officials can accept as valid types of identification.

Legal observers from the American Civil Liberties Union and other organizations spent the month monitoring the activities of the Minutemen and their allies. They reported several disturbing civil liberties violations by the vigilantes, including one incident where volunteers allegedly held a migrant against his will and photographed him wearing clothing with the slogan "Bryan Barton caught an illegal alien and all I got was this t-shirt," and even occasions where the Minutemen took migrants hostage and tried to attack them with dogs.

Furthermore, the Minuteman Project's activities disrupted the work of the legal immigration authorities. Volunteers unfamiliar with the provisions the Border Patrol already has in place tripped sensors, caused false alarms that taxed the efforts of law enforcement agents. One agent noted the toll of these mistakes: "Every sensor has to be addressed. It has taken away from our normal operations."

In spite of the group's radical views and racist ties, the Minutemen received resounding endorsement from prominent political figures, including at least ten members of Congress, including [U.S. Representative] Tom Tancredo [R-CO], chairman of the House Immigration Reform Caucus, and California Governor Arnold Schwarzenegger, who has been criticized by immigration rights groups for making comments "nothing short of base racism" in support of the Project. In addition, prominent conservative pundits and journalists, including Michelle Malkin, Cal Thomas, and George Metcalf, strongly defended the Minutemen—suggesting that the extremism of Spencer, Simcox, and Gilchrist is very much within the mainstream of conservative political discourse on immigration.

The conclusion of the Minutemen's month of vigilantism came as Congress continues to debate how to address the genuine problem of illegal immigration. In March, the Pew Hispanic Center estimated that there are about 10.3 million undocumented residents in the United States, with 57% coming from Mexico. Arizona has experienced one of the most rapid growths in its undocumented migrant population. One proposal being floated in Washington is the REAL ID Act, which passed the House in February [2005] and is currently pending in the Senate. Written by Representative James Sensenbrenner [R-WI], the legislation attempts to make it easier to send asylum-seekers back to the country they are fleeing, and makes it more difficult for the courts to review unlawful actions made by the government in deportation cases. [Democratic National Committee] Chairman Howard Dean has explicitly highlighted the similarities between the REAL ID Act and the Minuteman Project, saying that both create "an atmosphere of hostility." Dean also noted that the Act would provide incentives for vigilantes to corral immigrants without ensuring their identity, creating the potential for more Minutemen-style civil liberties violations. [The proposed Real ID Act (H.R. 418) was included as a provision of a supplemental appropriation bill (H.R. 1286), which was enacted by Congress, signed by the president, and became law (P.L. 109–13) in May 2005.

Progressives continue to wrestle with this issue. Some who advocate for change argue that we need to have a skills-based approach to immigration, encouraging the immigration of highly skilled workers from abroad who will be able to contribute significantly to American economic growth, while at the same time gradually reducing the number of unskilled workers. This is, of course, quite different from the more aggressive approach favored by conservatives and the Minutemen.

If there's anything to be learned from the sorry saga of the Minuteman Project, it's that efforts to make America a land of exclusion, not freedom, are pervasive even in the age of globalization. Declaring "victory" in their efforts on April 30, the Minutemen have now announced plans to expand their efforts northward to the U.S.-Canada border, and into other Southwestern states. Progressives must be just as vigilant in ensuring that this nation remains a genuine land of opportunity for millions of immigrants from around the world. In her famous 1883 poem "The New Colossus," Emma Lazarus offered a vision of an America open to receiving the "huddled masses yearning to breathe free," a "city on a hill" where people could come and create a better life free of poverty, sickness, and persecution. We must remain true to Lazarus' dream of opportunity—a dream that both defines us and unites us as Americans.

THE CONTINUING DEBATE:
Volunteer Border Patrol Groups

What Is New

The Minutemen's plan to patrol the U.S.-Mexico border during April 2005 set off alarm and criticism. Mexican President Vicente Fox of Mexico denounced such groups "immigrant hunters," President Bush declared, "I'm against vigilantes," and the American Civil Liberties Union dispatched staff to monitor the Minutemen. After the first period of monitoring had ended, according to the *Wall Street Journal*, "those on both sides of the issue [agree that] the Minuteman…initiative in Arizona came off largely without incident." The Minutemen did not try to detain suspected illegal immigrants. Instead they reported them and followed them until the Border Patrol arrived. According to that agency, over 1,000 such citizen reports led to over 2,000 intercepts during April in the 20-mile zone the Minutemen were patrolling. Skeptics noted that 900 Minutemen had patrolled a small area, and, the same coverage of the entire 1,400 mile long U.S.-Mexico border would take 60,000 people.

According to Simcox, the Minutemen plan future patrols along the border, want to organize consumer boycotts of employers who hire undocumented workers, and will try to mobilize voters nationally to press Washington to allocate enough resources to secure the border. This goal may strike a responsive cord with Americans, 61% of whom described the matter as "extremely" or "very" serious.

Where to Find More

Data on undocumented immigration is available from the Pew Hispanic Center's report, "Unauthorized Migrants: Numbers and Characteristics" at www.pewhispanic.org. A group that wants strong measures to stem illegal immigration is the Center for Immigration Studies at www.cis.org/. A group that disagrees is the National Immigration Forum at www.immigrationforum.org/. A review of U.S. policy is Wayne Cornelius, "Controlling 'Unwanted' Immigration: Lessons from the United States, 1993–2004," *Journal of Ethnic & Migration Studies* (2005). Chris Simcox sold the *Tombstone Tumbleweed* in September 2005, but the newspaper of the historic town made famous for the gunfight at the OK Corral is worth visiting at www.tombstonetumbleweed.com/.

What More to Do

The core debate for the future is whether to (1) spend the financial resources necessary to seal the border against future illegal immigration and also locate, detain, and repatriate the millions of undocumented immigrants already in the United States, (2) increase both the level of enforcement against and penalties on the many Americans and U.S. businesses that employ undocumented workers, (3) adopt one of the various proposals to "legalize" these immigrants by either granting them temporary workers/family status or even permanent residency/citizenship, (4) give enough aid to the countries the immigrants come from so that they can find economic opportunity at home, and/or (5) do no more or even less along the border and devote financial resources to other issues facing the country. How would you prioritize these five options?

MEDIA

SHIELDING JOURNALISTS' SOURCES FROM SUBPOENA:
Protecting Democracy *or* Impeding Justice?

PROTECTING DEMOCRACY

ADVOCATE: Norman Pearlstine, Editor-in-Chief, Time Inc.

SOURCE: Testimony during hearings on "Reporters' Shield Legislation: Issues and Implications," U.S. Senate Committee on the Judiciary, July 20, 2005

IMPEDING JUSTICE

ADVOCATE: James B. Comey, Deputy Attorney General, U.S. Department of Justice

SOURCE: Testimony during hearings on "Reporters' Shield Legislation: Issues and Implications," U.S. Senate Committee on the Judiciary, July 20, 2005

Journalists have long used "anonymous" or "confidential" sources to obtain information. They argue that unless they can assure their sources of anonymity, the flow of news will decrease because their sources will fear retaliation. Sometimes, such anonymous sources have been instrumental in major stories. Most famously, "Deep Throat" was an anonymous source for the press during the Watergate scandal that led President Richard M. Nixon to resign in 1974. The press did not identify that source (Mark Felt, former deputy director of the FBI) until he gave his permission in 2005. Historically, there has been little effort to, and no court support of, efforts to force journalists to reveal their sources in such cases.

The ability of journalists to shield sources in criminal matters is another issue. The matter first became a legal issue in the 1890s when a reporter for the Baltimore *Sun* was jailed for contempt of court after he refused to disclose his sources related to a voting bribery scandal and ensuing criminal investigation. Responding to his incarceration, Maryland in 1896 enacted the country's first "shield law" giving journalists the legal right to maintain confidential news sources, even during criminal investigation. Since then, almost all states have passed shield laws to protect reporters, although the extent of protection varies widely among the states.

On the federal level, the key Supreme Court ruling came in the *Branzburg v. Hayes* (1972), a case involving the refusal of a reporter for the Louisville *Courier-Journal* to reveal sources related to drug dealing. In a 5 to 4 decision, the court held that the First Amendment did not exempt journalists from having "to respond to grand jury subpoena and answer relevant questions." However, the court kept its focus on criminal investigating by adding, "Official harassment of the press undertaken not for purposes of law enforcement but to disrupt a reporter's relationship with his news sources would have no justification."

There the matter rested until the recent events that prompted this debate. They began in 2003 amid the controversy over whether or not the administration of President George W. Bush had reason to believe that Iraq had a nuclear weapons program. On July 6, 2003, the *New York Times* published an op-ed piece by former Ambassador Joseph Wilson claiming that the CIA had sent him to Niger in early 2002 to look into whether the Iraqis had tried to buy uranium from that country and that he had found no evidence of any attempted purchase. Soon thereafter, syndicated columnist Robert Novak reported that two high-level Bush officials had told the him that the CIA had sent Wilson on the recommendation of his wife, Valerie Plame. Novak described her as a spy, "an agency operative on weapons of mass destruction." Soon thereafter, *Time* published articles based on the investigative reporting of Matthew Cooper, Judith Miller, and others indicating that government officials had also revealed to *Time* that Plame was a CIA operative. One story-line suggested that officials leaked Plame's status in order to ruin her career by blowing her cover in retaliation for the op-ed piece written by her husband.

Knowingly disclosing the identity of U.S. spies violates the Intelligence Identities Protection Act, and federal investigators subpoenaed Cooper, Miller, and *Time*, demanding that they submit all documents related to the stories and reveal their sources. Such subpoenas are not common. According to Department of Justice data, federal officials and courts issued only 17 subpoenas between 1991 and 2001 asking for journalist's sources.

In the cases at hand, the reporters and *Time* declined to comply. In subsequent court actions, they all were held in contempt of court by a U.S. district judge, the U.S. Court of Appeals upheld that action, and the Supreme Court refused to take the case. *Time* gave way and submitted the documents it possessed. Cooper also complied with the court order after receiving a waiver of confidentiality from his source, White House senior political adviser Karl Rove. But Miller remained in contempt and was sent to jail and was still incarcerated when the testimony that makes the up following articles was given.

One response to the Plame affair was the introduction of the Free Flow of Information Act of 2005 in Congress. The legislation is designed to further limit the ability of the government to force journalists to reveal their sources. In the first of the following articles, *Time*'s editor-in-chief Norman Pearlstine tells the Senate that using confidential sources is necessary to enabling reporters to protect an essential element of democracy: providing vital information to the public so that people can make informed decisions about the government and thereby fully participate in democracy. Deputy U.S. Attorney General James Comey counters that he recognizes the importance of the press in a free society, but argues that sufficient protection for the press already exists and that new legislation to shield journalists' sources would upset the proper balance between the need for free dissemination of ideas and information in a democracy and the equally important need for effective law enforcement and the fair administration of justice.

POINTS TO PONDER

➤ Note the difference between the reporters right to shield sources about non-criminal matters and those under investigation as violations of the law.

➤ Think about whether by refusing to reveal sources, the media is not withholding important information that would help citizens evaluate the stories based on anonymous sources.

➤ Pay attention to the detailed commentary on the pending bill in James Comey's commentary. As the line goes, "the devil is in the detail," and you can favor some aspects of the bill and not others.

83

Shielding Journalists' Sources from Subpoena: Protecting Democracy

NORMAN PEARLSTINE

I...support...the proposed federal legislation that would protect journalists from being compelled to testify about confidential sources and other unpublished information obtained during newsgathering. This type of protection, which has been adopted in one form or another by 49 states and the District of Columbia, is commonly called a "reporter's privilege," but this is something of a misnomer. The laws are really intended to protect the public, not reporters, by ensuring the free flow of information about governmental activities and other matters of public concern and interest. I believe there is an urgent need for such protection at the federal level.

Until today, I had never testified in a Senate hearing or, for that matter, in any other legislative proceeding. As a journalist, I am far more comfortable reporting, writing, or editing news about the government than urging the government to adopt new laws. But the absence of federal legislation protecting sources has created extraordinary chaos, limiting the public's access to important information that is so necessary in a democratic society. The Supreme Court's sharply divided decision 33 years ago in *Branzburg v. Hayes* (1972) has mystified courts, lawyers and journalists alike. As a result, the federal courts are in a state of utter disarray about whether a reporter's privilege protecting confidential sources exists. The conflicting legal standards throughout the federal courts defeat the nearly unanimous policies of the states in this area. This uncertainty chills essential newsgathering and reporting. It also leads to confusion by sources and reporters, and the threat of jail and other harsh penalties for reporters who do not know what promises they can make to their sources. I recently witnessed the problems firsthand. As the Committee is no doubt aware, for almost two years, Time Inc. and its reporter Matthew Cooper fought against compelled disclosure of confidential sources in response to grand jury subpoenas in Special Counsel Patrick Fitzgerald's investigation of the Valerie Plame affair. The federal district judge presiding over the matter called this battle a "perfect storm" in which important First Amendment rights clashed with the important interest in law enforcement. We fought all the way to the Supreme Court and lost.

My decision to turn over confidential documents to the Special Counsel after we had pursued every possible legal remedy was the toughest decision of my career—and one I should never have had to make. The experience has only deepened my commitment to ensure protection for confidential sources and made clear to me the urgent need for federal legislation....[In the following commentary] I shall...discuss why the careful use of confidential sources is indispensable to ensuring that the press can fulfill its constitutionally established duty of providing vital information to the public so that people can make informed decisions about the government and thereby fully participate in democracy. I shall [also] explain why I so strongly believe that federal legislation is necessary—and long overdue.

THE IMPORTANCE OF PROTECTING CONFIDENTIAL SOURCES

It is Time Inc.'s editorial policy that articles in our publications should identify sources by name whenever possible. But sometimes we can obtain information only by promising confidentiality to a source, because many persons with important information won't speak to the press unless they are assured anonymity. Information given in confidence is especially valuable when it contradicts or undermines public positions asserted by governments or powerful individuals or corporations. Without confidential sourcing, the public would never have learned the details of many situations vital to its interests, from Watergate to the controversies that led to the impeachment (and then acquittal) of President [Bill] Clinton to the Enron and Abu Ghraib scandals.

Time Inc. has a long history of fighting to preserve press freedoms because we believe it is in the public interest to do so. It is no coincidence that the Supreme Court held in a case involving our company that freedom of the press was created "not for the benefit of the press so much as for the benefit of all of us." *Time Inc. v. Hill* (1967). We know that when gathering and reporting news, journalists act as surrogates for the public. Protecting confidential sources is thus intended not to protect the rights of news organizations, individual reporters or sources, but to safeguard the public's rights. [As argued by constitutional expert] Ronald Dworkin..., "The special position of the press is justified, not because reporters have special rights but because it is thought that the community as a whole will benefit from their special treatment, just as wheat farmers might be given a subsidy, not because they are entitled to it, but because the community will benefit from that." Our "Constitution specifically selected the press" to fulfill an "important role" in our democracy ...[according to the Supreme Court in] *Mills v. Alabama* (1966). [In that case, the court also said that] the press "serves and was designed to serve as a powerful antidote to any abuses of power by governmental officials as a constitutionally chosen means for keeping officials elected by the people responsible to all the people whom they were elected to serve." [In another case, *Estes v. Texas* (1965), the court commented that] the press "has been a mighty catalyst in awakening public interest in governmental affairs, exposing corruption among public officers and employees and generally informing the citizenry of public events and occurrences." [In a 1981 ruling], the Second Circuit Court of the Court of Appeals wrote, "[N]ews gathering is essential to a free press" and "[t]he press was protected so that it could bare the secrets of government and inform the people." Without an unfettered press, citizens would be far less able to make informed political, social, and economic choices. But the press's function as a vital source of information is weakened whenever the ability of journalists to gather news is impaired.

Some reliance on confidential sources is necessary to protect the press's ability to fulfill its constitutionally ordained role. Over the years *Time* and our other magazines have published many stories regarding issues of significant public interest that could not have been published unless we could rely on confidential sources. To cite a few examples from the weeks prior to the Supreme Court's denial of our petition for certiorari, I worked with colleagues at *Time* on important stories about a suicide bomber in Iraq, the treatment and interrogation of a detainee at Guantanamo [Bay, U.S. Naval Base], and the vulnerability of our nation's commercial nuclear facilities should they be subjected to terrorist attack. None of these stories could have been published without the use of information from confidential sources. As one court explained it:

> The interrelationship between newsgathering, news dissemination and the need for a journalist to protect his or her source is too apparent to require belaboring. A journalist's inability to protect the confidentiality of sources s/he must use will jeopardize the journalist's ability to obtain information on a confidential basis. This in turn will seriously erode the essential role played by the press in the dissemination of information and matters of interest and concern to the public.

Following my decision to obey the courts by providing the Special Counsel with the subpoenaed documents, I met last week with *Time's* Washington bureau, and later that day with many of its New York writers and editors. Many of them showed me e-mails and letters from valuable sources who insisted that they no longer trusted the magazine and that they would no longer cooperate on stories.

The chilling effect is obvious. Without confidentiality—that express promise or implied understanding that a source's identity won't be revealed—it will often be impossible for our reporters to sustain relationships with sources and to obtain sensitive information from them. As Professor Alexander Bickel observed in a celebrated essay:

> Indispensable information comes in confidence from officeholders fearful of superiors, from businessmen fearful of competitors, from informers operating at the edge of the law who are in danger of reprisal from criminal associates, from people afraid of the law and of government—sometimes rightly afraid, but as often from an excess of cau-

tion—and from men in all fields anxious not to incur censure for unorthodox or unpopular views. …Forcing reporters to divulge such confidences would dam the flow to the press, and through it to the people, of the most valuable sort of information: not the press release, not the handout, but the firsthand story based on the candid talk of a primary news source.

THE URGENT NEED FOR A FEDERAL SHIELD LAW

The need for a federal shield law has never been clearer. Judith Miller is in jail and Matthew Cooper would have been had his source not released him at the last minute from his bond of confidentiality. As we argued in our certiorari petition [to the Supreme Court], the law is a mess—so much so that the three judges on the D.C. Circuit panel each took a very different view of whether the federal common law recognizes a reporter's privilege. Some judges…believe that *Branzburg* bars not only First Amendment protection, but any form of judicially recognized privilege, and the Supreme Court has refused to revisit that decision, leaving federal legislation as the sole realistic possibility for a uniform federal rule. As the Supreme Court in *Branzburg* recognized, "[a]t the federal level, Congress has freedom to determine whether a statutory newsman's privilege is necessary and desirable and to fashion standards and rules as narrow or broad as deemed necessary to deal with the evil discerned and, equally important, to refashion those rules as experience from time to time may dictate."

Federal law recognizes many other evidentiary privileges, including privileges protecting spousal communications, and communications between social workers and those seeking counseling from them, doctors and patients, attorneys and clients, and clergy and penitents. These privileges may lead to the loss of evidence in some instances, but they are viewed as necessary to protect and foster communications deemed valuable to society as a whole. The same is true for communications between reporters and confidential sources.

When courts compel disclosure of confidential sources, it endangers our ability to do our jobs, and this practice inevitably stems the flow of information on public events vital to an informed citizenry and a healthy democracy. In this case, for instance, Cooper's story *A War on Wilson?* raised the important question whether government officials improperly retaliated against a critic of the Administration's decision to go to war.

The Plame case is part of a disturbing trend. In the last two years, dozens of reporters have been subpoenaed to reveal their confidential sources, many of whom face the prospect of imminent imprisonment. The use of such subpoenas in the Plame case represents a profound departure from the practice of federal prosecutors when this case is compared to other landmark cases involving confidentiality over the past 30 years. Neither Archibald Cox, the Watergate Special Prosecutor, nor Judge John Sirica sought to force *The Washington Post* or its reporters to reveal the identity of "Deep Throat," the prized confidential source. We are deeply concerned that the rulings in the Plame case will exacerbate the danger of prosecutorial excesses when it comes to issuing subpoenas in all types of cases. To be sure, the Department of Justice guidelines limit subpoenas to the press and require the Attorney General's approval of such subpoenas. But the courts in the Plame case held that these regulations are not judicially enforceable. And where a special (or "independent") counsel is leading the investigation, the Attorney General's

approval is no longer required, posing special dangers to the press. As Judge Tatel noted in the Plame case, "[I]ndependent prosecutors...may skew their assessments of the public interests implicated when a reporter is subpoenaed. After all, special prosecutors, immune to political control and lacking a docket of other cases, face pressure to justify their appointments by bagging their prey.

To make matters worse, reporters and their sources are subject to a tangle of contradictory privilege rules that vary widely depending on the jurisdiction in which they are subpoenaed. These differing rules lead to arbitrary, unpredictable and conflicting outcomes. This uncertainty has a chilling effect on speech, and ultimately results in less information reaching the public, as many individuals will hesitate to communicate with a reporter if a promise of confidentiality is good in some jurisdictions but not in others. In particular, a state-law reporter's privilege is of little value if it offers no reliable protection from forced disclosure in federal court.

The 34 states and the District of Columbia said it best in their amicus curiae brief urging the Supreme Court to grant review in the Plame case. All of these states and the District have adopted some form of reporter's shield law and these laws, "like those of the other fifteen jurisdictions that have them, share a common purpose: to assure that the public enjoys a free flow of information and that journalists who gather and report the news to the public can do so in a free and unfettered atmosphere. The shield laws also rest on the uniform determination by the states that, in most cases, compelling newsgatherers to disclose confidential information is contrary to the public interest. That the chief law enforcement officers for these 35 jurisdictions weighed in to endorse their reporter's shield laws is powerful evidence that these laws do not interfere with the government's ability to prosecute crimes.

At the same time, the states also declared in their brief that a "federal policy that allows journalists to be imprisoned for engaging in the same conduct that these State privileges encourage and protect 'buck[s] that clear policy of virtually all states,' and undermines both the purpose of the shield laws, and the policy determinations of the State courts and legislatures that adopted them." And they emphasized that the states "have a vital interest in this issue independent of protecting the integrity of their shield laws. Uncertainty and confusion...have marked this area of the law in the three decades that have passed since...*Branzburg*....This increasing conflict has undercut the state shield laws just as much as the absence of a federal privilege."

CONCLUSION

I strongly believe in the need for confidential sources and that we must protect our sources when we grant them confidentiality. This is an obligation I take with the utmost seriousness. I also believe we must resist government coercion. But defying court orders, accepting imprisonment and fines, shouldn't be our only way of protecting sources or resisting coercion. Put simply, the issues at stake are crucial to our ability to report the news to the public. Without some federal protection for confidential sources, all of this is in jeopardy. The time has come for enactment of a shield law that will bring federal law into line with the laws of the states and ensure the free and open flow of information to the public on the issues of the day.

Shielding Journalists' Sources from Subpoena: Impeding Justice

JAMES B. COMEY

INTRODUCTION

This statement will focus on S. 340, the "Free Flow of Information Act of 2005." An identical bill has been introduced in the House of Representatives as H.R. 581. S. 340 would establish a federal shield law that would preclude the federal government from issuing compulsory process to obtain information about sources from members of the news media. It would shift from the Department of Justice to the courts the authority to evaluate requests for subpoenas to members of the media and make final decisions during criminal investigations and prosecutions as to whether subpoenas should be issued. It would create a bar against any subpoena issued to certain third parties that reasonably could be expected to lead to the discovery of the identity of a source. It would apply to all forms of federal compulsory process, including court orders and national security letters used in terrorism and espionage investigations, to selected categories of news and informational outlets. The bill would create serious impediments to the department's ability to effectively enforce the law and fight terrorism.

[The proposed legislation] would significantly impair the flexibility of the Executive branch in enforcing federal law, both by imposing inflexible, mandatory standards in lieu of existing voluntary ones and by applying its restrictions on the use of compulsory process more broadly than existing regulations. The bill is bad public policy primarily because it would bar the government from obtaining information about media sources—even in the most

urgent of circumstances affecting the public's health or safety or national security—and would place an unreasonable burden upon the government to justify to the court, in a public evidentiary proceeding, that it requires non-source information from the media in connection with sensitive grand jury investigations.

The Department of Justice recognizes that the media plays a critical role in our society. The freedom of the press is a hallowed American right, and in a time when news can be sent around the world almost instantaneously, it is as important as ever that the American people be kept informed of what is happening overseas, in Washington, and in their hometowns. For this reason, the department's disciplined approach to subpoenas directed towards members of the news media carefully balances the public's interest in the free dissemination of ideas and information with the public's interest in effective law enforcement and the fair administration of justice.

For the last 33 years, the Department of Justice has authorized subpoenas to the news media only in the most serious cases. The guidelines [that the Department of Justice follows] require the Attorney General personally to approve all contested subpoenas directed to journalists, following a rigorous multi-layered internal review process involving various components of the department. [The proposed legislation] would disrupt the department's ability to balance the competing interests involved in a decision to subpoena a member of the media and would strip the department of its ability to obtain crucial evidence in criminal investigations and prosecutions. It would also effectively overrule the Supreme Court's decision in *Branzburg v. Hayes* (1972), which held that reporters have no privilege, qualified or otherwise, to withhold information from a grand jury. *Branzburg* has been followed consistently by the federal courts of appeals, and was recently reaffirmed by the United States Court of Appeals for the District of Columbia in *In re Grand Jury Subpoena, Judith Miller* (2005). Indeed, the bill would give more protection to the reporter's "privilege"—which has not been recognized by the Supreme Court—than exists for other forms of privilege that are recognized, *e.g.*, the attorney-client privilege or the spousal privilege.

These results are completely unjustified and would pose a great threat to public safety. In the absence of a credible demonstration that the subpoena power is being abused by the department in this area, such that sources have dried up, with the result that journalists are unable to do effective investigative reporting, there is no need for a legislative fix that substantially skews the carefully maintained balance against legitimate law enforcement interests. The next part of this statement will address the specific provisions of the bill.

SECTION 2

Section 2 of the bill is intended to…prevent the department from issuing subpoenas to members of the news media unless a court determines by clear and convincing evidence: (i) that there are reasonable grounds to believe, based upon non-media evidence, that a crime has occurred; (ii) that the testimony or document sought is essential to the investigation or prosecution; and (iii) that the department has unsuccessfully attempted to obtain the evidence from non-media sources. While, to some degree, subsection 2(a) is similar to the guidelines

the department follows in its governing regulation, the bill departs dramatically from the regulation's requirements, first, by requiring the department to make its case before a court, after providing the news media an opportunity to be heard, and, second, by imposing a new "clear and convincing standard" to meet the section's requirements. In effect, this provision would require public mini-trials whenever the department seeks relevant information in a criminal grand jury investigation or to justify a trial subpoena.

The bill would seriously jeopardize traditional notions of grand jury secrecy and unnecessarily delay the completion of criminal investigations. To meet the bill's "clear and convincing" standard, the department frequently will have to present other evidence obtained before the grand jury. It is unclear how the department can present such justifying evidence consistent with its secrecy obligations under Rule 6(e) of the Federal Rules of Criminal Procedure. Further, the provision would require that in order to issue to the media a trial subpoena for non-source information, such as a reporter's eyewitness testimony or video outtakes, the department must showcase its evidence prematurely. These new burdens could significantly cripple effective law enforcement and thereby wreak havoc on the public's interest in the fair administration of justice. We note that media outlets often are happy to provide certain types of non-sensitive information to the federal government, but are more comfortable doing so in response to a subpoena. By making it quite difficult to issue almost any type of subpoena, the bill would make it more difficult for media outlets to cooperate with the federal government. Subsection 2(b) is directed toward…limiting compelled evidence from a member of the media to: (i) verifying published information; or (ii) describing surrounding circumstances relevant to the accuracy of published information. But the regulatory provision [the department follows] has been interpreted consistently to permit compulsion of additional types of evidence if it is apparent that there are no other sources to obtain the information and that the information is otherwise essential to the case. While subsection 2(b) includes language that the limitation is applicable "to the extent possible," it is manifestly unclear under what circumstances the court would allow other types of evidence to be subpoenaed. The provision certainly would substitute the judgment of the court for that of the prosecutor in determining what evidence was necessary in a criminal investigation or prosecution.

SECTION 4

Section 4 would ban compelling members of the news media to identify their sources of information. It would preclude the department from compelling a journalist to identify a confidential source of information from whom the journalist obtained information. More importantly, it also would prevent the compulsion of any information that reasonably could lead to the discovery of the identity of the source. These limitations are not in the department's governing regulation and represent a significant departure from the state of federal law.

The effect of this provision cannot be overstated. A provision that bars process that might obtain "any information that could reasonably be expected to lead to the discovery of the identity of...a source" might effectively end an investigation, particularly one that involved release of national security information. Moreover, even if the intent of the investigation were not to identify a source, the investigation might be barred because it may compel information that a court may find could reasonably lead to the discovery of a source's identity.

This provision would create a perverse incentive for persons committing serious crimes involving public safety and national security to employ the media in the process.

Historically, in applying its governing regulation to requests involving source information, the department has carefully balanced the public's interest in the free dissemination of ideas with the public's interest in effective law enforcement. The department's regulation has served to limit the number of subpoenas authorized for source information to little more than a handful over its 33-year history. The authorizations granted for source information have been linked closely to significant criminal matters that directly affect the public's safety and welfare. Section 4 of the bill would preclude the department from obtaining crucial evidence in vital cases, and would overrule settled Supreme Court precedent that protects the grand jury's ability to hear every person's evidence in pursuit of the truth.

The harm that this provision might cause is demonstrably greater than the purported benefit it may serve. It is essential to the public interest that the department maintain the ability, in certain vitally important circumstances, to obtain information identifying a source when a paramount interest is at stake. For example, obtaining source information may be the only available means of abating a terrorist threat or locating a kidnapped child. Certainly, in the face of a paramount public safety or health concern or a national security imperative, the balance should favor disclosure of source information in the possession of the news media. For example, on September 11, 2001, the U.S. Attorney's Office for the Northern District of California requested authorization to subpoena facsimiles that were sent to a San Francisco, California television station from individuals who had predicted eight weeks earlier that September 11th would be "Armageddon." Under the bill, the government would have been unable to obtain that information.

This provision would go far beyond any common law privilege. As the United States Court of Appeals for the District of Columbia Circuit recently held in *Miller*, there is no First Amendment privilege for journalists' confidential sources, and if a common law privilege exists, it is not absolute and must yield to the legitimate imperatives of law enforcement. Further, comparing the bill to existing state shield laws is inapt. None of the states deals with classified information in the way that the federal government does, and no state is tasked with defending the nation as a whole or conducting international diplomacy. The bill makes no recognition of these critical federal responsibilities, and would allow no exceptions for situations that endanger the national security or the public's health and safety.

Finally, section 4's definition of a confidential source is overly broad. Under subparagraph 4(1)(B), any individual whom the journalist subjectively claims to be a confidential source automatically would be afforded that status. This is the case although the source may have not sought confidential status with the journalist or even cared whether his or her identity was disclosed.

SECTION 5

Section 5 appears to be an attempt to codify the regulation governing requests to subpoena the telephone toll records of a member of the news media. It would add other business transaction records between a reporter and a third party, such as a telecommunications service provider, Internet service provider, or operator of an interactive computer service for a business purpose.

Taken together with section 4's prohibition against obtaining information that rea-

sonably could lead to the identification of a source, this section largely ends the ability of law enforcement authorities to conduct *any* investigation involving third parties. For example, a ransom demand made to a kidnap victim's family home telephone could be investigated by compulsory process; a ransom demand made by an anonymous person to a media outlet could not be investigated by such compulsory process. This provision is inconsistent with common law and goes far beyond any statute in any State.

Like section 2, section 5 would require a public mini-trial every time the department sought telephone or other communications service provider records in a grand jury investigation or criminal trial. For the reasons articulated above, section 5 is also bad public policy. While section 5 would establish an exception to the notice requirement if the court determines by clear and convincing evidence that notice "would pose a substantial threat to the integrity of a criminal investigation," there are no built-in mechanisms to protect from public disclosure the very information that the department would be seeking to protect by resisting notice.

SECTION 6

Even if the information sought has already been published or disseminated, section 6 of the bill would continue the ban on compelling source material and would continue to require court approval for other media evidence. The purpose of this provision is unclear. Moreover, reporters could use the provision to provide selective testimony; they could choose what facts to disclose in testimony, while every court would be barred from ordering the reporter to provide any information that the reporter chose not to share. It is possible that the provision is intended to protect a reporter from disclosing source information that already has been publicly disclosed (inadvertently or otherwise) by someone else. Other well-established privileges are waived under certain circumstances when the information sought to be protected has been disclosed. We believe that the issue of waiver should be determined on a case-by-case basis.

SECTION 7

The definition of a "covered person" contained in the bill raises several distinct concerns. Most significantly, it would extend the bill's protections well beyond its presumably intended objective, that is, providing special statutory protections for the kind of news- and information-gathering activities that are essential to freedom of the press under the First Amendment. For example, "covered persons" protected by the bill include non-media corporate affiliates, subsidiaries, or parents of any cable system or programming service, whether or not located in the United States. It would also include any supermarket, department store, or other business that periodically publishes a products catalog, sales pamphlet, or even a listing of registered customers.

Far more dangerously, it would cover criminal or terrorist organizations that also have media operations, including many foreign terrorist organizations, such as al Qaida (which, from its founding, maintained a media office that published a newsletter). Indeed, the inherent difficulty of appropriately defining a "covered person" in a world in which the very definition of "media" is constantly evolving, suggests yet another fundamental weakness in the bill. What could be shielded here is not so much the traditional media—which already is protected adequately by existing Justice Department guidelines—as criminal activity deliberately or fortuitously using means or facilities in the course of the offenses that would cause the perpetrators to fall within the definition of the media under the bill.

In addition, the provisions of the bill reach well beyond the department of Justice. The bill applies broadly to any "federal entity," defined under the bill to include "an entity or employee of the judicial, legislative, or executive branch of the federal government with the power to issue a subpoena or provide other compulsory process." The bill also would reach beyond the guidelines in imposing its restrictions upon any requirement for a covered person to testify or produce documents "in any proceeding or *in connection with any issue arising under federal law.*" Section 2(a). For example, although section 3 of the bill attempts to exclude from coverage "requests for…commercial or financial information unrelated to news gathering or news and information dissemination," the meaning of this section is unclear and may not be sufficient to prevent the bill from empowering news companies to block legitimate antitrust investigations into their potentially anticompetitive mergers and business practices.

CONCLUSION

Recent events no doubt have raised the public's awareness of the issue of compelling evidence from journalists. There are legitimate competing interests involved in the ongoing dialogue on this issue. However, history has shown that the protections already in place, including the department's rigorous internal review of media subpoena requests coupled with the media's ability to challenge compulsory process in the federal courts, are sufficient and strike the proper balance between the public's interest in the free dissemination of ideas and information and the public's interest in effective law enforcement and the fair administration of justice.

THE CONTINUING DEBATE:
Shielding Journalists' Sources from Subpoena

What Is New

After 85 days imprisonment, Judith Miller was released in October 2005 after testifying before the grand jury and identifying her source as I. Lewis "Scooter" Libby, chief of staff for Vice President Dick Cheney. Miller indicated that Libby had given her permission to reveal his identify. Later that month, a grand jury indicted Libby for perjury and other crimes related to the investigation. The Free Flow of Information Act of 2005 remains in committee in both the House and Senate. Some sources speculate that the bill will pass both houses, but the urgent need to address the devastation by Hurricanes Katrina and Rita (see Debate 20), the tumult accompanying the indictment by House Majority Leader Tom Delay (R-TX) for election law violations, and other matters could sidetrack the legislation.

It is unclear how Americans feel about shielding journalists' sources in criminal investigation. A May 2005 poll found that 55% of those asked approved "of the use of anonymous sources in news stories," compared to 43% who disapproved and 4% who were unsure. But that did not address the nuanced issues of shielding a source during a criminal investigation. It is probable that public support of the press would be much lower. One reason is that Americans are skeptical of press motives, with another 2005 poll showing that 75% of Americans think the press is primarily motivated by attracting bigger audiences, with only 19% thinking that journalists mostly act to keep the public informed, and 6% unsure.

Where to Find More

A journalists' group at the center of the fight for shield law is the Reporters Committee for Freedom of the Press at www.rcfp.org. For printed commentary from the media's point of view of the impact of the Plame affair on reporter-source relations and on news gathering, read Rachel Smolkin, "Uncharted Terrain," *American Journalism Review* (October 2005). The opposite stand is taken by Dan Ackman, "Expose the Press Players," *Forbes* (February 2005). To explore Americans' attitudes about the news media and issues surrounding freedom of the press, read David A. Yalof and Kenneth Dautrich, *The First Amendment and the Media in the Court of Public Opinion* (Cambridge University Press, 2002).

What More to Do

Debate shield laws in the abstract, but also get into the details of specific legislation. Go to Thomas (http://thomas.loc.gov/), the basic Web site for Congress, and enter "Free Flow of Information Act" in the search window labeled "Search Bill Text 109th Congress (2005–2006)." Pick one of the related House or Senate bills, such as S. 1419 or H.R. 3323, then click "Text of Legislation" to access the bill. Debate it in class provision by provision. If you support the basic thrust of the legislation, try to build a majority coalition of your class members. Anyone can offer amendments to your bill.

8 INTEREST GROUPS

ETHNIC FOREIGN POLICY LOBBYING:
Misplaced Allegiance *or* All-American Tradition?

MISPLACED ALLEGIANCE

ADVOCATE: Geoffrey Wheatcroft, a British journalist
SOURCE: "Hyphenated Americans," *Guardian Unlimited* online, April 25, 2000

ALL-AMERICAN TRADITION

ADVOCATE: Yossi Shain, Aaron and Cecile Goldman Visiting Professor, Georgetown University; Professor of Political Science, Tel Aviv University
SOURCE: "For Ethnic Americans, The Old Country Calls," *Foreign Service Journal*, October 2000

E *pluribus unum* (out of many, one) reads the banner the eagle holds in its beak on the Great Seal of the United States. These words on the seal, which was adopted by the Congress in 1782, refer to the union of 13 former colonies into one United States. Whatever its initial meaning, *e pluribus unum* has come to symbolize what is sometimes called the "American melting pot." This is the idea that one nation, the American people, have been created by the assimilation of people of diverse national origins. More accurately, it might be said that the blending of foreign immigrants in the melting pot into one puree in which the original makings cannot be distinguished, has never been realized. Instead, Americans are something of a demographic stew, one in which carrots, potatoes, celery, and other ingredients often maintain their identity.

Scholars disagree about why this imperfect amalgamation has occurred. Whatever the cause, though, many Americans tend to think of themselves as not just Americans, but as Irish Americans, Italian Americans, Mexican Americans, African Americans, Jewish Americans, and many other kinds of Americans. The hyphen to denote these groups (as in Irish-American) has gone out of style, but its earlier use has left the term "hyphenated American" to designate the lingering identification of many Americans with the heritage of their immigrant ancestors. Identification with a specific country is the most common link, but there are others. Religion is one, with, for example, many Jewish Americans having a strong sense of community with Israel. Other groups have regional cultural connection. For example, because the history of slavery wiped out the ability of most blacks to trace their heritage to a specific location, what sense of identification that group does have is linked more to sub-Saharan Africa than a single country. Similarly, many Arab Americans identify with that broader cultural identity instead of, or along with, a specific country.

For many the foreign connection is quite recent. Some 12% of all U.S. residents were born elsewhere, and many others are second and third generation Americans. When the U.S. Census Bureau asked people to identify their cultural heritage, 80% did so. The most frequent answers were German (15%), Irish (11%), English (9%), Italian

(6%), Mexican (7%), Chinese (4%), Polish (3%) and French (3%). Another 7% of U.S. residents chose "American" as their ethnic heritage.

Throughout American history, hyphenated American groups have often acted as interest groups dedicated to influencing U.S. foreign policy to be favorable to their homeland and ancestral culture. For one, Jewish Americans who support Israel are represented by such organizations as the American-Israel Public Affairs Committee (AIPAC, http://www.aipac.org/), which declares itself, "America's Pro-Israel Lobby." Among the groups trying in part to counterbalance the efforts of AIPAC is the Arab American Institute (http://www.aaiusa.org/), which lists among its missions, "represent[ing] Arab American interests in government and politics" on such issues as "U.S. Middle East policy." To this list of ethnic lobbies could be added the Cuban American National Foundation, American Latvian Association, the TransAfrica Forum, the Armenian National Committee of America, the American Hellenic Institute (Greek Americans), the Irish National Caucus, the Polish American Congress, and myriad others.

The issue that the activity of these groups raises is the propriety of ethnic foreign policy lobbying. There can be little doubt that the language of the First Amendment guaranteeing the right "to petition the government for a redress of grievances," gives ethnic interests groups, as all interest groups, the right to lobby the U.S. government. Equally certain is that lobbying by groups of every ideological and policy persuasion is a key, and perhaps a necessary, element of the American democratic tradition and process. Some people, however, believe that lobbying for a policy to benefit a foreign government falls outside the boundaries of what is, or should be, acceptable. They charge that such pressures distort U.S. foreign policy in ways that can actually contravene U.S. national interests.

Such concerns are not new. For example former President Theodore Roosevelt was outraged at the opposition of German American groups, Irish American groups, and others to U.S. entry into World War I against Germany and as a British ally. In a 1915 speech, Roosevelt declared, "There is no room in this country for hyphenated Americanism." He asserted that "Our allegiance must be purely to the United States" and he condemned the "tangle of squabbling nationalities,…each at heart feeling more sympathy with Europeans of that nationality, than with the other citizens of the American Republic." Roosevelt even termed it "treason" for "an American citizen to vote as a German-American, an Irish-American, or an English-American."

POINTS TO PONDER

➤ Advocate Yossi Shain writes of a "flexible world of multiple loyalties." Think about this idea. Is it possible to simultaneously be a loyal American and loyal to another country? What if those two countries disagree?

➤ To argue that ethnic lobby groups sometimes advocate policies counter to the national interest necessarily assumes that there is an objective national interest. Is that so, or is the national interest subjective—that is, whatever the American policy process eventually decides it is?

➤ There are foreign policy lobby groups based on economic interests, ideological views, gender, and many other bases, as well as ethnicity. Are your views on the legitimacy of foreign policy lobbying the same for all these groups? If you differentiate, why?

97

Ethnic Foreign Policy Lobbying: Misplaced Allegiance

GEOFFREY WHEATCROFT

Although the old saying that hard cases make bad law might seem to apply to the case of Elian Gonzalez, it wasn't really so hard. The law held that he should be reunited with his father, that is what most Americans thought should be done and that is what has now happened. But the case leaves ugly scars, and it raises once again the question of what should be the rights—and responsibilities—of "hyphenated Americans." The boy would have joined his father in Cuba weeks ago if he hadn't become an emblem, or a pawn, for one of the most noisiest and most feared of such groups, the Cuban Americans.

The United States is a land of immigrants, with complicated feelings towards their ancestral lands. It is also a free country where interest-group politics have always flourished, which does not mean that the effects of these groups or lobbies have been benign. To the contrary, the pressure exerted by the "hyphenates" has been almost unfailingly malign, for the American republic and for American people as a whole.

It is made worse by the cravenness of American politicians. In *Of Thee I Sing*, the Gershwin brothers' very funny 1931 musical satire on American politics, the campaign song goes, "He's the man the people choose,/Loves the Irish, loves the Jews." Real-life American polls have all too often taken this jest as a true word.

The US's emergence as a great power dates from the first world war, which the country entered belatedly, and despite the wishes of many Americans. Tens of millions of German Americans obviously didn't want to fight against their fathers' fatherland. Millions of Irish Americans were scarcely keener to fight for the king of England, or millions of Jewish Americans for the tsar of all the Russians whose oppression most of them had fled. And indeed the US did not enter the war until after the 1917 February revolution and the fall of tsardom.

Then the fun began. Irish-American pressure led towards the creation of an Irish Free State. Whatever else may be said of this, it was by no means in the American national interest. During the second world war, the most important war the Americans ever fought, once they, again belatedly, entered it, that Irish state was sullenly neutral.

There has recently been much bitter criticism in America of Swiss neutrality during the war. Apart from the fact that Switzerland was surrounded by the Axis and had no choice between neutrality and annihilation, Swiss neutrality did no military harm to the Allied cause. By contrast, Irish neutrality delayed victory in the battle of the Atlantic and thus the defeat of Hitler, with all that implies.

After the Irish came the Czech Americans' turn. Largely thanks to them President Woodrow Wilson's 14 points included the 10th point: "The peoples of Austria-Hungary...should be accorded the freest opportunity of autonomous development." From this light-hearted undertaking came the destruction of the Habsburg monarchy.

The rights and wrongs of that aren't simple, but it is worth noting that the allegedly national "successor state" of Czechoslovakia thereby called into being no longer exists. Nor does Yugoslavia, the other state invented after the great war.

No other hyphenated group has been as politically powerful as the Jewish-American lobby. Although Washington politicians may tremble at the phrase "the 40m[illion] Irish Americans," they tremble more before the numerically fewer Jewish Americans. The American-Israeli Public Affairs Committee has won a reputation as the most formidable, and often the most ruthless, of all such pressure groups. Having spent some little time looking into this subject, I would merely say that the activities of that lobby will one day come to be seen as not having served the true interests of the United States, of Jewish America, or even, in the end, of Israel.

The behavior of Cuban America over Elian speaks for itself, and the lobby has anyway prevented a necessary rapprochement between the US and Cuba. What has been more shocking than the hysteria of Little Havana in Miami has been the fawning on the Cuban Americans by politicians, including both presidential candidates?

Yet even that is trivial compared with what may prove to be the true "legacy" (in the president's favorite word) of the Clinton administration. The eastward expansion of NATO [North Atlantic Treaty Organization by adding many new countries in Eastern Europe to the alliance] must rank, in a hotly contested field, as the craziest single piece of American statecraft since the invasion of Cambodia 30 years ago this week. After the end of the cold war, it has no good strategic or political justification but can only justifiably inflame Russian suspicions and means, strictly speaking, that we must go to war on behalf of Hungary in a border dispute with Slovakia.

Why has it happened? It was inspired partly by the president's desire to enrich what his wiser predecessor Eisenhower called the military-industrial complex, but more importantly by his ingratiating himself with ethnic lobbies. Historians will date NATO expansion [to include many

new countries in Eastern Europe in the alliance] to Clinton's groveling to a Polish-American audience in Chicago.

Even if the politics of hyphenated-America didn't produce such sorry practical consequences, it would be an affront to the "American idea." In direct contrast to European nationalism, the concept of "the American nation" is not based on ethnicity. Unlike European nation states, the American republic is founded not on a people, but on a proposition. This ideal has often been neglected, to put it mildly, and it may not say much to many black Americans, but it is noble in inspiration. If only American politicians remembered that more often.

In between sucking up to Cuban Americans and claiming to have invented the Internet, Vice-President Gore not long ago produced an exquisite howler. The country's motto is *E pluribus unum*, which means, he told his audience, "out of one, many." It was a true Freudian slip. He made a mistake, but in his ludicrous way he expressed a truth, about the fragmentation of America into all too many fractious and competitive components.

What the 18th-century creators of the American republic believed in was "out of many, one." One people would emerge from many different origins, sharing common creeds (that all men are created equal, entitled to life, liberty and the pursuit of happiness), rather than common gene pools. What the 20th century has seen is a regression to the primitive atavistic group loyalties which the new country was meant to avoid.

More than a hundred years ago, a federal judge told an Irish-American agitator that any American was entitled to sentimental sympathies for another country, but that every American's first political duty must be to the United States.

Ethnic Foreign Policy Lobbying:
All-American Tradition

Yossi Shain

American ethnics don't just lobby for their ancestral homelands—they also export American values.

Last March, when Marie Jana Korbelova returned to her birth city, Prague, this time as Madeleine Albright, U.S. secretary of State, Czech President Vaclav Havel declared, "I would personally consider it excellent [if Madeleine Albright could succeed me as President of the Czech Republic] because into this rather staid provincial environment this would bring an international spirit, someone who knows the world well, understands it, and would be able to act." In the Czech Republic, the president must be a Czech citizen over 40 years of age. Albright, a naturalized U.S. citizen, qualifies for Czech citizenship under the law that enables those who fled the communist regime after 1948 to reclaim citizenship. Albright smiled and said "I am not a candidate and will not be a candidate....My heart is in two places, and America is where I belong."

Havel's vision, that transnational allegiance to both an ancestral homeland and to the U.S. can exist without conflict, is quite remarkable. It represents not only his own liberal-humanistic vision of world affairs—where boundaries of state and culture are no longer so rigid—but also the perception that Americans are the best conveyors of this mentality. As members of an open liberal society where multiple ethnic identities are no longer suspect and where, in fact, ancestral identities are welcomed as the cornerstone of multiculturalism, Americans in the post-Cold War world are often perceived as the best rep-

resentatives of a more flexible concept of citizenship and loyalty.

Havel's extraordinary invitation is just one sign of a changing configuration of national and ethnic loyalties. For the United States, a nation of immigrants, the meaning of ethnic identity is being transformed. Old nativist fears—that Americans with emotional ties to their ancestral homelands cannot be fully loyal to the United States—are rapidly disappearing. Those people once disparagingly called "hyphenated Americans" feel increasingly free to organize and lobby on behalf of the "old country." Even within America's foreign policy establishment, one finds increasing acceptance of the legitimacy of ethnic lobbies and full participation by ethnically identifiable players such as Jews and Cuban-Americans.

But what is arguably the most interesting new development is that the flow of political influence is becoming more of a two-way street. American diasporas—of Arabs, Jews, Armenians, Chinese—are playing significant roles in their ancestral homelands. They bring American ideologies and influence into the politics of the mother country. At times—taking up the challenge that Secretary Albright declined—U.S. citizens have even returned to their countries of origin to play leading political roles.

DIVERSITY AND DIASPORAS

The signs of this more flexible world of multiple loyalties are easy to find. For example, The *Washington Post* reported this year a sharp increase in the number of young Americans who are spending summers in their parents' homeland. These parents apparently no longer fear that their children will be stigmatized; in fact, many now consider their children's bilingual abilities and familiarity with ancestral culture an asset in a globalized world order. Indeed, as America recognizes the value of diversity, homeland countries that previously restricted their kin abroad to single citizenship now permit them dual nationality. These countries have also enabled their kin diasporas to retain broad economic and political rights in their kin states, including absentee voting, even though the individuals have clearly established themselves as loyal citizens in the U.S.

The December 1996 passage of Mexican legislation permitting dual nationality is but one example. That law affects the lives of millions of Mexican-Americans—the fastest-growing voting bloc in American politics. With Mexican politicians now routinely courting support of the Mexican community in the United States, Mexico has laid to rest the image of the "pocho"—a derogatory term that questions the loyalty of diasporic Mexicans seen as having abandoned their roots in order to assimilate into American society.

There are many reasons that Mexico and other countries have reversed course and now encourage rather than prohibit dual nationality. Most importantly, they see numerous advantages in cultivating the continued loyalty of their kin diasporas. For countries such as Colombia, Nicaragua, the Dominican Republic and El Salvador, remittances and investments from kin communities in the United States play an important economic role. Diaspora money also now influences national politics and political campaigns in many countries, so politicians may want to win the approval of their financial backers abroad. More generally, they want to keep their diaspora's loyalty intact, and thus they use citizenship as an incentive for ethnic or national pride.

Many states [countries] also want to use the lobbying power of their kin, especially in the United States. Armenia, for example—which is involved in a bitter territorial struggle with a neighboring state—works hard to maintain the intensity of diasporic involvement in the motherland's cause.

During the past decade, Eastern European countries have evoked kinship ties even more dramatically by inviting expatriates in the U.S. to take leading roles in their countries of origin. Consider Milan Panic, a California pharmaceutical industrialist who became the prime minister of Yugoslavia in 1992; Alexander Eiseln, an American Army colonel who became the defense minister of Estonia in 1993; and Valdas Adamkus, a Lithuanian-American who moved to Lithuania in 1997 and was elected Lithuania's president in 1998. In the words of one Lithuanian voter, "He lived in America for a long time....He knows how the system works there. I think he will bring democracy from America to us." Also, in Armenia, former foreign minister Raffi Hovannisian and energy minister Sebuth Tashjian are both from California. These are of course rather rare cases of ethnically identified Americans taking posts in their countries of origin at a time when American political and business expertise is sought in nascent states or in new democracies emerging from the shadow of communism. Because of their American experience, these individuals with dual attachments are in a special position to help their ancestral homelands.

Leaders in other countries, realizing that ethnic Americans can be a powerful lobbying force, have at times encouraged their kin to become involved in U.S. foreign policy. However, they fail to recognize that in the process of empowerment, these ethnic Americans may become even more American, and in turn bring back unexpected messages and ideas, such as democratic reforms, much to the chagrin of the kin state. Take, for example, Arab-American relations with Saudi Arabia.

In April 1999, Jeddah's conservative newspaper Al-Madina ran an editorial entitled "A Clinton Victory and Arab Americans." Noting that the peace accord in Ulster showed the great political clout of Irish-Americans, the editorial stated, "The Arab minority in the United States must move toward influential centers in a society where domestic politics [is so crucial]." However, when Arab-American lobbyists like Jim Zogby and Khalil Jashan were welcomed by the Clinton administration as harbingers of peace in the Middle East and subsequently began to contemplate advocating greater openness in the Arab world, they were immediately rebuffed by Arab states, including Saudi Arabia.

FEAR OF HYPHENATED AMERICANS

The question of expatriate loyalty has evolved over the years. In the 19th and early 20th centuries, the idea of hyphenated Americans was used by nativists to question the allegiance of immigrants, despite the newcomers' claims that their ancestral identities were not incompatible with their loyalty to America. Even cultural assimilation in America did not shield many immigrants from feeling threatened because of a perceived affinity to their homelands. This was especially the experience of diasporas whose homelands were enemy states at war with the U.S. American fear of transnational allegiance was also behind the exclusionary laws of the late 1910s and the early 1920s. During World War I, the issue of dual loyalties became particularly prominent with the growing suspicion of pan-German organizations, which prompted America's demand for total assimilation and unqualified renunciation of German-American past loyalties. President Woodrow Wilson feared that American involvement against Germany might unleash "serious domestic clashes inside the U.S."

The most vivid example of misguided fear manifested itself during World War II after the attack on Pearl Harbor. The belief that Japanese-Americans might still be loyal to the ancestral homeland resulted in the relocation and internment of 120,000 Japanese-Americans. As recently as 1991, this animosity surfaced again (albeit in a much milder form), as Arab-Americans became vulnerable to attack during the Gulf War with Iraq.

During the Cold War years, ethnic Americans who sought a voice in foreign policy matters regarding a country of origin could gain access to decision-makers mostly when their views coincided with America's hostility to communism. Richard Allen, Ronald Reagan's first national security adviser, encouraged Cuban-Americans to build up an ethnic lobby that would serve as a tool furthering the administration's effort to delegitimize the Castro regime. Over time, Jorge Mas Canosa and the Cuban-American National Foundation became a major power broker in American foreign policy.

With the changing nature of America's ethnic mix—i.e., with the proliferation of non-European immigrants arriving mostly from Latin America and Asia, and with the growing advancement of minority groups, especially African-Americans—ethnic Americans began to consider a voice in foreign policy an additional form of empowerment. In America today, there are many new ethnic voices making themselves heard. Even groups which are satisfied with their accomplishments in the American economic arena no longer shy away from foreign policy. Thus, in contrast to their historical timidity in American public affairs, the 1.4 million Indian-Americans have found a political voice and are raising the stature of India in Washington.

ETHNIC LOBBIES' GROWING POWER

At a time when global foreign relations are no longer defined in strictly East-West terms [the cold war rivalry between the U.S.-led bloc and the Soviet-led bloc] and [when] U.S. foreign policy is characterized by a diminished cohesiveness, ethnic lobbies are becoming more important in influencing foreign policy makers. The fact that American society and politics permit, or even welcome, expressions of ethnic solidarity and no longer discourage preoccupation with motherlands lends itself to special diasporic influences on the U.S. foreign policy agenda. This reality has raised concerns about the ability of the U.S. to develop foreign policy in the "American national interest." Will its foreign policy be tainted and confused by partisan and divisive ethnic voices? On this point, Samuel Huntington says that by accepting the validity of multiculturalism and by heeding ethnic voices, American decision-makers are at risk of compromising American national interests.

Such concerns are usually exaggerated. In my book, *Marketing the American Creed Abroad: Diasporas in the U.S. and Their Homeland*, I document that ethnic Americans who engage in U.S. foreign policy are frequently carriers of American foreign policy messages and values, rather than being agents or fifth columns for their countries of origin.

For example, Iranian radicalism is said to be waning as reformist politicians win elections in Teheran. Even Iranian-Americans now see the possibility of building an ethnic lobby without compromising their American loyalties or without being suspected of treason by their kin in Iran. Especially when a homeland is at odds with America, first-generation exiles may feel compelled to remain silent, lest they be accused of being traitors at home or spies abroad. Over time, however, their offspring become sufficiently comfortable to organize as ethnic Americans, and eventually to act as a liaison between the U.S. and their homeland. In the case of the million-strong and economically thriving Iranian-American community, Negar Akhvi has recently noted that after the revolution of 1979, first-generation immigrants were too timid either to speak against Ayatollah Khomeini or to organize as diasporic Americans. Describing the younger generation of Iranian-Americans in Los Angeles, Akhvi maintains, "the fatigue and the stress that enveloped the generation that fled Iran has not been passed on to my own. My generation is less scared by the Revolution and at greater ease in democratic forums. In short, we are American enough to form a lobby, yet Iranian enough to care about what happens in our homeland."

Other American ethnic communities, both newcomers and those of long standing, have discovered they can unify and mobilize their particular community by pursuing goals related to the homeland as well as domestic issues in the U.S. That was certainly true of African-Americans as they effectively protested apartheid in South Africa in the mid-1980s. When in 1988 a number of American black leaders announced their preference for the appellation "African-American" over "black," the Rev. Jesse Jackson declared, "Every ethnic group in this country has a reference to some land base, some historical cultural base. African-Americans have hit that level of maturity." Indeed, in recent years African-American activists inside and outside Congress have gained high visibility and importance in the foreign policy arena. When in 1994 President Clinton was hesitant about restoring deposed President Jean-Bertrand Aristide in Haiti, it was the Congressional Black Caucus and the hunger strike of Randall Robinson, director of the

African-American lobby TransAfrica, which forced him to act.

The recent case of Elian Gonzalez [a Cuban boy who survived the sinking of the boat in which his mother and others fleeing to the United States died. The father, still in Cuba, and the Cuban government demanded the boy's return. The Cuban-American community strongly opposed his return, but he was eventually taken by U.S. Marshals and sent back to Cuba] is a fascinating example of how diaspora community leaders try to safeguard the exile mentality against the atrophy that would be quite natural for a community of immigrants after 40 years in the United States. It appeared that the Cuban-American community found itself at a critical juncture: Was its identity that of exiles and refugees nurturing their old rhetoric and the hope of return—or were they to become ethnic Americans plain and simple? For Cuban-Americans, the Gonzalez case served as the impetus for reassessing the question of their loyalty, and the community found itself in a precarious dilemma. The difficulty is that if Cuban-Americans are perceived as acting outside the laws of America regarding child custody, or in opposition to congressional tendencies to relax the economic sanctions against Cuba, they endanger the sympathy they enjoy as adherents of American interests and values and opponents of the Castro regime. That struggle over the loyalty and identity of Cuban-Americans is certain to continue.

In today's America it becomes more and more difficult to distinguish between domestic and foreign politics. America's divided government, which empowers single members of Congress and even local municipal leaders in foreign policy, enhances the stature and the clout of well-organized ethnic lobbies. These lobbies also benefit from the declining power of traditional foreign policy elites—the old "Eastern establishment." For example, the highly mobilized and well-funded Armenian-American community has gained its reputation over the past decade as the most important element in shaping U.S. foreign policy posture toward the newly independent states in the Caucasus and especially toward the conflict in Nagorno-Karabakh, a territory claimed by both Armenia and Azerbaijan. While Congress continues to support the lobby's position and prohibits direct U.S. assistance to Azerbaijan under Section 907, the Clinton administration strongly opposes Section 907 and has testified in favor of repeal of these sanctions. In his inaugural address in 1998, Armenian President Robert Kocherian emphasized the importance of "the unification of efforts of all Armenians, and ensuring the Armenian diaspora's active participation in the social, political and economic life of our republic. …Armenia should be a holy motherland for all Armenians, and its victory should be their victory."

JEWISH AMERICANS AND MIDDLE EAST POLICY

When U.S. foreign policy was determined by traditional professional elites, there was a tendency to perceive Jewish-American affinity with Israel as a liability, especially since the Foreign Service held that America's close ties to Israel could jeopardize its interest in the Arab world or the oil-rich countries. In the 1950s, U.S. foreign policy-makers under Eisenhower viewed Israel as, at best, a benign presence in the Middle East and, more commonly, as an irritant in America's strategic planning in the region. At the height of the Cold War, Jewish Americans were leery about breaking with the American official line. For instance, during the Suez Crisis of 1956, the Jewish-American lobby emphasized its allegiance to American interests and was reluctant to push Israel's case for fear of being labeled disloyal....

The emphasis on American allegiance by Jewish Americans could also be seen in Secretary of State Henry Kissinger's handling of the Middle East conflict. During the Nixon and Ford administrations, Kissinger downplayed his Jewish origin in his work on this policy area. Kissinger was attacked vehemently by the American-Israel Political Action Committee when he attempted to push Israel into a deal with the Arabs. In light of Israel's reluctance to accept an American dictate, AIPAC mobilized the Congress against President Ford's decision to reassess U.S. policy in the Middle East and U.S. relations with Israel. When 76 senators wrote to the president urging him to declare that "the U.S. acting in its own national interest stands firmly with Israel," Kissinger responded angrily. He berated Israeli Ambassador Simcha Dinitz and told him that the letter "will increase anti-Semitism, it will cause people to charge that Jews control Congress." As a result, Kissinger was accused of betrayal and hounded by demonstrators in Israel. His insistent loyalty to the United States thus resulted in his being pulled from both sides of the ethnic bridge.

The allegation that Jews cannot always be both good Americans and good Jews surfaced on various occasions when there was a contest between the White House and the Israel lobby. Today, however, as foreign policy-making in Washington is becoming more dispersed and influenced by, among other things, think tanks, public opinion and the media, ethnic lobbyists are no longer perceived as an inherent threat to the national interest, and the dreaded charge of "divided loyalties" is less and less persuasive. In fact, the end of the Cold War and deep splits within Israel regarding the direction of the Palestinian peace process and the character of the Jewish state have tended to divide the

U.S. Jewish community. Thus, when President Clinton wanted to demonstrate his frustration with former Israeli Prime Minister Benjamin Netanyahu, he could call upon certain Jewish-American community leaders to mobilize their constituencies to reprimand the Israeli government for its behavior.

At times, individuals associated with ethnic lobbies have even established themselves as leading experts in their respective kin states and, as such, are mobilized by the American government as more effective messengers in the United States or in their ancestral homelands. When persons of Jewish origins, such as Aaron Miller, Dennis Ross, or Martin Indyk (who was a member of the pro-Israel lobby before he established the Washington Institute for Near East Policy) are situated at the forefront of American foreign policy in the Middle East, the idea that committed Jews cannot be trusted as brokers in the Arab-Israeli peace process is no longer viable. Even Arab leaders and Arab-Americans have grudgingly accepted this as a fact of life, despite ongoing Arab-Israeli conflicts. Take, for example, Daniel Kurzer, America's current ambassador to Egypt, who is a deeply committed and publicly identified Jew. The prominence of these individuals in Middle East policy-making is a clear indication that in America at least, Jewish identity does not provoke serious suspicions of divided loyalties.

Finally, we should not forget that America's generally benign attitude toward questions of ethnic loyalty does have its limits. After Jonathan Pollard, an Israeli-American, was convicted of spying for Israel, it was not surprising that the Jewish-American community was much less merciful toward Pollard than was the Israeli government, which has been trying for years to secure his release from prison. More recently, Wen Ho Lee, the physicist formerly at Los Alamos National Laboratory who is alleged to have passed nuclear secrets to China, has reportedly caused a cloud of suspicion to be cast over other Chinese-American scientists. Despite these rare cases, the overall trend in the United States has clearly moved in recent decades in a more positive direction. There is an ever greater acceptance of the legitimacy of ethnic Americans in national policy-making, as well as a growing appreciation that in the present period of globalization, America's ethnic groups can strengthen and expand U.S. influence around the world.

THE CONTINUING DEBATE:
Ethnic Foreign Policy Lobbying

What Is New

Ethnic lobbying continues to exert influence on foreign policy. For example, recent studies have shown that foreign aid is connected to ethnic lobbies, not only in the United States, but also in other aid-giving countries. Other recent research has shown that ethnic lobbying groups influence U.S. economic sanctions policy.

In 1915, Theodore Roosevelt condemned lobbying by various European American groups. The changing demographic characteristics of Americans and the rising political activity and strength of non-European heritage groups has diversified ethnic lobbying. The TransAfrica Forum, for one, is a relatively new organization, which, its mission statement says, "focuses on U.S. policy as it affects Africa and the Diaspora in the Caribbean and Latin America" on behalf of "African-American community." Cuban Americans have for decades influenced U.S. foreign policy, and now they are being joined by such other Latino groups, such as the National Council of La Raza, which includes among its missions presenting "an Hispanic perspective on trade, assistance, and other international issues."

Where to Find More

A good place to begin would be Thomas Ambrosio's edited study, *Ethnic Identify Groups and U.S. Foreign Policy* (Praeger, 2002). Additionally, a recent book that frets about ethnic lobbying while also supporting its validity is Tony Smith, *Foreign Attachments: The Power of Ethnic Groups in the Making of American Foreign Policy* (Harvard University Press, 2000). A study that worries that strong multiculturalism, including on foreign policy, is endangering American national unity is Arthur M. Schlesinger Jr., *The Disuniting of America: Reflections on a Multicultural Society* (W. W. Norton, 1998). For an optimistic view of competing identities, read Peter J. Sprio, *Embracing Dual Nationality* (Carnegie Endowment for International Peace, 1998). Also positive toward ethnic lobbying is James M. Lindsay, "Getting Uncle Sam's Ear: Will Ethnic Lobbies Cramp America's Foreign Policy Style?," *Brookings Review*, Winter 2002. It is available on the Web at: http://www.brook.edu/. Also worthwhile and available on the Web is a summary of a conference on ethnic foreign policy lobbying. See David J. Vidal, "Defining the National Interest Minorities and U.S. Foreign Policy in the 21st Century: Project for Diversity in International Affairs" at: http://www.ciaonet.org/conf/vid01/.

What More to Do

The view of many people may be that ethnic foreign policy lobbying is neither always good nor always bad. Given that, one thing to do in class is to work with others to come up with a "do's and don'ts" list of such activities.

You will also find it enlightening to analyze the 2004 U.S. presidential race for evidence of influence by various foreign policy lobby groups on that contest. The Middle East, U.S.-Cuba relations, immigration, and numerous other foreign policy or mixed *inter*national/dom*estic* (intermestic) issues of interest to one or another ethnic groups played a role in the close outcome that kept George Bush in the White House and John Kerry in the Senate.

POLITICAL PARTIES

...ARY CLINTON AND THE 2008 PRESIDENTIAL ELECTION:
The Democrats' Best Bet *or* a Problematic Candidate?

THE DEMOCRATS' BEST BET

ADVOCATE: Carl Cannon, White House correspondent for the *National Journal*

SOURCE: "She Can Win the White House," *Washington Monthly*, July/August 2005

A PROBLEMATIC CANDIDATE

ADVOCATE: Amy Sullivan, editor, *Washington Monthly*

SOURCE: "Not So Fast," *Washington Monthly*, July/August 2005

Kermit the Frog has often sung a plaintiff tune that begins, "It's not easy being green." Members of the currently out-of-power political party in the United States can identity with Kermit's struggle because for them, "It's not easy being a Democrat." Once that was easier. Indeed the Democrats had a great run beginning with Franklin D. Roosevelt's entry into the White House in 1933. From then until 1969, a Democrat sat in the Oval Office for all but eight years (1953–1961, Dwight D. Eisenhower). Making life even happier for the Democrats, they also controlled both houses of Congress except for four years (1947–1949 and 1953–1955).

Then the political fortune of the Democrats began to decline. Republican Richard M. Nixon became president in 1969, and since then a Republican has been president two-thirds of the time (exceptions: Jimmy Carter, 1977–1981; Bill Clinton, 1993–2001). The power of the Democrats also declined in Congress, although they held on longer there. The Republicans took control of the Senate in 1981 and held it for six years. They then lost the majority to the Democrats for eights years but regained control in 1997 and have held it ever since. Democrats ceded power in the House even more slowly, but they lost it in 1997 and remain the minority party. Republicans also dominate marginally at the state level. In 2005, Republican state governors outnumber their Democratic counterparts 28 to 22. Of the various state legislative chambers, Republicans control 50, the Democrats 47; one is tied.

This tale of nearly 40 disappointing years for the Democrats brings us to the 2008 presidential election and the potential of New York Senator Hillary R. Clinton as the Democratic nominee. Prior to that, of course, there is the 2006 congressional elections. But with Republicans holding only 15 of the 33 Senate seats being contested that years, it would take a major upset for the Democrats to gain a majority. The House presents a better chance for a Democratic victory. Nevertheless, the Republicans have a 24-seat majority going into the election, and relative rarity of a member of Congress being unseated gives the edge to continued Republican control of the House. Thus 2008 is a key year for the Democrats. With President Bush ineligible to run again, the Democratic incumbent will not have to run against an incumbent president. Moreover of the 33 Senate seats up for election in 2008, Republicans are vulnerable because they hold 19 of them. Additionally, a winning Democratic presidential "coat tails," even if limited, could provide the margin of victory gain a majority in the House.

Is Senator Clinton the candidate most likely to lead Democrats to control of the White House and both houses of Congress in 2009? That is the issue which divides Carl Cannon, who believes she is, and Amy Sullivan, who contends that she is not.

Clinton was born on October 26, 1947, as Hillary Diane Rodham and grew up in Park Ridge, Illinois. She began her active political career while at Wellesley College, where she served as president of the Wellesley College Chapter of the College Republicans. During her junior year, however, Rodham became a Democrat. She first gained a glimmer of national note when her valedictory graduation speech at Wellesley was considered so outstanding that she was featured in a *Life* magazine article. After that, she attended Yale Law School, where she met future husband Bill Clinton, and from where she graduated in 1972. After marrying Clinton in 1975, she moved to Arkansas, where she practiced law.

Hillary Clinton became first lady in 1993, and was soon appointed by her husband to head the Task Force on National Health Care Reform. Its eventual recommendations were much too far reaching to be accepted by Congress and were soon abandoned. This ended any overt political role for Ms. Clinton until the very end of her husband's tenure in the White House. It was not, however, the last of her trouble during those years. There were charges of unethical, even illegal activities in the huge gain she had made in 1979, turning an investment of $1,000 into $100,000, trading cattle futures on the Chicago Mercantile Exchange. Later, in the so-called Whitewater scandal, Ms. Clinton was summoned to testify before a grand jury regarding any part she might have played in a real estate fraud involving a venture in which she and her husband were among the partners. Several of the partners went to jail, but the Clintons were not charged. Ms. Clinton's time in the White House was also troubled by her spouse's alleged and acknowledged extra-marital affairs, most notably with White House intern Monica Lewinsky. With her husband's years as president ending, Ms. Clinton sought and won the Democratic nomination for the U.S. Senate in New York, then handily beat her Republican opponent with 55% of the vote. It was widely thought then, as it is now, that she would try to use the New York Senate seat as a platform to launch a bid for the presidency.

POINTS TO PONDER

➤ For this early in a campaign, Senator Clinton has an unusually high percentage of "positive" and "negatives," people who like and dislike her. The authors disagree about what this means. Who is right?

➤ What, if anything, would it mean to have former president Bill Clinton in the White House as the "first gentleman"?

➤ To what degree if any is gender a reasonable standard to any voter to make a decision for or against supporting Clinton?

Hillary Clinton and the 2008 Presidential Election: The Democrats' Best Bet

CARL CANNON

In 1978, while covering California politics, I found myself on election night at the Century Plaza Hotel in Los Angeles, which was serving as a kind of election central. Waiting for the returns to come in, I was sitting in the lobby having a drink with my father—who, then as now, was the leading expert on Ronald Reagan. As iron cue, the former actor and ex-California governor came striding into the hotel. Even then Reagan looked the part: wide-shouldered, flanked by a security detail, sporting his trademark blue serge suit, every black hair in place.

The only thing missing, I thought, was the Marine Corps Band.

No one back east took Reagan nearly as seriously as he seemed to be taking himself. Despite a devoted following among what were then known as Goldwater Republicans, the Washington cognoscenti casually dismissed Reagan as too conservative, too old, a B-movie actor who once played second fiddle to a chimpanzee— "Who does he think he is?" I asked my dad. "The president of the United States?"

"No," came the reply. "He thinks he's the next president of the United States." After a pause, he added, "And he might be."

I remember that vignette every time a political sage says authoritatively that [Senator] Hillary Rodham Clinton [D-NY] will "never" be president.

This is a particularly entrenched bit of conventional wisdom, which seems to have metastasized into a kind of secret handshake. If you "know" Clinton can't be president, you're a member of the Washington in-crowd. If you don't, you're an outsider,

some boob from the sticks of, I don't know, Sacramento or somewhere. Suburban Chicago, maybe. You know the rap: She's too liberal, too polarizing, a feminist too threatening to male voters. Too much baggage. Too...*Clinton*.

And these are Democrats talking. Bizarrely, the party's insiders are going out of their way to tear down the credentials and prospects of one of their rare superstars. Conservative columnist Robert Novak van into this phenomenon recently while speaking to eight local Democratic politicians in Los Angeles. Novak told them matter-of-factly that Hillary was the odds-on favorite to be their party's 2008 nominee—and that no one was in second place. Novak was surprised by their reaction: Not one was for Mrs. Clinton. Why? "They think she is a loser," said one of the Democrats.

With some exceptions, the journalistic pack seems nearly as negative about Hillary Clinton's chances. I'm a charter member of an informal lunch group of writers who runs the gamut from conservative to liberal, and each month when we meet, Hillary's name arises. Around the table it goes: She can't be elected in a general election; men aren't willing to vote for a woman like Hillary; women don't think much of her marriage—or her, for staying in it; which red state could she possibly carry? What swing voter would she convince? Each month, I marshaled my arguments in favor of Hillary's candidacy until finally I began sparing my friends the whole rap by just noting—for the minutes of the meeting, as it were—that I disagree with them.

Perhaps my lunch mates, those worried activist Democrats, and the majority of Washington pundits are correct. But I don't think so.

They certainly weren't right about Reagan.

Conservatives (and liberals) would consider it heresy to compare Ronald Reagan and Hillary Clinton. And Reagan is certainly a hard act to follow. He combined Main Street sensibilities and a soothing Middle America persona with an uplifting vision of America's place in the world that earned him a stunningly decisive victory in 1980—and 60 percent of the vote when he ran for reelection four years later. Senator Clinton is a more polarizing figure, in more polarized times. Yet Clinton, like Reagan, can lay claim to the passions of diehard grassroots members of her party. With the exception of incumbents and vice presidents, no candidate since Reagan has had a hammerlock on his or her party's nomination this long before the election. And like Reagan, the charisma gap between her and any would-be challengers in her own party is palpable.

Of course, the question is not whether she can win in the primary. Most Democrats concede the primary is probably hers for the taking. "I don't know how you beat her for the Democratic nomination," former Senator Bob Kerrey [D-NE] told *New York* magazine. She's a rock star. But that, as the cognoscenti see it, is the problem. She can't lose the primary, and she can't win the general election. And so they look vainly for an alternative—Warner? Biden? Bayh? Oh my!—always circling back to the same despairing fear of another four years in the political wilderness. Democrats have raised this kind of defeatism to a high art. But it's time for Democrats to snap out of it and take a fresh look at the hand they've been dealt. Hillary Rodham Clinton can win the general elec-

tion no matter who the Republicans throw at her. The Democrats just might be holding aces.

POLL POSITIONED

The available data do not suggest she is unelectable—they suggest just the opposite. A Gallup poll done a week before Memorial Day showed Senator Clinton with a favorable rate of 55 percent. True, her unfavorable number is 39 percent, which is high enough for concern—but one that is nearly identical to Bush's on the eve of his reelection. And the unfavorable rating registered by Republican contender [Senator] Bill Frist [R-TN] was nearly as high as his favorable numbers, with 32 percent saying they'd never heard of him.

"Then there was this eye-opening question:

If Hillary Rodham Clinton were to run for president in 2008, how likely would you be to vote for her—very likely, somewhat likely, not very likely, or not at all likely?

Very likely	29%
Somewhat likely	24
Not very likely	7
Not at all likely	40
No opinion	1

53%

At the risk of laboring the point, 29 percent plus 24 percent adds up to a majority. I can hear my pals answering this as they read these numbers: "Yes, but that's before the conservative attack machine gets a hold of her…"

Well, no, it isn't. They've been going at her with verbal tire irons, machetes, and sawed-off shotguns for 12 years now. Senator Clinton's negatives are already figured into her ratings. What could she be accused of that she hasn't already confronted since she entered the public eye 14 years ago? Clinton today is in a position similar to Bush's at the beginning of 2004. Democrats hoped that more information about the president's youth would "knock him down." But voters had already taken the president's past into account when they voted for him in 2000. More information just wasn't going to make a dent. In fact, as the spring of 2005 turned to summer there were yet another book and a matched spate of tabloid broadsides. In the face of it all, Hillary appears, if anything, to be getting stronger. Indeed, the more the right throws at her, the easier it is for her to lump any criticism in with the darkest visions of the professional Clinton bashers.

Let's also look deeper into that Gallup survey because the closer you look at it, the more formidable Senator Clinton seems. Thirty percent of the poll's respondents consider Hillary a "moderate," while 9 percent described her a "conservative." Now, I'm not sure which newspapers that 9 percent have been reading (the *Daily Worker*?), but the fact that nearly 40 percent of the electorate does not identify her as liberal mitigates the perception that she's considered too far to the left to be a viable national candidate.

Such perceptions are hardly set in stone, however, and senators' voting records can come back to haunt them in the heat of a campaign as [Senator] John Kerry [D-MA] learned in 2004 and countless others have learned before him. It's no accident that the last sitting U.S. senator elected president was John F. Kennedy. Thus, Clinton's Senate voting record, and where it puts her on the ideological scale, is worth some additional scrutiny.

The most comprehensive annual analysis of voting records is undertaken by my magazine, *National Journal*, which for 2004 used 24 votes on economic issues, 19 votes on social issues, and 17 foreign policy-related roll calls to rate all 100 U.S. senators. Its resulting ranking of John Kerry as the Senate's most liberal member (at least during 2003) was a gift from on high for the Bush

campaign, and the Massachusetts senator spent the better part of his campaign trying to explain away this vote or that. But Senator Clinton is harder to pigeon-hole. For 2004, Clinton's composite liberal score was 71 percent—putting her roughly in the middle of the Democratic caucus. While adhering to her party's liberal dogma on issues such as race, gun control, and judicial appointees, Hillary lists slightly toward the center on economic issues, and even more so on national security and foreign-policy issues. There's no telling at this point how the war in Iraq will play in 2008, but one thing is certain: Senator Clinton won't struggle the way Kerry did to reconcile a vote authorizing the war with one not authorizing the $87 billion to pay for it. For better or worse, she voted "aye" both times.

Yet another piece of received Washington wisdom holds that the party could never nominate someone in 2008 who has supported the Iraq war. Perhaps. But history suggests that if Bush's mission in Iraq flounders, a politician as nimble as Clinton will have plenty of time to get out in front of any anti-war movement. If it succeeds, Hillary would have demonstrated the kind of steadfastness demanded by the soccer moms turned security moms with whom Bush did so well in 2004.

On domestic issues, Senator Clinton has also shown a willingness to step out of the safety zone. She is bolstering her bipartisan credentials by teaming up with Republicans from the other side of the aisle, such as [Senator] Lindsey Graham [R-SC] and Frist himself, making her more difficult to portray as some kind of radical. And while her liberal voting record on social issues remains intact, she has taken rhetorical steps toward the middle. The most notable example occurred during a January speech in Albany, in which she advised abortion-rights activists to seek "common ground …with people on the other side." While pledging to defend Roe v. Wade, Mrs. Clinton relented to abortion as a "sad, even tragic, act" and called on Democrats to embrace a moral language for discussing the issue. Some conservatives even seemed receptive. In some quarters, Hillary's centrist posture was portrayed as new; but it actually isn't: She butted heads with the Arkansas teachers' union in the mid-1980s over a proposal she led to improve teacher quality.

The abortion speech was reminiscent of her husband's 1992 campaign-trail criticism of Sister Souljah for advocating violence against white people. Her remarks simultaneously showed she was willing to talk common sense to a key Democratic interest group while putting herself in sync with the ambivalent sensibilities most Americans have toward abortion. And because of the high standing she enjoys among Democratic women, she was able to do it without any fear of liberal backlash. Let's face it: When a feminist with Hillary's credentials discusses abortion in the way she has, it causes people to sit up and take notice.

Which brings us to the ultimate question: Hillary's gender. Will Americans vote for a woman?

They certainly say they will: 74 percent told Gallup that they'd be either "somewhat" or "very" likely to vote for a woman in 2008. This number is actually on the low side compared to polls from the pre-Hillary era, for the obvious reason that Clinton casts a shadow over 2008, and many of the respondents are Republicans who plan to vote against her. Again, I can hear some of my friends murmuring that these voters aren't telling the truth. But that's precisely the kind of snobbish thinking that never gets Democrats anywhere, that is usually wrong, and that infuriates swing voters. My advice to my Democratic friends is to ignore your inner elitist, and trust the American people to tell the truth, and, moreover, to do the right thing.

In fact, there is no reason to doubt them, as they've been proving their willingness to pull the lever for female candidates for a long time. In 1999, when Hillary first entered the national scene, 56 women sat in the House of Representatives, and nine in the Senate. Only three women were governors, but many women were in the pipeline in state government: Nearly 28 percent of statewide elective offices in the country were occupied by women. In one state, Arizona, women held the top five statewide offices. And that pipeline produced. Six years later, there are 14 women in the Senate, and 66 in the House (along with another three non-voting delegates). There are eight, not three, women governors. "The day will come when men will recognize woman as his peer, not only at the fireside, but in councils of the nation," [Women's suffrage leader] Susan B. Anthony [1820–1906] once predicted. That day is fast approaching whether or not conservatives are ready for it, and whether or not liberals are willing to acknowledge it.

Nonetheless, anyone who maintains that the American electorate is ready for a female president (and this particular female candidate) must at some point confront the Electoral College map. This, my skeptical friends claim, is where Hillary's hopes run aground. Putting it plainly, they challenge anyone to come up with a red state that Hillary can carry—someplace, anyplace, where Senator Clinton could run stronger than the Kerry/Edwards ticket.

It is, of course, absurd to look at electoral politics at such an atomic level this far out. In due time, pollsters and the press will christen 2008's must-have swing voters and must-win swing states. But calibrating a candidacy to the last election is a fool's errand. The near-frozen electoral map of the last five years has been an historical anomaly, not the rule. So there's no reason to believe that a 2004 electoral map would be terribly useful three years hence.

But if we must, let's play along. What red state could Clinton snatch away from the GOP column? How about Florida? The Gold Coast considers itself part of New York anyway, and Clinton's moderate overtures might draw swing voters from upstate. Cuban Americans are no longer the sole Latino voting bloc in Florida—and even Cubans are no longer monolithic. If not Florida, how about Iowa and New Mexico? They are centrist, bellwether states—and states Hillary's husband carried both times he ran. Meanwhile, the Republican Party hardly has a lock on Ohio, which went for Clinton twice, and which was close in 2000 and 2004.

The fact is, there are a thousand movable parts in a presidential campaign, but the two most indispensable are (1) a candidate with charisma, money, and a broad following in his or her party; and (2) a ticket that espouses values and policies that Middle Americans agree with. A candidate, the polls now suggest, like Hillary Clinton.

Or [Senator] John McCain [R-AZ].

THE BUBBA FACTOR

After dissecting an upcoming race, any good horse player will look at the *Racing Form* again and figure out if he (or she) missed anything: Who could beat the obvious horse? For the 2008 presidential run, there is an answer that jumps off the page: If the Republican faithful are smart enough to nominate him, John Sydney McCain III would probably be their most formidable candidate—if he gets the GOP nomination, a big "if."

It's fanciful to suggest that anyone is unbeatable this far out, even McCain. While he makes the media swoon, the Arizona senator would have to thread a pretty tight needle to get to the White House. A Quinnipiac Poll taken in March showed a McCain-Clinton election virtually tied, 43–41. These are good numbers, but they're hardly in the Colin Powell range. The Republican conservative base remains leery of him. That this antipathy is self-defeating (or even inexplicable) makes it no less real. In addition, the easiest circumstances to envision that would benefit McCain would be if there were widespread disillusion with Bush. But the issue most likely to bring that about—a dire result to the occupation in Iraq—probably doesn't help McCain anyway: If anything, he's been more hawkish on foreign policy than the president. Even if other factors—a rotten economy or a scandal—led to a McCain general election candidacy, a GOP meltdown might carry McCain to the nomination, but it wouldn't help him against Hillary Clinton. First, if conservatives could muster only halfhearted passion for the man (not unlike the less-than-enthusiastic support John Kerry received from many Democrats), well, we've seen that movie. No candidate is without vulnerabilities, and certainly Hillary has hers. (I'll leave their enumeration to my counterpart, Amy Sullivan.) The difference between a winning and losing campaign, though, is whether you have the strategy to weather the inevitable rough waters.

On the USS *George W. Bush*, Karl Rove is considered the indispensable navigator. But when one looks on the Democratic side, who is a match for the man Bush called "The Architect" of his triumph? What recent Democrat has shown such an ability to see the political chessboard 20 moves ahead and plot a winning game plan? Only one, and to find him, Senator *Clinton* need only look to the other side of the breakfast table.

President Clinton doesn't come without strings attached. While it is an article of faith among the Clintonistas that Al Gore hurt his own campaign in 2000 by not using Bill Clinton more on the stump, there was plenty of polling to back up Gore's gambit. While Clinton could stir up the party faithful, his presence wasn't always a net plus. Hillary faces a similar dilemma when it comes to her husband—and a lot closer to home. But in addition to being able to draw upon Clinton's strategic gifts, Senator Clinton would almost certainly not make the more serious mistake Gore made: not being able to successfully make use of the Clinton administration's record of 22 million new jobs; steady income growth for workers of every level; precipitous declines in the welfare rolls; and an expanded NATO [North Atlantic Treaty Organization] alliance that ushered in the post–Cold War geopolitical map.

Will Americans remember the optimism and idealism espoused in 1992 by The Man From Hope [a reference to Hope, Arkansas, the childhood home of Bill Clinton], and the way Clinton would parry policy questions with long, coherent, informative answers? Or will they remember their disgust at the revelations about the infamous blue dress, and how Clinton often shaded the truth?

No repentance, however sincere, could spare Bill Clinton from his eternity as fodder for the tabloids and late-night monologues. But he seems to be growing increasingly sure-footed and confident in his role as elder statesman. He has formed a friendship with the man he defeated for the office, and a productive working relationship with the current president. If he is to help his wife, all Clinton needs to do is remind us of his better angels, as he did during his tour of tsunami-devastated South Asia.

This brings us back to Hillary herself. Even if Bill Clinton rises to the occasion, voters are going to remember the yin and the yang of our 42nd president, and they are going to chew on the fact that the woman who wants to be our 44th is married to him. She will be asked about the marriage. How she answers will go a long way toward determining the viability of her candidacy. In his astute book [*The Survivor*: Random House, 1992] on the Clinton presidency, John F. Harris recounts how aides broached the subject of her marriage as Hillary prepared to run for the Senate. How would she answer this basic question: Why had she stayed with him?

"Yes, I've been wondering that myself," Hillary says playfully.

Then Bill interjects: "Because you're a sticker! That's what people need to know—you're a sticker. You stick at the things you care about."

Clintonites love this story, but there are a couple of things wrong with it. First, Bill Clinton is providing the answer, but it's not his answer to give. Second, it's a talking point. The Clintons are good at slogans, but this is a question women will have for Hillary Clinton, women looking to identify with her. A sound bite answer just might confirm voters' fears that her marriage is a sham, and that she's an opportunist. On the other hand, if the answer emerges that she loves Bill Clinton, despite his flaws, and that she's in an imperfect marriage—well, most marriages are imperfect. Moreover, if she suggests that the deciding factor was her concern for their daughter, well, that's the kind of pro-family cred that really matters. Cute answers won't cut it. Authenticity will. And there's every reason to believe both Clintons could summon it when talking about the daughter to whom they are so obviously devoted.

Finally, there is one perceived pitfall—and that's Hillary's penchant for the jugular. Party activists admire her for this, but successful general election candidates learn to temper the instincts that result in outbursts like the "vast, right-wing conspiracy."

In upstate New York, Senator Clinton has charmed independent Yankee farmers and small-town Republican businessmen from Buffalo with an inclusive, upbeat style of campaigning and governing. This is the dress rehearsal for running nationwide, yet when she gets going on the red meat circuit Senator Clinton retains a fondness for ad hominem attacks and paranoid world views.

"There has never been an administration, I don't believe in our history, more intent upon consolidating and abusing power to further their own agenda," Clinton said at a recent Democratic fundraiser. "Why can't the Democrats do more to stop them? I can tell you this: It's very hard to stop people who have no shame about what they're doing....It is very hard to stop people who have never been acquainted with the truth." The crowd loved it, but this rant manages to ignore Nixon, while simultaneously sounding Nixonian. Hillary can definitely have a tin ear.

Hillary Clinton, whether she realizes it or not, is relieved of the obligation to pander in this way. She has paid her dues to the Democratic Party, and she doesn't have to prove her bona tides to anyone. From now on, she only need emulate Reagan, a fellow Illinois native, who campaigned with positive rhetoric and a smile on his face, trusting that the work he'd done cultivating his base would pay off, and that he needed mainly to reassure independent-minded voters. When we in the press corps tried to bait Reagan into going negative by asking why he'd abandoned the party of his youth, he invariably smiled, cocked his head, and gave the same line. "I didn't leave the Democratic Party," Reagan would say. "The Democratic Party left me."

As a girl, Hillary Rodham was a Goldwater Republican. She could use the same line in reverse. It might remind swing voters why they are looking, once again, at casting their lot with a candidate named Clinton. She can do this because Democrats are poised to back her already, and because much of the rest of America is watching, open-minded, half-hoping that she gives them a reason to support her, too.

Hillary Clinton and the 2008 Presidential Election: A Problematic Candidate

Amy Sullivan

For a first-time candidate and controversial first lady, Hillary Clinton's bid for the open New York Senate seat in 2000 was going surprisingly well. From the beginning, she had staked out a seemingly impossible strategy; given who she was: ignore the press, go straight to the voters, and focus exclusively on issues, never on herself. "You make a mistake if you let any campaign become about you," she told Michael Tomasky, one of the reporters who followed her that year. Given that even campaigns not involving Hillary Clinton sometimes manage to become about Hillary Clinton, it was difficult to imagine how she could pull off this feat. Still, she stuck doggedly to policy talk, boring the press corps but impressing New York voters. Two weeks before Election Day, she enjoyed a comfortable lead, polling eight points ahead of opponent [Republican candidate, Representative] Rick Lazio.

And that's when Lazio decided to take matters into his hands and make the race about Clinton whether she liked it or not. His campaign put together a commercial intended to target her biggest vulnerability: white suburban women. All throughout the campaign, this demographic had been the most skeptical; in focus groups, even women who liked Clinton said she reminded them of an unpleasant woman in their lives—a mother-in-law or a stern Catholic nun or a judgmental neighbor. The ad sought to remind them that, deep down, they didn't really like Hillary Clinton, that they thought she was too ambitious. On the screen, a woman making dinner in a kitchen talked on a phone, her tone angry:

"We started out at the bottom and worked our tushes off to get somewhere. No, but Hillary, she wants to start at the top, you know, the senator from New York?"

The ad was the most personal of the race, and it worked. Within days, Clinton's lead had shrunk to three points, within the margin of error. Although she recovered to win the Senate seat with 55 percent of the vote, Clinton's advantage among women was only half that of Al Gore's, who won New York's female vote by a margin of 65 to 31.

Five years later, Senator Clinton is a major player on the political scene. Her name is first on the lips of anyone who talks about the 2008 race for the White House. Potential rival John McCain says she would make a fine president. Conservatives such as [former Speaker of the U.S. House of Representatives] Newt Gingrich and Bill Kristol [editor of *The Weekly Standard*] are talking up Clinton, warning their partisan colleagues that she would be a formidable opponent. That's not surprising—after all, Republicans have long fantasized about the prospect of taking on Hillary Clinton again at a national level. But now, talk of her candidacy has gone from conservative wishful thinking to serious discussions within her own party, which is anxious to end its losing streak and is considering the advantages of closing ranks behind an early frontrunner. One glance at polls showing that 53 percent of Americans are willing to consider putting Clinton in the White House makes visions of sugar plums and oval offices dance in the heads of Democratic Party leaders. The high name recognition, impressive early poll numbers, and desperate party all carry the Senate whiff of inevitability that accompanied George W. Bush's campaign for the 2000 election.

In the face of this momentum, someone has to say it, so here goes: Please don't run, Senator.

Don't get me wrong. I'm a longtime Hillary Clinton fan. As in a back-when-she-was-still-wearing-headbands fan. I have found her warm and utterly charming in person; more than that, she understands the challenges facing Democrats in a way that few others in the party do, and her ability to absorb policy nuances rivals her husband's. This country is long past due for a female president, and I would love to see Hillary Clinton in that trailblazing role (and not just because it would make Ann Coulter break out in giant hives). But—at the risk of getting myself permanently blackballed by her loyal and protective staff while Clinton can win nearly any debate that is about issues, she cannot avoid becoming the issue in a national campaign. And when that happens, she will very likely lose.

NO SUCH THING AS UNDECIDED

It's not exactly news that Hillary Clinton is a polarizing figure. Ever since Newt Gingrich's mother whispered to Connie Chung on national television that she thought Mrs. Clinton was, well, a bitch, Americans have understood that the ex-first lady provokes intense emotions on all sides. Still, it's not hard to see why Hillary boosters are tempted to think that voters might be willing to take a new look at her and why politically astute people are turning cartwheels over the idea of her candidacy.

Over the last five years, Clinton has developed into perhaps the most interesting politician in America. She has a reputation for bipartisanship in the Senate, forming partnerships with some of her most conservative Republican colleagues, including Bill Frist (R-Tenn.), Rick Santorum (R-Pa.), and Sam Brownback (R-Kan.). She has quietly, but firmly, assumed a leadership role in her own caucus. And she has shown vision and backbone in a party that is accused of having none.

Years before most Washington Democrats started worrying about the party's reputation on "moral values," Clinton was bringing Jim Wallis and other progressive religious leaders to talk with her colleagues about reclaiming the concepts of faith and values. She voted for the Iraq war when that wasn't a popular position for a Democrat to take, and has been willing to speak uncomfortable truths in difficult venues. In January, she told a crowd of over 1,000 assembled pro-choice activists that the way they have been talking about abortion is wrong, that many Americans won't even listen to them until they admit that it would be better if most women didn't have to face the "sad, even tragic choice" of having one. More recently, she cosponsored the "Workplace Religious Freedom Act" after intense lobbying from women's groups that oppose the legislation.

There's no one tougher. No one understands better that Middle America cares about both economic issues and cultural concerns. At the same time, no one is better at firing up the liberal base. Add to all of that approval ratings in the high 50s, and it sounds like you have the makings of a sure-fire winner for the Democrats.

And if it were any other candidate, that might be true. But with Hillary Clinton, everything's more complicated.

Let's look at those poll numbers that have Democrats pasting "Hillary '08" bumper stickers onto their Subaru Outbacks and Republicans pulling their Whitewater files out of the basement. Right now, Clinton is leaving her fellow Democratic contenders—including Sens. John Kerry (D-Mass.), John Edwards (D-

N.C.), and Joseph Biden (D-Del.)—in the dust. In polls that ask voters to identify which potential Democratic nominee they would back in 2008, she regularly clocks in at around 40 percent while her closest competitor rarely breaks the 20 percent mark.

It's important to remember, however, that polls taken this early in the process tend simply to reflect how well known a candidate is. (Kerry is surely as well-known as Clinton, but may be suffering in the polls from Democratic loser fatigue.) In 1997, for instance, George W. Bush led most polls of Republican prospects, in large part because many respondents thought they were being asked about his father. Hillary Clinton occupies the spot held by Al Gore at this point in the 2004 election cycle. She may well be the candidate most Democrats want to see as their nominee; or she could just be the one they know best. Right now, it's too early to know for certain.

In addition, while her "favorables" are good—57 percent of Americans have a positive impression of her—her negatives are disturbingly high as well. This long before an election, most voters have yet to make up their mind about a candidate. Even as close to the primaries as December 2003, 66 percent of voters didn't know what they thought of John Kerry. That's not the case with Clinton. While at this point in George W. Bush's first presidential campaign, Bush also had favorable ratings around the mid-50s, an additional 30 percent of voters said they either hadn't made up their minds about him or they didn't know who he was. Compare that to Hillary: Only 7 percent of respondents aren't sure what they think of her, and—not surprisingly—no one says they haven't heard of her.

Never in American political history has a candidate faced such a decided electorate at this early a point in a presidential race. That's a disadvantage when you consider that one of the lessons of 2004 was that

once voters develop a perception about a candidate, it's as immovable as superglue. No one who thought George W. Bush was a likable, friendly guy could be convinced that he was corrupt or misleading. And once John Kerry became identified in voters' minds as a "flip-flopper," no amount of arguing could change that image. It's a problem for any candidate. For Senator Clinton, it could be fatal. Americans know exactly what they think of her. And nearly 40 percent say they would never consider voting for her.

SHAKING HANDS, CHANGING MINDS

Of course, there is one proven way that Hillary Clinton has damaged voters' perceptions. In her first Senate race, the strategy was simple: Meet as many voters as possible, and ignore the scandal-focused press. It paid off—when Clinton hunched her campaign, only 41 percent of New Yorkers were prepared to vote for her; she won in November 2000 with 55 percent of the vote after having visited each of the state's 62 counties, many of them repeatedly.

Operation Smother the Voters worked in large part because the real Hillary Clinton is a far cry from the caricature of a manipulative, power-hungry, shrewish woman that has been propagated by the right. One of the unexpected benefits of being demonized and attacked by conservatives for more than a decade turns out to be that voters are surprised and relieved when she doesn't fly into town on a broomstick. Tomasky relates the response of voters when they actually met the woman they'd heard so much about for eight years in *Hillary's Turn*, his excellent book about Clinton's 2000 campaign. "People had expected Hillary to instruct and talk, and, let's face it, to come across as pushy and judgmental," he wrote. "So when she paid genuine attention to the things people were saying, she really threw them." Indeed, the first time I met the Clintons, the president distractedly shook some hands after a speech and then left fairly quickly while the first lady was the one who displayed the vaunted Clinton political skills—chatting easily about policy details, focusing intently on what my colleague and I had to say, and then throwing her arms around our shoulders for a photo that looks more like three college friends than two awed congressional staffers and a first lady.

The strategy also succeeded because many voters—weaned on a diet of conservative talking points during the 1990s—expected Clinton to be a liberal of the bluest sort, to the left of Ted Kennedy and unable to understand their concerns. What they found was that her positions on welfare, crime, and foreign policy, among other issues, were far more centrist than liberal. In addition, while most professional political observers dismissed her "Listening Tour" as a stunt, Clinton actually used it to query New Yorkers about their problems and obsessively study up on local issues.

All of this is impressive. But if the ability to work a rope line or a town hall meeting was the key ingredient to winning a national race, our political history would be quite different. In *What It Takes*, his chronicle of the 1988 presidential race, the journalist Richard Ben Cramer describes watching Dick Gephardt entrance voters with his earnest, determined approach and piercing blue eyes. "Sweet Jesus, he is terrific," Cramer writes. "There aren't ten voters in the country who would work against him, once he's had them face-to-face." Similarly, last winter, many political reporters chalked up John Kerry's surprising comeback in Iowa to the fact that he'd spent countless evenings in individual homes, talking to voters until he had convinced each person to support him. No candidate, however, meets every voter face-to-face en route to the White House.

Anyone running for office would prefer to meet as many voters as possible in person. The stakes are higher for Hillary Clinton: She has to meet personally with voters in order to have a chance of changing their minds about her. If she runs for the White House, the vast majority of Americans will learn what they know about her campaign through the media. And that's where the second half of Senator Clinton's New York strategy falls apart.

"NURSE RATCHED"

When a candidate's name recognition is at 100 percent in a statewide campaign, she can afford to turn a few campaign saws about the media upside-down. For the 2000 Clinton campaign, no press was good press; "the smaller the circus, the better," one of her staffers told Tomasky. They considered it a victory when the traveling press corps—bored by the lack of news made by Clinton's "Listening Tour" and its endless focus on the minutiae of dairy compacts and traffic conditions on the Canadian border—winnowed from 250 reporters to 70 to about a dozen permanent scribes. Although the *New York Post*, and columnist Dick Morris in particular, nipped at Clinton's heels for the length of the campaign, she was able to conduct her image transformation largely in a vacuum.

It's safe to say that wouldn't be the case in 2008. The only way to reach voters in a nationwide campaign is through the media, both through purchased airtime and what is referred to as "free" media—coverage of campaign events and interviews with print and television reporters. It's a two-sided coin for candidates. They need journalists in order to get their messages across to the majority of Americans who won't get a chance to hear them in person, but they have no control over what gets reported or how it's framed in the press. Any Democrat running in the general election would face that challenge, although they might not yet know precisely how the press would cover their candidacy. Senator Clinton, however, knows all too well what to expect. Her instincts were correct in 2000: When you're Hillary Clinton, "free" media always comes with a cost.

Journalists are often no different from voters in general—when they form an impression of a politician, many reporters filter coverage through what they think they know about the candidate. Reporters "knew" Al Gore was a serial exaggerator, that Kerry was an out-of-touch, aristocratic elitist, and that Bush was an amiable goof. They may not let ideological leanings color their coverage, but personal biases can affect what they choose to report and the narratives they choose to tell.

Jill Lawrence, one of *USA Today*'s campaign correspondents in 2004, has observed that very few political reporters wrote about the way Kerry used religious language—even though, she noted, it occurred every week on the campaign wail—because they assumed that Democratic candidates weren't deeply religious. "The stereotype of the Democratic Party is so deep that it never broke through," she said. That's already happening with Clinton, whose religious references and comments on abortion generated headlines early in 2005. Most news outlets characterized her remarks as a distinct break from the past—implying that she was transforming herself for a White House run—even though she is a former Sunday School teacher who has spoken publicly about religion for decades and her comments on abortion were consistent with her husband's mantra that abortion should be "safe, legal, and rare?"

Chemistry is also important for the press corps. Reporters are attracted to straight-talkers like [Senator] John McCain [R-AZ],

Rudy Giuliani [former Republican mayor of New York City], and—in 2003, at least—Howard Dean [former Democratic governor of Vermont]. Inaccessibility is definitely a turn-off; in the early years of the Clinton administration, the First Lady famously fought with the *Washington Post* over the release of documents about Whitewater. Her chilly relationship with the press has warmed considerably during her first term in the Senate, but Hillary Clinton still has far more skeptics than fans have the press corps.

Sometimes they go far beyond reportorial cynicism. The *Washington Post's* reporter assigned to cover Clinton's first Senate race, [*Washington Post* reporter] Michael Grunwald, provides one illustration of how the press corps already feels about her. Describing the first lady as "bor[ing] New York into submission, droning on endlessly about focus-grouped Democratic issues," Grunwald accused her of "baldly deceptive and intentionally vacuous behavior" and "an intellectually and emotionally dishonest scheme to get a job without a résumé" and charged that "her only consistent ideology was a faith in political popularity." Ouch. More recently, on the Feb. 20, 2005, installment of "The Chris Matthews Show," a panel discussed Hillary's candidacy while calling her "Nurse Ratched" [an unflattering reference to a domineering, repressed character in the 1975 film *One Flew Over the Cuckoo's Nest*] and a "castrating female persona" things really got going when journalist Gloria Borger mimicked Clinton's laugh and mannerisms while her colleagues sniggered.

And that's coming from members of the mainstream media. The conservative press—never shy when it comes to Hillary Clinton—has spent the spring teeing up for another game of Hillaryball. The trial of David Rosen, the fundraiser for Clinton's 2000 campaign, who was accused of hiding about $800,000 of costs for a campaign event held in Los Angeles, came first. In the three months leading up to the verdict (Rosen was acquitted), the FOX News Channel ran more than a dozen segments on Rosen, including a "Hannity & Colmes" segment titled "Are Hillary's Presidential Chances Over?" Rosen's eventual acquittal merited barely a hiccup on FOX, which simply replaced Rosen coverage with segments on the next Clinton scandal story—yet another bestselling book taking on the Senator.

THE HILLARY EFFECT

Edward Klein's *The Truth About Hillary: What She Knew, and How Far She'll Go to Become President* [Sentinel, 2005] is, even by the low standards of the genre, vile. In seeking to portray Hillary Clinton as a cold, manipulative woman who will do anything for power, Klein relies on wholly unsubstantiated accusations of corruption, lesbianism, and marital rape. Most conservatives who gleefully anticipated the book's release are now distancing themselves from it. And liberals have derived some joy from scenes such as right-wing talk show host Scan Hannity sharply questioning Klein over his use of sources.

Klein apparently didn't get the memo about anti-Hillary strategy. Frontal assaults and reckless accusations are sooo 1990s, definitely déclassé. More to the point, they make conservatives sound scary and are counterproductive. But while Democrats are surely hoping that these attacks will spur a backlash and sympathy for Clinton, the more likely outcome is a draw. Americans may have lost their appetite for books like *Madame Hillary: The Dark Road to the White House* [by R. Emmett Tyrrell, Jr., and Mark W. Davis, 2004] and *Hillary's Scheme: Inside the Next Clinton's Ruthless Agenda to Take the White House* [by Carl Limbacher, 2004], but many of them share the under-

lying concern about Clinton's motives and character. Likewise, while a Republican nominee would benefit from anti-Hillary donations—in the last few months of the 2000 race, Lazio averaged $1 million each week in hard money contributions from Hillary-haters outside of New York— Senator Clinton's prodigious fundraising has the potential to neutralize that effort.

Conservatives won't trot out supposed lesbian lovers in 2008; they'll go after her more subtly. They know that 40 percent of the country can't stand Senator Clinton, another 40 percent adores her, and the remaining 20 percent (which, according to those recent polls, seem to feel generally positive about her) is made up of fairly soft support. The best way to turn that support into opposition is to voice those age-old questions about the Clintons: She's inappropriately power-hungry and ambitious— remember that Tammy Wynette crack? He lacks moral character—do you really want him roaming the White House again? And don't forget health care—who elected her to that post anyway?

Another golden oldie—the charge that the Clintons will say anything to get ahead—is already being revived elliptically by conservatives. The day after Senator Clinton's news-making abortion speech this past January, conservatives were all over the media, charging that she was undergoing a "makeover" of her political image. "I think what we're seeing is, at least rhetorically, the attempt of the ultimate makeover," Gary Bauer told the *Washington Times. Investors Business Daily* editorialized: "When husband Bill did it, it was called triangulation....Now another Clinton running for president is telling different audiences what they want to head." In the six months since, the "makeover" charge has been repeated more than 100 times in the press. Give them another six, and "makeover" will be the new "flip-flop."

The target audience for these whispers and insinuations—and, let's not be naive, occasional television commercials—is a familiar demographic: suburban women. Democrats lost ground in the 2004 elections among white, married, working women, and it's generally accepted that to win back the White House, the party needs a nominee who can appeal to these women. There's no reason to think that Republicans wouldn't revive the same kind of personal attacks that Lazio brought out in the last week of the 2000 campaign. In that race, the Hillary effect that resulted in the loss of suburban women was masked by gains among upstate men. She'll have a much harder time winning their counterparts in those essential swing states, which makes it even more important that she be able to count on the women's vote. If the Republican strategy in 2008 results in the same outcome as 2000—if, in other words, Clinton's advantage among women was half that of Gore's—the

margin of victory in states like Iowa, Minnesota, New Mexico, and Wisconsin will disappear. Game, set, match.

No, Democrats, it's not fair. Hillary Clinton is smart, she's paving a promising new path for her party, she's a much better campaigner than anyone ever expected, and she's already survived more personal assaults than anyone should have to endure. But wishing the country would grow up and get over the 1990s already, that she could wage a campaign of issues and be evaluated on her political merit, won't make it so. What's more, those daydreams—pleasant as they are to contemplate on a sunny afternoon—cast a shadow over the Democratic field that makes it difficult for a potentially viable candidate to emerge.

It's too early for anyone to say with certainty that Hillary Clinton can't win the White House. But it's far too early—and dangerous—to conclude that she's the best chance that Democrats have.

THE CONTINUING DEBATE:
Hillary Clinton and the 2008 Presidential Election

What Is New

It would be surprising if Hillary Clinton did not seek the presidency in 2008. First, however, Clinton has to be reelected to the Senate in 2006. Few analysts doubt she can win, but a victory with less than the 55% of the vote she amassed in 2000 will dull her luster somewhat. Several other factors will also influence her prospects in 2008. One is whether Americans will elect a woman as president. Polls show that most Americans say they would vote for a woman, but it is the "no" or "doubtful" categories that worry Democrats. A 2005 poll found that 73% of respondents said they would be "very" or "somewhat" likely to vote for a woman nominated by their party for president. But 20% were "not very" or "not at all" likely to do so, with 7% unsure. To offset that minimum of 20%, Clinton would have to attract substantial "pro-woman" votes from Republicans and unaffiliated voters. A second factor is Clinton's record. Among other things, the electorate is moderate, and the Republicans will portray her as a liberal. Her record in the Senate tends to support that portrayal. In its analysis of Clinton's voting record, the liberal group, Americans for Democratic Action, rates her four year (2001–2004) "liberal quotient" at 95%. From the opposite perspective, the American Conservative Union rates her conservative score at only 6%. Also standing in Clinton's way is the 2004 vice presidential nominee John Edwards and the many other Democrats who would like their party's nomination in 2008. Finally, if nominated, she will have to defeat the Republican candidate. Among the most mentioned names are Senators John McCain (Arizona), former New York City Mayor Rudolph Giuliani, and Secretary of State Condoleezza Rice.

Where to Find More

Autobiographies are worth reading if not fully believing, and Hillary Clinton's is *Living History* (Simon & Schuster, 2003). In somewhat the same genre, visit her 2006 Senate reelection site at www.hillaryclinton.com/ and her Senate office site at http://clinton.senate.gov/. An official Hillary Clinton for president organization is Votehillary at www.votehillary.org/. Directly rebutting Clinton's autobiography is *Rewriting History* (Regan Books, 2004) by Dick Morris, a former top political adviser to President Clinton. A Web site that takes a dim view of the senator is at Stop Hillary Now at www.stophillarynow.net/.

What More to Do

Whether you support or oppose Senator Clinton, you have two fairly immediate chances to affect her political future and perhaps the country's too. One opportunity is to get involved in the 2006 New York Senate race, the other is to participate the 2008 presidential campaign, including the nomination and election. If you are not sure, gather information about Clinton, form an opinion, then get active.

10 VOTING/CAMPAIGNS/ELECTIONS

THE ELECTORAL COLLEGE:
Abolish *or* Preserve?

ABOLISH

ADVOCATE: Becky Cain, President, League of Women Voters

SOURCE: Testimony during hearings on "Proposals for Electoral College Reform: H.J. Res. 28 and H.J. Res. 43" before the U.S. House of Representatives Committee on the Judiciary, Subcommittee on the Constitution, September 4, 1997

PRESERVE

ADVOCATE: Judith A. Best, Professor of Political Science, State University of New York at Cortland

SOURCE: Testimony during hearings on "Proposals for Electoral College Reform: H.J. Res. 28 and H.J. Res. 43" before the U.S. House of Representatives Committee on the Judiciary, Subcommittee on the Constitution, September 4, 1997

Sometimes figuring out your course grade in college can get pretty complicated. Your raw score on tests may not exactly equate to your final "curved" grade. Determining the final score in the Electoral College can be a little like this. The raw score (the popular vote) and the final score (the vote of the electors) never match up. In 1980, for example, Ronald Reagan received 90.1% of the electors' votes, while getting only 51.6% of the popular vote. It is even possible in the Electoral College to have a higher raw score than anyone else yet lose. Al Gore received 51,003,238 popular votes to only 50,459,624 votes for George Bush in the 2000 presidential election. Yet Bush received 50.4% of the electoral vote compared to 49.4% for Gore.

Then, like in some college grading, the Electoral College has other variables. For example, electors selected by the voters in many states can legally vote for someone other than the candidate to whom they are pledged. Such unexpected votes are not common, but they have occurred in 10 elections. For example, a disgruntled elector from Alabama who was supposed to vote for Democratic candidate Adlai Stevenson in 1956 instead cast his ballot for Walter B. Jones, a judge from his hometown who was not even running.

These oddities and other quirks bring up three questions. What is the Electoral College? Where did it come from? Should we keep it? The first two questions are easier. The Electoral College is an indirect process for selecting the U.S. president. Each state selects a number of electors equal to its representation in Congress, and the District of Columbia gets three electors, for a total of 538 electors. The exact process for choosing electors varies by state, but as a general rule each party or candidate selects a slate of electors. It is for one of these slates that the people vote in November. In all states except Maine and Nebraska, there is a "winner-take-all" system in which the slate that receives the most votes wins. Then the individual electors cast their separate ballots for president and vice president in December. The ballots are sent to Congress, where they are counted in early January. It takes a majority of all electoral votes (270) to win. If no individual receives a majority, then the House selects a president from among the candidates with the three highest electoral votes. Each state casts one vote in the House, and it requires a majority of the states (26) to win. The Senate, with each member voting individually, chooses a vice president from among the top two electoral vote recipients. It is not possible to detail here all the possible permutations, but the choice has gone to the House twice (1800 and 1824), and on three occasions (1876, 1888, and 2000) the candidate with the most popular votes has lost the electoral vote.

The Electoral College was established for two reasons. One is that it stressed the role of the states. They can choose electors as they wish and are not even obligated to have popular elections. The second motive for the Electoral College was to insulate the selection of president from the people. As Alexander Hamilton explained in *Federalist* #68 (1788), he and others worried that the "general mass" would not "possess the information and discernment requisite to such complicated investigations," raising the possibility of "tumult and disorder."

The question is whether to abolish or preserve the Electoral College. Throughout its history, the process has been controversial, and it has provoked over 700 proposals in Congress to reform or eliminate it. Yet it survives. The following articles lay out their respective attack on and defense of the Electoral College, but beyond those substantive arguments, the process continues for two additional reasons. One is that changing it would require a constitutional amendment, most probably through a two-thirds vote by each house of Congress and ratification by three-fourths of the state. Obtaining such supermajorities is very difficult. The second procedural reason the Elector College survives is that, for contradictory reasons, it appeals to many states. States with big populations, such as California with its 55 electoral votes (more than 20% of those needed to win), believe they gain political advantage through their hefty share of the electoral votes. States with small populations also see political advantage. Wyoming may have only 55/100ths of one percent of the electoral vote, but that is more than three times the state's 17/100ths of one percent of the U.S. population. States in a middle position come out mathematically about right. For example, New Jersey with 8.1 million people and 15 electoral votes has 2.86% of the population and 2.78% of the electoral votes. Thus the Electoral College seems either politically favorable or neutral to almost every state, making an amendment even more difficult to pass and ratify.

POINTS TO PONDER

➤ Becky Cain, testifying in 1997, predicts a fiasco if, once again, a candidate were to lose the electoral vote while winning the popular vote. Three years later that occurred, yet there were no widespread protest demonstrations. Why not?

➤ Judith Best contends that abolishing the Electoral College would diminish the influence of minority groups. Why might this occur?

➤ Which is more important, the aspect of federalism that is part of the Electoral College vote calculation or the principle of "one person—one vote"?

The Electoral College:
Abolish

BECKY CAIN

Mr. Chairman, members of the subcommittee, I am Becky Cain, president of the League of Women Voters.

I am pleased to be here today to express the support of the League [League of Women Voters of the United States] for a constitutional amendment to abolish the Electoral College and establish the direct election of the President and Vice President of the United States by popular vote of the American people.

The League of Women Voters of the United States is a non-partisan citizen organization with 150,000 members and supporters in all fifty states, the District of Columbia and the Virgin Islands. For over 75 years, Leagues across the country have worked to educate the electorate, register voters and make government at all levels more accessible and responsive to the average citizen.

Since 1970, the League has supported an amendment to the Constitution that would abolish the Electoral College and establish a direct, popular vote for the President and Vice President of the United States. The League arrived at this position through its time-honored study and consensus process. Leagues in over 1,000 communities across the country participated in the study and came to the same conclusion: our method of electing a President must be changed to ensure a more representative government.

Political developments since the 1970s have only underscored the need for the elimination of the Electoral College system. The downward trend in voter participation, coupled with increased cynicism and skepticism amongst the public about the ability of elected leaders to provide meaningful representation are the warning signs of a potential electoral fiasco.

Picture if you will a future national election in which a presidential candidate receives a majority of the popular vote, but is denied the 270 votes necessary for election by the Electoral College. This has already happened once in our nation's history, when, in 1888, Grover Cleveland outpolled Benjamin Harrison in the popular vote but lost the Electoral College vote by 233 to 168. It caused a public furor then, when political office was often gained through back-room deals and closed-door maneuvering. Imagine the public outcry today, after a long primary campaign and a grueling race for the Presidency. Imagine the public's rage at being denied their candidate of choice.

Now go one step further. Consider a close three-way race for President in which no candidate earns the necessary Electoral College votes to win. This has happened twice before in our nation's history, in 1801 and 1825, when the House of Representatives chose Thomas Jefferson and John Quincy Adams, respectively. While the League believes both of these men were great presidents, we are troubled about the potential for a future presidential candidate with the highest number of popular votes to lose the election in a House of Representatives dominated by one or another political party.

In the twentieth century, we have only narrowly avoided a series of constitutional crises in which the Electoral College could have over-ruled the popular vote.

- In the 1916 presidential election, a shift of only 2,000 votes in California would have given Charles Evans Hughes the necessary electoral votes to defeat Woodrow Wilson, despite Wilson's half-million vote nationwide plurality.
- In 1948, a shift of only 30,000 votes in three states would have delivered the White House to Governor [Thomas] Dewey, in spite of the fact that he trailed President Truman by some 2.1 million popular votes.
- In 1960, a shift of only 13,000 votes in five states (5,000 in Illinois, 5,000 in Missouri, 1,200 in New Mexico, 1,300 in Nevada and 200 in Hawaii) would have made Richard Nixon president.
- In 1968, a shift of 42,000 votes in three states (Alaska, Missouri and New Jersey) would have denied Nixon an Electoral College victory and thrown the election into the House of Representatives.
- In 1976, a shift of only 9,300 votes (5,600 from Ohio and 3,700 from Hawaii) would have elected Gerald Ford, even though he trailed Jimmy Carter in the popular vote by 1.6 million ballots.

Apart from the public outcry that would be caused by a circumvention of the popular will, there are a number of other serious flaws in the Electoral College system.

The Electoral College system is fundamentally unfair to voters. In a nation where voting rights are grounded in the one person, one vote principle, the Electoral College is a hopeless anachronism.

The current system is unfair for two reasons.

First, a citizen's individual vote has more weight if he or she lives in a state with a small population than if that citizen lives in a state with a large population. For example, each electoral vote in Alaska is equivalent to approximately 112,000 people. Each electoral vote in New York is equivalent to approximately 404,000 eligible people (based on 1990 census data). And that's if everyone votes!

The system is also unfair because a citizen's individual vote has more weight if the percentage of voter participation in the state is low. For example, if only half of all people in Alaska vote, then each electoral vote is equivalent to roughly 56,000 people.

Moreover, the electoral vote does not reflect the volume of voter participation within a state. If only a few voters go to the polls, all the electoral votes of the state are still cast.

Finally, the Electoral College system is flawed because the constitution does not bind presidential electors to vote for the candidates to whom they have been pledged. For example, in 1948, 1960 and 1976, individual electors pledged to the top two vote getters cast their votes for third place finishers and also-rans. Defecting electors in a close race could cause a crisis of confidence in our electoral system.

For all these reasons, the League believes that the presidential election method should incorporate the one-person, one-vote principle. The President should be directly elected by the people he or she will represent, just as the other federally elected officials are in this country. Direct election is the most representative system. It is the only system that guarantees the President will have received the most popular votes. It also encourages voter participation by giving voters a direct and equal role in the election of the President.

Of course, a direct popular vote does not preclude the possibility of a close three-way race in which no candidate receives a majority, or even a plurality, of the votes. The League believes that if no candidate receives more than 40 percent of the popular vote, then a national run-off election should be held.

Until there is a constitutional amendment to abolish the Electoral College, the League supports the early establishment of clear rules and procedures for the House and Senate to handle their responsibilities in electing the President and Vice President if there is no majority vote in the Electoral College.

Procedures should be established to avoid the last-minute partisan wrangling that would inevitably take place. In addition, we believe any congressional vote for President must take place in full public view, with individual representative's votes entered into the Congressional Record.

When the constitution was first written, our nation was a vastly different kind of democracy than it is today. Only white, male property owners could vote. The 15th Amendment gave black men the right to vote. The 17th Amendment provided for direct popular election of the Senate. The 19th Amendment gave women the vote. The 26th Amendment established the right of citizens 18 years of age and older to vote.

The time has come to take the next step to ensure a broad-based, representative democracy. Fairness argues for it. Retaining the fragile faith of American voters in our representative system demands it. We urge the House and the Senate to pass a constitutional amendment abolishing the Electoral College system and establishing the direct popular election of our President and Vice President.

The Electoral College: Preserve

JUDITH A. BEST

Critics of the electoral vote system believe that the principle of democratic legitimacy is numbers alone, and therefore they think the system is indefensible. On the contrary, the electoral vote system is a paradigm—the very model—of the American democracy, and thus is quite easy to defend. For all practical purposes it is a direct popular federal election. (The Electors are mere ciphers, and the office of elector, but not the electoral votes, can be abolished.) The critics' principle of democratic legitimacy is inadequate because it is apolitical and anti-federal. Logically it boils down to: the majority must win and the minority must lose no matter what they lose. It is a formula for majority tyranny. But majority rule is not the principle of our Constitution. Rather it is majority rule with minority consent. The critics, however, think that because the system does not follow an arithmetical model it may produce the "wrong" winner. In fact, I contend, because it is federal it produces the right winner.

The following passage from my recent book, *The Choice of the People? Debating the Electoral College* explains my point:

Politics and mathematics are two very different disciplines. Mathematics seeks accuracy, politics seeks harmony. In mathematics an incorrect count loses all value once it is shown to be wrong. In politics even though some people are out-voted they still have value and must be respected in defeat. Efforts must be made to be considerate and even generous to those who lost the vote, to make then feel they are part of the community, for if they feel alienated they may riot in the streets. Further, mathematical questions, like those in all the sciences, deal with truth and falsehood. But politics is an art, not a science. Political questions do not deal primarily with truth and falsehood, but with good and bad. We do not ask whether a political decision on war or taxation or welfare or agricultural subsidies is true. We ask, is the policy good for the country? And, will it actually achieve its purpose?

Those who confuse politics and mathematics, the head counters, operate on an unstated assumption that the will of the people is out there like some unsurveyed land, and all we need do is send out the surveyors with accurately calibrated instruments to record what is there. They also assume that our democratic republic is a ship without a specific destination. Whatever most of the people want, most of the people must get, and the minority be damned. Mathematical accuracy being their sole criterion for legitimacy, they make a great fuss about politically imposed devices, intermediary institutions like the electoral vote system with its federal principle and its winner-take-all rule. From their perspective, such majority building and structuring devices complicate their self-assigned task, distort the accuracy of their count and possibly produce the "wrong" result.

If their assumptions were correct they would have a point. But their assumptions are false. Ours is a ship of state bound for a port called Liberty. On such a ship majority rule doesn't suffice without the consent of the minority. Their assumption about the will of the people is particularly false in this vast and varied country, in a continental republic populated by a people who do not share a common religion, race, or ethnic heritage, in a commercial republic populated by people with diverse and competing economic interests. In such a country the will of the people and the will of the majority can be two very different things. Therefore, the will of the people—that one thing which all can share, which is the goal of liberty for all—must be constructed and periodically reconstructed. This requires a political, not a mathematical process.

In this country, it requires a federal political process. The federal principle is one of the two fundamental structural principles of our Constitution (the other being the separation of powers). The proposals to abolish the Electoral College are proposals to abolish the federal principle in presidential elections. All of our national elective offices are based on the federal principle—they are state based elections for we are a nation of states. Thus our national motto: *E Pluribus Unum*.

The federal principle in presidential elections forces presidential candidates to build broad cross-national political coalitions. Thereby it produces presidents who can govern because of their broad cross-national support. In politics as well as in physics there is such a thing as a critical mass. In presidential elections numbers of votes are necessary but not sufficient. To create the critical mass necessary for a president to govern, his votes must be properly distributed. This means he must win states and win states in more than one region of the country.

Under the federal presidential election system, a successful candidate can't simply promise everything to one section of the country and neglect the others. Analogy: Why are professional football teams required to win games in order to get into the playoffs and win the Super Bowl? Why not simply select the teams that scored the most points during the regular season? Any football fan can tell you why. Such a process wouldn't produce the right winner. Teams would run up the score against their weakest opponents, and the best teams in the most competitive divisions would have the least chance to get into the playoffs. Such a system isn't the proper test of the team talent and ability. A nonfederal election is not a proper test of support for the president.

If we abandon the federal principle in presidential elections, we will be abandoning a national consensus building device by allowing candidates to promise everything to the populous Eastern megalopolis, or to promise everything to white Christians, or to suburbanites who are now half of all the voters. These are formulas for inability to govern or even civil war. And a system, like direct popular election, based on raw unstructured numbers alone rather than on the structuring federal principle, would effectively reduce the influence of minorities who often are the swing votes in closely divided states—groups like farmers who are only 2 percent of national population or blacks who are only 12 percent.

We need to remember that when we change the rules, we change the game and the game strategy and the skills needed to win. Under the federal principle successful candidates must have consensus building skills. The goal of politics in this country is harmony—majority rule with minority consent. But when and why would a minority consent to majority rule? The answer is only if the minority can see that on some occasions and on some vital issues it can be part of the majority. It is irrational to consent to a game in which you can never win anything at all. To gain minority consent, the Framers created many devices to allow minorities to be part of the game, devices that give minorities more influence than their raw numbers would warrant including the state equality principle for representation in the Senate and the state distracting principle for the House of Representatives. (The majority party in the House is often "over-represented" if our measure is raw numbers of votes nationally aggregated.) Then, of course, there is the state equality principle in voting on constitutional amendments. And there is the three-fourths requirement for passage of amendments. Such devices are designed to give minorities an influential voice in defining the national interest. The president is a major player in defining the national interest, and therefore it is necessary that the presidency be subjected to the moderating influence of a federal election system.

An equally important outcome of a state based election system is that it serves to balance local and national interests. It is not just racial, religious, ethnic or occupational minorities that must be protected, there are local minorities whose consent must be sought; the people in small states must be protected against misuse of the phrase "the national interest." My favorite example is the problem of nuclear waste which none of us want in our backyards—not in my state. The rest of us can outvote Utah—so let's turn Utah into our national nuclear waste dump. This is majority tyranny in action. Nuclear waste is a national problem and the burden of solving it should not be placed on the people of one state without their consent. Since the president is a major player in making national policy, it is just as important that he be sensitive to balancing

national and local interests, and the federal election system is designed to make it so. The right winner is a presidential candidate who recognizes the necessity and often the justice in balancing national and local interests. As Jefferson said, "the will of the majority to be rightful must be reasonable." The federal principle even and especially in presidential elections is a device for building reasonable majorities.

The opponents of the electoral vote system are head counters who confuse an election with a census. In a census our goal is mere accuracy. We want to know how many people are married or divorced, or have incomes over or under $20,000, or are Catholic or Protestant etc. In short, we want to break down the population into its multiple individual parts. In an election, especially a presidential election, we want to bring the people together. We want to build consensus, to build the support necessary and sufficient for our president to govern.

The proponents of direct national election think their system solves problems, but in fact it creates problems that are addressed or avoided by the federal election system. Presidential elections have multiple goals. Obviously we want to fill the office with someone who can govern, but we also want a swift, sure decision, and we want to reduce the premium on fraud, and most of us want to support the two party system—a major source of national stability and a consensus, coalition-building system.

From this perspective, the current system has been very successful. Since 1836 with the almost universal adoption of the state unit rule, awarding all of a state's electoral votes to the winner of the popular plurality, we have had never had a contingency election. That's a proven record of 160 years. And we know the reason why: the magnifier effect of the state unit rule, a.k.a. the winner-take-all system. The victor in the popular vote contest for president will have a higher percentage of the electoral vote. The Magnifier effect does not exaggerate the mandate—popular vote percentages are widely reported, not electoral vote percentages. The magnifier effect is not like a fisherman's story in which the size of the fish grows with the telling. Rather it is like the strong fishing line that serves to bring the fish, whatever its size, safely to shore. It supports the moderate two-party system, and balances national and state interests. And it makes the general election the only election.

Of course, there would be no magnifier effect under direct non-federal election, and the result is that contingency elections would become the rule. Under one proposal there would be a national run off if no candidate received 50 percent of the popular vote. This provision would turn the general election into a national primary, proliferate candidacies and weaken or destroy the two-party system. It would also increase the potential for fraud and result in contested general elections with every ballot box in the United States having to be reopened and recounted under court supervision. Even the Left-handed Vegetarians Party could bring a court challenge because 1 percent or less of the popular vote could trigger a runoff election. And there would be a reason to challenge. In a runoff election even candidates who are not in the contest can win something by making a deal with one of the remaining two in return for support in the runoff. Not only would this mean an extended period of uncertainty about who the president will be—a temptation to foreign enemies, but also little time for the orderly transfer of power.

Most proponents of direct election, recognizing that to require a majority of the popular votes would produce these problems, suggest a 40 percent instead of a 50 percent runoff rule. The fact that most supporters of direct election are willing to make this concession indicates the seriousness of the problems attending contingency elections. This is a compromise of their principle—the arithmetical majority principle. Logically, on their principle, whenever no one polls 50 percent plus one vote there should be a runoff election.

And 40 percent is not a magical figure. It could be 42 or 44% with similar result—frequent runoffs. It is true that only one president, Lincoln, (who was not on the ballot in 10 states) failed to reach-the 40 percent plurality figure. However, history under the current system cannot be used to support the 40 percent figure because when you change the rules you change the game. Under the current rules we have had 17 minority presidential terms—presidents who came to the office with less than 50 percent of the popular vote. The last two are Clinton's terms. The list includes some of our best presidents, not only Lincoln, but also Wilson (twice), Polk and Truman. Seventeen minority presidential terms out of 42 presidents! The unit rule magnified their popular pluralities into electoral vote majorities because they won states.

But under direct nonfederal election there would be no magnifier effect. Potential candidates would recognize that multiple entries would be likely to trigger a runoff wherein one losing candidate could win a veto promise, another a Supreme Court nomination and a third a special interest subsidy in return for an endorsement in the runoff. And there is no reason to believe all such deals would be struck in the open. There would be no incentive for coalition building prior to the general election. The two major national parties would lose all control over the presidential nomination process—their lifeblood. Factional candidates, single issue candidates, extremist candidates would serve as spoilers. As one commentator noted, on the day prior to the election, the *New York Times* would have to publish a twenty-page supplement simply to identify all the candidates.

Add to this the second chance psychology that would infect voters, and you have the formula for a national ordeal. Second chance psychology arises from the recognition that a popular vote runoff is a real possibility. Many a voter, thinking he will have another chance to vote in a runoff, will use his general election vote to protest something or other—to send a message.

Recounts would be demanded not only to determine who won, but also whether any candidate actually polled the 40% minimum, and if not which two candidates would be in the runoff—Under the unit rule magnifier effect which discourages multiple candidacies, we have already had five elections in which the popular vote margin was less than one percent. In the 1880 election the margin was one tenth of one percent. If such could happen under the current system where it is unlikely to trigger a runoff, it surely will happen under a 40 percent rule with a hair trigger runoff system. Weeks or months could pass with the outcome in doubt. One candidate could claim victory and start naming his cabinet only to be told some weeks later that he would have to participate in a runoff.

Further, the electorate wearies of prolonged elections. Even in the sports world players as well as teams reach a point where they want an end to it, and so accept sudden death rules. It is so important to fill the office on a timely basis that we have even had one president, Gerald Ford, who was not confirmed by a national election. Ford succeeded to the office on the resignation of his predecessor, Richard Nixon, but unlike vice presidents who had succeeded before him, he had been nominated by Nixon and confirmed by congressional vote under the provisions for filling vice presidential vacancies in the Twenty-fifth Amendment.

No election system is perfect, but the current system has borne the test of time. It has never rejected the winner of a popular vote majority. In every case but one it gave the victory to the winner of the popular plurality. And that one case proves the rule. Cleveland, who lost in the electoral vote, won the popular vote while running a sectional campaign. He did not seek to broaden his support; he focused his message on one section of the country. Unintentionally, he thereby sent a message about the current system to all future presidential candidates: Remember 1888! Don't run a sectional campaign! Further, he won the popular vote by only eight tenths of one percent! This was an election that verged on a tie. Since a timely decision is so important, a reasonable tiebreaker is the win states federal principle.

The proposed amendments would deform not reform the Constitution. It is not just the presidency that is at risk here if the federal principle is illegitimate in presidential elections, why isn't it illegitimate for Senate and House elections? Why should a state with half a million people have the same representation in the Senate as a state with twenty million people? Why should every state have at least one representative in the House? Why shouldn't states with very small populations have to share a representative with folks in another state? And why should each state regardless of its population size have an equal vote on constitutional amendments? The Framers knew the answer to these questions—the federal principle. It is true that the electoral vote system did not work out in precisely the fashion that the Framers anticipated, but it did evolve in conformity to the federal principle and the separation of powers. I have no doubt that they would recognize this if they were here today. It evolved in conformity with the federal spirit of the constitution, the "great discovery," the Framers themselves made.

For this, let us turn to Alexis de Tocqueville, who commenting [in *Democracy in America*, 1835] on the federal principle in the Constitution, called it "a wholly novel theory, which may be considered as a great discovery in modern political science." He goes on to explain that combines the best of both worlds. He says that its advantage is to unite the benefits and avoid the weaknesses of small and large societies. He learned this not only from observation, but also from reading James Madison in *Federalist 39*, who said that our form of government "is, in strictness, neither a national nor a federal Constitution, but a combination of both."

Madison's word "combination" is the key. The federal principle is a "great discovery," because it is a combination like an alloy—my term not his. We create alloys because we want to combine the advantages and avoid the weakness of two different things. We fuse copper and zinc to create brass because brass is harder, more malleable and more ductile than copper. We create steel alloys for the same reason. The federal system is an alloy. It not only makes us strong as a nation, it also allows us to be diverse and flexible, to experiment. It thereby increases our freedom without destroying our national unity. Tocqueville was right; it was a "great discovery" of modern political science. Let us preserve it.

THE CONTINUING DEBATE:
The Electoral College

What Is New

Generally, the country reacted mildly to the oddities of the 2000 election. A few proposals to abolish the Electoral College were introduced in Congress, but they died in committee. Nor did the public react strongly. When one poll pointed out the popular vote/electoral vote mismatch and asked Americans about their reaction, 51% said the outcome was "fair," 46% thought it "unfair," and 3% were unsure. Yet, numerous polls also found about 60% of respondents in favor of instituting direct popular election of the president. Thus Americans were willing to abide by the rules but also favored changing those rules. It is unclear, though, if most people understand the implications of such a change. One poll that asked respondents if they understood the Electoral College found that 69% said they did, just 27% said they did not, and 4% were uncertain. Yet when another poll asked people what the Electoral College did (correct answer: elect the president), only 20% gave the right answer, 35% gave an incorrect answer, and 46% confessed they did not know. Whether the oddities of the 2004 election, especially the issues involving Ohio, spark an effort to change the electoral system remains to be seen.

Where to Find More

An edited book in which contributors discuss various alternatives to the Electoral College and the implications of each is Paul D. Schumaker and, Burdett A. Loomis, *Choosing a President: The Electoral College and Beyond* (Chatham House, 2002). For a defense of the Electoral College, read Gary L. Gregg's edited volume, *Securing Democracy: Why We Have an Electoral College* (Westview, 2001). A valuable Web site for further research is that of the Office of the Federal Register in the National Archives at http://www.archives.gov/federal_register/. The site even has an interactive function that you can use to try to predict the electoral vote count in the next presidential election. Also excellent is the information on the Electoral College on the site of the Federal Election Commission at: http://www.fec.gov/elections.html.

What More to Do

Calculate your state's percentage of the national population and its percentage of the electoral vote. Based on this equation, would your state gain or lose political advantage if the Electoral College were to be abolished?

In addition to debating the future of the Electoral College, it is important to consider the alternatives. If the Electoral College were abolished, how would you determine who is on the ballot? That is now governed by state law, and the candidates vary from state to state. In 2004, there were 20 candidates on one or more state ballots. Some were one-state candidates, such as the Prohibition Party's Earl Dodge, who received 208 votes in Colorado. A national ballot qualifying procedure that was too difficult would restrict democratic choice. A standard that was too easy might replicate the gubernatorial recall election in California in 2003, with 135 candidates on the ballot. Then there is the question of what to do in races with three or more contenders. Does the candidate with the most votes win, even if that is less than 50.1%, or should there be a run-off system to eventually achieve a majority vote? Just since World War II, no presidential candidate has received a majority in 6 (1948, 1960, 1968, 1992, 1996, 2000) of the 14 presidential elections. So, if not the Electoral College, then what?

11   CONGRESS

CONGRESSIONAL TERM LIMITS:
Promoting Choice *or* Restricting Choice?

PROMOTING CHOICE

ADVOCATE: Paul Jacob, Executive Director, U.S. Term Limits

SOURCE: Testimony during hearings on "Limiting Terms of Office for Members of the U.S. Senate and U.S. House of Representatives," U.S. House of Representatives, Committee on the Judiciary, Subcommittee on the Constitution, January 22, 1997

RESTRICTING CHOICE

ADVOCATE: John R. Hibbing, Professor of Political Science, University of Nebraska

SOURCE: Testimony during hearings on "Limiting Terms of Office for Members of the U.S. Senate and U.S. House of Representatives," U.S. House of Representatives, Committee on the Judiciary, Subcommittee on the Constitution, January 22, 1997

One way this debate could have been entitled was with a riddle: "When Does Restricting Voter Choice Improve Democracy?" An alternative riddle/title might have been, "When Does Unrestricted Voter Choice Diminish Democracy?" Those who advocate limiting the number of terms members of Congress may serve argue that incumbents have advantages that make it nearly impossible for challengers to unseat them, thereby limiting the "real" choice of voters. Opponents counter that, among other drawbacks, term limits abridge the voters' democratic right to choose whomever they wish to represent them for as long as they wish.

Statistically, once someone gets elected to Congress they have an extraordinarily good chance of being reelected again. For example, during elections between 1980 and 2002, about 90% of all incumbent members of Congress sought another term, and of those who did, voters returned 93% of the representatives and 89% of the senators. Moreover, incumbents in House races received an average of 71% of the vote in 2002. The senators in office in 2003 had amassed an average 62% of the vote in their previous election. Also indisputable is the fact that the average number of years a person spends in Congress has increased over time. During the 1800s only 3% of representatives and 11% of senators served more than 12 years. Those figures jumped to 27% and 32% during the 1900s, and since 1947 to 35% and 41% respectively.

There are numerous reasons why incumbents have an advantage, which, in sum, create a positive view by most people of their individual members of Congress. One survey found that 62% of respondents approved of the job their members of Congress were doing, only 17% disapproved, and 21% were not sure. This is remarkable given that only 43% of those respondents approved of the job Congress as an institution was doing, with 33% disapproving and 24% unsure.

Term limits have long applied to the tenure of many chief executives. The presidency had a two-term tradition until Franklin Roosevelt sought and won four terms. Soon thereafter, the Twenty-Second Amendment (1951) made the two-term limit mandatory. Additionally, 36 states have term limits for governor. Recently, the idea of also limiting the terms of state and national legislators began to become prominent. California and Oklahoma passed the first such legislation in 1990. It was an idea whose time had come, and soon 20 other states followed suit. Most of these restrictions were enacted by direct democracy techniques, including initiatives and referendums.

Opponents of term limits quickly challenged their constitutionality. In 1995 by a 6 to 3 vote in *U.S. Term Limits, Inc. v. Thornton*, the U.S. Supreme Court struck down the limits that Arkansas (and by implication all other states) had placed on terms in the U.S. Congress. Term limits on state legislatures, by contrast, are matters primarily of state constitutional law, and in this realm, the federal courts and most state courts have upheld term limits.

The Supreme Court decision means that it would be necessary to amend the Constitution in order to limit the number of terms that members of the U.S. Senate and House of Representatives can serve. Part of the "Contract with America" put forth by the successful Republican congressional campaign in 1994 was a pledge to work for such a constitutional amendment, with a limit of two terms (12 years) for senators and 6 terms (12 years) for members of the House. Numerous such proposals were introduced in Congress in 1995, and others have been submitted since then. But none have gathered sufficient support. The "hot topic" of the 1990s faded somewhat in face of the daunting prospect of getting two-thirds of each of the two houses to pass a constitutional amendment and thereby truncate their own political careers. This fate has, among other things, increased the calls to adopt national direct democracy procedures (see Debate 19) and to amend the Constitution so that states can initiate amendments to the U.S. Constitution (see Debate 20). What many see as the problem of entrenched legislators remains, however. The senior senator in the 108th Congress, Robert Byrd, has held his seat since 1959 when Dwight D. Eisenhower was president, and the dean of the House, John Dingle, began his tenure four years before that in 1955 when the current president, George W. Bush was nine years old. As a historical note, the record for the longest combined service in Congress (57 years) is held by Carl Hayden, who served in the House from the time of Arizona's admission to the union in 1912 to 1927, then was in the Senate until 1969. The oldest member ever of Congress was South Carolina Strom Thurmond, who retired at age 100 in 2003 after 48 years in the Senate.

POINTS TO PONDER

➤ Would term limits enhance or diminish Congress' power compared to the president?

➤ John Hibbing notes that senior members of Congress are often more effective in terms of getting legislation passed. Is this because they gain expertise or because they use the power structure to limit the role of junior members?

➤ What impact do you think term limits would have on the proportion of underrepresented groups (such as women and racial and ethnic minorities) in Congress?

Congressional Term Limits: Promoting Choice

PAUL JACOB

America has one clear and decisive advantage over the rest of the world: Our political system.

Our system is unique a democratic republic with constitutional limits on the federal government. It's a system designed to maximize individual freedom and citizen control of government at all levels. Our forebears not only set up this system of protected freedoms, but also recognized the need for change, for continual reform, and for constitutional amendment in order to preserve and enhance our freedom.

George Washington said in his farewell address, "The basis of our political systems is the right of the people to make and alter their constitutions of government." President [Abraham] Lincoln explained: "The country, with its institutions, belongs to the people who inhabit it. Whenever they shall grow weary of the existing government, they can exercise their Constitutional right of amending it." As Thomas Jefferson said to those who object to amending the Constitution, "We might as well require a man to wear still the coat which fitted him when a boy."

The vast majority of Americans today want to amend their Constitution. They want congressional term limits of three terms for House members and two terms for Senators.

EXPERIENCE WITH TERM LIMITS

Term limits is not a new idea. Democracy as far back as Aristotle has known term limits, or rotation in office. Certainly our Founders appreciated rotation in office. John Adams, Ben Franklin, Thomas Jefferson all spoke to the need for limited tenure in public office. Today, term limits are the law of the land for the President, 40 state governors, 20 state legislatures and thousands of local elected officials including many large cities most notably New York and Los Angeles. Americans support congressional term limits not only for what they hope it will do to the culture in Congress, but for what it has already done at other levels of government.

According to Jody Newman, former head of the National Women's Political Caucus, "Our political system is tremendously biased in favor of incumbents." While this has slowed the progress of women and minorities into elected office, term limits are helping to bring more women, minorities and people from all walks of life into politics. This has been the case in cities like New Orleans and Kansas City where record numbers of minorities now hold office as well as the legislature in California which, according to the *Los Angeles Times*, now includes "a former U.S. Air Force fighter pilot, a former sheriff-coroner, a paralegal, a retired teacher, a video store owner, a businesswoman-homemaker, a children's advocate, an interior designer…and a number of businessmen."

Term limits are bringing more competition, and arguably fairer competition. A recent study by Kermit Daniel of the University of Pennsylvania and Joan R. Lott of the University of Chicago concluded: "California's legislative term limits have dramatically reduced campaign expenditures, while at the same time that more candidates are running for office and races are becoming more competitive. The changes are so large that more incumbents are being defeated, races are closer, more candidates are running, and there are fewer single candidate races than at any other time in our sample."

In Ohio, state legislative term limits were credited with helping pass serious ethics reform. "Term limits established a kind of public-interest momentum" according to Ohio Common Cause executive director Janet Lewis, whose group had led the fight against term limits. Robert McCord, a columnist with the *Arkansas Times* declared "the Arkansas House of Representatives has been reborn" after the state's voters enacted a six-year House limit and representatives were quick to dismantle the seniority system.

Anecdotal and empirical evidence abounds that term limits have reduced partisanship, gridlock, and special interest influence. At the same time, more people are running for office, additional reforms are following in the term limits wake, and the disastrous predictions of opponents are being quietly forgotten.

Unfortunately, Congress continues to be locked in partisan warfare, ethics problems, and largely uncompetitive elections. Congress needs term limits.

CONGRESS HAS A CONFLICT OF INTEREST

When the amendment process of the Constitution was originally debated [in 1787], delegate George Byron of Pennsylvania had tremendous vision. He saw the potential of a congressional conflict of interest and warned, "We shall never find two-thirds of a Congress voting for anything which shall derogate from their own authority and importance."

Even with consistent and overwhelming public support, about three out of four Americans believe Congress will refuse to propose a constitutional amendment for term limits. Why? Because Congress has a clear conflict of interest. Term limits is

about limiting your personal power and the power of any individual who takes your place in our system.

Most members of Congress do support the concept of term limits and have for some time. After all, Congress voted by two-thirds of both Houses to propose the Twenty-Second Amendment limiting the President to two terms, eight years, in office. More recently (in the 104th Congress) [1995–1996], 355 members of the House voted to limit committee chairs to three terms. Yet, while supporting and imposing the concept on others, many members do not want limits to apply to them personally.

The congressional conflict of interest results in many members of Congress favoring limits twice as generous as most voters, that is, if they favor any limits at all. Congress has also shown a tremendous ability for political maneuvering on the issue.

Last Congress, the House of Representatives failed to represent their constituents as term limits were defeated by outright opponents and "loved to death" by some questionable friends. The three-term House limit enacted by 15 states and supported by gigantic percentages of voters was opposed by a majority of Republicans, as well as Democrats. Only the freshman Republicans were in sync with the wishes of the American people 72 percent voting for a three-term limit, a constitutional majority itself demonstrating the benefit of regular rotation in office.

This conflict also can be found in some members' demand that Congress, rather than the voters, set the limits. As David Mason of the Heritage Foundation wrote, "At a February 28 [1995] House Judiciary Committee mark-up session on these proposals, a coalition of opponents and wavering supporters amended the McCollum bill, so that it…explicitly would preempt state term limit laws (the original bill was silent on state powers)." What Mr. Mason didn't report was Representative McCollum proposed this amendment to his own bill that would have specifically struck down the shorter term limit imposed on him by the voters of Florida. That the House GOP's point-man on the issue would seek to preempt his own state's term limit law passed by a 77 percent vote is a striking example of his conflict of interest.

The commitment of the House Republican Leadership, especially Speaker Newt Gingrich, has been the subject of much doubt. Television producer Brian Boyer, who spent a great deal of time with Gingrich while filming a 1995 documentary, said, "It was very surprising, and this was, remember, from very long conversations with Gingrich, to learn that he personally is not in favor of term limits." Gingrich's spokesperson Tony Blankley told the *American Spectator* in July of 1994 that term limits was "something conceptually [Newt] doesn't like." Columnist Robert Novak wrote in the *Washington Post*, "Republican leaders profess to want 12 years, but it is clear they prefer no limits at all."

A number of Republicans in the leadership voted against every term limit bill as did five committee chairs. Only one member of the leadership, Majority Leader Dick Armey, and only one committee chair voted for the three-term House limit passed by most states. Yet while Mr. Armey said he would have stripped a member of a committee chairmanship had they like Senator Mark Hatfield voted against the Balanced Budget Amendment, there was no such pressure brought to bear for term limits.

Freshman Michael Forbes of New York told the *New York Times* after the failed House vote, "Candidly, this leadership didn't want [term limits] anymore than the old leadership did." But the American people were not fooled—a *Washington Post*/ABC News poll found close to two-thirds believe neither Republicans nor Democrats in Congress really tried to pass term limits.

THREE TERMS VS. SIX TERMS

The question as to the proper length of the term limits is not merely: What should the limits be? Rather, the essential question is: Who should set the limits? U.S. Term Limits is dedicated to the proposition that the people, not Congress, should set the limits.

Some observers of the battle in Congress over whether House terms should be limited to three terms or six terms have posited that the term limits movement is split. This is simply not the case. The term limits movement is strongly united behind three terms. Only in Congress (and especially among longtime members whose support for any limit whatsoever is questionable) is there significant approval of six terms and fierce opposition to three terms.

Throughout the rest of America, support for three terms far surpasses support for six terms. The American people, pro-limits scholars and virtually every state term limit group in the country supports a three-term limit in the House and a two-term limit in the Senate. Poll after poll demonstrates public support for three terms over six. A 1996 Fabrizio-McLaughlin poll of 1,000 adults nationally found supporters favored three terms 81 percent to 16 percent over six terms.

Not surprisingly, election results bear this out. In every head to head vote three terms has won over six terms. Colorado voters went to the polls in 1994 and voted to lower their limits from six terms to three terms. The arguments in favor of a six-term House limit are so barren, that one such Beltway advocate brazenly and erroneously claims this is "compelling" evidence of support for the longer limit.

ONLY IN WASHINGTON

South Dakota has voted on both a 12-year House limit and a 6-year House limit in separate elections where one would not replace the other. The 6-year limit received 68 percent of the vote to 63 percent for the 12-year limit. After the Wyoming legislature voted to double its state House limits from three terms to six, voters said keep the three-term limit 54 to 46 percent. This even after the sitting governor and three former governors came out in favor of the longer limits.

In fact, the latest trend for politicians opposed to term limits is to pretend to favor term limits, but only longer ones like 12 Years. In New York City, Peter Vallone, Council President and adamant term-limit opponent, was unsuccessful in his attempt to defeat term limits in 1993. Just this past election, he sought to extend the limits from eight years to twelve years. Even with a purposely slanted and misleading ballot title, the voters saw through the council's scheme and rejected this term extension. The same effort to claim support for the term limits concept in order to extend the limits has been and is being repeated in many cities and states with term limits. The voters continue to oppose these term extensions.

The intellectual support for a shorter House limit is also very substantial. A working group of 31 scholars formed by Empower America in December of 1994 studied the term limits issue and concluded, "We put term limits on our agenda, and would even go so far as to favor the specific proposal to limit terms to 6 years in the House and 12 in the Senate."

Mark Petracca, a professor at the University of California-Irvine and a leading scholar on limits, told Congress "my preference is strongly for a limit less expansive than 12 years or 6 terms in the House....A six-term or 12-year limit in the House...won't do much to deprofessionalize the House. Neither may it do much to remedy the other exigencies driving the term limits movement."

David M. Mason of the Heritage Foundation points to "Senate-envy" as the number one reason House members favor the much longer six-term limit and reminds us, "The incumbents' plea for experience only echoes arguments of term limits opponents."

Senator Fred Thompson of Tennessee pointed out one of the reasons people oppose a six-term limit and support three terms. In his 1995 House and Senate testimony, he stated, "Limiting House Members to six terms, instead of the three terms as I have proposed, would leave the seniority system intact and do little to level a playing field that has huge advantages for incumbents." Missouri Senator John Ashcroft recognizes a three-term limit would reduce the incentive for gerrymandering congressional districts for the benefit of incumbents, stating, "it would be one of several benefits exclusive to the 3/2 term proposal..."

Of the major Republican candidates for president in 1996, Lamar Alexander, Pat Buchanan, Steve Forbes, Phil Gramm, and Alan Keyes all supported a limit of three House terms. As Pat Buchanan told the Senate, "Now, what about this 12-year proposal? Well, let me associate myself with what...Lamar Alexander...said. I am unalterably opposed to 12 years. I am for 6 years and out. I know that folks say let's treat both Houses the same way. But the Founding Fathers did not treat both Houses the same way."

There are a plethora of other important policy reasons for enacting a three-term limit as opposed to six terms. Three-term limits will mean greater turnover, more competitive elections, more and quicker campaign reform, and a larger dose of fiscal sanity.

The "Legislative Backgrounder" attached as an appendix to this testimony details further evidence of the public policy benefits associated with a three-term rather than six-term limit.

In reality, many in Congress supposedly favoring a six-term limit appear to not support term limits at all. Representative Bill Barrett of Nebraska has supported the six-term McCollum bill, but wrote in 1995, "I understand voters are frustrated and dissatisfied with the performance of Congress, but I doubt term limits are the answer." Another cosponsor of the McCollum bill is Representative David Camp of Michigan who like Barrett voted against the three-term limits passed in his state. Camp told the *Michigan Midland Daily News* [May 23, 1995], "Voters understand that if they want to limit a member of Congress' term, they can vote for the opponent." These are not the statements of term limit enthusiasts.

In the face of popular and intellectual reasons that three-term limits are superior, the main argument advanced by the longer limit advocates in Congress is that they will simply refuse to support any limits shorter than 6 terms regardless of any support or rationale evidenced against them. This is presented as realism and practicality, but at its core it's the intellectual integrity of a hijacker. Congress in such a case is saying, "The people may have right on their side, but we have the power to ignore them."

INFORMED VOTER LAWS

Nobel prize-winning economist Milton Friedman recognizes the congressional conflict, but also appreciates the ingenuity of the American people in declaring, "Congress is never, not in a million years, going to impose term limits on itself unless it has to."

After the vote in the House in 1995, the American people understood they would have to take matters into their own hands, and they did. The result? In 1996, nine states passed Informed Voter Laws sometimes called Term Limits Accountability Laws. These states are Alaska, Arkansas, Colorado, Idaho, Maine, Missouri, Nebraska, Nevada and South Dakota.

The laws are very simple. First, they instruct members of Congress to support a specific 3/2 term limits amendment written precisely in the initiative. With differing opinions among members of Congress in the past, and the built-in conflict of interest, the voters of these states seek to make the term limits amendment they want explicitly clear.

Secondly, these laws create a procedure for informing the voters if their instructions on term limits are simply disregarded. If members from these states fail to support the 3/2 amendment or attempt to enact watered-down limits longer than 3/2, the Secretary of State will inform the voters by printing "DISREGARDED VOTER INSTRUCTION ON TERM LIMITS" next to the incumbents' names on the ballot.

Candidates who are not incumbents are allowed to sign a pledge to abide by the voters' instructions when they file for the office. If they do not so pledge, the voters will again be informed by the Secretary of State printing "DECLINED TO PLEDGE TO SUPPORT TERM LIMITS" next to their name on the ballot.

Some will argue these laws are unconstitutional. The opponents of term limits have long used the lawsuit as their primary weapon. Already the voters are being sued by special interests and politicians in a number of states trying to overturn the people's vote. But let me suggest the courts will not save politician-kind this time.

Prior to the 1996 election, the Arkansas Supreme Court declared the state's Informed Voter Initiative unconstitutional and removed it from the ballot. The state court argued the measure would cause "potential political deaths" if elected officials did not heed the instructions of an informed public. To this end, I can only say I certainly hope so. But the U.S. Supreme Court did not allow the Arkansas court to deny the people a vote on this measure. In a highly unusual move, the High Court 7 to 2 issued an emergency stay of the state court decision and the voters got their opportunity to cast ballots for or against the Informed Voter Law.

On November 5, more than 60 percent of Arkansans voted to add the Term Limits Informed Voter amendment to their state constitution. Now the U.S. Supreme Court has been petitioned to take the case, and we believe the people of Arkansas will prevail on the merits.

The response to these Informed Voter Laws has been universal shock and horror from the political establishment. What is there to cause such objection? These laws offer congressmen non-binding instructions from the people they work for and are charged with representing. The republican right of instruction is nothing new and surely no elected official could object to his or her constituents making their desires known regarding their government and their very own representative.

The informational aspect of the initiative has been attacked as the Scarlet Letter. Yet term limit enemies do not argue the information is anything but accurate. Their claims that such an "instruct and inform" tactic is coercive are all predicated on their understanding that the public deeply favors term limits and will likely use the accurate information to oppose those not representing their position. Do incumbents have a right to block truthful information harmful to them from the voting public? If citizens are free to make their instructions known, are they to be denied any knowledge as to how their elected representatives have acted? There is no public good in promoting public ignorance on term limits.

Some have argued that the voters will demand similar information on a whole host of issues. They imagine ballot information such as "VOTED TO RAISE TAXES" or "SUPPORTED CONGRESSIONAL PAY RAISE" next to candidates' names. What if it were so? Isn't public education a good thing? If the voters want more information, then they should have it. Yet, similar voter instructions were given and ballot notations used 90 years ago by the Progressives in pursuit of the Seventeenth Amendment for popular election of U.S. Senators and not until now on term limits have citizens returned to this device. The reasons are obvious. Voters understand they must call the tune if they can hope to overcome the political self-interest of members on the issue.

Harry Truman was called "Give 'em Hell Harry." But Truman remarked, "I never did give anybody hell. I just told the truth and they thought it was hell." These Informed Voter Laws likewise only tell the truth, and while they have popular support, term limits opponents will think they're hell. With public knowledge, politicians lose their wiggle-room on an issue that truly matters to voters.

The American people want a constitutional amendment for a three-term limit in the House and a two-term limit in the Senate. The sooner this body proposes such an amendment, the sooner Congress can be reconnected to this great country. For as the great Englishman Edmund Burke said: "In all forms of Government the people [are] the true legislator."

I ask you to put aside all political games and offer a proposal the American people have endorsed. If this Congress chooses to vote it down, so be it. At least the people will have a clean vote on real term limits.

Congressional Term Limits: Restricting Choice

JOHN R. HIBBING

I urge you to do what you can to keep the terms of members of Congress from being limited to a set number. I will organize my case against term limits around three points: the value of congressional experience, the uncertain consequences of term limits for representation, and the inability of term limits to improve the public's opinion of Congress.

CONGRESSIONAL EXPERIENCE

The term limit movement believes it is important to have a constant infusion of "new blood" in Congress lest the body become stale and set in its ways. Opponents of term limits worry that too much new blood would lead to a decrease in both legislative quality and institutional memory as inexperienced members wrestle with devilishly complex issues. Which side is correct? What is the optimal level of membership turnover for an institution like Congress? Most of the debate on these questions has proceeded without any firm evidence for the value of congressional experience. I would like to interject some evidence now.

About 10 years ago, I attempted to determine the manner in which members of this house changed as their careers in Congress unfolded. I found that, with a few exceptions of course, most members did not change much ideologically. Liberals stayed liberal and conservatives stayed conservative. Early career roll call patterns were good predictors of late career roll call patterns. Surprisingly, perhaps, early career electoral results were also good predictors of late career electoral results. It is not the case

that many members transform marginal seats into safe seats. The chances of losing office because of an election are nearly as great for senior members as they are for junior members. Attention to the district, as measured by the number of trips home, diminishes with increasing tenure but only by a little. Most senior members work quite hard at maintaining a presence in the district. Finally, the odds of a member being involved in some type of scandalous behavior do not increase with tenure. Junior members are just as likely as senior members to be scandal-ridden. The popular vision of an inert, uncaring, corrupt, and electorally unchallengeable senior member is simply inaccurate. On each of these counts, senior members are almost no different from junior members.

This statement does not apply, however, when attention shifts to legislative activity, that is, actually formulating and passing legislation. Here I found substantial differences between junior and senior members. Senior members, it turns out, are the heart and the soul of the legislative process. They are more active on legislation (giving speeches, offering amendments, and sponsoring bills), they are more specialized (a greater portion of their legislative attention goes to a focused substantive area), and they are more efficient (a greater percentage of their legislation becomes law). These patterns, I might add, persist even when senior members do not become leaders on committees or subcommittees, so it is not just that member activity reflects the positions of power that some senior members hold. The reasons for altered legislative contributions are broader than that and have to do, simply, with increased legislative experience.

Now, I will be the first to admit that many of these indicators of legislative involvement are badly flawed. It is impossible to measure quantitatively a representative's overall legislative contribution. As members know better than anyone, the legislative process is too rich and subtle to be captured by counting speeches or calculating legislative batting averages. But we must try to understand the relative contributions of senior members if we are to know the consequences of statutorily prohibiting the service of senior members, and here it can be said with some confidence that senior members have more active, focused, and successful legislative agendas. Junior members tend to introduce bills on topics about which they know very little. The subject matter of these bills is all over the map and the bills have precious little chance of making it out of committee let alone becoming law. These are empirical facts. We need more senior members; not fewer.

UNCERTAINTY ABOUT CONSEQUENCES

Many people support the term limit movement because they believe it would make members more responsive to the people. The argument is that Congress has grown out of touch and that if members served only short time periods, along the lines of the citizen legislatures of old, they would be more in touch with the needs and concerns of ordinary people. But there are others who support the term limit movement for exactly the opposite reason. [Columnist] George Will is probably the best-known proponent of the position that term limits should be enacted in order to make Congress less sensitive to the desires of ordinary people. Will and others believe that mandatory term limits would embolden representatives, giving them the nerve to go against public opinion. Only when members know their stint in Congress will soon end, the argument is, will members stop pandering to unrealistic public demands for both lower taxes and more government services. I do not know which side is correct about the consequences of term limits for the proximity of Congress to the people but I do know that the inability of those in the term limit movement to agree amongst themselves on whether Congress is too close or not close enough to the people together with their inability to know whether term limits would in actuality reduce or increase the distance between the people and their Congress should give us pause. Before we enshrine a reform in the Constitution of the United States, should we not at least expect the champions of that reform to know what they want to accomplish?

Public Opinion of Congress

My current research interests have to do with the reasons the public tends to be displeased with Congress. People believe Congress has been captured by special interests, extremist parties, and professionalized politicians and that ordinary folks have been lost in the shuffle. They want changes that would restore the public's role in the process. The only way we can restore public confidence in Congress, some reformers argue, is to enact measures, like term limits, that are central to the public's populist agenda.

It is my belief that term limits would not improve the public's opinion of Congress in the long run. Much public unrest stems from the belief that Congress creates conflict. The common notion is that agreement exists among the masses but that when special interests, parties, and ambitious politicians come together in Congress they manage to construct disagreement where it need not exist. But the truth of the matter is that, while interest groups, parties, and politicians sometimes create conflict, most of the time they only reflect the people's diverse views. Survey research indicates clearly that people are deeply divided over how to solve almost every major societal problem. This disagreement would exist whether or not term limits were enacted. In fact, I contend the public would be even more disillusioned than they are currently once they saw political conflict continuing unabated long after term limits were enacted.

The real solution is to educate people on the extent of their own disagreements and on the difficulties faced by elected officials in moving from these disagreements to responsible, brokered solutions to problems. People harbor beliefs that reforms such as term limits will be able to reduce conflict and the accompanying deliberation (bickering) and compromise (selling out) that they find so objectionable. Nothing could be further from the truth. Rather than pretending there is a magic solution to political conflict, we need to educate the people on the necessity of having learned, experienced legislators who can work their way through the challenging assignment of coming to agreement in the face of public ignorance and uncertainty.

THE CONTINUING DEBATE:
Congressional Term Limits

What Is New

The 2004 elections demonstrated the relative safety of incumbents. Of the 34 senators whose terms were up, 26 sought new terms, and 25 were reelected. There was also scant turnover in the House, to which voters returned 99% of the 400 incumbents who ran again. For the 108th Congress (2003–2005), the average length of service in the House was 9.2 years and the average senator had been serving 10.9 years. If a term limit using the most often discussed parameters (12 years in either chamber) existed, it would mean 163 of 435 members of the House would be barred from seeking reelection in 2004, as would be 70 of 100 senators in their next election.

Since the late 1990s, term-limit advocates have had more defeats than victories. The "informed voter measures" favored by advocate Paul Jacobs did not withstand the test of constitutionality. Those in Missouri were challenged and ruled unconstitutional by the U.S. Supreme Court in *Cook v. Gralike* (2001). As for term limits as such, the Supreme Courts of Massachusetts, Oregon, and Washington struck them down as violating their respective state constitutions. Idaho's legislature repealed limits in 2002, and Utah's legislature followed suit in 2003. The last states to hold a referendum on term limits were Mississippi in 1999 and Nebraska in 2000. In Mississippi, 55% of the voters rejected term limits, making the state the first to do so by direct democracy. Taking the opposite stand, 56% of Nebraska's voters supported term limits. This leaves 16 states with limits in place. A final note is that the concept remains popular with the public. When a 2003 survey asked about term limits, 67% of the respondents said term limits were a "a good idea," 27% thought them a "bad idea," 3% replied "it depends," and 4% were unsure.

Where to Find More

A good new study that presents a series of empirical studies of the impact of term limits on state legislatures is Rick Farmer, John David Rausch, Jr., and John C. Green (eds.), *The Test of Time: Coping with Legislative Term Limits* (Lexington, 2003). U.S. Term Limits, the group represented by advocate Paul Jacob, has a helpful Web site at: http://www.termlimits.org/. You can also find good information on the site of the National Conference of State Legislators at http://www.ncsl.org/programs/legman/about/termlimit.htm.

What More to Do

Think about one or more members of Congress whom you admire or who, because of their seniority, are powerful advocates of positions you support but who, at the end of their current term, will have been in their chamber 12 years or longer. Would you want them to be forced to retire because of term limits?

Consider your two senators and one member of the House. How do they stand with the 12-year rule? Also figure out which of the several U.S. senators who are being mentioned as possible presidential candidates in 2008 would have already had to retire under the 12-year rule or would have to do so in 2006. Would term limits affect the quality of future presidents?

12   PRESIDENCY

QUALIFIED TO BE PRESIDENT:
Natural-Born Citizens Only *or* All Citizens?

NATURAL-BORN CITIZENS ONLY

ADVOCATE: Matthew Spalding, Director, Center of American Studies, The Heritage Foundation

SOURCE: Testimony during hearings on "Maximizing Voter Choice: Opening the Presidency to Naturalized Americans," before the U.S. Senate Judiciary Committee, October 5, 2004

ALL CITIZENS

ADVOCATE: John Yinger, Professor of Economics and Public Administration, The Maxwell School, Syracuse University

SOURCE: Testimony during hearings on "Maximizing Voter Choice: Opening the Presidency to Naturalized Americans," before the U.S. Senate Judiciary Committee, October 5, 2004

It is a constant theme in the mythology of American democracy: Any boy or girl can grow up to be president. American children learn about such humble beginnings as Abraham Lincoln being born in a log cabin. And politicians trumpet them. For example, the first line of Richard Nixon's autobiography, *RN*, is, "I was born in the house my father built." Similarly, President Jimmy Carter's wife Rosalyn has recalled that in the elementary school both she and the president attended, their teacher Julia Coleman would tell her students, "We had to be prepared for the outside world. She reminded us that in a country as great as ours, 'any…one of [us], might grow up to be President of the United States'."

As it turns out, though, it is not true that any American boy or girl can theoretically grow up to be president. Young Henry Kissinger could not, even though he would one day become Secretary of State. Neither could Madeleine Albright, the girl who grew up to be the first female Secretary of State. More currently, the youths who grew up to be Governor Jennifer Granholm of Michigan and California's Governor Arnold Schwarzenegger are also ineligible. Indeed, well over a hundred million boys and girls growing up in the United States throughout its history have been unable to aspire to lead their country.

What stands between Governor Granholm, Governor Schwarzenegger, and millions of other Americans from being inaugurated as president is Article II, section 1 of the Constitution, which reads, "No person except a natural-born citizen, or citizen of the United States at the time of the adoption of this Constitution, shall be eligible to the office of president." With all Americans who were foreign-born in 1789 long gone, this means that anyone who is not a citizen of the United States by birth cannot become president. According to the 2000 census, this includes 28.4 million resident of the United States, or about 10% of the population, who are foreign-born, legal immigrants. Of these, 10.6 million have already become citizens, and another 17.6 million are eligible for U.S. citizenship when they have completed the naturalization process under U.S. laws. Oddly, although the process of becoming a citizen is officially called *naturalization*, that does not imply that those granted citizen are natural-born citizens.

It should be noted that this does not mean that being born in a foreign country as such creates the barrier. The rules are complex, but generally children born of American parents anywhere are American citizens, and they would almost certainly be considered natural born. Among other things, the First Congress enacted legislation in 1790 specifying, "The children of citizens of the United States that may be born beyond sea, or outside the limits of the United States, shall be considered as natural-born citizens of the United States." Beyond this, there are some cases where who are natural-born citizens and who are statutory citizens (naturalized, have become citizens according to provisions of statutory law) is not totally clear because the courts have never dealt with this issue. For example, there is disagreement about whether Puerto Ricans born in Puerto Rico can become president because they were made citizens by statute in 1917, and because Puerto Rico is a commonwealth of the United States, not fully part of it.

Why were foreign-born citizens constitutionally barred from becoming president? The answer is not entirely clear because the direct historical record from the documents of the Constitutional Convention and the *Federalist Papers* is nearly nonexistent, as the advocates in the two accompanying articles explain. But they also discuss the general feeling among historians about the origins of the clause based on indirect evidence.

The issue of the ineligibility of naturalized citizens for the presidency has regularly arisen in Congress, as it did in 2000 when Representative Barney Frank (D-MA) introduced House Joint Resolution 68 to allow foreign-born citizens to become president. That proposal engendered the hearings from which the two articles below are drawn. Like other such proposals, however, Frank's died in committee after the hearings. At least one reason this idea has never gotten very far is public opinion about it. An October 2003 national poll found that 64% of respondents opposed making naturalized citizens eligible to be president, with 29% in favor and 7% unsure.

To return briefly to the idea that every boy and girl can become president, that bit of Americana does not mean that parents or their children necessarily want that to happen on a personal level. In a 1999 survey, 53% of adults thought their children could grow up to be president, but only 30% wanted them to do so. Teenagers were more optimistic about their chances, with 62% thinking they could someday be president. But they were even more turned off than their parents by the prospect, with only 17% wanting to one day occupy the Oval Office.

POINTS TO PONDER

➤ Advocates Matthew Spalding and John Yinger both extensively detail the views of the framers of the Constitution on the subject of eligibility for the presidency. More than two centuries later, how relevant are such views?

➤ Do you think there is a relationship between people's views on this topic and their views on some other debates, especially Debate 5 on immigration?

➤ If John Yinger is correct that allowing naturalized citizens to become president is a matter of equal rights, should the age restriction also be abolished to make adult citizens ages 18 through 34 eligible to be president?

Qualified to Be President:
Natural-Born Citizens Only

MATTHEW SPALDING

More than any other nation in history, this country and its system of equal justice and economic freedom beckons not only the downtrodden and the persecuted—indeed, all those "yearning to breathe free"—but also those who seek opportunity and a better future for themselves and their posterity.

By the very nature of the principles upon which it is established, the United States encourages immigration and promotes the transformation of those immigrants into Americans—welcoming newcomers while insisting on their learning and embracing America's civic culture and political institutions, thereby forming one nation from many peoples.

"The bosom of America is open to receive not only the opulent and respectable stranger," George Washington wrote, " but the oppressed and persecuted of all Nations and Religions; whom we shall welcome to a participation of all our rights and privileges if, by decency and propriety of conduct, they appear to merit the enjoyment."

Yet there is one legal limitation on the potential rights of immigrant citizens: only those who are native born can become president of the United States. Why the exception to this otherwise universal principle? The immediate answer seems to be clear: Poland, where in 1772, as the historian Forrest McDonald explains, "the secret services of Austria, Prussia and Russia had connived to engineer the election of their own choice for king, whereupon the entirety of Poland was partitioned and divided among those three powers." Indeed, South Carolina delegate Charles Pinckney worried that "in not many years

the fate of Poland may be that of the United States."

Perhaps with this in mind, John Jay, then Superintendent of Foreign Affairs wrote to Washington, as president of the Convention, urging that it would be "wise & seasonable to provide a strong check to the admission of Foreigners into the administration of our national Government; and to declare expressly that the Command in chief of the American army shall not be given to, nor devolve on, any but a natural born Citizen." Thus the phrase, as Justice Joseph Story later explained in his *Commentaries on the Constitution*, "cuts off all chances for ambitious foreigners, who might otherwise be intriguing for the office."

But there is something more going on here as well, that points back to the Founders' general views about immigration. The purpose of immigration policy, as Hamilton put it succinctly, was for immigrants "to get rid of foreign and acquire American attachments; to learn the principles and imbibe the spirit of our government." The immediate fear was a foreign takeover, but the larger concern was foreign influence.

At the Constitutional Convention there was a lively and illuminating debate about the eligibility of foreign immigrants for federal office. Elbridge Gerry wanted to restrict membership to those born in the United States, while Gouverneur Morris and Charles Pinckney advocated a qualifying period of at least 14 years before eligibility. George Mason was all for "opening a wide door for emigrants; but did not choose to let foreigners and adventurers make law for and govern us." Indeed, were it not for the many immigrants who had acquired great merit in the Revolution, he, too, would be "for restraining the eligibility into the Senate to natives."

Other, more numerous delegates vigorously criticized this position. Scottish-born James Wilson knew from experience "the discouragement and mortification [immigrants] must feel from the degrading discrimination now proposed." Benjamin Franklin opposed such illiberality and argued that when a foreigner gives a preference to America "it is a proof of attachment which ought to excite our confidence and affection." James Madison wanted to maintain the "character of liberality" of the state governments and "to invite foreigners of merit and republican principles among us," while West Indies-born Alexander Hamilton spoke of attracting respectable immigrants who would "be on a level with the First Citizens."

These views prevailed and the Constitution required relatively modest residency periods for immigrant citizens who aspired to the federal legislature: seven years for the House and nine years for the Senate. This was long enough, Madison later wrote in The Federalist, to assure that legislators are "thoroughly weaned from the prepossessions and habits incident to foreign birth and education."

But again, why the natural born citizenship requirement for the presidency? In the House of Representatives and the Senate, members check each other and diffuse the influence of any one individual. Not so in the case of the president. With a single executive, at the end of the day, there are no checks, no multiplicity of interests that would override the possibility of foreign intrigue or influence, or mitigate any lingering favoritism—or hatred—for another homeland.

The attachment of the president must be absolute, and absolute attachment comes most often from being born and raised in—and educated and formed by—this country, unalloyed by other native allegiances. "The safety of a republic," as Hamilton observed, "depends essentially on the energy of a common national sentiment; on a uniformity of principles and habits; on the exemption of the citizens from foreign bias, and prejudice; and on that love of country which will almost invariably be found to be closely connected with birth, education, and family." The natural born citizen requirement for the presidency seeks to guarantee, as much as possible, this outcome where it matters most.

And while the practical circumstances have changed—there is no threat of a foreign royal taking the reins of power—the underlying concerns about foreign attachments and favoritism, and the need for absolute allegiance and loyalty in the executive, still make sense....

Let me add [two other brief points]:

1. Opening the presidency to naturalized citizens, who in theory but often not in practice have renounced their past allegiances, compels us to consider the question of Dual Citizenship. This is a significant issue and...could be a particularly thorny problem. If the natural born citizen requirement violates the idea that anyone can become an American, so the reality of multiple citizenships violates the idea that becoming an American is meaningful.

2. I am concerned about the politicization of this question....It should not be resolved based on immediate calculations to advance or hinder the political aspirations of any particular individual or party....

Qualified to Be President:
All Citizens

JOHN YINGER

1. INTRODUCTION

One of the cornerstones of American democracy is the "self-evident truth" in the Declaration of Independence that "all men are created equal." This truth leads directly to the principle that all citizens should have equal rights. The U.S. Constitution made historic contributions, of course, to the establishment of this principle, by, among other things, setting up the popular election of members of the House of Representatives and by allowing even naturalized citizens, after a waiting period of a few years, to run for the Senate or the House of Representatives.

It is equally true, of course, that the Founding Fathers did not fully implement the equal-rights principle, and throughout its history, this nation has moved toward completing this task. The Constitution's most important limitations on this score obviously were that it allowed the states to disenfranchise people on the basis of sex and race. The Fourteenth, Fifteenth, and Nineteenth Amendments to the Constitution, along with extensive civil rights legislation, have been passed to remove these limitations. The vast majority of American citizens now embrace the principle that all citizens should have equal rights, and our equal-rights legislation has made us a beacon of hope for people around the world striving for freedom and justice.

[We should follow]…the path toward equal rights, namely, ensuring that naturalized American citizens have exactly the same rights as natural-born American citizens. The only difference in rights between these two groups is that naturalized citizens can-

not run for president or vice president. This difference comes from the clause in the Constitution that limits the presidency to natural-born citizens, along with the Twelfth Amendment to the Constitution, which implicitly extends this limitation to the office of Vice president. Thus, the quintessential dream of our democracy, the dream of being able to grow up to be president, is withheld, for no good reason, from millions of naturalized American citizens.…

The provision in the Constitution that limits presidential eligibility to natural-born citizens grew out of the Founders' fear of foreign influence. As I will show in this statement, however, the Founders expressed serious doubts about this provision, and, as the Founders' own arguments make clear, this provision is both unwise and unnecessary. We should not let a misplaced fear of foreigners prevent us from removing this anachronistic provision from the Constitution and thereby reaffirming the principle of equal rights for all American citizens.

2. THE FOUNDERS' DOUBTS ABOUT THE NATURAL-BORN CITIZEN REQUIREMENT

The issue of presidential eligibility was first raised at the Constitutional Convention fairly early in the deliberations. On July 26, 1787, George Mason of Virginia moved that a committee "be instructed to receive a clause requiring certain qualifications of landed property and citizenship of the United States in members of the legislature." Two other delegates, Charles Pinckney and Charles Cotesworth Pinckney of South Carolina, then "moved to insert by way of amendment the words Judiciary & Executive so as to extend the qualifications to those departments." This motion carried unanimously. Hence, the Founders' first instinct was to allow all citizens, naturalized and natural-born, to run for president. Moreover, the first draft of the presidential eligibility clause, which appeared on August 22, includes only a time-of-citizenship requirement.

The version of the presidential eligibility clause that excludes naturalized citizens did not appear until the final grand compromise on September 4, less than two weeks before the Constitution was signed by most of the delegates. This version was accepted unanimously with no record of any debate. In fact, however, the Founders provided considerable evidence concerning their feelings about restricting the rights of naturalized citizens, and most of these feelings were negative. In this section, I discuss three examples of this evidence: the grandfather clause concerning presidential eligibility, the Founders' recognition that second-class citizenship for naturalized citizens violates the equal-rights principle, and the Founders' demonstrated trust in naturalized citizens.

The Grandfather Clause

The first source of evidence about the Founders' views concerning the treatment of naturalized citizens comes from the presidential eligibility clause itself, which reveals that the Founders did really not want to prevent all naturalized citizens from running for president. To be specific, this clause grants presidential eligibility to any "Citizen of the United States at the time of the Adoption of this Constitution."

This "grandfather" clause gave presidential eligibility to tens of thousands of naturalized citizens, included seven of the people who signed the Constitution. If the Founders thought that, among people meeting the fourteen-year residency

requirement, naturalized citizens were inherently unqualified to be president or that naturalized citizens were inherently more likely than natural-born citizens to be subject to foreign influence, then they would not have included this provision.

According to this clause, presidential eligibility was granted to all naturalized citizens at the time the Constitution was adopted in 1789. Based on information available from the U.S. Census, I estimate that roughly 60,000 foreign-born American citizens were eligible to run for president in the elections of 1796 and 1800. Moreover, about 1,500 of these people were born in France and about 10,000 were born in Great Britain, countries that were at odds with the United States in those years.

Thus, the grandfather clause granted presidential eligibility to about 60,000 foreign-born citizens, including citizens from countries in conflict with the United States. The Founders' ambivalence about limiting presidential eligibility to natural-born citizens is evident in the presidential eligibility clause itself for anyone to see.

Statements that Second-Class Citizenship for Naturalized Citizens Violates the Equal-Rights Principle

Although the records of the Constitutional Convention contain no mention of a debate about the presidential eligibility clause itself, they contain evidence about the Founders' views concerning second-class citizenship for naturalized citizens.

This evidence comes from the debates concerning the time-of-citizenship requirements for the Senate and the House of Representatives....The key issue in these debates was whether to set long or short time-of-citizenship requirements. The delegates all agreed that long requirements placed an extra burden on naturalized citizens, but some delegates thought this extra burden was appropriate and others did not.

A few of the delegates raised the issue of restricting eligibility to natural-born citizens, but no delegate moved to include such a restriction in the Constitution, and only one delegate, Elbridge Gerry of Massachusetts, made a statement in support of such a restriction.

In contrast, numerous delegates spoke out against long time-of-citizenship requirements and, implicitly, against stronger restrictions on naturalized citizens, such as making them ineligible altogether. The most eloquent statements on this matter come from James Madison, who is often called the father of the Constitution. Madison declared that a severe restriction on the rights of naturalized citizens would be "Improper: because it will give a tincture of illiberality to the Constitution." He was seconded by Benjamin Franklin "who was not against a reasonable time [that is, a reasonable time-of-citizenship requirement], but should be very sorry to see any thing like illiberality inserted in the Constitution."

Another important argument about naturalized citizens was then made by Edmond Randolph of Virginia, who "could never agree to the motion for disabling them for 14 years to participate in the public honors. He reminded the Convention of the language held by our patriots during the Revolution, and the principles laid down in all our American Constitutions." Randolph is referring to the state constitutions passed shortly after the Declaration of Independence, none of which placed limits on the rights of naturalized citizens....

At the time of independence, eleven of the thirteen original colonies adopted new state constitutions. Not one of these constitutions restricted the rights of naturalized citizens. Two cases are particularly instructive. In Virginia, a draft constitution was written by Thomas Jefferson in June, 1776. This document has special historical significance because it contains a preliminary version of the grievances that would appear in the Declaration of Independence the next month. In addition, this draft includes the following naturalization clause:

> All persons who by their own oath or affirmation, or by other testimony shall give satisfactory proof to any court of record in this colony that they propose to reside in the same 7 years at the least and who shall subscribe the fundamental laws, shall be considered as residents and entitled to all the rights of persons natural born.

The draft goes on to say that "every person so qualified to elect shall be capable of being elected" and thereby explicitly makes naturalized citizens eligible for all statewide offices. Although this specific wording was edited out of the final version of the Virginia Constitution, its spirit remained, and this constitution does not place any restrictions on the rights of naturalized citizens.

In the case of New York, the constitution of 1776, which was drafted by John Jay, gives the right of suffrage to "every male inhabitant of full age, who shall have personally resided within one of the counties of this State for six months" and who is a "freeholder," that is, a person who owns property. This constitution also says that the "freeholders" must elect the governor, with no explicit statement about the governor's qualification. Among other powers, the governor was declared to "be general and commander-in-chief of all the militia, and admiral of the navy of this State." Finally, this constitution gives the state legislature the power to naturalize foreigners and to make them "subjects of this state," with no qualifications concerning their rights.

John Jay's role in drafting this constitution is intriguing because many historians believe that Jay is responsible for the natural-born citizen requirement in the U.S.

Constitution thanks to a letter he wrote George Washington, who presided over the Constitutional Convention. Jay, who was well known but not a delegate to the Convention, suggested that foreign influence could be minimized by limiting the "command in chief of the American army" to "a natural born citizen." Thus, John Jay's own position appears to be contradictory: he saw no need for a natural-born citizen requirement for New York's governor and commander in chief, but then, a decade later, called for such a requirement for the nation as a whole.

In short, speaking though the state constitutions and the debate at the Constitutional Convention, many of our Founding Fathers considered restrictions on the rights of naturalized citizens to be violations of the fundamental principle of equal rights for all citizens. As Madison put it many years later, "Equal laws, protecting equal rights, are found, as they ought to be presumed, the best guarantee of loyalty and love of country."

Demonstrated Trust in Naturalized Citizens

Presidents George Washington, John Adams, and James Madison revealed their lack of concern about nativity by, among other things, offering high-level federal positions to some of the foreign-born delegates to the Constitutional Convention. Washington appointed William Paterson and James Wilson to the U.S. Supreme Court; he made James McHenry Secretary of the Army; he offered to make Robert Morris Secretary of the Treasury and then gave the job to Alexander Hamilton when Morris turned him down. Adams kept McHenry and Hamilton in his cabinet, later appointed Hamilton as Inspector-General of the Army, and made William Davie first a brigadier general and then Peace Commissioner to France. Finally,

Madison offered Davie an appointment as a major-general, but this offer was declined.

An even more dramatic declaration of the Founders' ambivalence, if not outright hostility, toward the natural-born-citizen requirement came out of the U.S. Senate in 1798. In this year, the Senate was full of men who had participated in the founding of the United States. Two senators (John Langdon of New Hampshire and Charles Pinckney of South Carolina) had been delegates to the Constitutional Convention. All but three of the remaining senators had served in at least one of the following: the American Army during the Revolutionary War, the Continental Congress, a state convention to ratify the U.S. Constitution, and the House of Representatives. In December, these men elected a naturalized citizen, John Laurance of New York, to be President Pro Tempore of the Senate.

This action is particularly significant for two reasons. First, the grandfather clause applied to Laurance. He was born in England in 1750, sailed to America in 1767, and was admitted to the bar in 1772—all well before the adoption date of 1789. Second, the Presidential Succession Act of 1792 placed the President Pro Tempore second in the line of succession to the presidency. For a brief period in 1798, therefore, a naturalized citizen, John Laurance, stood behind only Vice President Thomas Jefferson in the sequence of succession.

During this year, the notorious XYZ affair stirred up American patriotism, and tensions between the United States and both Great Britain and France were very high. In the summer of 1798, the Senate responded by passing the infamous Alien and Sedition Acts, which authorized the president to deport "dangerous" aliens and also imposed penalties for "malicious writing." Moreover, the year before, William Blount, a natural-born citizen who had been a delegate to the Constitutional

Convention, was expelled from the Senate for the "high misdemeanor" of conspiring with the British.

Despite the turbulence of the times, however, the Senate clearly believed that a man with a distinguished record of service to the United States, namely Laurance, should not be disqualified for the presidency simply because he was born in another country, even a country at odds with the United States.

3. THE CASE FOR REMOVING THE NATURAL-BORN CITIZEN REQUIREMENT

Thanks to 9/11, this country once again finds itself in a time characterized by concern about the influence of foreigners in the United States. Why is this a good time to eliminate the natural-born citizen requirement? In this section, I evaluate key argument for and against such a change.

Arguments for Removing the Natural-Born Citizen Requirement

The natural-born citizen requirement (including its implicit extension to the vice president in the Twelfth Amendment) is the only provision in the Constitution, or in our laws, for that matter, that explicitly denies rights to an American citizen based on one of that citizen's indelible characteristics. The equal-rights principle is fundamental to our democracy, and throughout our history we have struggled to extend it. By sanctioning one exception to this principle, we leave open the door to other exceptions. We will strengthen out democracy by closing this door.

The Fourteenth Amendment, which is one of the crowning achievements in this nation's struggle to promote equal rights, says, in part, all persons born or naturalized in the United States, and subject to the jurisdiction thereof, are citizens of the United States and of the state wherein they

reside. No state shall make or enforce any law which shall abridge the privileges or immunities of citizens of the United States; nor shall any state deprive any person of life, liberty, or property, without due process of law; nor deny to any person within its jurisdiction the equal protection of the laws.

This amendment prohibits the states from treating naturalized citizens any differently from natural-born citizens. The same prohibition should apply to the federal government. As the U.S. Supreme Court said in another context, "it would be unthinkable that the same Constitution would impose a lesser duty on the federal government." In the case of the natural-born citizen requirement, however, the Constitution does impose a lesser duty on the federal government than the duty imposed on the states by the Fourteenth Amendment. This "unthinkable" contradiction should be removed.

Eliminating the natural-born citizen requirement from the Constitution would also send a powerful message to people around the world about this nation's commitment to equal rights. We will judge all or our citizens on their merits, this change would say, not on their place of birth. In these troubled times, a statement of this type can only serve to enhance our reputation as the world's standard bearer for democratic values.

Arguments against Removing the Natural-Born Citizen Requirement

Some people have argued recently that we need to keep the natural-born citizen requirement because it makes this country safer. This argument is simply not true.

The delegates to the Constitutional Convention obviously wanted to protect the United States from foreign influence. This concern played an important role in many of their decisions, including the creation of a strong central government, the design of the Electoral College, and the system of checks and balances.

The relationship between foreign influence and the provisions in the Constitution is discussed at length in the Federalist Papers, which are, of course, key documents in interpreting the Founders intentions. Essays 2 through 5, which were written by John Jay, were titled "Concerning Dangers from Foreign Force and Influence." Although the main focus of these essays is on the need for a strong central government to protect a nation from foreign military action, they also suggest that a strong central government can help protect a nation from "foreign influence." Concern about foreign influence also appears in essay 20, written by Hamilton and Madison; essay 43 by Madison; and essays 66, 68, and 75 by Hamilton.

The role of the presidential selection mechanism, and in particular of the Electoral College, in limiting foreign influence is explicitly discussed by Hamilton in essay 68. Neither this essay, however, nor any of the others, refers to the natural-born citizen requirement. To these three influential Founders, this requirement is not important enough to mention. Even John Jay, whose letter may have inspired the requirement, does not bring it up.

Despite all the protections built into the governmental system created by the Constitution, some people still insist that we gain additional protection from the natural-born citizen requirement. If naturalized citizens were allowed to run for president, these people argue, foreign powers might scheme to have their citizens elected here. In fact, however, this Manchurian Candidate imagery has two major flaws. The first flaw was articulated by…Representative Charles T. Canady [R-FL]…during hearings…on this issue in 2000. According to Canady, eliminating the natural-born citizen require-

ment would not give naturalized citizens "a right to be president"—only a right to run for president.

Moreover, any naturalized citizen running for president would face an extremely high burden convincing a majority of the American people that he or she is the best candidate for president. This point was made by Madison [in 1787]. "For the same reason that they [men with foreign predilections] would be attached to their native country, our own people would prefer natives of this Country to them. Experience proved this to be the case. Instances were rare of a foreigner being elected by the people within any short space after his coming among us."

The second flaw in the Manchurian Candidate image is that any foreign power wishing to undermine our government is more likely to use a natural-born citizen than a naturalized one, precisely because of the suspicion falling on naturalized citizens. This argument was forcefully made by Madison at the Constitutional Convention. He said that "He was not apprehensive …that foreign powers would make use of strangers as instruments for their purposes. Their bribes would be expended on men whose circumstances would rather stifle than excite jealousy and watchfulness in the public."

Restricting the rights of all naturalized citizens out of the fear than one of them might try to undermine our government by running for president is an extreme form of profiling with no basis in logic or history. Does it make sense to discriminate against 12.8 million naturalized citizens, including over 250,000 foreign-born adoptees, because one of them might both harbor negative attitudes toward this country and decide to run for president? Of course not: It makes no sense at all. The natural-born citizen requirement may make some people feel better, but it adds nothing of substance to the extensive protection provided by our constitutional election procedures, by our checks and balances, and by the judgment of the American people.

Another argument against changing the natural-born citizen requirement is that it is a poor subject for a constitutional amendment, either because it is tied to the political fortunes of a particular person or because it is just not important enough to justify altering the Constitution.

A constitutional amendment to eliminate the natural-born citizen requirement might, depending on its time-of-citizenship requirement, enable two current governors, Arnold Schwarzenegger of California and Jennifer Granholm of Michigan to run for president. Both of these governors are naturalized citizens. Some people have argued for or against an amendment because of their feelings about one of these governors. In my view, however, this amendment is about principle, not politics.

We do not disqualify other potential presidential candidates on the basis of their experience or their stands on substantive issues, and we should not disqualify Governors Schwarzenegger or Granholm, either. The principle of equal rights for all American citizens should not have an exception based on nativity—or on any other indelible characteristic—and these two governors should be allowed to run for president if they choose to do so.

This principle does not imply, of course, that voters would have to ignore a candidate's nativity, and, as Madison said long ago, it might be more difficult for Governors Schwarzenegger and Granholm than for a natural-born candidate to convince voters that they would act in our country's best interests. Instead, the principle of equal rights simply requires than neither of these governors nor any other citizen be automatically disqualified from the presidency because of their place of birth.

The argument that presidential eligibility is not substantive enough for a constitutional amendment also does not hold up under scrutiny. The distinguished, non-partisan organization called the Constitution Project has developed a series of guidelines for constitutional amendments. According to these guidelines, a constitutional amendment "should address matters...that are likely to be recognized as of abiding importance by subsequent generations," "should be utilized only when there are significant practical or legal obstacles to the achievement of the same objectives by other means;" "should not be adopted when they would damage the cohesiveness of constitutional doctrine as a whole;" and "should embody enforceable, and not purely aspirational, guidelines."

An amendment to eliminate the natural-born citizen requirement clearly meets all of these tests. The equal-rights principal is a matter of "abiding importance." Because the natural-born citizen requirement is in the Constitution, there are significant legal obstacles to obtaining equal rights through other means. As pointed out earlier, this requirement contradicts the Fourteenth Amendment, so eliminating it would actually enhance constitutional doctrine as a whole. And an amendment to eliminate this requirement would obviously be easy to enforce....

4. A SIMPLE MATTER OF EQUAL RIGHTS

The principles on which our democracy is founded need to be protected, extended, and reaffirmed....[by amending the Constitution and thus supporting one of our most fundamental principles, namely, the principle that all American citizens should have equal rights.

In practical terms, the right to run for president is not the most important right a citizen can have. After all, the vast majority of American citizens will never attempt to run for president. In symbolic terms, however, the right to run for president is vitally important.

Commentators, politicians, and teachers are fond of saying that the United States is a country where anyone can grow up to be president, because this expression conveys the essence of our democracy. This expression clearly sends the signal that political offices in this country are not inherited or restricted to a select few, but instead are open to anyone who can convince the voters of his or her merit.

THE CONTINUING DEBATE:
Qualified to Be President

What Is New

Numerous new proposals to make foreign-born citizens eligible to become president have been introduced in recent years. Sponsors in the House have ranged from liberals such as Barney Frank (D-MA) to conservatives such Darrell Issa (R-CA). In the Senate, Orrin Hatch (R-UT) introduced the "Equal Opportunity to Govern" amendment, designating a 20-year citizenship waiting period before eligibility. Although Hatch is politically friendly with Arnold Schwarzenegger, and even though the 20 years that Hatch proposed in 2003 neatly fits with period since the governor became a citizen in 1983, the senator denied that the possibility of a President Schwarzenegger was connected to the proposed constitutional amendment. Still, doubters dubbed Hatch's proposal the "Arnold amendment."

More important than the Schwarzenegger factor, changing demographics have brought new prominence to the issue. Changed immigration laws have increased the percentage of foreign-born citizens, and that figure continues to grow. Moreover, politics is becoming more diverse, with an increased number of naturalized citizens in prominent positions. Ironically, two members of President George W. Bush's cabinet whose office put them in the line of succession to the presidency are constitutionally excluded. These two Cabinet members are Secretary of Labor Elaine Chao, who was born in Taiwan, and Secretary of Housing and Urban Development Mel Martinez, who is a native of Cuba.

Where to Find More

You can find out more on the attempt in the House and Senate during the 109th Congress (2005–2007) or any previous Congress to amend the constitution on this issue by going to Thomas, the Web site of Congress, at http://thomas.loc.gov/. For the proposal made in 2005, search for House Joint Resolutions 2, 15, and 42.

There is surprisingly little written on this subject. Among the few short essays available is Erin Montgomery, "Immigrants for President?" *The Weekly Standard*, October 24, 2003, which is available on the Web at http://www.weeklystandard.com/Search/FreeSearch.asp, then keyboarding in the author's name in the search window. If the proposed amendments submitted in Congress begin to move toward passage, there will be an upsurge of articles and other sources that can be accessed, among other ways, by entering such word combinations as "natural born," "president," and "amendment" into the leading search engine, Google.

What More to Do

There are two suggestions here about what more to do, and they parallel similar suggestion in many of the other debates herein. First, stimulate your intellect by finding out more about what is going on and the arguments pro and con, then debating or discussing the issue with your friends and classmates. At least as important, perhaps more so, is to get involved in the national debate by letting your members of Congress know what you think, by writing an op-ed piece for a newspaper or other publication, by joining a group that is active on the issue, or by taking any one of the myriad other steps available to ensure you have a voice. It is, after all, your country; it is a democracy, albeit an indirect one; and the mantra for each citizen in a democracy with this and every other issue in this volume should be, **You Decide!**

13   BUREAUCRACY

THE DEPARTMENT OF EDUCATION AND TITLE IX:
Champion of Equality *or* Overzealous Crusader?

CHAMPION OF EQUALITY

ADVOCATE: Judith Sweet, Vice-President for Championships and Senior Women Administrator, National Collegiate Athletic Association

SOURCE: U.S. Department of Education, Secretary's Commission on Opportunity in Athletics, Hearings, August 27, 2002

OVERZEALOUS CRUSADER

ADVOCATE: Amanda Ross-Edwards, Visiting Professor of Political Science, Fairfield University

SOURCE: "The Department of Education and Title IX: Flawed Interpretation and Implementation," an essay written especially for this volume, October 2003

We tend to think that elected representatives serving in Congress and, to a degree, the elected president, make federal rules. However, in terms of sheer volume, non-elected agency officials make most government rules. Off these functionaries, the president appoints about 600, with career civil servants making up the rest of the 2.8 million civilian federal employees.

One measure of the deluge of bureaucratic rules is the *Federal Register*, the annual compilation of new rules, rule changes, and other authoritative bureaucratic actions. Just for 2003, the *Federal Register* was an immense 75,795 pages of regulations addressing almost every conceivable subject. So great is the impact of the rulemaking and implementation authority of the bureaucracy that some analysts refer to it as the fourth branch of government.

Administrators make binding rules in two ways. One is by issuing regulations that, in theory, simply add detail to the general intent of laws passed by Congress. In practice, many analysts say, agency-made rules take laws in a direction that Congress did not anticipate or even want. The second way that bureaucrats make rules is by how they implement the law. As with regulations, implementation is supposed to follow the intent of the law, but whether that is true is sometimes controversial. You will see presently that advocate Amanda Ross-Edwards charges that the Department of Education has both formulated rules and implemented them in a manner that has subverted Congress' original intent when it enacted Title IX of the Education Amendments (Act) in 1972. This legislation declared that no one "shall, on the basis of sex, be…subjected to discrimination under any education program or activity receiving Federal financial assistance." It is language that covers most activities at all levels of education, although here we will focus on athletics in higher education.

The legislation also, as most acts do, authorized and directed agencies "to effectuate the provisions of [this act]…by issuing rules, regulations, or orders of general applicability which shall be consistent with achievement of the objectives of the statute."

What is not in dispute here is the value of the basic law. It was enacted to protect girls and women from discrimination by schools and colleges, which was widespread as late as the 1960s. For example, after Luci Baines Johnson, the daughter of President Lyndon Johnson, married in 1966, Georgetown University's nursing school denied her re-admission on the grounds that school regulations barred married women (but not married men) from being students. And it was not until 1970 and a federal court order that the University of Virginia even admitted undergraduate women, much less let them play sports.

There can also be no argument that since the passage of Title IX there has been a dramatic increase in the number of women participating college sports and in the percentage of student athletes who are women. Judith Sweet attributes these changes to the enforcement of Title IX, but Amanda Ross-Edward contends that the expansion of women's athletics was already underway and that the changes reflect social norms more than the legislation.

What is very much in dispute here is whether the Department of Education's Office for Civil Rights, which since 1994 has been responsible for enforcing Title IX, has followed congressional intent when interpreting the law and formulating regulations and policies. Also at issue, albeit less directly so, is the matter of how equal opportunity should be measured. In this sense, this debate is distinctly related to Debate 17 on education policy and affirmative action admissions. Critics of both the way that Title IX has been enforced and many aspects of affirmative action charge that numerical quotas are used overtly or covertly and that they are neither legal nor just.

POINTS TO PONDER

➢ Amanda Ross-Edwards argues men are being subjected to reverse discrimination. What is the basis of the charge, and do you agree?

➢ Currently, only 45.8% of college students are men. Should this mean that 54.2% of all college scholarship athletes should be women?

➢ If not by proportionality, how would you evaluate a school's compliance with Title IX?

The Department of Education and Title IX: Champion of Equality

Judith Sweet

I've loved sports all my life. As a young girl I dreamt of representing my high school and college on a sport team. I never had that opportunity because there were no teams at either the high school or college level.

While I would welcome the opportunity to share my perspective based on those life and campus experiences that Cynthia alluded to, my remarks today will focus on the NCAA.

On behalf of the National Collegiate Athletic Association and its more than 1200 member colleges, universities, conferences, and affiliated organizations, I'm pleased to have the opportunity to provide the Commission with comments about the impact of Title IX on intercollegiate athletics from the Association's perspective.

For those of you who may not be as familiar with the NCAA as others of you are, allow me to briefly note that the NCAA is a membership driven association. The NCAA derives its authority, including all national policy, entirely from the will of the membership through the vote of institutional or conference representatives.

The vast majority of decisions regarding athletics programs, including which sports to sponsor or to cease sponsoring, are made at the campus level. Member institutions have complete autonomy over their programs except where the broader membership has set standards through national policy.

Allow me also briefly to describe the role of intercollegiate athletics for women 30 years ago when Title IX was signed into law. There were no college athletic scholarships to speak of for women, no NCAA champi-

onships for women, and very few opportunities for competition.

In 1971/72 a survey of the NCAA member institutions showed that only 29,977 women were participating in sports and recreational programs compared to over 170,000 men, more than five times as many men as women.

The athletics opportunities for women were few, and the prospects for growth were dismal. With numbers like that, it might be fair to wonder what college woman would show any interest at all in athletics.

What a difference 30 years of legislative impetus, opportunity and support make. Today nearly 150,000 women are competing in sports at NCAA member schools.

While some individuals suggest that women do not have a strong interest in sports participation, the numbers prove otherwise. In the last ten years alone female NCAA participants have increased by more than 55,000. The number of collegiate women's soccer teams has grown from 80 in 1982 to 824 in 2002.

The number of girls participating in sports at the high school level exceeds 2.7 million. As opportunity has increased, interest has increased. Of the 87 championships in 22 sports conducted by the NCAA, 43 are exclusively for women, and bowling will be added to the women's championship in 2003/04.

And...the Committee on Women's Athletics has also indicated that they will look at the number of scholarships being provided in all of our sports. The NCAA membership has demonstrated a commitment to both men's and women's Olympic sports through legislation that allows the continuation of championships in Olympic sports even if the number of sponsoring institutions does not meet minimum requirements for championship events.

Clearly Title IX has promoted opportunities for female athletes over the last 30 years, but there is much more still to be done to ensure that men and women who attend NCAA member schools have equitable access to athletics participation.

Although women comprise 54 percent of the undergraduate student population at NCAA member schools on average, as you have heard, they account for only 4 percent of the athletics participants. They receive only 40 percent of the scholarships; they receive only 36 percent of the operating dollars, and have only 32 percent for recruiting budgets.

Like any social legislation designed to change the deeply imbedded status quo, Title IX has had and still has its critics. Over the last 30 years the voices of dissent have been less strident regarding the law itself and have grown more concerned with the standards used to measure compliance.

The Department of Education standards consider an athletics program to be in compliance with Title IX if its student athletes by gender are in proportion to the make-up of the undergraduate student body or if the program can demonstrate a history of expanding its program to meet the needs of the under-represented gender or if the program can demonstrate that it has fully and effectively accommodated interests and abilities of the underrepresented gender.

Critics argue that the focus of courts and the Office of Civil Rights has been on a proportionality test and that it has become the de facto single test used to determine compliance. The unintended consequence of Title IX they say has been the cutting of the so-called nonrevenue men's sports in order to get the number of athletics participants

for an institution more in line with the undergraduate population by gender.

Others have claimed that increased expenses in providing opportunities for women to comply with Title IX have resulted in a reduction of spending for men's sports. In fact, financial reports from 1972 to 1993 show that in Division 1-A for every new dollar spent on women's sports, three new dollars were spent on men's sports.

Before I discuss the findings of the report on this issue from the United States GAO [General Accounting Office, an investigate agency of Congress] in March 2001, allow me to share with you a message from the NCAA executive committee, one of the primary decision making bodies within the government structure and comprised of university Presidents and Chancellors.

In a discussion about the work of the Commission at their meetings earlier this month, the President spoke strongly of the value of Title IX and urged the Office of Civil Rights to apply consistent Title IX enforcement and interpretations in all regions of the country.

Regarding decisions by member institutions to cut men's sports, this group of college and university CEOs noted that institutions have dropped sports for various reasons, such as institutional philosophy, program priorities, finances, infractions, safety, lack of conference opportunities, inadequate facilities, insurance costs, and others, but the single most important message that they wanted me to deliver on their behalf was this: Don't blame Title IX for institutional decisions to cut programs.

The President's position is supported by findings of the GAO report. The United States Congress included provisions in the higher education amendments of 1998 that required the GAO to study participation in athletics, including schools' decisions to add or discontinue sports teams. They examined the membership of both the NCAA and the NAIA. Among the GAO's findings are these: Athletics participation for both men and women have increased since 1981. The total number of teams has increased for both men and women.

Since 1992, 963 schools added teams and 30 discontinued teams. Most were able to add teams, usually women's teams, without discontinuing any teams.

The report found that the level of student interest was the factor schools cited most often as greatly or very greatly influencing their decisions to add or discontinue both men's and women's teams.

The conclusions are clear. The decisions to discontinue specific sports are made at the institutional level for a variety of reasons.

If the decision is made to eliminate sports for gender-equity reasons, it is because institutions have chosen this path rather than pursuing other options, not because Title IX dictates such action.

The task before the Commission is an important one. In a perfect world Title IX would not be necessary. There would be enough resources and the will to do the right thing and thus meet everyone's needs. Social legislation exists, of course, because we do not live in that perfect world.

In the charge to this commission the Department of Education acknowledges that extraordinary progress has resulted from the passage of Title IX. While we like to think that this progress would have taken place without Title IX because it was the right thing to do, the fact is that opportunities and support for girls and women in athletics are still not equitable with those provided for men, even though it was 30 years since the law was passed.

Your charge appears to bear more on the federal standards for measure of compliance than on the necessity for the law. The degree to which the Commission can give direction to colleges and universities in achieving compliance with Title IX, emphasizing application of any of the three prongs, would remove the misunderstanding that proportionality is the only way to comply. The law is clear; the intent is to correct inequities.

The NCAA stands ready to assist the Commission any way it can as you deliberate. The ultimate test for compliance with Title IX may have been summed up best by an NCAA gender-equity task force in 1992. It defined gender equity in the following manner: An athletics program can be considered gender equitable when the participants in both men's and women's programs would accept as fair and equitable the overall program of the other gender. No individual should be discriminated against on the basis of gender, institutionally or nationally, in intercollegiate athletics.

As I conclude my comments, I urge you to consider the following: Would participants in both our men's and women's programs accept as fair and equitable 40 percent of the participation opportunities, 36 percent of the operating dollars, and 32 percent of the recruiting dollars? Would we expect that of them?

The Department of Education and Title IX: Overzealous Crusader

Amanda Ross-Edwards

In 1973, one year after passage of Title IX, tennis professional Billie Jean King received a congratulatory call from President Nixon for being the first female athlete to win one hundred thousand dollars in prize money in a single year. In 2003, Justine Henin-Hardenne received one million dollars in prize money for winning a single event, the U.S. Open in Women's Tennis. It is clear that women's opportunities in sports have increased in the 31 years since Title IX was enacted. It is also clear that in the past ten years Title IX's interpretation and implementation have become flawed. Contrary to Title IX's original aim of equal opportunity for women in education, the courts and the Office for Civil Rights at the Department of Education have equated equal outcomes in the form of statistical proportionality as their primary means of measuring compliance with Title IX statute.

Title IX prohibits sex discrimination in education by institutions that receive federal funding. Although Title IX passed in 1972, it was not until 1975 that the Department of Health, Education and Welfare published implementing regulations. These regulations, however, were vague and thus provided very little guidance on how schools should enforce the law against sex discrimination in athletics. It was not until 1979 that the department's Office of Civil Rights (OCR) established its Title IX Athletics Policy Interpretation. According to Jessica Gavora, a senior policy advisor at the Department of Justice, "although this interpretation lacks the legal status of an official government regulation, it has been treated by succeeding adminis-

trations and by the courts as the government's final word on implementing Title IX in athletics." This document declares that schools may comply with Title IX in one of three ways: 1) proportionality; 2) showing a recent history of adding women's athletic teams; or 3) proving that the interests of the student body were being met. Gavora notes in her book, *Tilting the Playing Field*, that "Officials in the OCR insist that the three-part test is progressive; compliance they say, is measured in stages. If a school is unable to comply under the first test, it may do so under the second and, failing there, it has a final opportunity under the third test. In any case, a school need pass only one of the three tests to be in compliance with the law." Historical evidence, however, demonstrates that this isn't true; statistical proportionality has become a requirement for compliance under Title IX statute.

The Office for Civil Rights has never explicitly defined proportionality; however, the courts have generally agreed at this point that proportionality is an athletics participation rate that is within plus or minus five percent of the sex ratio of the student body. Proportionality, thus, does not count the number of opportunities available to men and women, but rather the actual number of individual men and women competing in sports. In order to comply under the proportionality rule, the percentage of women participating in athletic programs should be proportional to the percentage of women enrolled in the college or university. If 51 percent of the student body is made up of women, but only 45 percent of the athletes are women, then the college or university would not be in compliance with Title IX.

As noted, in theory a school must only meet one of the three prongs. In practice, however, as the result of significant court cases and executive interpretation, the proportionality rule has become a "safe harbor" for a school's compliance with Title IX. In 1991, Brown University cut two women's teams and two men's teams for budgetary reasons. At the time, Brown University had 15 sports teams for women, compared to the average 8.3 for other NCAA Division I schools. In fact, the number of women's varsity teams at Brown outnumbered the men's. Only Harvard had a broader and more generous women's athletic program.

Despite Brown's exemplary program of women's athletics, Amy Cohen, along with seven other women from the teams that had been cut, filed a lawsuit against Brown charging non-compliance with Title IX. They argued that the proportion of women participating in sports at Brown was less then the proportion of female students. At the time the lawsuit was filed, 51 percent of Brown students were women, while only 39 percent of Brown's athletes were women. According to the plaintiffs, if 61 percent of the athletes at Brown were male, then cutting two men's teams and two women's teams merely perpetuated a preexisting inequality.

The relevance of this case is the context within which it was decided and the impact of its outcome on the future actions of other schools regarding men and women and sports. In 1992, the Supreme Court decided the case of *Franklin v. Gwinnett County Public Schools*, which involved Christine Franklin's claim that the Gwinnett County Public School district owed her punitive damages for not protecting her from her teacher's repeated harassing behavior even after she reported the incidents. The Supreme Court ruled in her favor and thus

set precedent for women to receive monetary compensation for Title IX violations.

By the time the Brown case arose, lawyers, such as Arthur Bryant, executive director of the Trial Lawyers for Public Justice (TLPJ), had fully recognized the possibilities associated with Title IX statute. In the early 1990's, Bryant and TLPJ had filed a number of successful Title IX actions against colleges and universities. Their strategy involved filing a case against a university or college that had cut a women's team and demanding that the team be reinstated. The case usually never made it to court because college administrators wanted to avoid the publicity and the legal costs. The women's teams were thus reinstated and Bryant received his attorney's fees.

Aside from the issue that a primary motive behind these cases was monetary gain for Bryant, there is also the question of how Bryant found out about these cases. In the Brown case, a woman named Kathryn Reith, a Brown alumna and director of advocacy for the Women's Sports Foundation, was responsible for creating the case. As a representative of an interest group interested in women's athletics, she wanted female athletes to file federal complaints under Title IX. It was not until the Franklin decision that money provided the needed added incentive for individuals to file complaints. Reith and Bryant thus looked for the ideal client in the Brown University case and chose Amy Cohen, the former captain of the Brown gymnastics team. In the Brown case, therefore, it was not female athletes pressuring the school and the government for more opportunities; instead it was pressure group incentive and monetary interest that led to the creation of this case. Women were not demanding more athletic opportunity; money and organized interests motivated policy reinterpretation.

Unlike the other suits filed by Bryant, Brown University administrator Vartan

Gregorian refused to settle. In court, Cohen's lawyers argued that Brown could correct the discrimination against women by refunding the women's gymnastics and volleyball teams and continuing to create teams for women until proportionality was reached. Brown's lawyers responded that this was a complete misapplication of the law. The three prong test was clearly a misrepresentation of congressional intent. The authors of Title IX legislation stated clearly in the congressional record that Title IX did not mean quotas. Furthermore, athletics is only one part of Title IX's larger applicability to the academic realm. For instance, dance programs have proportionately more women than men, and engineering programs have proportionately more men than women. So why is disproportionate involvement in sports targeted as an indication of discrimination?

In 1995, the lower courts found in favor of Amy Cohen. Brown University immediately filed an appeal. In January 1996, while waiting for the decision of the first circuit of the U.S. Court of Appeals, Norma Cantu, head of the Office of Civil Rights (OCR), issued a clarification of the three part test in which she reinterpreted the third prong. Appointed as President Clinton's Chief Title IX enforcer, Cantu had established a proactive approach to Title IX enforcement. According to Gavora, within the first nineteen months of Cantu's tenure, "OCR began 240 reviews of schools from which no civil rights complaints had been filed." This was in sharp contrast to the Reagan and Bush administrations that waited to initiate investigations until complaints were filed against schools and universities.

Prior to Cantu's reinterpretation, schools were required to meet the interests and abilities of women only to the same degree as they met the interests and abilities of men. Cantu's directive instructed that the interests of only the underrepresented sex be fully accommodated. This reinterpretation served as an indication that compliance with Title IX required more than the provision of equal opportunity for women in athletics; it required remedial action. Cantu also put both the NCAA and its member institutions on notice that the federal government backed the Title IX compliance evolving in the courts. Ten months later, the First Circuit of the U.S. Court of Appeals confirmed the lower courts decision and in April 1997, the Supreme Court denied review thereby letting the lower court's ruling stand. The message was not lost on other schools and their lawyers. Since then, the safest and surest way to comply with Title IX has been by ensuring that statistical quotas are met.

As a result, colleges have proceeded to cut men's teams as the surest means of complying with Title IX. For instance, in the hearings before the U.S. Department of Education, Secretary's Commission on Opportunity in Athletics, Christine Stolba, a senior Fellow with the Independent Women's Forum, testified that between 1993 and 1999, 53 men's golf teams, 39 men's track teams, 43 wrestling teams and baseball teams have been eliminated. The University of Miami's diving team, which had produced 15 Olympic athletes, has also been eliminated. Furthermore, in 2001, the General Accounting Office, reported that between 1981 and 1999, 171 men's wrestling programs, 83 men's tennis teams and 56 men's gymnastics teams, had been eliminated.

These men, whose opportunities to play sports are being denied, have a valid argument that they are victims of reverse discrimination. Men's teams are being cut and opportunities to play are being denied in order to create the required number of male and female athletes. Not only is this inequitable, but it may also have an impact on the Olympic movement in the United States. College athletics is a primary source for our nation's Olympic athletes; therefore, as the number of men's teams is reduced, the number of potential Olympic athletes is also reduced.

Some argue that this is a spending choice. Colleges and universities facing budget cuts choose to cut men's teams rather than cut money and players to sports like football that bring revenue and name recognition to the school. On the one hand, large division 1-A football programs could do a lot to alleviate some of the division between the two sides of this debate by curbing some of the excesses in their programs. On the other hand, division 1-A football programs are more of an exception to the rule. According to Bill Curry, a former college football coach and ESPN game analyst, in 2002, only 17.2% of college football teams were Division 1-A. These are the teams that need the large number of scholarships to field championship teams. Two-thirds of these programs produce revenue for their universities.

When it comes to complying with Title IX under the proportionality rule, however, it is not a budget issue; it is a Title IX issue. Money is beside the point; Title IX deals with the number of bodies on the playing field. As an example, in 1994, Marquette University cut its men's wrestling team. There was no budget issue. At the time, it was the alumni who funded the wrestling team. The real issue was that the number of male wrestlers, more than 30, skewed the overall number of male-to-female athletes at Marquette. Women made up 54% of Marquette's student body compared to only 46% of its student athletes. Marquette University, thus, dropped wrestling in order to comply with Title IX and remain NCAA certified. Furthermore, Marquette University does not have a football team, so football cannot be blamed as a blanket issue.

Also relevant is the number of male versus female walk-on athletes. Studies show that men's team rosters are bigger than women's because more men walk-on than women. If it was really about budget issues then schools wouldn't be turning away non-scholarship, walk-on athletes who don't cost the school very much. Cost has nothing to do with it. Instead, it has to do with a quota over which men's participation cannot go and under which women's participation cannot go. Why should men be penalized because they walk on and women don't?

In response, supporters of the current method of implementation argue that women's demonstrated interest in sports is not a true measure of equality because it fails to consider the potential for female athletic participation. They contend that women turn out to play sports at a lower rate than men as a result of past discrimination against female athletes. It is true that, culturally, in the past women were not encouraged to play sports. Only recently have women athletes become truly accepted role models for future generations. The UCONN women's basketball team, for instance, only began charging for its games in 1993. By the late 90's, every game was sold out. According to this argument, therefore, Title IX needs to ensure that the opportunity exists for women to achieve their full athletic potential. If the opportunities are created, women will want to play these sports. In other words, if you build it, they will come.

Congress, however, did not pass a law thirty years ago that said it was the responsibility of colleges and universities to create interest in athletics. It passed a law that barred discrimination based on sex. The point is not whether or not making sure women reach their full athletic potential is a good idea or not. It's about interpreting the law correctly. If we want schools and universities to create athletic opportunities for women then we need to pass a law for that purpose. Title IX isn't that law. Furthermore, Congress has never amended Title IX in the years since 1972; instead, the executive branch has progressively changed Title IX's meaning through successive reinterpretations of its implementation policy. The eventual consequence of the U.S. Department of Education's Secretary's Commission on Opportunity in Athletics will be further development in Title IX's meaning.

Those who oppose changing the current interpretation of Title IX, such as Judith Sweet, argue that Title IX policy has been directly responsible for changing women's opportunities in education and sport. Title IX's compliance standards should, therefore, not be changed because athletic opportunities for girls and women in athletics are not yet equitable. Evidence suggests, however, that by the time Title IX passed in 1972 the revolution in women's sport had already begun. Women's participation in sport began to increase significantly before Title IX's passage in 1972 and well before the executive enacted Title IX's final policy interpretation in 1979 which established

Title IX's enforcement guidelines. For instance, according to Gavora, "between 1971 and 1972, the number of girls playing high school sports jumped almost threefold, from 294,015 to 817,073." Furthermore, the number of women participating in intercollegiate athletics doubled in the five years *before* Title IX from around 15,000 to 30,000. Although it was the government that created the statute and regulations to enforce the principal of not using the people's money to deny access, it was the changing social environment that led women to seek such access in the first place.

It is clear that Title IX is still needed as a means of ensuring equal opportunities for women in education and athletics. There must be, however, a better way of implementing this law. If courts and policy makers recognize that Title IX guarantees equal opportunity, but does not necessarily guarantee equal outcomes, then they can return to the original intent of Title IX and restore the integrity of this policy's interpretation and implementation.

THE CONTINUING DEBATE:
The Department of Education and Title IX

What Is New

In 2002, the uproar over the application of Title IX prompted the secretary of education to create the Commission on Opportunity in Athletics to examine the implementation of Title IX. The 18-member panel was divided evenly between men and women. Early in 2003, the Commission gave Paige several recommendations, two of which drew furious dissent from some of the commissioners, numerous interest groups, and several prominent members of Congress, both Democrat and Republican. One was that the Department of Education be allowed to formulate a "reasonable variance" from existing Title IX standards to measure compliance. Opponents of this change argued that "close enough" was not a satisfactory benchmark. The second controversial recommendation was to authorize the secretary to establish "additional ways of demonstrating equity." Proponents of Title IX fretted this vaguely worded standard could be used to gut enforcement. Whether he agreed with these criticisms or was averse to a political donnybrook, the secretary soon announced that he would not act on the controversial recommendation. However, in 2005 the department did issue new standards for measuring compliance. It touted them as more flexible, but the American Association of University Women charged that they "lower the bar for schools, making it easier for schools to prove compliance" and represent "the latest in a series of attempts to weaken Title IX."

Where to Find More

Information about Title IX and the Commission on Opportunity in Athletics is available on the Department of Education site: http://www.ed.gov. A good overview of the controversy is Welch Suggs, *A Place on the Team: The Triumph and Tragedy of Title IX* (Princeton University Press, 2005). For a group that criticizes Title IX, go to the Web site of the Independent Women's Forum at http://www.iwf.org/issues/titleix/index.shtml. The opposite stance is taken by the National Women's Law Center. Among other things, its Web site (http://www.nwlc.org/) lists 30 colleges which it charges are not (as of 2002) in compliance with Title IX.

What More to Do

One thing to do is to visit the Web site of the National Women's Law Center to see if your school is on the list of 30 colleges the Center says are in particular violation of Title IX. Look at the data provided at the site. Assuming it is true, do you agree with the Center? You can also contact the office of your school's athletic department to get comparable data for your college. How does it stand? Also, you can help the Department of Education come up with Title IX enforcement standards on which everyone can agree. Draft a department regulation detailing how compliance will be measured.

14

JUDICIARY

FILIBUSTERING FEDERAL COURT NOMINEES:
Frustrating the Majority *or* Protecting the Minority?

FRUSTRATING THE MAJORITY

ADVOCATE: Orrin G. Hatch, U.S. Senator (R-UT)
SOURCE: *Congressional Record*, May 10, 2005

PROTECTING THE MINORITY

ADVOCATE: Harry F. Byrd, U.S. Senator (D-WV)
SOURCE: *Congressional Record*, March 1, 2005

This debate has two related parts. One is the filibuster as such. It is a tactic legislators use to try to defeat a measure by "talking it to death," that is, continuing to speak on the subject to force the majority to compromise or even give way in order to resume normal operations. The second part of this debate is whether filibusters, even if sometimes reasonable, are appropriate to block nominees for the federal bench because of their judicial philosophy.

Filibusters: One of the often-cited adages of democratic governance is "majority rule with respect to minority rights." Today we tend to equate "minority" with groups that are disadvantaged based on race, ethnicity, sexual orientation, or some other inherent characteristic. To the framers of the Constitution, "minority" had a broader meaning. It included any group in the minority, such as property owners, and even minorities with a belief in a philosophical principle or even in an issue position. What is controversial is which should prevail when majority rule conflicts with minority rights. Taking one view, Thomas Jefferson held, "It is my principle that the will of the majority should always prevail." James Madison differed, contending that in democracies "the great danger is that the majority may not sufficiently respect the rights of the minority."

During their first 50 years or so, neither house of Congress limited debate, although there is no indication this process was consciously tied to protecting minorities. During this time, legislators tried occasionally to defeat legislation by using a filibuster, a word derived from the Spanish *filibustero* (freebooter or pirate). In response, the House in 1842 adopted procedures to close debates by majority vote. By contrast, the Senate continued unlimited debate until 1917, and then required a two-thirds vote of those senators "present and voting" to invoke "cloture" (halting debate). The cloture rule was modified in 1975 to permit stopping debate by three-fifths of all senators. This currently means 60 votes unless there is a vacancy.

Filibustering Judicial Nominees Because of their Judicial Philosophy: The second part of this debate involves the more modern use of filibusters to try to block the confirmation of judges based on their political/ideological/judicial outlook. Currently, this involves the question of whether it is acceptable for Democrats, who are a minority in the Senate, to use filibusters to try to block the conservative nominees for federal judgeships made by a Republican President George W. Bush.

It is the power of federal judges that make their nominations so important. As Supreme Court Chief Justice Charles Evans Hughes once put it, "We are under a Constitution, but the Constitution is what the judges say it is." This translates into the ability to make policy based on the courts' *power of interpretation*, their ability to find meaning in the words of the Constitution and legislative acts, and the courts' *power of judicial review*, their authority to decide whether laws passed by Congress and actions taken by officials are constitutional. Adding to the importance of judicial nominations is that most appointees continue to influence policy long after the president that appointed them and the senators that confirmed them have departed from the political stage.

Nevertheless, by most estimates it has only during the past half century or so that judicial nominations have become frequently and increasingly controversial. At least one reason is the contention that the courts have played a growing role in creating policy rather than merely interpreting the law. Some analysts also point to the growing partisanship in Congress and even in the country. Whatever the reason may be, all Supreme Court nominations now undergo intense scrutiny, with six Supreme Court nominees rejected since 1968. Especially during the terms of Bill Clinton and George W. Bush, resistance to appointments has also increasingly affected nominations to lower courts. Moreover, opposition to nominees has increasingly extended beyond their legal competence and judicial temperament to include their personal and political philosophy. More than any single issue, the question of where a nominee would uphold *Roe v. Wade* (1972), the abortion rights decision (see Debate 3) has become a "litmus test" for many senators.

The immediate debate here that pits Senator Orin Hatch against Senator Harry Reid resulted from Republican frustration with filibusters that blocked several nominations by President Bush for the U.S. Court of Appeals for the Federal Circuit. In response, the republican leadership in the Senate threatened to employ a complex parliamentary maneuver that would have allowed their party to bar filibusters of judicial nominations. Democrats characterized the threat to Senate tradition as so severe that it was a "nuclear option" and issued counter threats about using filibusters and other parliamentary tactics to halt Senate business if the Republicans went forward with their threat. This standoff, which imperiled the ability of the U.S. government to function normally, is the setting for the readings that follow.

POINTS TO PONDER

➤ Be consistent. For example, if you favor Democrats being able to filibuster the nominees of Republican president, then consistency dictates that you also agree to Republicans filibustering future nominees of Democratic presidents.

➤ Consistency would also arguably favor taking the same stand on whether senators should vote for or against judicial nominees based on their ideology alone and whether it is acceptable to filibuster on the basis of ideology. Should liberal legislators vote against conservative judges and vice versa?

➤ Consider having members of the Court of Appeals and Supreme Court serve set terms of, say, 10 years as a way to limit the impact of any one judge/justice and to ease the intensity of the conflict over judicial appointments.

Filibustering Federal Court Nominees:
Frustrating the Majority

ORRIN G. HATCH

Yesterday [May 9, 2005] marked the fourth anniversary of President [George W.] Bush's first judicial nominations, a group of 11 highly qualified men and women nominated to the U.S. courts of appeals. As I said in the East Room at the White House on May 9, 2001: I hope the Senate will at least treat these nominees fairly. Many of our Democratic colleagues instead chose to follow their minority leader's order issued days after President Bush took office, to use "whatever means necessary" to defeat judicial nominees the minority does not like.

While the previous 3 presidents saw their first 11 appeals court nominees confirmed in an average of just 81 days, today, 1,461 days later, 3 of those original nominees have not even received a vote, let alone been confirmed. Three have withdrawn.

In 2003, the minority [the Democrats] opened a new front in the confirmation conflict by using filibusters to defeat majority-supported judicial nominees. This morning I will briefly address the top 10 most ridiculous judicial filibuster defenses. Time permits only brief treatment, but it was difficult to limit the list to 10.

No. 10 is the claim that these filibusters are part of Senate tradition. Calling something a filibuster, even if you repeat it over and over, does not make it so. These filibusters block confirmation of majority-supported judicial nominations by defeating votes to invoke cloture or end debate. Either these filibusters happened before or they did not.

Let me take the evidence offered by filibuster proponents at face value. [Let us examine the historical record of]....some representative examples of what Democrats repeatedly claim is filibuster precedence....Some examples are more ridiculous than others. Stephen Breyer is on the Democrats' list of filibusters, suggesting that the Senate treated his nomination the way Democrats are treating President Bush's nominations today. The two situations could not be more different. Even though President [Jimmy] Carter nominated now-Justice Breyer [since 1994] but then attorney Breyer, law professor Breyer, [for a seat on the U.S. Court of Appeals, First Circuit] in November 1980, after losing his bid for reelection—that is when he nominated him—and after Democrats lost control of the Senate, we voted to end debate and overwhelmingly confirmed Stephen Breyer just 26 days after his nomination. And I had a lot to do with that. The suggestion that confirming the Breyer nomination for the party losing its majority now justifies filibustering nominations for the party keeping its majority is, well, just plain ridiculous.

No. 9 on the list of the most ridiculous filibuster defenses is that they are necessary, they [the Democrats] say, to prevent one-party rule from stacking the Federal bench. Now, if you win elections, you say the country has chosen its leadership. If you lose, you complain about one-party rule. When your party controls the White House, the president appoints judges. When the other party controls the White House, the president stacks the bench—at least that seems to be the attitude.

Our Democratic colleagues say we should be guided by how the Democratic

Senate handled Franklin Roosevelt's attempt to pack the Supreme Court. It is true that FDR's legislative proposal [in 1937] to create new Supreme Court seats failed, and without a filibuster, I might add. But as it turned out, packing the Supreme Court required only filling the existing seats. President Roosevelt packed the Court all right, by appointing no less than eight Justices in 6 years—more than any president, except George Washington himself.

[With regard]…to FDR's court packing without a filibuster.…let me just make some points. During the 75th, 76th, and 77th Congresses [1937–1943], when President Roosevelt made those nominations, Democrats outnumbered Republicans by an average of 70 Democrats to 20 Republicans. Now, that is one-party rule. Yet the Senate confirmed those Supreme Court nominees in an average of just 13 days, one of them on the very day it was made and six of them without even a roll-call vote. That is not because filibustering judicial nominations was difficult. In fact, our cloture rule did not then apply to nominations. A single member of that tiny, beleaguered Republican minority could have filibustered these nominations and attempted to stop President Roosevelt from packing the Supreme Court—just a single member could have. [Instead]…the number of filibusters against President Roosevelt's nominees [was] zero.

No. 8 on this list is the claim that without the filibuster the Senate would be a patsy, nothing but a rubberstamp for the president's judicial nominations. To paraphrase a great Supreme Court Justice: If simply stating this argument does not suffice to refute it, our debate about these issues has achieved terminal silliness. Being on the losing side does not make one a rubberstamp.

For all of these centuries of democratic government, have we seen only winners and rubberstamps? Was the famous tag line for ABC's Wide World of Sports "the thrill of victory and the agony of rubberstamping"? Democrats did not start filibustering judicial nominations until the 108th Congress. Imagine the history books describing the previous 107 Senates as the great rubberstamp Senates. Did Democrats rubberstamp the Supreme Court nomination of Clarence Thomas in 1991 since they did not use the filibuster? That conflict lasting several months and concluding with that 52-to-48 confirmation vote did not look like a rubberstamp to me.

Some modify this ridiculous argument by saying this applies when one party controls both the White House and the Senate. They make the stunning observation that senators of the president's party are likely to vote for his nominees. The assistant minority leader, Senator [Richard] Durbin [D-IL], recently said, for example, that Republican senators are nothing but "lapdogs" for President Bush.

Pointing at others can be dangerous because you have a few fingers pointing back at yourself. Counting both unanimous consent or roll-call votes, more than 37,500 votes were cast here on the Senate floor on President Clinton's judicial nominations. Only 11 of them, just a teeny, tiny, three one-hundredths of 1 percent, were "no" votes from Democrats—only 11 of 37,500. Were they just rubberstamping lapdogs in supporting President Clinton?

The Constitution assigns the same roles to the president and the Senate no matter which party the American people put in charge of which end of Pennsylvania Avenue.

In the 1960s, the Democrats were in charge, yet Minority Leader Everett Dirksen [R-IL] refused to filibuster judicial nominees of Presidents [John F.] Kennedy or [Lyndon B.] Johnson. Was he just a rubberstamp?

In the 1970s, the Democrats were in charge, yet Minority Leader Howard Baker [R-TN] refused to filibuster President Carter's judicial nominees. Was he just a rubberstamp?

In the 1980s, the Republicans were in charge, yet Minority Leader Robert Byrd [D-WV] did not filibuster President [Ronald] Reagan's judicial nominees. Was he just a rubberstamp?

And a decade ago, the Democrats were again in charge, yet Minority Leader Bob Dole [R-KS] refused to filibuster President [Bill] Clinton's judicial nominees. Was he a rubberstamp?

To avoid being a rubberstamp, one need only fight the good fight, win or lose.

No. 7 on the list of most ridiculous judicial filibuster defenses is that these filibusters are necessary to preserve our system of checks and balances. That is an argument we have heard from the other side. Any civics textbook explains that what we call "checks and balances" regulates the relationship between the branches of Government. The Senate's role of advice and consent checks the president's power to appoint judges, and we exercise that check when we vote on his judicial nominations.

The filibuster is about the relationship between the majority and minority in the Senate, not about the relationship between the Senate and the president. It actually interferes with being a check on the president's power by preventing the Senate from exercising its role of advice and consent at all. Former Majority Leader Mike Mansfield [D-MT] once explained that by filibustering judicial nominations, individual senators presume what he called "great personal privilege at the expense of the responsibilities of the Senate as a whole, and at the expense of the constitutional structure of the federal government." In September 1999, the [Democratic] senator from Massachusetts, [Ted] Kennedy, expressed the same view when he said:

> It is true that some senators have voiced concerns about these nominations. But that should not prevent a roll call vote which gives every senator the opportunity to vote "yes" or "no."

Those were the words of our colleague from Massachusetts, Senator Kennedy: Give every senator the opportunity to vote yes or no. That was then; this is now....

No. 6 on the list is that these filibusters are necessary to prevent appointment of extremists. What our Democratic colleagues call "extreme" the American Bar Association calls "qualified." In fact, all three of the appeals court nominees chosen 4 years ago who have been denied confirmation received the ABA's highest "well qualified" rating. Now, that was the gold standard under the Democrats when Clinton was president. The same Democrats who once called the ABA rating the gold standard for evaluating judicial nominees now disregard it and call these people extreme.

Did 76 percent of Californians vote to keep an extremist on their supreme court when they voted to retain Justice Janice Rogers Brown [one of President Bush's filibustered nominees for the Court of Appeals], an African-American woman, a sharecroppers' daughter, who fought her way all the way up to the Supreme Court of California?

Did 84 percent of all Texans and every major newspaper in the state support an extremist when they reelected Justice Priscilla Owen [another filibustered Bush nominee to the Court of Appeals] to the Texas Supreme Court—84 percent?

The Associated Press reported last Friday that the minority leader [Senator Harry Reid, D-NV] reserves the right to filibuster what he calls "extreme" Supreme Court nominees. Now, that is quite an escape hatch, if you will, since the minority already defines any nominee it does not like as "extreme." This is simply a repackaged status quo masquerading as reform.

If senators want to dismiss as an extremist any judicial nominee who does not think exactly as they do, that certainly is their right. That is, however, a reason for voting against a confirmation, not for refusing to vote at all. As our former colleague, Tom Daschle [D-SD], said, "I find it simply baffling that a senator would vote against even voting on a judicial nominee."

No. 5 on this list of most ridiculous judicial filibuster defenses is the claim that these filibusters are about free speech and debate. If senators cannot filibuster judicial nominations, some say, the Senate will cease to exist, and we will be literally unable to represent our constituents.

The same men who founded this republic designed this Senate without the ability to filibuster anything at all. A simple majority could proceed to vote on something after sufficient debate. Among those first senators were Oliver Ellsworth of Connecticut, who later served on the Supreme Court, as well as Charles Carroll of Maryland and Richard Henry Lee of Virginia, who had signed the Declaration of Independence. When they ran for office, did they know that they would be unable to represent their states because they would be unable to filibuster?

These filibusters are about defeating judicial nominations, not debating them. The minority rejects every proposal for debating and voting on nominations it targets for defeat. In April 2003, my colleague from Utah, Senator [Robert] Bennett [R], asked the minority leader, how many hours Democrats would need to debate a particular nomination. His response spoke volumes. [He commented,] "[T]here is not a number [of hours] in the universe that would be sufficient." Later that year, he said, "We would not agree to a time agreement...of any duration." Just 2 weeks ago, the minority leader summed up what really has been the Democrats' position all along: "This has never been about the length of the debate."

He is right about that. This has always been about defeating nominations, not debating them. If our Democratic colleagues want to debate, then let us debate. The majority leader said we will give 100 hours for each of these nominees. Let's debate them. Let us do what Democrats once said was the purpose of debating judicial nominations. As my colleague from California, Senator Barbara Boxer [D], put it in January 1998, "[L]et these names come up, let us have debate, let us vote."

No. 4 on the list is that returning to Senate tradition regarding floor votes on judicial nominations would amount to breaking the rules to change the rules. As any consultant worth even a little salt will tell you, that is a catchy little phrase. The problem is that neither of its catchy little parts is true. The constitutional option, which would change judicial confirmation procedure through the Senate voting to affirm a parliamentary ruling, would neither break nor change Senate rules. While the constitutional option has not been used to break our rules, it has been used to break filibusters. [The constitutional option refers to the Republican threat to have the president of the Senate, Vice President Richard Cheney, rule the filibuster of nominees to be unconstitutional and thus out of order. Under Senate rules, it would require a majority vote to overturn that ruling.]

On January 4, 1995, the senator from West Virginia, Senator Byrd, described how, in 1977, when he was majority leader, he used this procedure to break a filibuster on a natural gas bill. Now, I have genuine affection and great respect for the senator from West Virginia, and he knows that. But....since I would not want to describe his repeated use of the constitutional option in a pejorative way, let me use his own words. Here is what he said back in 1995:

> I have seen filibusters. I have helped to break them. There are few senators in this body who were here [in 1977] when I broke the filibuster on the natural gas bill....I asked Mr. [Walter] Mondale, the Vice president, to go please sit in the chair; I wanted to make some points of order and create some new precedents that would break these filibusters. And the filibuster was broken—back, neck, legs, and arms....So I know something about filibusters. I helped to set a great many of the precedents that are on the books here.

Well, he certainly did. I was here. And using the constitutional option today to return to Senate tradition regarding judicial nominations would simply use the precedents the distinguished senator from West Virginia put on the books.

No. 3 on the list of most ridiculous judicial filibuster defenses is that the constitutional option is unprecedented....In 1977, 1979, and 1987, the then majority leader, Senator Byrd, secured a favorable parliamentary ruling through a point of order and a majority of senators voted to affirm it. He did this even when the result he sought was inconsistent with the text of our written rules. In 1980, he used a version of the same procedure to limit nomination-related filibusters. Majority Leader Byrd made a motion for the Senate to vote to go into executive session and proceed to consider a specific nomination. At the time, the first step was not debatable but the second step was debatable. A majority of senators voted to overturn a parliamentary ruling disallowing the procedural change Majority

Leader Byrd wanted. Seven of these [Democratic] senators serve with us today....They can explain for themselves how voting against restricting nomination-related filibusters today is consistent with voting to restrict them in 1980.

No. 2 on the list is that preventing judicial filibusters will doom legislative filibusters. As you know, there are two calendars in the Senate. One is the legislative calendar. I would fight to my death to keep the filibuster alive on the legislative calendar to protect the minority. But then there is the executive calendar, which is partly the president's in the sense that he has the power of appointment and nomination and sends these people up here and expects advice and consent from the Senate. Advice we give. Consent we have not given in the case of these nominees who have been filibustered, or so-called filibustered.

[The contention] that preventing judicial filibusters...will doom legislative filibusters....[is] pure bunk. Our own Senate history shows how ridiculous this argument really is. Filibusters became possible by dropping the rule allowing a simple majority to proceed to a vote. The legislative filibuster developed, the judicial filibuster did not. What we must today limit by rule or ruling we once limited by principle or self-restraint—for 214 years, that is. The filibuster is an inappropriate obstacle to the president's judicial appointment power but an appropriate tool for exercising our own legislative power. I cannot fathom how returning to our tradition regarding judicial nominations will somehow threaten our tradition regarding legislation. The only threat to the legislative filibuster and the only votes to abolish have come from the other side of the aisle. In 1995, 19 senators, all Democrats, voted against tabling an amendment to our cloture rule [to cut off debate] that would prohibit all filibusters of legislation as well as nominations. Nine of those senators still serve with us and their names are right here on this chart.

I voted then against the Democrats' proposal to eliminate the legislative filibuster, and I oppose eliminating it today. The majority leader, Senator [Bill] Frist [R-TN], also voted against the Democrats' proposal to eliminate the legislative filibuster. In fact, that was his first vote as a new member of this body. I joined him in recommitting ourselves to protecting the legislative filibuster. I urge…the Democrats to follow the example of our colleague from California, Senator [Barbara] Boxer [D], who recently said that she has changed her position, that she no longer wants to eliminate the legislative filibuster.

In 1995, *USA Today* condemned the filibuster as "a pedestrian tool of partisans and gridlock meisters." The *New York Times* said the filibuster is "the tool of the sore loser." I hope these papers will reconsider their position and support the legislative filibuster.

The No. 1 most ridiculous judicial filibuster defense is that those wanting to filibuster Republican nominees today opposed filibustering Democratic nominees only a few years ago. In a letter dated February 4, 1998, for example, the leftwing urged confirmation of Margaret Morrow to the U.S. District Court for the Central District of California. They urged us to "bring the nomination to the Senate, ensure that it received prompt, full and fair consideration, and that a final vote on her nomination is scheduled as soon as possible." Groups signing this letter included the Alliance for Justice, Leadership Conference on Civil Rights, and People for the American Way. As we all know, these leftwing groups today lead the grassroots campaign behind these filibusters that would deny this same treatment to President Bush's nominees. Their position has changed as the party controlling the White House has changed.…

I opened the debate on the Morrow nomination by strongly urging my fellow senators to support it. We did, and she is, today, a sitting Federal judge, as I believe she should be. The same Democrats who today call for filibusters called for up-or-down votes when a Democrat was in the White House.…

Let me…give some [other] illustrations [of the Democrats' changing position]. In 1999, Senator Diane Feinstein [D-CA], said of the Senate, "It is our job to confirm these judges. If we don't like them, we can vote against them." She [also] said, "A nominee is entitled to a vote. Vote them up, vote them down." Senator Charles Schumer [D-NY] properly said in March 2000, "The president nominates and we are charged with voting on the nominees." I have already quoted Senator Boxer once, but in 2000 she said that filibustering judicial nominees, "would be such a twisting of what cloture really means in these cases. It has never been done before for a judge, as far as we know—ever." And [Senator Herbert] Kohl [D-WI], said in 199, "Let's breathe life back into the confirmation process. Let's vote on the nominees.…"

The same view comes from three former Judiciary Committee chairmen, members of the Democratic leadership. A former committee chairman, Senator [Joseph] Biden [D-DE], said in 1977 that every judicial nominee is entitled "to have a shot to be heard on the floor and have a vote on the floor." Former chairman [Ted] Kennedy [D-MA] said in 1998, "If senators don't like them, vote against them. But give them a vote." And my immediate predecessor as chairman, Senator [Patrick] Leahy [D-VT], said a year later, judicial nominees are "entitled to a vote, aye or nay." Finally, the minority leader, Senator Reid, expressed in March 2000 the standard that I hope we can reestablish: "Once they [nominations] get out of committee, bring them down here and vote up or down on them."

The majority leader, Senator Frist, recently proposed a plan to accomplish precisely this result. But the minority leader dismissed it as—I want to quote this accurately now—"a big fat wet kiss to the far right." I never thought voting on judicial nominations was a far-right thing to do.

These statements speak for themselves. Do you see a pattern here? The message at one time seems to be let us debate and let us vote. That should be the standard, no matter which party controls the White House or the Senate.

As I close, let me summarize these 10 top most ridiculous judicial filibusters in this way. Blocking confirmation of majority-supported judicial nominations by defeating cloture votes is unprecedented. In the words of the current Judiciary Committee chairman, Senator [Arlen] Specter [R-PA], "What Democrats are doing here is really seeking a constitutional revolution." We must turn back that revolution. No matter which party controls the White House or Senate, we should return to our tradition of giving judicial nominations reaching the Senate floor an up-or-down vote. Full, fair, and vigorous debate is one of the hallmarks of this body, and it should drive how we evaluate a president's judicial nominations.

Honoring the Constitution's separation of power, however, requires that our check on the president's appointment power not highjack that power altogether. This means debate must be a means to an end rather than an end in itself. Senators are free to vote against the nominees they feel extreme, but they should not be free to prevent other senators from expressing a contrary view or advising and consenting. In this body, we govern ourselves with parliamentary rulings as well as by unwritten rules. The procedure of a majority of senators voting to sustain a parliamentary ruling has been used repeatedly to change Senate procedure without changing Senate rules, even to limit nomination-related filibusters....

We confirmed, in 6 years of Republican control of the Senate, 377 judges for President Clinton. That was five less than the all-time confirmation champion Ronald Reagan. All of these people [judicial nominees of President Bush] who are up have well-qualified ratings from the ABA, all had a bipartisan majority to support them. What is wrong with giving them an up-or-down vote and retaining 214 years of Senate tradition? What is wrong with that? I think it is wrong to try and blow up that tradition the way it is being done.

Filibustering Federal Court Nominees: Protecting the Minority

Harry F. Byrd

In1939, one of the most famous American movies of all time, *Mr. Smith Goes to Washington*, hit the box office. Initially received with a combination of lavish praise and angry blasts, the film went on to win numerous awards and to inspire millions around the globe. The director, the legendary Frank Capra, in his autobiography, *Frank Capra: The Name Above the Title*, cites this moving review of the film, appearing in the *Hollywood Reporter*, November 4, 1942:

> Frank Capra's *Mr. Smith Goes to Washington*, chosen by French Theaters as the final English language film to be shown before the recent Nazi-ordered countrywide ban on American and British films went into effect, was roundly cheered....Storms of spontaneous applause broke out at the sequence when, under the Abraham Lincoln monument in the Capital, the word, "Liberty," appeared on the screen and the Stars and Stripes began fluttering over the head of the great Emancipator in the cause of liberty. Similarly, cheers and acclamation punctuated the famous speech of the young senator on man's rights and dignity. "It was....as though the joys, suffering, love and hatred, the hopes and wishes of an entire people who value freedom above everything, found expression for the last time."

For those who may not have seen it, *Mr. Smith* is the fictional story of one young senator's crusade against forces of corrup-

tion and his lengthy filibuster—his lengthy filibuster—for the values he holds dear.

My, how things have changed. These days, Mr. Smith would be called an obstructionist. Rumor has it that there is a plot afoot to curtail the right of extended debate in this hallowed chamber, not in accordance with its rules, mind you, but by fiat from the chair [the presiding officer, the vice president, through] the so-called nuclear option....This morning I asked a man, "What does nuclear option mean to you?" He said: Oh, you mean with Iran? I was at the hospital a few days ago with my wife, and I asked a doctor, "What does the nuclear option mean to you?" He said, "That sounds like we're getting ready to drop some device, some atomic device on North Korea." Well, the so-called nuclear option purports to be directed solely at the Senate's advice and consent prerogatives regarding federal judges. But the claim that no right exists to filibuster judges aims an arrow straight at the heart of the Senate's long tradition of unlimited debate.

The Framers of the Constitution envisioned the Senate as a kind of executive council, a small body of legislators, featuring longer terms, designed to insulate members from the passions of the day. The Senate was to serve as a check on the executive branch, particularly in the areas of appointments and treaties, where, under the Constitution, the Senate passes judgment absent the House of Representatives.

James Madison wanted to grant the Senate the power to select judicial appointees with the [president] delegated to the sidelines. But a compromise brought the present arrangement: appointees selected by the [president], with the advice and consent of the Senate confirmed. Note that nowhere in the Constitution of the United States is a vote on appointments mandated.

When it comes to the Senate, numbers can deceive. The Senate was never intended to be a majoritarian body. That was the role of the House of Representatives, with its membership based on the populations of states. The Great Compromise of July 16, 1787, satisfied the need for smaller states to have equal status in one House of Congress, the Senate. The Senate, with its two members per state, regardless of population, is, then, the forum of the states.

Indeed, in the last Congress 52 members, a majority, representing the 26 smallest states, accounted for just 17.06 percent of the U.S. population. In other words, a majority in the Senate does not necessarily represent a majority of the population of the United States.

The Senate is intended for deliberation, not point scoring. The Senate is a place designed, from its inception, as expressive of minority views. Even 60 Senators, the number required under Senate rule XXII for cloture [closing debate], would represent just 24 percent of the population if they happened to all hail from the 30 smallest states.

So you can see what it means to the smallest states in these United States to be able to stand on this floor and debate, to their utmost, until their feet will no longer hold them, and their lungs of brass will no longer speak, in behalf of their states, in behalf of a minority, in behalf of an issue that affects vitally their constituents.

Unfettered debate, the right to be heard at length, is the means by which we perpetuate the equality of the states. In fact, it was 1917, before any curtailing of debate was [allowed], which means that from 1789 to

1917...the Senate rejected any limits to debate. Democracy flourished along with the filibuster. The first actual cloture rule in 1917 was enacted in response to a filibuster by those people who opposed the arming of merchant ships. Some might say they opposed U.S. intervention in World War I, but to narrow it down, they opposed the arming of merchant ships.

But even after its enactment, the Senate was slow to embrace cloture, understanding the pitfalls of muzzling debate. In 1949, the 1917 cloture rule was modified to make cloture more difficult to invoke, not less, mandating that the number needed to stop debate would be not two-thirds of those present and voting but two-thirds of all senators. Indeed, from 1919 to 1962, the Senate voted on cloture petitions only 27 times and invoked cloture just 4 times over those 43 years.

On January 4, 1957, Senator William Ezra Jenner of Indiana [R] spoke in opposition to invoking cloture by majority vote. He stated with great conviction:

> We may have a duty to legislate, but we also have a duty to inform and deliberate. In the past quarter century we have seen a phenomenal growth in the power of the executive branch. If this continues at such a fast pace, our system of checks and balances will be destroyed. One of the main bulwarks against this growing power is free debate in the Senate....So long as there is free debate, men of courage and understanding will rise to defend against potential dictators....The Senate today is one place where, no matter what else may exist, there is still a chance to be heard, an opportunity to speak, the duty to examine, and the obligation to protect. It is one of the few refuges of democracy.

Minorities have an illustrious past, full of suffering, torture, smear, and even death. Jesus Christ was killed by a majority; Columbus was smeared; and Christians have been tortured. Had the United States Senate existed during those trying times, I am sure that these people would have found an advocate. Nowhere else can any political, social, or religious group, finding itself under sustained attack, receive a better refuge.

Senator Jenner was right. The Senate was deliberately conceived to be what he called "a better refuge," meaning one styled as guardian of the rights of the minority. The Senate is the "watchdog" because majorities can be wrong and filibusters can highlight injustices. History is full of examples.

In March 1911, Senator Robert Owen of Oklahoma [D] filibustered the New Mexico statehood bill, arguing that Arizona should also be allowed to become a state. President [William H.] Taft opposed the inclusion of Arizona's statehood in the bill because Arizona's state constitution allowed the recall of judges. Arizona attained statehood a year later, at least in part because Senator Owen and the minority took time to make their point the year before.

In 1914, a Republican minority led a 10-day filibuster of a bill that would have appropriated more than $50,000,000 for rivers and harbors. On an issue near and dear to the hearts of our current majority, Republican opponents spoke until members of the Commerce Committee agreed to cut the appropriations by more than half.

Perhaps more directly relevant to our discussion of the "nuclear option" are the 7 days in 1937, from July 6 to 13 of that year, when the Senate blocked Franklin Roosevelt's Supreme Court–packing plan.

Earlier that year, in February 1937, FDR sent the Congress a bill drastically reorgan-izing the judiciary. The Senate Judiciary Committee rejected the bill, calling it "an invasion of judicial power such as has never before been attempted in this country" and finding it "essential to the continuance of our constitutional democracy that the judiciary be completely independent of both the executive and legislative branches of the Government." The committee recommended the rejection of the court-packing bill, calling it "a needless, futile, and utterly dangerous abandonment of constitutional principle…without precedent and without justification."

What followed was an extended debate on the Senate floor lasting for 7 days until the majority leader, Joseph T. Robinson of Arkansas [D], a supporter of the plan, suffered a heart attack and died on July 14. Eight days later, by a vote of 70 to 20, the Senate sent the judicial reform bill back to committee, where FDR's controversial, court-packing language was finally stripped. A determined, vocal group of senators properly prevented a powerful president from corrupting our nation's judiciary.

Free and open debate on the Senate floor ensures citizens a say in their government. The American people are heard, through their senator, before their money is spent, before their civil liberties are curtailed, or before a judicial nominee is confirmed for a lifetime appointment. We are the guardians, the stewards, the protectors of the people who send us here. Our voices are their voices. If we restrain debate on judges today, what will be next: the rights of the elderly to receive social security; the rights of the handicapped to be treated fairly; the rights of the poor to obtain a decent education? Will all debate soon fall before majority rule?

Will the majority someday trample on the rights of lumber companies to harvest timber or the rights of mining companies to mine silver, coal, or iron ore? What about the rights of energy companies to drill for new sources of oil and gas? How will the insurance, banking, and securities industries fare when a majority can move against their interests and prevail by a simple majority vote? What about farmers who can be forced to lose their subsidies, or western senators who will no longer be able to stop a majority determined to wrest control of ranchers' precious water or grazing rights? With no right of debate, what will forestall plain muscle and mob rule?

Many times in our history we have taken up arms to protect a minority against the tyrannical majority in other lands. We, unlike Nazi Germany or Mussolini's Italy, have never stopped being a nation of laws, not of men. But witness how men with motives and a majority can manipulate law to cruel and unjust ends. Historian Alan Bullock writes that Hitler's dictatorship rested on the constitutional foundation of a single law, the Enabling Law. Hitler needed a two-thirds vote to pass that law, and he cajoled his opposition in the Reichstag [Germany's legislature] to support it. Bullock writes that "Hitler was prepared to promise anything to get his bill through, with the appearances of legality preserved intact." And he succeeded.

Hitler's originality lay in his realization that effective revolutions, in modern conditions, are carried out with, and not against, the power of the state: the correct order of events was first to secure access to that power and then begin his revolution. Hitler never abandoned the cloak of legality; he recognized the enormous psychological value of having the law on his side. Instead, he turned the law inside out and made illegality legal.

That is what the nuclear option seeks to do to rule XXII of the Standing Rules of the Senate. The nuclear option seeks to alter the rules by sidestepping the rules, thus making the impermissible the rule,

employing the nuclear option, engaging a pernicious, procedural maneuver to serve immediate partisan goals, risks violating our nation's core democratic values and poisoning the Senate's deliberative process.

For the temporary gain of a handful of out-of-the-mainstream judges, some in the Senate are ready to callously incinerate each and every senator's right of extended debate. Note that I said every senator. For the damage will devastate not just the minority party;...it will cripple the ability of each member, every member, to do what each member was sent here to do—namely, represent the people of his or her state. Without the filibuster—it has a bad name, old man filibuster out there. Most people would be happy to say let's do away with him. We ought to get rid of that fellow; he has been around too long. But someday that old man filibuster is going to help me, you, and every senator in here at some time or other, when the rights of the people he or she represents are being violated or threatened. That senator is then going to want to filibuster. He or she is going to want to stand on his or her feet as long as their...lungs will carry their voice.

If the nuclear option is successful here, no longer will each Senator have that weapon with which to protect the people who sent him or her here. And the people finally are going to wake up to who did it. They are going to wake up to it sooner or later and ask: "Who did this to us?"

Without the filibuster or the threat of extended debate, there exists no leverage with which to bargain for the offering of an amendment. All force to effect compromise between the parties will be lost. Demands for hearings will languish. The President of the United States can simply rule by executive order, if his party controls both Houses of Congress and majority rule reigns supreme. In such a world, the minority will be crushed, the power of dissenting views will be diminished, and freedom of speech will be attenuated. The uniquely American concept of the independent individual asserting his or her own views, proclaiming personal dignity through the courage of free speech will forever have been blighted. This is a question of freedom of speech....And the American spirit, that stubborn, feisty, contrarian, and glorious urge to loudly disagree, and proclaim, despite all opposition, what is honest, what is true, will be sorely manacled.

Yes, we believe in majority rule, but we thrive because the minority can challenge, agitate, and ask questions. We must never become a nation cowed by fear, sheeplike in our submission to the power of any majority demanding absolute control. Generations of men and women have lived, fought, and died for the right to map their own destiny, think their own thoughts, speak their own minds. If we start here, in this Senate, to chip away at that essential mark of freedom—here of all places, in a body designed to guarantee the power of even a single individual through the device of extended debate—we are on the road to refuting the principles upon which that Constitution rests. In the eloquent, homespun words of that illustrious, obstructionist, Senator Smith, in *Mr. Smith Goes to Washington*, "Liberty is too precious to get buried in books. Men ought to hold it up in front of them every day of their lives and say, 'I am free—to think—to speak. My ancestors couldn't. I can. My children will.'"

THE CONTINUING DEBATE:
Filibustering Federal Court Nominees

What Is New

The immediate confrontation between Democrats and Republicans that sparked the debate you have just read ended in compromise. In late May 2005, a group of seven Democratic senators and seven Republicans agreed to a deal that allowed three of President Bush's stalled nominees to proceed to a vote and confirmation, while two others remained subject to filibuster and, thus, in effect, blocked. More importantly, the seven Democrats pledged not to filibuster future Bush nominees except under "extraordinary circumstances." In turn, the Republicans promised to oppose the nuclear option. Although there was and remains considerable uncertainty about what constitutes "extraordinary circumstances," the leadership of the two parties eventually agreed and a legislative crisis was averted.

That set the stage for what many observers were anticipating: one or more vacancies on the Supreme Court. These soon came when Associate Justice Sandra Day O'Conner retired and when, within weeks, Chief Justice William Rehnquist died. It is unclear whether the threat of a filibuster had any impact on the choices of President Bush, but he made a careful point of consulting the leadership of both parties in the Senate about potential nominees. Chief Justice John G. Roberts, Jr. appeared relatively moderate and was easily confirmed. However, after Bush's other nominee, Harriet E. Miers, withdrew under attack from conservative groups, the president nominated decidedly conservative Samuel A. Alito, Jr. in her place. That led one analyst to predict both that a Democratic filibuster was "highly likely" and that the Republican would respond with the "nuclear option."

Where to Find More

Two good studies of the appointment process are David Yalof, *Pursuit of Justices: Presidential Politics and the Selection of Supreme Court Nominees* (University of Chicago Press, 1999) and Joyce A. Baugh, *Supreme Court Justices in the Post-Bork Era: Confirmation Politics and Judicial Performance* (Peter Lang, 2002). For a group that would support the opposition to conservative judges, go to http://www.pfaw.org/pfaw/general/, the site of the liberal group, People for the American Way. The opposite view is held by the Committee for Justice at http://www.committeeforjustice.org/.

What More to Do

Begin by asking yourself whether the nomination and confirmation process for judges works well. Particularly think about whether it is possible to select non-ideological judges and justices through what is inherently a political process. If the process is wanting, what would you do to fix it?

15 STATE AND LOCAL GOVERNMENT

TAKING PROPERTY BY EMINENT DOMAIN FOR ECONOMIC DEVELOPMENT:
Serving the Public Good *or* Abuse of Government Power?

SERVING THE PUBLIC GOOD

ADVOCATES: Connecticut Conference of Municipalities and 31 other state municipal leagues

SOURCE: Amicus Curiae brief to the U.S. Supreme Court in *Kelo v. New London* (2005)

ABUSE OF GOVERNMENT POWER

ADVOCATE: Institute for Justice, representing Suzette Kelo and 8 other petitioners

SOURCE: Brief of Petitioners to the U.S. Supreme Court in *Kelo v. New London* (2005)

Private property has something of an air of sanctified ground in the United States. Signs reading, No Trespassing, Keep Out, No Entry, or simply Private Property are ubiquitous. Sayings like "A man's home is his castle" are often heard. There is also a long line of political theory that supports property rights. One of the great democratic philosophers, John Locke, theorized in his *Second Treatise on Civil Government* (1690) that people carried with them into society certain rights that could not be taken away. He believed that natural law, inherent laws of nature, created rights and mandated that "no one ought to harm another in his life, health, liberty or possessions." Locke was not an absolutist. While he believed that the community could not take away an individual's rights, he made an exception if the individual transgressed, for example, by taking another life, restricting someone else's liberty, or "hord[ing] up more [property] than he could make use of" for "whatever is beyond this is more than his share and belongs to others."

Other political theorists have thoroughly disagreed about the near inviolability of private property. Jean Jacques Rousseau argued in *The Social Contract* (1762) that the concept of private property was divisive and that strife among people had intensified after "the first man...enclosed a piece of ground, [proclaimed]...'This is mine,' and found people simple enough to believe him."

In between those two extremes, the United States and other democratic countries have tried to craft laws that protect private property but allow the government to take that property provided that the purpose is for the public good and owners are paid for it. This is expressed by the Fifth Amendment to the Constitution, which, closely paraphrasing Locke, reads in part: "No person shall...be deprived of life, liberty, or property, without due process of law; or shall private property be taken for the public use, without just compensation." In the United States the right of the government to require the compulsory sale of land is called "eminent domain," a phrase that relates to the right of the monarch (an eminence) to acquire land within his/her realm (domain). The word "condemnation" describes the act of a government designating property it will acquire under its authority of eminent domain.

Although the legality of condemning property under eminent domain is well established, what is uncertain is what "public good" means in the Fifth Amendment. The meaning of those two words is at the heart of this debate. In the mid-1990s the city of New London, Connecticut, began to seek ways to improve its deteriorating downtown and waterfront areas. To assist it, the city hired the New London Development Corporation (NLDC), a private nonprofit organization. In 2000, the city accepted the NLDC's recommendations, which included condemning under eminent domain over 100 pieces of private property, including private homes, in the waterfront area and turning the land over to private developers. They, in turn, would build hotels, office complexes, and other structures according to broad plans approved by the city. New London believed this would help revitalize the city. Most of the homes and other buildings in the area were old, but they were not rundown.

Most of the businesses and individuals who had homes or other property in the area, known as Fort Trumbull, soon agreed to terms with the city. But Susette Kelo and a few others did not. They valued their homes more than their monetary worth and sued New London. The petitioners claimed that transferring their property to private developers did not constitute "public use" of the condemned property and thus violated the doctrine of eminent domain. The city argued that its economic development constituted public use because the town and its tax base would be improved by upgraded use of the area and by the tearing down of what were old, but not woefully rundown, homes and other buildings. A Superior Court in Connecticut found for the petitioners, but the Connecticut Supreme Court overturned that decision. Kelso and the others then took the case to the U.S. Supreme Court, setting the stage for the debate here. The first reading is an amicus curiae (friend of the court) brief filed with the U.S. Supreme Court by the Connecticut Conference of Municipalities and 31 other organizations representing cities and towns in other states and urging the court to uphold New London's actions. Replying is the Institute for Justice, whose attorneys represented Kelso and the other petitioners. The institute argues in its brief to the court that taking property that is not blighted for economic redevelopment is not permissible under eminent domain.

POINTS TO PONDER

➤ Near its beginning, the brief by Connecticut Conference of Municipalities outlines various definitions of "public use" ranging from a broad interpretation to a narrow one. Think about which one seems most reasonable, then see if you have changed your mind once you have finished reading the countervailing readings.

➤ The two readings comment on the degree of public participation and other factors in the process used to exercise eminent domain in this and other cases. Think about whether you agree that how the decision is made has any bearing on whether it was constitutional or not.

➤ To a degree this debate involved a clash between individualism (focus on the good of individuals) versus communitarianism (focus on the good of the community). Ponder where you think the line should be between protecting individual rights and promoting the general welfare.

Using Eminent Domain to Take Property for Economic Development: Serving the Public Good

CONNECTICUT CONFERENCE OF MUNICIPALITIES AND 31 OTHER STATE MUNICIPAL LEAGUES

I. HISTORY TEACHES THAT "PUBLIC USE" SHOULD BE GIVEN A BROAD INTERPRETATION THAT INCLUDES ECONOMIC DEVELOPMENT

The briefs filed in this case can be read to imply that this [Supreme] Court in [several recent cases upholding the use of eminent domain] abdicated a constitutional role it had previously performed in protecting property owners from overly zealous exercises of the power of eminent domain, and that the law should now be restored to its former glory. Nothing could be further from the truth. Petitioners [those opposing the use of eminent domain in this case] are the ones who seek a sharp break with settled constitutional understandings. They are urging the adoption of novel constitutional limitations on the exercise of eminent domain that have never had, and never should have, any basis in federal constitutional law.

A. The Rise and Fall of "Use by the Public"

There is little evidence that the Framers understood the words "for public use" in the Just Compensation Clause to incorporate any kind of substantive limitation on the ends to which the power of eminent domain may be devoted. [The "just compensation clause" is the language in the Fifth Amendment that specifies: "nor shall private property be taken for public use, without just compensation."] These words may have been intended merely to describe the type of taking for which just compensation must be given—a taking of specific private property by public authority as opposed to some other type of taking, such as a taking by tort or taxation. Nevertheless, "for public use" has been read throughout our history as imposing an implied limitation on the exercise of eminent domain— that it can be used only for public and not private uses—and this Court has accepted this interpretation. As an implied limitation on the power of eminent domain, the core case of a forbidden private use has always been clear: when the government takes A's property and gives it to B, with no public justification other than the legislature's preference for B over A. What has been less clear is just what sort of justification is necessary to elevate a taking from the A to B category and transform it into a public use.

Historically speaking, three different interpretations of "public use" can be discerned. The most restrictive interpretation requires that the government actually hold title to the property after the condemnation. The next-most restrictive definition is that public use means "use by the public." Under this definition, public title to the property is irrelevant; what is decisive is whether property is accessible as a matter of right to the public. The third and broadest definition is that public use means public benefit or advantage. Under this conception, neither title to the property after condemnation, nor access to the property by the general public, is necessary. Instead, property can be taken for any objective that the legislature rationally determines to be a sufficient public justification.

The narrowest possible definition—that public use means public ownership—has always been regarded as a fairly uncontroversial type of taking. Many routine examples of eminent domain—such as the acquisition of land for a highway—fit this definition. But public ownership has almost universally been regarded as too narrow to serve as a comprehensive definition of public use. Starting in the early years of the nineteenth century, States frequently delegated the power of eminent domain to privately-owned turnpike, canal and railroad corporations.

Later, such delegations were extended to privately-owned gas, electric, and telephone utilities. The widespread practice of delegating the power of eminent domain to these sorts of privately-owned common carriers and public utilities meant that courts almost never regarded public title to condemned property as a complete definition of public use.

During the colonial and early national periods, the understanding about the permissible scope of eminent domain appears to have been, at least implicitly, the broad view—that the power could be used for any purpose consistent with public benefit or advantage. The issue received little attention by courts, presumably because land was plentiful and eminent domain was little used. Around 1840, however, a judicial reaction began to set in. Many state courts began to endorse the more restrictive "use by the public" test. This permitted eminent domain to be delegated to railroads, turnpike companies, and the like, because these were common carriers subject to duties to serve the public on a nondiscriminatory basis. But, by definition, it would not permit eminent domain to be used by other types of enterprises, such as manufacturing plants or mining operations.

Almost immediately, those state courts which had endorsed the "use by the public" reading began to encounter cases in which the test appeared to be unduly restrictive.

The Mill Acts, which permitted riparian [on the bank or shore of a body of water] owners to build dams flooding the property of upstream owners, were a primary focus of controversy. With respect to grist mills that ground grain for area farmers, one could characterize the enterprise as being subject to common carrier-type duties, and hence as satisfying the "use by the public" criterion. But as the nineteenth century unfolded, Mill Acts increasingly came to include other types of mill dams, such as those powering textile plants and other types of manufacturing operations. Courts that had embraced the "use by the public" test struggled with these applications.

Similar problems were encountered when public utility companies began to acquire easements for electric and telephone distribution lines across private property, and many states, especially in the West, adopted statutes broadly permitting eminent domain to be used to facilitate the construction of mining operations, irrigation projects, and drainage districts. State courts that had adopted the "use by the public" test engaged in a variety of contortions in an effort generally to sustain these exercises of eminent domain. By the beginning of the twentieth century, as one commentator observed, "there had developed a massive body of case law, irreconcilable in its inconsistency, confusing in its detail and defiant of all attempts at classification."

The coup de grace to the "use by the public" test was delivered in the 1930s. Beginning with the National Industrial Recovery Act, followed by the Housing Acts of 1937 and 1949, Congress began appropriating significant federal funds to state and local government authorities to assist in the process of slum removal and construction of public housing. Many of these projects entailed the use of eminent domain either to clear deteriorated properties and/or to acquire sites for public housing. State courts uniformly rejected claims that these condemnations violated the public use limitation. From this point on, the "use by the public" test faded into obscurity. It is today the law in at most only a few States.

B. This Court Has Consistently Embraced the Broad View of Public Use

Throughout the roughly 100 years that witnessed the rise and fall of the "use by the public" standard in the state courts, this [the Supreme] Court never once sought to impose such a restriction on eminent domain as a matter of federal constitutional law. Cases decided by this Court around the turn of the twentieth century involving the development of natural resources are particularly instructive. These cases involved challenges to the use of eminent domain to construct a ditch to remove water from a drainage district, to construct ditches to bring water to irrigation districts, and to build an aerial bucket line to transport minerals taken from a mine. They establish three propositions of importance to the present controversy.

First, in none of the cases did the general public have any right of access to the property condemned [taken by eminent domain]. The Court specifically rejected the contention that a lack of public access made the exercise of the power of eminent domain constitutionally problematic.... Given that the two contending approaches to interpretation of public use at the time were the "use by the public" test and the public benefit or advantage test, the Court's explicit rejection of the narrow test represented a firm embrace of the broad public benefit or advantage interpretation.

Second, the Court stressed that the conditions that might justify the exercise of eminent domain vary greatly from one section of the country to another, making it inappropriate to lay down a single federal rule binding on all states. In [one case], the

Court upheld a Utah statute which had been applied to permit the condemnation of a ditch to convey water for irrigation to a single farm.

Third, the public rationale for the takings in each of these cases was the state's determination that the property was needed in order to enhance the productivity of particular resources. The Court recognized that the takings in these cases could not be justified on public health and safety grounds or on the ground that large numbers of persons directly benefited from the takings. Instead, in each case the condemnation was justified because,...it was needed to promote economic development. Each of these decisions therefore stands for the proposition that condemnation for the sole purpose of economic development is a legitimate public use, provided a state so determines and this judgment is a rational one in light of the circumstances of the property and the needs of the public....

As the federal government grew in the scope of its activities, this Court also began to encounter public use challenges to the exercise of eminent domain by federal authorities. The Court in these cases adhered to the broad conception of public use, permitting eminent domain to be used for a variety of ends, including acquiring land for a park, acquiring the site of the Battle of Gettysburg for a national memorial, acquiring land to retransfer to persons whose property had been flooded by a federal reservoir, and acquiring homes that had been cut off from access to the outside world by a federal reservoir.

From its earliest encounters with the public use issue, the Court's understanding of the applicable standard of review remained essentially unchanged. In [one case], the Court said: "[W]hen the legislature has declared the use or purpose to be a public one, its judgment will be respected by the courts, unless the use be palpably without reasonable foundation." [What this means is that] the determination of what ends constitute a public use is for the legislature to make, without any artificial restrictions on legislative choice such as the "use by the public" test. Legislative determinations of public use are subject to judicial review, but only under the highly deferential rationality standard that applies to constitutional challenges to social and economic legislation more generally.

In [recent] years…litigation over the public use issue has settled into a stable pattern. Federal courts have played a minor role in the process, and have been highly deferential to legislative determinations of public use. There are thirty-one published federal appellate decisions resolving public use controversies since [1954]. Only one of these decisions holds that a condemnation is not for a public use, and that decision turns largely on the conclusion that the taking was not an authorized public use under Indiana state law. The outcome in state courts, not surprisingly in a federal system, is somewhat more variable. There have been 513 state appellate decisions resolving public use controversies since [1954], the vast majority of which interpret "public use" language in state constitutions rather than the parallel language found in the federal Constitution. These decisions are also deferential to legislative determinations of public use, but less so than federal appellate decisions. Altogether, about one in six of these decisions (17%) holds that a challenged taking is not for a proper public use, mostly under state constitutional law.

In short, the law of public use has been and largely remains state constitutional law, reflecting the vagaries and traditions of each individual state. State courts have not failed to scrutinize the use of eminent domain to assure that states do not take property from A and give it to B without an adequate public justification. They have in fact invalidated a sizable number of takings as lacking a sufficient public use. The Connecticut Supreme Court's decision in this case [upholding New London] reflects the kind of careful consideration that state appellate courts continue to give to these issues. Federal courts, however, have stood to one side, and have allowed the state courts to police this issue.…

II. HEIGHTENED PUBLIC USE REVIEW IS NOT THE ANSWER TO MISUSE OR OVERUSE OF EMINENT DOMAIN

Eminent domain is admittedly an unsettling power. To be wrenched from one's home or business by order of the government is a deeply disruptive experience—with or without the payment of compensation. Such coercive power should be used sparingly. Heightened judicial review under the public use requirement, however, would provide a poor mechanism for protecting property owners against the misuse or overuse of eminent domain. Such review would aid only the lucky few who could persuade a panel of judges that the purpose of a particular exercise of eminent domain is not sufficiently "public." To be displaced by eminent domain is a potentially disorienting event for any property owner who experiences it, whatever the justification for the condemnation. What is needed are more general mechanisms that will assure that eminent domain is used as a last resort, not a first resort, and that mitigate the harshness of eminent domain for all who experience it.

Fortunately, there is reason to believe that those mechanisms are already in place. They do not work perfectly, and there is unquestionably room for refinements that would provide additional protections for property owners. But constructive solutions to eminent domain abuse or overuse lie in directions other than developing novel substantive limitations on the ends to which eminent domain can be used, or injecting federal courts into local land use planning processes through a heightened standard of review.

A. Keeping Eminent Domain as a Second-Best Option

[One factor that limits the use of eminent domain is that] as a general rule, it is cheaper to acquire resources through voluntary exchange in the market than it is to obtain them through eminent domain. Market exchange is of course not without cost. But the costs of eminent domain are generally greater....Eminent domain is generally more expensive because the power is [restrained] by a variety of procedural requirements that entail significant cost and delay for agencies seeking to acquire resources....Also [governments] must make an actual determination that condemnation is for a public use before exercising the power of eminent domain. We do not believe that a restrictive judicial gloss should be imposed on the meaning of public use, or that courts should apply a heightened standard of review to public use determinations. But we do believe it is important that some politically accountable body determine that the exercise of eminent domain is for a public use, and that judicial review of such determinations remain available, even if under a deferential standard. The prospect of judicial review and potential invalidation of public use determinations, especially in state courts where review has been more intrusive than in federal courts, adds another important increment to the expected costs of acquiring resources through eminent domain.

Perhaps the most constructive contribution courts can make in protecting against misuse or overuse of eminent domain is to insist that the procedural requirements associated with the exercise of eminent domain be faithfully followed in every case. These requirements not only provide valuable protections ex post for individual property owners when they have been singled out for condemnation. Perhaps more importantly, by increasing the costs and the delay associated with acquiring resources by eminent domain, they provide important protection to all property owners, by creating a powerful incentive for authorities with condemnation authority to use market transactions wherever possible. Strict enforcement of procedural requirements, in other words, makes eminent domain largely self-regulating, in the sense that it will only be used in situations where the costs of negotiated exchange are prohibitive.

B. Integrating Eminent Domain into Land Use Planning

Another source of protection for all property owners is to assure, to the extent possible, that eminent domain is exercised only in conjunction with a process of land use planning that includes broad public participation and a careful consideration of alternatives to eminent domain. Integrating the decision to use eminent domain into a sound planning process has a number of desirable consequences. Such a process can help minimize the use of eminent domain, by identifying alternatives to proposed development projects, such as relocating or re-sizing projects, or perhaps forgoing them altogether. It can also reduce public concerns about the use of eminent domain, by providing a forum in which the reasons for opposition can be considered, offering explanations for the proposed course of action and possible alternatives, and perhaps instilling a greater degree of understanding on the part of both the proponents and opponents of the proposed project.

We think that the presence of these features is relevant to this Court's consideration of whether the public use determination of New London and the New London

Development Corporation was a rational one. New London and its Development Corporation engaged in an extensive planning process before determining that it was necessary to exercise the power of eminent domain; they provided multiple opportunities for public participation in the planning process; and they gave extensive consideration to alternative plans before settling on the final plan.

Using Eminent Domain to Take Property for Economic Development: Abuse of Government Power

INSTITUTE FOR JUSTICE
REPRESENTING SUZETTE KELO AND 8 OTHER PETITIONERS

QUESTION PRESENTED

What protection does the Fifth Amendment's public use requirement provide for individuals whose property is being condemned, not to eliminate slums or blight, but for the sole purpose of "economic development" that will perhaps increase tax revenues and improve the local economy?

I. THE CONDEMNATION OF PETITIONERS' HOMES FOR THE SOLE PURPOSE OF ECONOMIC DEVELOPMENT VIOLATES THE PUBLIC USE REQUIREMENT OF THE FIFTH AMENDMENT.

The Connecticut Supreme Court held that the use of eminent domain in the hope that private development may generate taxes and jobs and improve the local economy did not violate the public use requirement of the Fifth Amendment. But this [the U.S. Supreme] Court has never gone so far. Thus, this...[the U.S. Supreme Court] should take this opportunity to reject the use of eminent domain purely for private business development because that is not a public use.

A. The Use of Eminent Domain for Private Economic Development Obliterates the Line Between Public and Private Takings.

While substantial deference must be given to legislative determinations of public use, this Court has consistently held that private takings [must conform with]...the public use requirement....As set forth below, in upholding eminent domain for private economic development, the majority of the Connecticut Supreme Court effec-

tively nullified the public use clause by making it virtually impossible to distinguish a public use from private takings. [This] opinion places all home and small business owners at risk, especially property owners of more modest means.

In addition to making a profit for themselves and their shareholders, businesses, if they are successful, generate tax revenue, employ individuals, and contribute to the overall economic vitality of a community. Indeed, the incidental benefits that flow to the government and the community from private businesses are commonly recognized as virtues of a free enterprise system. Under the standard adopted by the [Connecticut Supreme Court], however, private business development is transformed into a public use simply because of the "secondary" or "trickle-down" benefits a business may produce.

According to [that decision], so long as the City declares in good faith that there are economic benefits to be realized from condemnations and there is no overwhelming evidence that the takings were intended only to benefit a private party, any lower-tax generating use, such as a home or small business, could be taken and given to a larger private business that might be able to put the land to more "productive" use.

A fundamental flaw [of this reasoning] is that once the spin-off benefits of large private businesses become per se public uses, there really is no difference between intending to benefit a private party and intending to promote economic development.

In this case, [New London] clearly intends to benefit Pfizer, by meeting all of its "requirements" in developing the Fort Trumbull area. But the motivation in doing so was to reap the supposed trickledown benefits Pfizer-related development would bring to the area. When the "public uses" of greater tax revenue and employment are achieved only through the success of private parties, a distinction between an intent to benefit a private party and an intent to benefit the public becomes meaningless. As a result, eminent domain for economic development has no limiting principle.

Economic development condemnations [taking property under eminent domain] also do not have any geographic limitations. Unlike condemnations for blight, which are confined to certain areas that meet statutorily-defined criteria, the eminent domain power for economic development applies to all areas. Thus, all of downtown Greenwich or New Haven, the suburbs of Hartford, the farms of the northwestern part of the state, or any other area in Connecticut, regardless of its condition, is subject to eminent domain for commercial, financial or retail enterprises. By encouraging a vision of eminent domain where virtually any property can be taken for virtually any private business, the [Connecticut Supreme Court] invites abuse by governmental bodies and private parties....

Indeed [in this case], the whole idea behind economic development projects is replacing lower-income residents with higher-income ones and smaller, lower-tax stores and services with larger businesses. If a government agency can decide property ownership solely upon its view of who would put that property to more productive or attractive use, the inalienable right to own and enjoy property to the exclusion of others will pass to a privileged few who constitute society's elite. The rich may not inherit the earth, but they most assuredly will inherit the means to acquire any part of it they desire.

B. The Use of Eminent Domain for Economic Development Purposes Is Not Supported by this Court's Eminent Domain Jurisprudence Concerning the Transfer of Condemned Land to Private Parties.

In addition to conflating public and private use, eminent domain for economic development has no support in this [the U.S. Supreme] Court's previous statements as to what constitutes a public use under the Fifth Amendment. Eminent domain can unquestionably be used for traditional public uses such as the construction of public buildings and the creation of national parks. Moreover, this Court has noted that the public use clause of the Fifth Amendment does not absolutely prohibit the transfer of condemned land to private parties. But this Court has permitted the use of eminent domain to take private land and subsequently transfer it to other private parties only in specific and limited circumstances. Economic development is neither specific nor limited, and it falls under none of the categories this Court has previously approved....

The first category [occurs when] condemned land is constitutionally transferred to a private entity because "public necessity of the extreme sort" requires collective action. The primary example in this category is the construction of "instrumentalities of commerce," such as railroads, gas lines, and canals, all of which require coordination of land assembly.

The second category involves the private transferees that remain subject to strict operational controls in carrying out the public use. These cases typically concern the instrumentalities of commerce mentioned above or other closely regulated entities such as water or power companies that might be privately-owned, but are nonetheless performing vital public services. In these instances, a public body such as a utility commission must maintain sufficient control of the private company to ensure that the public services are provided.

[A third category] is when…the government…[takes] property necessary to clear "slums" and subsequently transfers the cleared or improved property to another private party. A slum was defined [by this Court] as "the existence of conditions injurious to the public health, safety, morals and welfare." In [this case, New London is] not operating under Connecticut's urban renewal law nor claiming that the purpose of the condemnations is the removal of blight.

In sum, the ordinary benefits that derive from private enterprise cannot constitute a public use under the Fifth Amendment. If all private business development is a "public use," it will be virtually impossible to distinguish between a public use and a private one. That result would violate this Court's repeated admonishments that private takings are prohibited by the Constitution. The use of eminent domain for private business development also conflicts with this Court's prior jurisprudence that permits the transfer of property from one private owner to another in only limited and specific circumstances. This Court should reject private economic development as a public use.

II. EVEN IF THIS COURT HOLDS THAT EMINENT DOMAIN FOR ECONOMIC DEVELOPMENT IS NOT CATEGORICALLY UNCONSTITUTIONAL, THESE PARTICULAR CONDEMNATIONS STILL DO NOT CONSTITUTE A PUBLIC USE.

Petitioners endorse a clear, bright-line rule that the trickle-down benefits of successful business do not make private business a public use. Nonetheless, if this Court holds that economic development could constitute a public use, it still should find that

these condemnations do not satisfy the constitutional requirement….[because] the condemnations lack minimum standards to ensure realization of public benefit, and the actual use of the property would not result in the purported public benefits.

A. "Public Use" Has Independent Significance in the Text of the Fifth Amendment.

Constitutional interpretation begins with the text, and this case concerns the meaning of "public use" in the Takings Clause [of the Fifth Amendment]—"Nor shall private property be taken for public use without just compensation." This Court presumes that every term in the Constitution has meaning and that nothing is superfluous. In the case of eminent domain, government is permitted to take property only for the enumerated purpose of "public use." Using the term "public use" presupposes the existence of something else—a private use; otherwise, "public use" would have no content at all. Accordingly, this Court consistently has held that the Takings Clause prohibits eminent domain for private use.…

The judicial interpretation of "public use" has, of course, expanded in the years since the Constitution was ratified, most notably to encompass the removal of slums and blight. But it is still an independent clause that retains an independent meaning. As the use of eminent domain moves further and further from the text, however, courts should take greater care to ensure that the exceptions are not allowed to swallow the rule.

B. Eminent Domain for Economic Development Should Not Receive the Same Deference as More Conventional Uses of the Power.

Even if this Court finds that economic development as a general matter can be a public use, there is no doubt that economic development condemnation projects are much more "private" than those for privately owned transportation or utilities. Economic development condemnations are intimately tied to private interest, private benefit, and private economic success. Because such condemnations have unique risks, those risks must be countered by a stronger connection between the use of eminent domain and the benefits sought to be achieved....

C. Economic Development Condemnations Carry Greater Constitutional Risk.

All eminent domain actions have the potential to expose condemnees [those whose property is being taken] to significant and uncompensable losses....[For example,] the pain of losing one's cherished home, the separation from family members and community, and other intangible but profound personal losses are not and cannot be shared or compensated. Indeed, the personal value of property ownership was a vital part of our nation's founding....If the petitioners [in this case] lose their homes, they will suffer just these types of personal and uncompensable losses. For example, there is no way to "justly" compensate petitioner Wilhelmina Dery, a woman in her late 80s and in poor health, for being forced out of the only home she has ever known....

There are at least two significant differences between many economic development condemnations and other, more conventional uses of eminent domain. First, economic development projects are uncertain ventures that often do not live up to their original promises. Second, in economic development condemnations, public benefits, if they occur at all, depend on the actions of third parties rather than the [government]....

III. THE SKY WILL NOT FALL IF THIS COURT RULES IN FAVOR OF PETITIONERS, WHILE A RULING AFFIRMING THE CONNECTICUT SUPREME COURT WILL OPEN THE FLOODGATES.

It is important to note the limited nature of petitioners' challenge. Petitioners challenge the condemnation of their homes for economic development alone. They do not challenge other government methods of trying to promote economic development. They do not challenge condemnations to eliminate blighted and harmful conditions. Connecticut and the five other states that have ruled that government may condemn for economic development all have urban renewal statutes that will remain in place.

In contrast, a ruling upholding the decision below will indicate to lower courts throughout the country that have not ruled on this issue that there is no bar under the U.S. Constitution against the use of eminent domain to raise more tax revenue or to improve the local economy, thus placing at risk all home and small business owners outside of the limited number of states that prohibit these takings. Henceforth, private business development will itself be a public use, and property may be forcibly acquired for private business, as long as the government claims that the project will lead to an increase in tax revenues or jobs. Such a claim will not be difficult to make. Every city desires more tax dollars, and a more "productive" use can be imagined for almost every property in the country. Only an utterly unimaginative and incompetent condemnor could fail to come up with a justification, and the public use requirement will be reduced to the question of whether the government body has a "stupid staff."

CONCLUSION

If the "public use" requirement means anything, it means that the government may not take A's home and give it to B, because B is likely to employ more people and produce more tax revenue. Condemnation for economic development goes far beyond anything this Court has previously considered. Such a radical leap is unwarranted, and unsupported by our Constitution.

THE CONTINUING DEBATE:
Taking Property by Eminent Domain for Economic Development

What Is New

In June 2005, the Supreme Court decided by 6 to 3 in favor of New London. Writing for the majority, Associate Justice John Paul Stevens held that "public use" can be equated with "public purpose," and that the city had acted legally because, "There is no basis for exempting economic development from our traditionally broad understanding of public purpose." Dissenting, Associate Justice Sandra Day O'Connor charged that the court had abandoned a "basic limitation on government power," and that "all private property is now vulnerable to being taken and transferred to another private owner, so long as it might be upgraded."

The decision caused a sensation, and it remains unclear whether the ultimate winners will be New London or Kelo and the other holdouts. In Connecticut, state legislators and Governor Jodi Rell called for a moratorium on the use of eminent domain by all municipalities in the states until laws could be rewritten to better protect property owners. Rell also threatened to cut off $65 in state funding for the New London redevelopment effort. Nevertheless, the NLDC served eviction notices on Kelo and other petitioners in September 2005. At the federal level, several bills were introduced in Congress to withhold federal development funds from states that allow private property to be taken in circumstances similar to those in the Kelo case. During Senate Judiciary Committee hearings, Kelo urged Congress to "protect our homes." Taking the opposite view during the hearings, Mayor Eddie Perez of Hartford, Connecticut, argued that the issue has been distorted by "frenzied rhetoric and misinformation" and eminent domain used for redevelopment "helps cities create jobs, grow business and strengthen neighborhoods."

Where to Find More

For an overview of eminent domain, read Richard Epstein, *Takings: Private Property and the Power of Eminent Domain* (Harvard University Press, 1989). You can read the Supreme Court's decision in *Kelo v. New London* and the concurring and dissenting opinions on the Web site of Cornell University Law School at www.law.cornell.edu/supct/html/04-108.ZO.html. Commentary on eminent domain from the Institute for Justice, the organization that represented Kelo, is available at www.ij.org/. For an opposing view, visit the site of the National League of Cities at www.nlc.org.

What More to Do

It is easy to take the side of the "little guy" battling "bid, bad" government, but consider this case in the abstract. A struggling small city tries to improve itself and benefit the vast majority of its residents through an ambitious redevelopment project that will bring jobs and new municipal revenue. It his blocked, however, by a handful of intransient people who won't sell their property for a fair price. The project is lost, and the city continues to struggle to provide decent municipal service to its residents, a large part of whom, as in most cities, are poor. Are the holdout individualistic heroes or communitarian hardheads?

ECONOMIC POLICY

CONSTITUTIONALLY REQUIRE A BALANCED BUDGET:
Fiscal Sanity *or* Fiscal Irresponsibility?

FISCAL SANITY

ADVOCATE: William Beach, Director, Center for Data Analysis, Heritage
Foundation

SOURCE: Testimony during hearings on the "Balanced Budget Amendment"
before the U.S. House of Representatives Committee on the Judiciary,
Subcommittee on the Constitution, March 6, 2003

FISCAL IRRESPONSIBILITY

ADVOCATE: Richard Kogan, Senior Fellow, Center on Budget and Policy
Priorities

SOURCE: Testimony during hearings on the "Balanced Budget Amendment"
before the U.S. House of Representatives Committee on the Judiciary,
Subcommittee on the Constitution, March 6, 2003

In a moment of candor, U.S. budget director David Stockman confessed in 1981,
"None of us really understands what's going on with all these numbers." Today's
budgets are even more daunting, given that they are three times larger (revenue: $1.8
trillion; expenditures: $2.1 trillion) than the one that perplexed Stockman. A few
questions and answers about the budget will help provide a foundation for thinking
about a balanced budget amendment. Unless noted, all data relates to the fiscal year
(FY) 2003 budget (October 1, 2002 to September 30, 2003).

How important is the budget to the U.S. economy? It is the most important
aspect of the economy. Budget outlays account for 19.5% of the U.S. gross domestic
product (GDP, the value of the wealth produced within a country).

How much has the budget grown? The budget has outpaced inflation and the
population. At $1.8 trillion, the FY2000 budget outlays were almost 3.5 million
times larger than the 1792 budget ($5.2 million). Even controlled for inflation, the
FY2000 budget was 1,101 times larger than in 1792. On a per capita basis, and again
controlling for inflation, the $6,406 per U.S. resident that the federal government
spent in FY2000 was 196 times more than in 1792.

Where does the money come from? Individual income taxes are the biggest
source (49%). Other sources are corporate taxes (10%), payroll taxes (*e.g.*, social security and Medicare, 36%), and miscellaneous taxes (5%).

Where does the money go? Human resources (*e.g.*, health, welfare, and social
security) consume 65% of the budget. Other outlays are national defense (17%),
physical resources (*e.g.*, environment and transportation, 5%), interest on the national debt (8%), and other functions (5%). The most important shift in spending in
recent decades has been the relative decrease in defense spending (48% of outlays in
FY1963) and increase in human resources spending, (28% that year).

What are some relevant budget concepts? One set is the *discretionary budget* and the *mandatory budget*. The first involves programs that receive specific annual appropriations. The second involves "entitlement" programs funded by a formula (*e.g.*, food stamps) and also expenditures the government is legally obligated to make (*e.g.*, paying interest on the national debt). Discretionary programs make up 37% of expenditures. Note that Congress, at its discretion, can change the formulas and thus the costs of entitlement programs or even abolish them. The second set of concepts is *on-budget* and *off-budget* receipts and expenditures. On-budget accounts are those that flow in and out of the U.S. Treasury. Off-budget accounts either go through special "trust funds," such as the social security account, or through such corporate-like activities as the U.S. Postal Service. On-budget accounts equal 74% of receipts and 83% of expenditures.

What is the history of budget surpluses and deficits? Since 1900, there has been a budget deficit about 70% of the years, including every year since 1970 except FY1998–FY2001. The estimated budget deficit for FY2003 is $304 billion, about $1,050 per U.S. resident.

How does the government fund the deficit? It borrows money. The government borrows some from itself by, for example, dipping into the social security trust fund. The rest it borrows by selling bonds to the public. In late 2001, the national debt was $5.8 trillion ($20,500 per American). Of that the government owed itself $2.5 trillion and the public $3.3 trillion. Interest on the public debt was $108 billion. Foreign investors hold 30% of the bonds. The national debt is 56% of the GDP, the same proportion as in 1960.

What is the history of trying to control the budget? In recent decades, attempts to legislatively control the budget began amid the perennial and mounting deficits between FY1970 and FY1997. They peaked in FY1992 at $290 billion, equal to about 21% of the budget. During these years, Congress passed several budget control acts. Each had some impact on restraining the budget, but none has provided a permanent solution. The surplus achieved during FY1998–FY2001 was more the result of revenues generated by one of the most prosperous decades in U.S. history than budget control. Attempts to add a balanced budget amendment to the Constitution have failed. The House passed such an amendment in 1997, but it was defeated in the Senate by one vote.

POINTS TO PONDER

➤ Think about who favors and opposes a constitutional balanced budget amendment. Is the idea inherently conservative or liberal?

➤ Compare the dangers William Beach argues result from deficit spending and those Richard Kogan sees if a balanced budget amendment is adopted.

➤ Consider politics and ask yourself why president and Congress have such a difficult time balancing the budget.

Constitutionally Require a Balanced Budget: Fiscal Sanity

William Beach

There are many things that the 108th Congress [2003–2004] can do for the long-term well being of those represented by the members: among them are strengthen our national and domestic security, provide tax relief that yields a stronger economy, and enact needed reforms to key programs that affect the country's neediest citizens. However, this Congress certainly would secure its place in history and fulfill its obligation to govern for the general good if it referred to the states for ratification an amendment to the Constitution that requires the federal government to operate within a balanced budget.

My testimony today is divided among three headings: 1) the constitutional importance of vigorous debate over competing priorities; 2) the statistical evidence that supports a rapid movement toward a balanced budget amendment; and 3) the role that dynamic revenue estimation plays in the process of achieving annual budget balances.

THE PLACE OF SPENDING DEBATES IN THE HEALTH OF THE CONSTITUTION

I know that many fiscal conservatives view the balanced budget amendment as justified principally on financial grounds. It is virtually uncontroversial that governments at all levels should practice the spending disciplines of well-run businesses. This practice is especially important at the federal level, if for no other reason than the enormous influence that federal spending has on other governments and the economy generally. Spending limitations encourage better accounting controls and auditing

processes, which assure that the monies allocated to address the priorities of voters are, indeed, well spent.

However, I believe that a larger, constitutional goal is served by amending the constitution to require a balanced budget: representative government works only as well as it allows a full airing of its citizens' divergent views, particularly in open debates over competing public policy priorities. Without a way to limit spending, such debates are unlikely to occur.

Suppose an extreme situation in which there exist no limitations on the ability of the federal government to spend taxpayers' funds except the capacity of taxpayers to produce revenues. In such a world, no one's spending goals would go unachieved in the short run. There would, as a consequence, be no debate over the direction the nation should go in meeting the needs of its elderly citizens, its educational systems, or its national defense. And, without debate and the deep social, economic, and policy inquiry such debate engenders, we would likely be unable to sustain our republican form of government.

Of course, such an extreme world cannot exist for long, if for no other reason than boundless spending by government inevitably destroys the economy out of which revenues flow. The point of this scenario, however, applies equally well to more realistic gradients of the extreme case. The ability of a government to avoid hard decisions about priorities because it can borrow to meet its revenue shortfalls also diminishes debate over competing views of our country's future and current priorities. This borrowing ability may, as well, enable organizations with powerful lobbying capabilities to squeeze millions of dollars in subsidies from Congress and the Administration with the public scrutiny that debate can produce.

ARE THERE REASONS FOR BEING CONCERNED?

These constitutional considerations should be justification enough to adopt a balanced budget amendment, even if reality had yet to catch up with the possibilities outlined above. However, the evidence is mounting that those fiscal disciplines that may once have protected these vital constitutional processes have yielded utterly to growth in spending that far exceeds required levels.

Let me highlight a few facts:

• The outlays of the federal government today are slightly more than 23 times greater than they were in 1960.

• Government spending after adjusting for inflation has increased by nearly five fold since 1960, while the population has grown by a factor of 1.6.

• Per capita federal spending now stands at $7,600. In 1960, per capita federal spending stood at $510.

• Per capita share of publicly held federal debt now stands at $13,720. In 1960, this share stood at $1,310.

• Total publicly held debt in 1960 was about $236.8 billion. In 2003 it equals about $3.88 trillion.

• Worse news on the debt is on the way. By 2020, most of the baby boom generation will be retired and drawing monthly checks from Social Security. By 2030, the total Medicare enrollment will be more than double the current Medicare population. Neither Medicare nor Social Security is expected to survive the onset of the baby boom

without massive infusions of additional cash or major structural reform. The unfunded liabilities of Social Security alone are now in excess of $21 trillion over the next 75 years.

The recent Congresses have shown little will to reverse or even slow this explosion in federal spending. The 107th Congress completed a four-year spending spree that exceeds every other four-year period since the height of World War II. Between 2000 and 2003, federal spending grew by $782 billion. This growth in spending is equivalent to $73,000 in household spending, which, again, was exceeded only during the darkest hours of the Second World War.

If the spending record of the period 1960 through 2000 fails to convince members of Congress that spending growth is beyond their collective abilities to control, the past four years should abundantly make the case.

THE ROLE OF DYNAMIC REVENUE ESTIMATION IN THE BUDGET PROCESS

Exceptionally rapid growth in government spending, such as we've seen in the last four years, bears down heavily on the general economy and, thus, on federal revenue growth. The consumption of goods and services by government generally comes at the expense of consumption and investment by private companies. This redirection of economic resources should be a concern to policy makers because private companies generally use identical resources more productively than government. When government uses economic resources instead of private firms, the growth of the economy slows below its potential, which reduces potential employment and tax revenue growth.

Members of Congress and the general public do, however, change public policy from time to time in order to achieve a specific end, like winning a war or encouraging an expansion of economic activity that call for spending above revenues. When the public and the Congress begin considering these policy changes, a better, more informed debate will be had if those involved in the decision process are able to see estimates of how their proposed changes would affect budget outcomes.

For reasons well beyond this hearing, Congress has resisted the adoption of dynamic tax and budget analysis in the past. However, the 107th Congress made great progress in bringing macroeconomic analysis into the tax policy debate, and a beginning also was made in introducing this analytical discipline into the preparation of the annual budget.

I raise this emerging capability here because it relates directly to the constitutional and fiscal importance of evaluating competing budget priorities. If the budget committees and those other bodies that propose tax policy changes were to use macroeconomic analysis as a routine part of their deliberations, I am confident the Congress would make better decisions between competing budget priorities than they do now.

Let me briefly illustrate how dynamic economic analysis could inform the annual debate over the federal budget. The Center for Data Analysis at The Heritage Foundation recently completed an econometric analysis of President Bush's proposed economic growth plan. This plan contains a number of major changes to current tax law, including the end to the double taxation of dividends. We introduced these tax law changes into a model of the U.S. economy that is widely used by Fortune 500 companies and government agencies to study such changes. Here are few of the interesting effects we found that would likely stem from adopting the President's plan:

- Employment would grow by nearly a million jobs per year over the next ten years, which adds significantly to the tax base of federal and state governments.

- The drop in the unemployment rate reduces government outlays for unemployed workers at all levels of government.

- Investment grows much more strongly under a tax regime without the double taxation of dividends than with such a policy, which expands the growth rate of the general economy, thus offsetting some of the deleterious effects of rapidly growing federal spending.

- The payroll tax revenues grow more rapidly with President Bush's plan than without, thus adding about $60 billion more to the trust funds than currently forecasted.

- Most importantly, the forecasts of fiscal doom made by many of the plan's critics fail to materialize. The additional economic growth produced by the plan reduces the ten-year "cost" to about 45 percent of its static amount.

- This economic feedback also reduces the growth of new publicly held debt that the plan's critics expect. Instead of a trillion dollars in new debt, the economic growth components of the plan produce significantly under 50 percent of that amount. In fact, the plan supports the creation of $3 in after-tax disposable income for every $1 of new debt, while still reducing all publicly held debt by 28 percent between 2004 and 2012.

While this testimony has touched on only a few of the many arguments that can be advanced in support of a balanced budget amendment, I trust that the thrust of my interest in this constitutional outcome is clear. We need the amendment not only to contain the growth in spending (a worthy goal all by itself), but also to protect our constitutional process of vigorous public debate over important policy alternatives. A budget process constrained by a balanced budget amendment and accompanied by the routine use of standard macroeconomic analysis would be more likely to produce the size and quality of government that most Americans desire.

Constitutionally Require a Balanced Budget:
Fiscal Irresponsibility

RICHARD KOGAN

The question before us today is whether the Constitution should be amended to require that the federal budget be balanced every year....

First, let me very briefly explain how restrictive the text of the current proposed amendment really is. By requiring that each year's expenditures be covered by that year's income, the amendment would preclude borrowing, even during times of unusual duress, such as wars or recessions; moreover, it would effectively preclude saving for the future, because the money saved in the present *could not be used* to cover future costs.

No state or local government, no family, and no business is required to operate under such restrictions. Every family borrows to finance the purchase of a house—that's what a mortgage is—and many borrow to finance higher education; every state, city, or county borrows to pay for school, road, or hospital construction or parkland acquisition; and most growing businesses borrow to finance new capital construction or acquisition.

Moreover, the amendment would prohibit dipping into past savings, since under the amendment *this* year's costs must be covered entirely by *this* year's income. Yet most families dip into savings to pay for a child's college education and certainly to cover costs during retirement; every state that "balances" its budget in fact can use its rainy day fund to help cover costs during a recession; and businesses often use retained earnings from prior years to finance expansions. This amendment makes saving for the future

pointless because the saved money could never be used: it would be unconstitutional to use rainy day funds, or to use the accumulating assets in the Social Security trust fund to help cover the costs of the baby boomers' retirement. In effect, it would prohibit this generation from building up public savings, or paying down public debt, for the express purpose of providing assets to make the burden on future generations lighter.

Second, such a restrictive amendment is truly inferior economics—it would require the government to reduce consumption during recessions, thus slowing the economy even further, throwing more people out of work, and in some cases running the risk of turning a recession into a full-blown depression. This Administration is exactly right when it says that Congress should not raise taxes during a recession. By the same token, Congress should not cut public spending during a recession. Either action takes purchasing power out of the hands of consumers at exactly the wrong time. In effect, the amendment would ban automatic stabilizers, such as unemployment compensation. Likewise, the amendment would give the seal of approval to over-stimulating the economy during an inflationary boom, risking an acceleration of inflation that could be seriously destabilizing.

Even though the states operate under much less restrictive rules, the actions states are forced to take during the current recession—raising taxes and cutting education, health care, social services, and infrastructure—are harming the economy and slowing the recovery; this fact makes it doubly important to maintain robust automatic stabilizers at the federal level.

Third, the experience of the last twenty years illustrates that setting targets for a budget surplus, or deficit, or balance, is not workable but that limiting the cost of legislation works far better. From the mid 1980s through 2000, three Presidents and many Congresses gradually worked to undo the damage of the first half of the 1980s, mostly by taking hard votes but partly by writing statutory rules or rules of House and Senate procedure providing guidance that Congress very largely followed. Especially after Gramm-Rudman-Hollings I and II were replaced by the far more workable system of appropriations caps and a rule of budget neutrality for tax and entitlement legislation—the so-called PAYGO rule—the budget moved from deficit to surplus. The relative failure of GRH I and II is important because those laws, like the amendment before us, attempted to set a specific fiscal target for the budget. The relative success of caps and the PAYGO rule illustrates that targeting the *cost of legislation*—rather than the overall level of the surplus or deficit—is a far superior road to the desired result. If this subcommittee is truly concerned about future deficits, it should work with the Budget and Rules Committees and the Administration to re-impose reasonable appropriations caps and the rule of budget neutrality. More importantly, Members should eschew any new tax cuts or entitlement increases, such as a prescription drug benefit, except to the extent that they are fully offset.

Fourth, almost every state has a political system in which the governor is inherently much more powerful than the legislators, most of whom are part-time legislators with other jobs. This is a logical consequence of allowing governors great freedom to implement or not implement elements of the budget, depending on circumstances, given various state balanced-budget requirements. By analogy, this amendment could lead to a vast strengthening of presidential powers and a weakening of congressional authority. This worries me; Congress is not very efficient, but its very inefficiency was deliberate, to minimize hasty and ill-considered actions. This has worked well for a few centuries, and I see no need to fundamentally change the balance of power.

Fifth, it is possible that power won't be shifted from the Congress to the President, but rather from the Congress and President to the courts. My guess is that the courts would find the amendment unenforceable, making this exercise mere show. But if the courts believed the Constitution prohibited an unbalanced budget except to the extent Congress voted by supermajority to approve it, then the risks of this amendment would be profound. We have absolutely no way of knowing what a court would do to balance the budget when Congress refused, or more likely, when the budget fell out of balance despite Congress' best efforts. I have attached a paper raising many of the legal avenues that can be imagined—court-ordered surtaxes or benefit cuts; court-ordered enactment of tax increases or spending cuts that the President had vetoed; court-ordered enactment of tax increases or benefit cuts that Congress had designed but had been defeated; court-ordered invalidation of appropriations bills, entitlement increases, and tax cuts; or contempt citations.

Sixth, whether the Courts will enforce the balanced budget amendment or not, there are a wide variety of gimmicks Congress can use to evade it. Among these are borrowing by another name, e.g. lease-purchase contracts; paying for costs through contingent liabilities, e.g. loan guarantees or insurance contracts; timing shifts that move costs from the present to the future, e.g. back-loaded IRAs and the new so-called "savings account" proposals; off-loading federal programs onto nominally independent "government-sponsored enterprises" such as REFCORP [Resolution Funding Corporation: an agency created in 1989 to issue bonds needed to raise funds to deal with the crisis caused by the collapse of numerous savings and loan institutions.]; and the perennial favorite, unfunded mandates on states, localities, businesses, and individuals. In fact, if this amendment were enacted, it could ultimately be referred to as the Unfunded Mandates Act of 2003. [Unfunded mandates are requirements to act without providing funding to carry out the mandated actions].

Seventh, let us leave aside the constitutional question for the moment and ask the public policy question. *Should* the Federal Government aim to balance its budgets? Clearly not during a recession, as I have said. How about on average over the business cycle? Even here, I think that a balanced budget would be the wrong general target. A better target would be to run surpluses, not balance, for the remainder of the decade, in an attempt to pay off much or all of the debt before the baby boom generation retires. The purpose, in this case, is to reduce or eliminate future federal payments for interest on the debt and thereby allow future tax revenue to be used entirely to pay for public benefits and needs, such as Social Security or defense. Because the federal government is a major supporter of people in retirement and because there will be a bulge in retirees at the end of the decade, federal costs will inevitably grow starting in about a decade. If we can reduce federal costs for interest at the same time that the federal costs of Social Security and Medicare are growing, we can afford *part* of the increased costs of Social Security and Medicare without having to raise taxes.

Thus, the question is whether we should pay somewhat higher taxes now (when I am paying them) in order to pay off the debt, or wait a decade or more to raise taxes, when I will be retired but my children will be paying taxes. It seems to me only fair that I and my generation be willing to reduce the tax burden on my children and their generation by being willing to pay somewhat higher taxes now so that we can reduce or eliminate the debt before we retire.

In short, if we are discussing budget policy rather than artificial budget rules, we happen to be in one of the rare decades in which surpluses are generally a better goal than balanced budgets. A surplus doesn't mean we are collecting "extra, unneeded" taxes; it merely means that the taxes we are collecting now will be needed for our future retirement.

This policy discussion illustrates one reason the constitutional amendment is a bad idea: circumstances change over time. During some decades, balance might be generally a good goal, but one should also take into account the private saving rate and needs of the future. In the particular circumstance we are in, where we can predict with certainty that the need for public expenditures will increase in the future compared with current needs, it makes sense for the nation to save for the future by paying down debt. Unlike the right to free speech or the right to a lawyer (which can be viewed as a permanent right), the appropriate general target for fiscal policy depends on circumstances, so it is inherently wrong to enact any such target into the Constitution.

Finally, a constitutional balanced budget amendment is fundamentally unworthy of a democracy. Our Constitution currently allows *every* public policy question—war versus peace, the levels and types of taxes, the purposes and amount of public expenditures, what constitutes a federal crime, whether to admit a new state to the Union—to be decided by majority vote. (True, the rights of individual citizens are protected against a majority decision to discriminate, and it takes a 2/3 vote to override a presidential veto. But these aspects of the Constitution do not favor one set of public policy preferences over any other.) Under a constitutional Balanced Budget Amendment, citizens with one preference on public policy (let us say, those who favor a tax cut or an increase in unemployment benefits during a recession, or merely allowing revenues to fall naturally and the normal unemployment compensation law to continue to operate) would have fewer legal rights than citizens with the opposite viewpoints because they would need more votes to win. This is so inherently unfair that it should be rejected out of hand. Equal legal rights, including the right to have our votes count the same amount as anyone else's votes, is fundamental.

THE CONTINUING DEBATE:
Constitutionally Require a Balanced Budget

What Is New

Concern over chronic budget deficits was quieted for a time by the cumulative $558 billion budget surplus of FY1998–FY2001. Then the budget plunged back into deficit spending and big deficit have continued and are projected to continue at least through the end of the decade. One factor was unexpected and costly events, especially the 9/11 terrorist attacks in 2001, the Iraq War and stabilization effort beginning in 2003, and the devastation caused by Hurricane Katrina in 2005. Another factor was the inability of the country's political leadership to agree on fiscal priorities. Democrat blamed tax cuts passed by the Republicans for much of the spending gap, and Republicans blamed the Democrats in Congress for blocking cuts in social welfare spending that the president had called for. The net result was that for FY2002 through FY2005, spending exceeded federal revenues by nearly $1.4 trillion, with FY2005 (−$427 billion) the worst year. If current U.S. Office of Management projections are correct (and they do not yet factor in the cost of Hurricane Katrina), then FY2006 through FY2010 will add almost another $1.4 trillion to the national debt, for a cumulative deficit for FY2002–FY2010 of $2.76 trillion. For those years, the Congressional Budget Office (CBO) puts the cumulative deficit at $2.99 trillion. A sobering thought is that using the OMB data, the average deficit during those 9 years comes to over $840 million a day.

Where to Find More

Data and commentary about the budget, budget history, and projected budgets are available at the OMB site (http://www.whitehouse.gov/omb/) and the CBO site (http://www.cbo.gov/). To learn the details of the balanced budget introduced in the House of Representatives in 2003, go to Thomas, the Web page of Congress, at http://thomas.loc.gov/, click "Search Bills and Resolution," choose the 108th Congress, and enter in "HJ Res 22" (House Joint Resolution 22) in window labeled "Bill Number." Further information is available on the Web sites of the two advocates' centers: Richard Kogan's Center on Budget and Policy Priorities (http://www.cbpp.org/) and William Beach's Center for Data Analysis, Heritage Foundation (http://www.heritage.org/research/).

What More to Do

There are few if any easy budget choices. It is easy to say, "Slash welfare spending and make those people get jobs" or "Vastly increase taxes on those fat-cat rich people and corporations and make them pay their fair share." Such statements do not make real budgets. To "get real," do two things. One, in your class take the budget for the current year (FY2006) and revise it. If you want to balance it, you will need to hike taxes or cut spending. So decided who gives and who gets. Second, debate and, if you wish, amend House Joint Resolution 22, the proposal in the 108th Congress to add a balanced budget amendment to the Constitution. While you are at it, tell your members of Congress what you think.

17 CRIMINAL JUSTICE POLICY

THE DEATH PENALTY:
Racially Biased *or* Justice Served?

RACIALLY BIASED

ADVOCATE: Julian Bond, Professor of History, University of Virginia and Distinguished Professor-in-Residence, American University

SOURCE: Testimony during hearings on "Race and the Federal Death Penalty," before the U.S. Senate Committee on the Judiciary, Subcommittee on Constitution, Federalism, and Property Rights, June 13, 2001

JUSTICE SERVED

ADVOCATE: Andrew G. McBride, former U.S. Associate Deputy Attorney General

SOURCE: Testimony during hearings on "Race and the Federal Death Penalty," before the U.S. Senate Committee on the Judiciary, Subcommittee on Constitution, Federalism, and Property Rights, June 13, 2001

Murder and capital punishment share four elements. They are: (1) a planned act (2) to kill (3) a specific person who (4) is not immediately attacking anyone. Should then murder and capital punishment be judged just or unjust by the same standard?

The first question is whether killing is ever justified. The doctrine of most religions contain some variation of the commandment, "Thou shalt not kill." For moral absolutists and pacifists, this prohibition is unbendable. They would not kill another person under any circumstances. Most people, however, are moral relativists who evaluate good and evil within a context. They do not condemn as immoral killing in such circumstances as self-defense and military combat.

What about premeditated acts by individuals? Most societies condemn these as murder even if the other person has harmed you. To see this, assume that a murderer has killed a member of your family. You witnessed it and thus are sure who is guilty. If you track down the murderer and execute him or her, by law now you are also a murderer. Yet 67% of Americans favor capital punishment, which is the state carrying out roughly the same act.

Arguably the difference is the willingness of most people to apply different moral standards to individuals acting privately and society acting through its government. This distinction is an ancient one. For example, God may have commanded "Thou shalt not kill" for individuals (Exodus 20:13), but in the very next chapter God details "ordinances" to Moses, including, "Whosoever strikes a man so that he dies shall be put to death" (Exodus 21:12). The point here is not whether you want to accept the words that Exodus attributes to a deity. After all, just two verses later, God also decrees death to "whoever curses his father or his mother." This would leave few teenagers alive today. Instead, the issue to wrestle with is whether and why it is just or unjust for a government, but not an individual, to commit an act with the four elements noted in the first paragraph. For those who see no moral distinction between actions by individuals and a society, capital punishment is wrong no matter how heinous the crime is, how fair the legal system is, or what the claimed benefits of executing criminals are.

There are others, though, who do not argue that capital punishment is inherently immoral. Their view is that executions have no positive effect. To think about this point, you have to first decide what it is you want capital punishment to accomplish. One possibility is to deter others from committing similar crimes. The other possibility is punishment as a way of expressing the society's outrage at the act. A great deal of the debate at this level is about whether capital punishment is a deterrent. It is beyond the limited space here to take up that debate, but to a degree it misses the point of why most Americans who favor capital punishment do so. When asked in a 2001 poll why they support it, 70% replied it is "a fitting punishment" for convicted murders, while only 25% thought, "the death penalty deters crime," and 4% were unsure.

Yet another line of attack on capital punishment is that the system is flawed. Some contend that mistakes get made, and innocent people are sometimes convicted and executed. Then there is the argument represented in this debate made by Julian Bond and disputed by Andrew McBride that, as conducted in the United States, the process from investigation, through trial and sentencing, to the carrying out of the death penalty is racially tainted. There can be little doubt that the demographic characteristics of those executed are not in proportion to their group's percentage of the society. Between 1977 and 2001, African Americans (about 12% of the population) made up 36% of those executed. Because federal criminal justice statistics classify Latinos as "white," it is hard to find the impact of executions on that group. However, Texas and California give some clues. Combined, the two states' population is 49% white, 9% African American, 28% Latino, and 16% other identifiers. The two states' combined death row population is 37% white, 38% African American, 22% Latino, and 4% others. It must be said that the disproportionate number of blacks executed does not by itself prove racial bias. Fully 98% of all those executed are men, yet there is little to argue the system is biased against males. Instead, consider the arguments of Bond and McBride carefully.

POINTS TO PONDER

➤ What evidence does Julian Bond provide to support his claim that "the death penalty serves as a shield for attitudes on race" in the United States.

➤ Given the disproportionate percentage of blacks executed, how does Andrew McBride justify his argument that "there is no credible statistical evidence of racial bias in the enforcement of the federal death penalty"?

➤ What, if anything, would make you change your view on capital punishment?

The Death Penalty:
Racially Biased

JULIAN BOND

Thank you for inviting me to offer my perspective as Chairman of the Board of the National Association for the Advancement of Colored People (NAACP) and as a member of Citizens for a Moratorium on Federal Executions (CMFE).

The NAACP is the nation's oldest and largest civil rights organization. We have long been opposed to the death penalty and are horrified by its all too frequent and easily documented racially discriminatory application. We do not believe it deters crime. It targets and victimizes those who cannot afford decent legal representation. It is used against the mentally incompetent. It tragically sends the innocent to death.

The death penalty serves as a shield for attitudes on race. It is used most often in states with the largest African-American populations and disproportionately used when the accused is black and the victim is white. In addition to being bad domestic policy, it increasingly alienates the United States from our allies and lessens our voice in the international human rights arena.

I am also a member of Citizens for a Moratorium on Federal Executions (CMFE). CMFE is a coalition of dozens of American public figures who joined together last fall when Juan Raul Garza was scheduled to be the first individual executed by the United States Government in nearly 40 years. Some members of CMFE support the death penalty in specific circumstances; others are unalterably opposed. Nonetheless, we spoke with one voice in urging President Clinton to declare a moratorium on federal executions.

Among the 40 people who signed CMFE's first letter to President [Bill] Clinton, delivered on November 20, 2000, were former high-ranking members of the Justice Department, former Clinton administration officials, the Dean of the Yale Law School, a Nobel Laureate, Congressional Gold Medal and Presidential Medal of Freedom recipients, civil rights, religious and civic leaders, former U.S. Senators, and prominent individuals in the world of arts and entertainment. Since last November, CMFE's roster has expanded to include an even broader spectrum of civil rights and religious leaders, the Founder and President of the Rutherford Institute, the Editor of the *American Spectator*, and a former United States Ambassador.

There can be no question that CMFE was able to assemble this cross-section of prominent U.S. citizens to call for a moratorium on federal executions because the public is prepared to carefully re-examine the use of capital punishment in this nation. At no time since the death penalty was reinstated by the Supreme Court in 1976 have Americans voiced such grave doubts about the fairness and reliability of capital punishment. At the state level, those doubts are reflected in the unprecedented moratorium on executions put into place by Governor Ryan of Illinois, in death penalty moratorium bills introduced and enacted in state legislatures, and in studies commissioned by Governors in other states. At the national level, Senator [Dianne] Feingold [D-CA] has introduced a bill calling for a moratorium on federal executions and Senator [Patrick] Leahy

[D-VT] has introduced legislation that would require greater protections for those prosecuted for capital crimes at the state and federal levels. Professional, community and civil rights organizations, including the League of United Latin American Citizens (LULAC), the National Urban League, the NAACP, the Black Leadership Forum, the Leadership Conference on Civil Rights and the American Bar Association, have called on the Executive Branch to suspend federal executions, and religious organizations have intensified their long-standing calls for a death penalty moratorium.

When CMFE addressed President Clinton on November 20, we were responding to the September 12 release of the Department of Justice survey that documented racial, ethnic and geographic disparities in the charging of federal capital cases. The CMFE wrote: "Unless you take action, executions will begin at a time when your own Attorney General has expressed concern about racial and other disparities in the federal death penalty process. Such a result would be an intolerable affront to the goals of justice and equality for which you have worked during your Presidency. Consequently, we urge you to put in place a moratorium until the Department of Justice completes its review of the federal death penalty process."

As I speak to you today, of course, the first federal execution in almost 40 years has been carried out. The man put to death was not Mr. Garza, who now faces execution in less than a week's time, on June 19 [Garza was executed that day at the U.S. Penitentiary in Terre Haute, Indiana].

Mr. Garza did not precede Timothy McVeigh to the death chamber in Terre Haute because, on December 7, 2000, President Clinton stayed Mr. Garza's execution for six months. While the President announced that he was not prepared to halt all federal executions, he nonetheless told the nation that further examination of possible racial and regional bias in the federal death penalty system "... should be completed before the United States goes forward with an execution in a case that may implicate the very questions raised by the Justice Department's continuing study. In this area there is no room for error."

Nothing has transpired since President Clinton's December 7 statement and grant of reprieve that warrants going forward with Mr. Garza's execution nor with carrying out the death sentence of any of the other 19 individuals on federal death row. We reject any suggestion that the report released by Mr. Ashcroft on June 6 constitutes a reliable or thorough study of possible racial and regional bias in the federal death penalty system. Nor does it answer the troubling questions raised by the Justice Department's September 12 survey.

On December 8, the day following the President's decision to stay Mr. Garza's execution, I was one of several CMFE representatives, who, along with Congressman John Conyers, met with former Attorney General Reno, former Deputy Attorney General Holder and other Justice Department attorneys to discuss President Clinton's announcement and plans for a more comprehensive investigation of the federal death penalty, which would include the participation of outside experts. Members of the Department of Justice acknowledged that this critical task could not be accomplished by the end of April of this year, the timetable set by President Clinton when he announced the December reprieve for Mr. Garza.

The result of that discussion with Attorney General Reno and Deputy Attorney General Holder was memorialized in the CMFE's letter to President Clinton, dated January 4, 2001.

We next learned that on January 10, 2001, the National Institute of Justice assembled a group of experts from within and without the Department of Justice to discuss the parameters of the comprehensive investigation that the Attorney General, Deputy Attorney General and the President had announced was needed.

At his confirmation hearing, then-Attorney General-designate John Ashcroft stated that evidence of racial disparities in the application of the federal death penalty "troubles me deeply." Acknowledging he was "unsure" why more than half the federal capital prosecutions were initiated in less than one-third of the states, the Attorney General asserted that he was also "troubled" by this evidence.

He expressed his approval of a "thorough study of the system," and proclaimed, "Nor should race play any role in determining whether someone is subject to capital punishment."

On June 4, 2001, CMFE wrote to President Bush, reiterating our call for a moratorium on federal executions. We raised the concern that the Attorney General's actions and statements subsequent to his confirmation hearing "cast doubt" on "the Administration's commitment to the principles he set forth at his confirmation hearing." We noted that "[t]here has been no indication that the Department intends to continue the necessary independent investigation of racial and geographic bias in the death penalty, which was to have been administered by the National Institute of Justice. Moreover, Attorney General Ashcroft's statements to members of Congress, including his testimony before the House Appropriations Committee in early May, suggest that even the internal inquiry that the Department of Justice embarked upon will consist of little more than a re-analysis of the same data already examined and found to demonstrate 'troubling' racial and geographic disparities." Just two days later, on June 6

2001, the Department of Justice released a flawed study purporting to demonstrate that federal administration of the death penalty was bias-free.

Now, Attorney General Ashcroft claims that "there is no evidence of favoritism towards white defendants in comparison with minority defendants." But such evidence does exist, and its existence raises serious doubts about fairness in our criminal justice system.

Without guarantees of fairness, there can be no public confidence in the administration of justice.

That lack of confidence is heightened and the guarantees of fairness are lessened by the Department of Justice's recent report on the Federal Death Penalty System.

Evidence of race-of-victim discrimination was ignored. Differences among geographical regions in which the penalty is sought by United States' Attorneys, approved by the Attorney General, and imposed by juries were ignored. Stark racial differences in death-penalty avoidance by whites and minorities who enter a plea to a non-capital charge were not fully examined or explained. The entrance of racial disparities at discrete stages in decision-making was evaded. Arguments for further study by researchers assembled by the Department of Justice were ignored.

Before Tuesday [June 11, 2001, the day Timothy McVeigh was executed], the United States had not executed anyone for nearly 40 years. What is the hurry, especially when life and liberty are at stake? When asked at his confirmation hearing, "Do you agree with President Clinton that there is a need for 'continuing study' of 'possible racial and regional bias' because 'in this area there is no room for error?'" the Attorney General unequivocally answered, "Yes!"

Attorney General Ashcroft has broken his pledge to the United States Senate. There has been no "thorough study of the system." It has fallen to you to assure Americans that, at least when it comes to the ultimate penalty in our federal system, justice is blind to race and ethnicity.

You cannot fix everything that is wrong in our justice system, but you can do this.

The Death Penalty:
Justice Served

Andrew G. McBride

INTRODUCTION

I am honored to appear...today on the important subject of the fair and even-handed enforcement of the federal death penalty....

I believe that the death penalty serves an important role in the spectrum of penalties that the federal criminal justice system has available. Recent studies indicate the death penalty does in fact play a role in the general deterrence of capital crimes. We know the death penalty accomplishes specific deterrence, for it eliminates the possibility that a known-killer will kill again in prison or upon eventual release. The death penalty offers an additional measure of protection for our federal law enforcement officers—who are often faced with the prospect of arresting violent felons who are already facing life imprisonment. Most importantly, the death penalty sends a message of society's outrage and resolve to defend itself against the most heinous of crimes. As we have seen most recently in the [Oklahoma City federal building bomber Timothy] McVeigh case, it gives survivors a sense of justice and closure that even life imprisonment without parole cannot accord. As a former prosecutor who has tried capital cases, and as a citizen, I share the concern [everyone here] that the death penalty be enforced in a fair, even-handed, and race-neutral manner. At the same time, I am wary of the misuse of race and racial statistics as a "stalking horse" for those who are opposed to the death penalty in all circumstances. Honest opposition to capital punishment on moral grounds is

one thing, throwing charges of racism at federal law enforcement officers and federal prosecutors in order to block enforcement of a penalty the Congress has authorized and the American people clearly support, is another. I fear that some of my fellow panelists today have let vehement opposition to all capital punishment blind them to some simple facts about enforcement of the federal death penalty.

THERE IS NO CREDIBLE STATISTICAL EVIDENCE OF RACIAL BIAS IN THE ENFORCEMENT OF THE FEDERAL DEATH PENALTY

The dangers of statistical analyses are perhaps best captured in the old saying "Figures never lie but liars often figure." [We] should be very wary of the results of regression analysis or other statistical devices applied to capital punishment. No two capital defendants are the same. No two capital crimes are the same. Federal law and the Eighth Amendment require that juries be allowed to consider every aspect of the crime, the background and competence of the defendant, and even impact evidence regarding the victim, in arriving at the correct punishment. Regression analysis posits that each factor relevant to the imposition of the death penalty can be identified and then given an assigned weight, such that very different cases can be meaningfully compared. This premise is simply false. There are literally millions of legitimate variables that a prosecutor or jury could consider in seeking or imposing capital punishment. If we truly believed that they could all be identified and weighted, we would allow computers to deliberate and impose penalty. Instead, we quite properly rely upon human judgment, the judgment of the prosecutor, the death penalty committee in the Department of Justice, the Attorney General, the district court judge, and a fairly-selected jury from the venue where the crime occurred. In my opinion, and in my experience for seven years as a federal prosecutor, I saw no evidence that the race of defendants or victims had any overt or covert influence on this process. I believe the charge is fabricated by those who wish to block enforcement of the federal death penalty for other reasons.

I would ask [you] to keep four points in mind as it evaluates these very serious, but, in my opinion, wholly unsupported charges. First, pointing to statistical disparities between racial percentages of capital defendants and racial percentages in the population at large is utterly specious. The population at large does not commit violent felonies—only a small percentage of both the white and non-white communities are ever involved in violent crime. The sad fact is that non-whites are statistically much more likely to commit certain crimes of violence that might lead to death penalty prosecutions. African Americans make up approximately 13 percent of the nation's population. Yet, according to the FBI's 1999 uniform crime reports, there were 14,112 murder offenders in the United States in 1999, and of those offenders for whom race was known, 50 percent were black. Given that most murders are intra-racial, it is not surprising that of the 12,658 murder victims in 1999, 47 percent were black.

Capital crimes also are more likely to occur in urban areas that are more densely populated and tend to have higher minority populations. According to the FBI data, 43 percent of murders in 1999 were recorded in the South, the most heavily populated area of the country. The same data shows that the Nation's metropolitan areas reported a 1999 murder rate of 6 victims per 100,000 inhabitants, compared to rates of 4 per 100,000 for rural counties and cities outside metropolitan areas.

One cannot simply ignore these facts in evaluating the performance of our criminal justice system. Indeed, if the numbers of federal capital defendants of each race precisely mirrored their representation in society as a whole, that would be truly a cause for alarm. It would suggest real "racial profiling" in the death penalty.

Second, the federal government does not have general jurisdiction over all violent crimes committed within its jurisdiction. From 1988 to 1994, the only federal death available was for murder in relation to certain drug-trafficking crimes. This period coincided with the worst drug epidemic in our Nation's history—the spread of crack cocaine from New York and Los Angeles to all our major urban centers. Most of the participants in the drug organizations that distributed crack cocaine were black, and most of the homicides connected with this drug trade were black-on-black homicides. Approximately half of the defendants presently on federal death row were convicted of a drug-related homicide.

The Department of Justice study released last week indicates that the Eastern District of Virginia [a federal district court area] is a prime example of an area where the type of crime at issue and the needs of state and federal law enforcement have shaped the statistics. I was a prosecutor in that district for a period of seven years, and I can assure [you] that I never saw any racial bias in the investigation or charging stages by federal agents or prosecutors during my tenure there.

Drug-related homicide was a major problem in the urban areas of Richmond, Norfolk, and Virginia Beach. Many of these homicides were unsolved and had in fact been committed by interstate drug gangs with roots as far away as New York, Los Angeles, and even Jamaica. Joint task forces, composed of federal agents, state police, and local detectives investigated these cases under the supervision of federal prosecutors. Local leaders and politicians, including leaders of the African American community, welcomed this effort to focus federal resources on inner-city crimes and the unsolved murders of African-American citizens. These prosecutions were a classic example of the federal government lending support where support was needed and requested and the crimes had a significant interstate element. The results of aggressive federal prosecutions have included cutting the murder rate in Richmond, Virginia in half from its high in the early 1990's.

Third, the available statistical evidence indicates that whites who enter the federal capital system (both pre- and post-1994) are significantly more likely to face the death penalty than minority defendants. Thus, even opponents of the federal death penalty seem to concede that there is no racial bias in the Department of Justice procedures for determining whether or not to seek the death penalty. Instead, they posit racial bias in the decision to make a case federal in the first place. It is obvious that these critics have never served as a state or federal prosecutor. The same federal prosecutors who make the initial intake decision regarding state or federal prosecution also make the initial decision on the death penalty and prepare the recommendation memorandum to the Attorney General's standing committee. The proposition that they are severely racially biased in the former (the intake decision when capital status is unsure) but are not biased in the latter (when the decision to seek the death penalty is actually

made) is absurd. Intake decisions are made by supervisors in the United States Attorney's Offices, who often have fixed protocols with their state counterparts regarding certain crimes. The fact that a group of bank robbers is multi-jurisdictional, or that an organization's trafficking level of cocaine has gone above 10 kilograms of crack are factors likely to result in federal prosecution. Race is never a factor and the notion that federal law enforcement agents are making "racist" intake decisions (by themselves) is a baseless charge that displays a shocking lack of knowledge of how our federal/state criminal justice system actually works.

Fourth, [you] should not place any stock in statistical patterns or comparisons. A "pool" of approximately 700 federal capital cases is too small a cohort for any serious statistician to produce any reliable conclusions. Moreover, all such studies suffer from the flaw noted above—they assume that all the factors that influence capital punishment can be quantified. It is clear that they cannot be. Rather than focus on largely meaningless statistical games, we should focus on continuing and improving the procedures in place at the Department of Justice to ensure that every capital eligible crime is submitted and reviewed, and that every decision to seek the death penalty is fully justified by the facts and circumstances of the case.

CONCLUSION

In my opinion as a former federal prosecutor, there is no racial bias in the federal capital system. The decision to seek federal prosecution itself is made by federal prosecutors based on largely fixed criteria regarding the interstate nature of the crime or other objective, non-racial factors. The decision to actually seek the death penalty for a capital eligible crime has several layers of review and includes a standing committee that ensures fairness and continuity. Statistical evidence is of little or no probative value in this area and is, in my opinion, being manipulated by those who simply oppose the federal death penalty for any crime. The American people overwhelmingly support capital punishment and Congress has made it available for a limited set of federal crimes. I believe that the Department of Justice has enforced these laws in an unbiased manner to date and that it will continue to do so under the leadership of Attorney General [John] Ashcroft.

THE CONTINUING DEBATE:
The Death Penalty

What Is New

Globally, about half the world's countries have a death penalty, and about 40% use it at least occasionally. The United States is among the countries most likely to execute prisoners. According to Amnesty International, there were 3,797 known legal executions in 25 countries in 2004. China had by far the most (3,400), followed by Iran (159), Vietnam (64) and the United States (59).

The number of death row inmates in U.S. prisons grew from 692 in 1980, to 2,246 in 1990, to 3,415 in 2005. The racial composition of the condemned is 42% African American, 44% white, 12% Latino, 1% Asian American, and 1% Native American. In another U.S. development, the Supreme Court rule in *Roper v. Simmons* (2005) that executing prisoners for crime committed as juveniles (under age 18) was unconstitutional.

Where to Find More

To review the legal background of capital punishment, including the US. Supreme Court's suspension of the death penalty in *Furman v. Georgia* (1972) and its reinstatement of capital punishment in *Gregg v. Georgia* (1976), go to Cornell University's Legal Information Institute at http://www.law.cornell.edu and enter "death penalty" in the search function. The view that the Supreme Court is moving toward finding all executions unconstitutional is expressed in Wendy Davis, "Inching Away From Death?" *ABA Journal* (September 2005). An overview of the death penalty use throughout U.S. history and attitudes about it is found in Stuart Banner, *The Death Penalty: An American History* (Harvard University Press, 2003).

A pro-death penalty position is taken by Joshua Marquis, "The Myth of Innocence," *Journal of Criminal Law & Criminology* (Winter 2005), and the opposite view is taken by Eliza Steelwater, *The Hangman's Knot: Lynching, Legal Execution, and America's Struggle with the Death Penalty* (Westview Press, 2003). For a group on each side of the issue, visit the Web sites of Pro-Death Penalty.com at www.prodeathpenalty.com/ and the Death Penalty Information Center at www.deathpenaltyinfo.org/. A site worth visiting is that of the Texas Department of Criminal Justice at www.tdcj.state.tx.us/stat/deathrow.htm. You can hyperlink from the name of each of the more than 300 people executed since 1982 to a picture, personal information, the crime each committed, and their last statement. It puts a "face" on the data about both those convicted of murders and the victims.

What More to Do

Discuss all the various permutations of the death penalty debate, including whether it is ever justified under any circumstances and, if so, under what circumstances; whether it is only justified by utilitarianism (it deters later murders) and/or as punishment per se, and whether the fact that executions are not proportionate among various demographic groups is evidence that capital punishment should be abolished. Also, get active. The federal government and 38 states have death penalty laws on the books; 12 states and the District of Columbia do not. Find out the law in your state and support or oppose it.

18   EDUCATION POLICY

AFFIRMATIVE ACTION ADMISSIONS:
Promoting Equality *or* Unfair Advantage?

PROMOTING EQUALITY

ADVOCATES: 41 College Students and 3 Student Coalitions

SOURCE: Amicus Curiae brief to the U.S. Supreme Court in *Grutter v. Bollinger* (2003)

UNFAIR ADVANTAGE

ADVOCATES: 21 Law Professors

SOURCE: Amicus Curiae brief to the U.S. Supreme Court in *Grutter v. Bollinger* (2003)

Surveys show that nearly all Americans support the idea of equal opportunity, but the data on the circumstances of various groups casts doubt on whether the country has yet to achieve it. Economically, for example, the average household income of whites is 63% greater than that of African Americans and 69% greater than that of Hispanics. The 24% poverty rate among black and Latino households is triple that for white households. There are also income gaps for the employed. For every dollar made by the average white worker, blacks make 72 cents, and Latinos make 65 cents. As for unemployment, the spring 2004 rate of white unemployment was about 4.3%, compared to 9.8% for blacks and 5.8% for Latinos. Moreover, significant disparities in poverty, income, and unemployment have persisted as far back as the data goes.

To address such gaps, the federal government began to promote affirmative action in 1961 when President John F. Kennedy issued Executive Order 10925 requiring that federally financed projects "take affirmative action to ensure that hiring and employment practices are free of racial bias."

Later, state and local governments also adopted affirmative action programs, and they and the federal government extended them to education and other areas. Title IX, featured in Debate 16, was part of that effort. Whether because of these policies or more general social changes, the position of women and minorities in education has improved somewhat. Women now make up a majority of college undergraduates and 44% of graduate students. Asian Americans are a greater percentage of both undergraduate and graduate students than they are in the general population. However, improvement for blacks and Latinos has been slower. Between 1980 and 2000, African Americans rose from 9.9% to 13.4% of undergraduates, and Latino enrollment went from 3.7% to 8.6%. This enrollment gap has created a large disparity in college graduates, with 28% of whites over age 25 having a bachelor's degree, compared to 16.5% of African Americans, and 10.6% of Hispanics. At the professional school level, white enrollment between 1980 and 2000 dropped from 81% to 73.9%, while black enrollment grew from 5.8% to 7.2%, and Latino enrollment climbed from 3.9% to 4.7%. This leaves minorities particularly underrepresented in law, medicine, and other professions. Among lawyers, 5.4% are blacks, and 3.9% are Latinos. African Americans are 6.3% of the physicians, and Hispanics are 3.4%. As a reference point, the population in 2000 was 69% white, 12.3% African American, 12.5% Hispanic, and 3.3% Asian American, with other groups making up the balance. Women were 51.9% of the population.

While Americans strongly support the theory of equal opportunity, many have disagreed with the application of affirmative action programs in education and other areas. As a result, there have been a number of court challenges alleging unconstitutional "reverse discrimination." The first significant education case was *Regents of the University of California v. Bakke* (1978), which involved the rejection of a white applicant to medical school that reserved 16% of its places for minority students. In a 5–4 decision, the Supreme Court ruled somewhat confusingly that (a) numerical quotas were not constitutional but that (b) race could legitimately be considered during the admissions process. The following articles trace the legal background more, but the ambiguities in the *Bakke* ruling created disagreements among various Circuit Courts of Appeals over what could and could not be done with respect to affirmative action admissions. This set the groundwork for two "companion" cases involving the University of Michigan. One, *Gratz v. Bollinger*, focused on undergraduate admission and involved the university giving minority students 20 points on a 150-point admissions score. The second, *Grutter v. Bollinger*, related to law school admissions but did not involve a stated quota or a point scheme, only the goal of achieving a "critical mass" of minority students.

The articles below relate to *Grutter*, although most of its underlying rationale also applied to *Gratz*. The two articles are *amicus curiae* (friend of the court) briefs filed by those who were not direct parties to the case but who the court agreed had an important concern. The first, supporting the university's affirmative action program, was filed by a coalition of three student groups and 41 individual students. The second, opposing the university, was written by 21 law professors.

POINTS TO PONDER

➤ Read the briefs as a Supreme Court justice. What is your decision in *Grutter v. Bollinger* and why?

➤ Assuming the only difference *Gratz v. Bollinger* is the explicit use of a point system, would you make the same decision as in *Grutter* and why?

➤ What should affirmative action mean as a policy directive?

Affirmative Action Admissions:
Promoting Equality

41 COLLEGE STUDENTS AND 3 STUDENT COALITIONS

STATEMENT OF THE CASE

When plaintiff filed suit in *Grutter v. Bollinger* in 1997, 41 individually named black, Latino, Native American, Arab American, Asian Pacific American, other minority and white students and three coalitions—United for Equality and Affirmative Action (UEAA), Law Students for Affirmative Action, and the Coalition to Defend Affirmative Action and Integration & Fight for Equality By Any Means Necessary (BAMN), sought and eventually won the right to present our defense of the Law School's affirmative action plan.

Beginning on the 16th of January 2001, a day after the Martin Luther King holiday, the *Grutter v. Bollinger* case went to trial. One month later, after 15 days of trial, and 24 witnesses, the case concluded. The student intervenors fought for the district court trial in order to disprove the plaintiff's claim of "reverse discrimination" and to lift the profound stigma that the attack on affirmative action has placed on the shoulders of minority students. We presented the overwhelming majority of evidence at trial: 15 of the 24 witnesses were called by us, and we used 28 hours and 48 minutes of the 30-hour limit imposed by the district court.

As the student intervenors will show, the plaintiff has not proved that she has been a victim of discrimination—and the United States has not offered a viable alternative to affirmative action. The facts show that if the plaintiff prevails in this Court, the Law School will quickly and inevitably resegregate. That conclusion is confirmed by the resegregation of the universities that has resulted from the end of affirmative action in California, Texas, and Florida. If the plaintiff prevails, gains toward integration will be reversed and replaced by a massive return to segregation starting in the most selective universities and spreading throughout higher education and into the society as a whole.

I. RACE AND THE LAW SCHOOL APPLICATION POOL

For two-thirds of black students and 70 percent of Latino students, the path to the future leads through segregated elementary and secondary schools. The worst segregation, which was once in the South, is now in the major industrial states of the Northeast and Midwest. Michigan [has] 83 percent of its black students attending segregated schools. For Latinos, segregation by race and ethnicity is compounded by segregation by language, with 50 percent of the Latinos in California speaking Spanish at home. For Native Americans, over half live in cities where they face segregation like that faced by blacks and Latinos, while just under half remain in impoverished government-run reservations and boarding schools.

The segregation concentrates and compounds the effects of poverty. While poverty disadvantages the poor of all races, poor whites are more dispersed residentially, and their children are far more likely to enroll in schools that have a substantial number of middle-class students. That is far less likely for black, Latino, and Native American students.

Even for black students from middle- and upper-middle-class families, substantial disadvantage exists. For equivalent incomes, black families have less wealth, less education, and fewer relatives who can provide financial and other assistance in times of trouble. Even when middle-class black people or Latinos move to nearby suburbs, the suburbs are, or quickly become, segregated and the school systems quickly decline. Even for the very few black families who move to stable white, upper-middle-class suburbs with good school systems, there remain racial isolation, stereotyping, tracking, and stigma.

In testimony at trial [in the Federal District Court] on behalf of the student defendants, Professor Gary Orfield of the Harvard University School of Education summarized the impact of segregation:

> There never was a separate but equal school system. That's because of many things. It's because the poverty levels in segregated schools are much higher....[T]here are fewer minorities in teacher training. There are many fewer teachers who choose to go to work in schools of this sort. Most teachers who start in segregated schools leave faster. The curriculum that is offered is more limited. The probability that the teacher will be trained in their field is much more limited. The level of competition is less. The respect for the institution in the outside world is less. The connections to colleges are less. There are more children with health problems....The population is much more unstable....The kids don't have books....There [are] no facilities....[I]t is like a different planet, a different society.

Segregation—separate and unequal schools—means that there are far fewer black, Latino, and Native American students who graduate from college. The national

pool of students who could apply to a school like Michigan is disproportionately white—and many of the comparatively small number of black, Latino, and Native American students in that pool attended segregated elementary and secondary schools.

II. BIAS IN MICHIGAN'S ADMISSIONS SYSTEM WITHOUT AFFIRMATIVE ACTION

A. A Segregated School in a Segregated Profession

Before the advent of affirmative action, there were very few black students who graduated from college, fewer still who applied to law school, and almost none who were admitted to law school.

In the 1950s and early 1960s, except for the law schools at the historically black colleges and universities, the nation's law schools were essentially all white and all male. In 1960, the nation had 286,000 lawyers, of whom 2180 were black and not more than 25 were Native American. The number of Latinos was not recorded but was unquestionably minuscule. Before 1968, each year there were about 200 black law graduates in the nation.

From 1960 through 1968, the Law School graduated 2687 law students, of whom four were black and none were Latino or Native American.

B. The LSAT

In the early 1960s, the University of Michigan Law School admitted students based on a rigid index that combined undergraduate grades with an LSAT score. At that time, the School was not nearly as selective as it would become. But as more students went to college—and as affirmative action began to open the doors to minorities and to women of all races—the number of applicants to all law schools expanded dramatically. The schools became more selective and the LSAT became far more important.

The plaintiff and the United States call the LSAT "objective"—but they offer no proof to support the claim that it is an "objective" measure of anything important or that it is "race-neutral" in any way. In fact, all the evidence at trial showed the reverse.

The uncontested evidence presented at trial by the student defendants also demonstrated that test scores had little predictive value. In an uncontested study, Professor Richard Lempert, a member of the committee that drafted the 1992 policy, testifying for the students at trial, established that an applicant's LSAT score did not correlate with later success as a lawyer, measured by income, stated satisfaction, or political and community leadership.

C. Undergraduate Grades

The other major "objective" criterion in the traditional Law School admissions system is the undergraduate grade point average (UGPA). While the racial gap on that average is much smaller than the LSAT gap, the gap is still significant when admissions are very competitive, as they have been at the Law School for many years.

The racial segregation in K–12 education causes part of the racial gap in UGPAs; but the conditions on the nation's campuses also contribute to the gap. Black, Latino, and Native American students feel and are isolated; and the cumulative effect of a daily run of slights and profiling takes its toll on black and other minority students. As the district court conceded, while the effect cannot be quantified for each student, racial prejudice depresses the undergraduate grades and overall academic performance of minority students who apply to Law Schools.

The grids prepared by the plaintiff's chief witness, Dr. Kinley Larntz, reflect the gap in test scores and grades and stand as a measure of the cumulative effect of discriminatory tests, segregated education, social inequality, and the depressing effect of racial prejudice on the undergraduate grades and overall academic performance of minority students.

III. THE LAW SCHOOL AFFIRMATIVE ACTION PROGRAM

Under pressure from students on the campus and the civil rights movement, the law faculty began an intense series of debates that stretched from the 1960s through the current date about how to deal with the realities outlined above.

In the course of those debates, faculty members repeatedly recognized that numerical credentials discriminated against black and other minority applicants, "caus[ing] [their] actual potential...to be underestimated, especially when gauged by standard testing procedures...thought to be 'culturally biased.'"

In 1973, the [University of Michigan] Law School graduated 41 black students and its first Latino student. In 1975, it graduated its first two Asian-Americans, followed by its first Native American in 1976. The increasing number of black and other minority students cleared the way for the admission of increasing numbers of women of all races.

After this Court handed down its decision in *Bakke* in June 1978, the faculty formulated a policy to comply with the decision.

In 1992, the faculty adopted the plan that is now in effect. The plan calls for consideration of each applicant as an individual; attempts to seek many forms of diversity; and states the School's commitment to enrolling a "critical mass" of black, Latino, and Native American students, who would not be admitted to the Law School in significant numbers without that commitment.

IV. WHAT ENDING AFFIRMATIVE ACTION WOULD MEAN

In ruling for the plaintiff, the district court conceded that the elimination of affirmative action at the Law School would result in an immediate reduction in underrepresented minority enrollment of over 73 percent. But this would only be the start. The end of affirmative action at selective colleges would dramatically reduce the pool of minority applicants to the Law School, driving the number of minority law students down still further. Within a few years at most, the Law School would again be nearly as segregated as it was in the 1960s.

In 1997, the ban on affirmative action announced by the University of California (UC) Board of Regents went into effect. The following year, only one black student enrolled at Boalt Hall. Minority enrollment at the UCLA School of Law dropped dramatically.

The few black and other minority students who remain at California's most selective campuses have faced increased racism caused by the elimination of affirmative action.

Dr. Eugene Garcia, the Dean of the Graduate School of Education at Berkeley, testified that black, Latino, and Native American students have been forced from the flagship campuses of the UC system onto its two least selective campuses. As the state's population continues to grow, the "cascade" will continue until the vast majority of black, Latino, and Native American students are forced out of the UC system altogether.

The UC faculty and administrations opposed the ban and sought to undo its effects. At Berkeley, the school downplayed the importance of grades and test scores; at UCLA, the school attempted to substitute the consideration of socio-economic status for the consideration of race. Because neither approach could serve as a substitute for affirmative action, both schools found it impossible to enroll a class including more than token numbers of black and other minority students.

SUMMARY OF THE ARGUMENT

In this case, the plaintiff is asking the Court to reinterpret the American Constitution to the dramatic detriment of black, Latino, and other minority people and women of all races. If the Court does what [the] plaintiff asks, it will resegregate, divide, and polarize our country. The authority of the Court would be compromised.

Segregation and inequality are increasing in education. Irrespective of the legal forms used to enforce, to maintain, or passively to justify the separate and unequal condition of education at virtually every level, the fact stands as a profound insult and provocation to the minority youth of America and to the best of the nation's legal and political traditions. Minority children are, in their increasing majority, relegated to second-class, segregated schools—today's version of the back of the bus. The very small handful of black, Mexican American, and Native American students who have made it to the front of America's education bus—institutions like the University of Michigan Law School—are now being told by the plaintiff to get out of their seat and move to the back of the bus.

The demographic fabric of America is changing. By the middle of this century, no racial grouping will be in the majority. America will be a more diverse society; it must not become a more segregated society. We must strive to make equality more, not less, of a reality, or we will surely face renewed social convulsions.

The movement to defend affirmative action and integration has awakened and stirred into action every sector of this society. What unites these many peoples in defense of affirmative action is the conviction that the Constitution's pledge of equality should have meaning and currency in our collective American future. Our progress as a nation depends on the realization of this prospect.

Affirmative Action Admissions: Unfair Advantage

21 LAW PROFESSORS

INTEREST OF *AMICI CURIAE*

Amici curiae are law professors with a professional interest in promoting learning environments free from the taint of racial discrimination. *Amici* are committed to the principles of equality under law embodied in the Constitution, and oppose invidious racial discrimination of any kind. In particular, *amici* oppose as unconstitutional the race-based admissions policies employed by the University of Michigan School of Law and many other institutions of higher learning. A list of the *amici* and their institutional affiliations is provided as an appendix to this brief. The institutional affiliations are for identification purposes only. The views expressed in this brief are those of the individual *amici* and do not necessarily reflect the views of the institutions at which they teach.

SUMMARY OF ARGUMENT

This Court should hold that "diversity" is not a compelling state interest sufficient to justify race-based discrimination. First, "diversity" is employed by universities as a shorthand term for discrimination on the basis of race, is indistinguishable from the use of quotas, and is not a remedial interest. Second, racial "diversity" in the classroom does not constitute academic diversity; to the contrary, it is based on racial stereotyping and fosters stigmatization and hostility. Furthermore, even stereotypically assuming it resulted in a greater diversity of views and information, such a result is not a compelling interest that would outweigh constitutional rights in this or other contexts. Finally, "diversity" is a race-balancing interest that would, by its own terms, require race discrimination for eternity.

ARGUMENT

The Court has held repeatedly that racial classifications are *"presumptively invalid* and can be upheld only upon an extraordinary justification"* (*Shaw v. Reno*, 1993). Race-based classifications can survive strict scrutiny only if they are narrowly tailored to serve a compelling state interest.

The University of Michigan School of Law ("Michigan") employs race-based classifications in its admissions policies, and race often is the deciding factor between the admission of one applicant and the rejection of another with equal or better qualifications. The questions for this Court, therefore, are whether Michigan's asserted interest is constitutionally "compelling" and whether its admissions program is narrowly tailored to serve that interest.

Amici [we]respectfully submit that this Court should state in words so clear that they cannot be misunderstood by university administrators that the use of racial preferences, classifications, or "pluses" for the purpose of achieving a racially diverse student body is prohibited by the Fourteenth Amendment. The failure of the Court to address the "diversity" question head-on could have devastating consequences for the rights of individuals of all races who participate in the admissions process. Since *Bakke* [*University of California v. Bakke*, 1978], the "diversity" principle in practice has been used to create a loophole through which universities continue to discriminate broadly and openly on the basis of race.

I. MICHIGAN'S DIRECT PURSUIT OF RACIAL DIVERSITY NECESSARILY ENTAILS RACIAL CLASSIFICATIONS

The pursuit of "diversity" in general is a broad and potentially varied exercise that can turn on any number of characteristics or traits. Universities can seek geographic diversity, intellectual diversity, athletic and artistic diversity, and even socio-economic diversity. Those qualities are directly relevant to the educational mission and are not themselves constitutionally suspect. But the direct pursuit of *racial* diversity as an end unto itself, and as a supposed means of creating other types of diversity, is quite different. That pursuit involves taking a single characteristic—race—that the Constitution and this Court have declared unrelated to legitimate bases for distinguishing among individuals, and relying upon it not withstanding such admonitions.

A. Pursuit of "Diversity" Is a Euphemism for Race-Based Decisionmaking

Making disingenuous use of Justice Powell's lone dictum regarding "diversity," [in the *Bakke* decision], universities such as Michigan have adopted the seemingly benign language of pursuing diversity in general as a misleading euphemism for decision-making processes and goals based overtly on race. It is the view and experience of *amici* here that whatever nods of the head universities make toward more general notions of diversity, their affirmative action programs, such as the one in this case, remain targeted at a narrow vision of *racial* diversity *regardless* of the consequences of such programs for other types of diversity.

Numerous experienced law professors, including even those who support racial preferences in admissions, have recognized and acknowledged that the language of educational diversity in the admissions context is generally used as a cover for direct racial decision-making. Such professors speak not merely as academics who have studied the issue, but as first-hand observers within law school communities and administrations, and often as direct participants of the very admissions processes they describe. Professor Alan Dershowitz of Harvard has been forthright about the deceptive use of the "diversity" label in connection with race-driven admissions programs:

> The *raison d'être* for race-specific affirmative action programs has simply never been diversity for the sake of education. The checkered history of "diversity" demonstrates that it was designed largely as a cover to achieve other legally, morally, and politically controversial goals. In recent years, it has been invoked—especially by professional schools—as a clever post facto justification for increasing the number of minority group students in the student body.

Professor Samuel Issacharoff, of Columbia and formerly of Texas, makes a similar point. One of the attorneys who defended the University of Texas School of Law's racedriven admissions policy, has nonetheless has acknowledged that "diversity" is the current jargon for racial discrimination: "[O]ne of the clear legacies of *Bakke* has been to enshrine the term 'diversity' within the legal lexicon to cover everything from curricular enrichments to thinly-veiled set-asides."

Other experienced law professors with diverse views of the affirmative action issue in general have recognized the same truth.

Professor Jed Rubenfeld of Yale, who defends "affirmative action" on non-diversity grounds not advanced by Michigan in this case, notes the disingenuousness of the claim that race-driven admissions advance true "diversity" measured by any criteria *other than* race. "[T]he pro-affirmative action crowd needs to own up to the weaknesses of 'diversity' as a defense of most affirmative action plans. Everyone knows that in most cases a true diversity of perspectives and backgrounds is not really being pursued."

In the end, even the proponents of affirmative action, if they are being candid, recognize that the "diversity" pursued by programs such as Michigan's is directly race-based in both its means and its ends, favoring or disfavoring particular races for their own sake without concern for diversity of qualities other than race. While such programs may pay lip-service to intellectual or experiential qualities other than race, they invariably collapse back to using race for its own sake, or as a proxy for other, pertinent, qualities without regard to whether such racial stereotyping is true or permissible.

B. Direct Pursuit of Racial Diversity Is Functionally Indistinguishable from Racial Quotas

"Diversity"-based admissions policies such as the one at Michigan necessarily begin and end with some perceived level of optimal diversity among the characteristics—in this case race—that they use to classify candidates. In order to achieve its claimed interest in diversity, Michigan must have at least some sense of what constitutes the proper representation of each race before it can decide that certain racial groups are "under-represented" and the student body thereby insufficiently diverse. Professor Issacharoff candidly acknowledges the point:

The problem with diversity as a justification for a challenged affirmative action program is that it is an almost incoherent concept to opera-

tionalize, unless diversity means a predetermined number of admittees from a desired group....[S]elective institutions must approach the applicant pool with predetermined notions of what an appropriately balanced incoming class should look like.

The only way to ensure adequate "representation" among the races at the end of the admissions process is to begin with an institutional definition of "diversity" that necessarily produces the desired proportions of racial representation in a class of admitted students. Michigan's "diversity" policy is symbolic of the numbers game that has become synonymous with admissions policies that employ racial preferences. For example, members of Michigan's admissions staff receive "daily reports," which track applicants by race. Dennis Shields, the former director of admissions at Michigan, has acknowledged that "as an admissions season progressed, he would consult the daily reports more and more frequently in order to keep track of the racial and ethnic composition of the class." Mr. Shields said that he did this to ensure that a "critical mass" of minority students were enrolled. "Diversity in education" through race-driven admissions is meaningless without quotas or something constituting the functional equivalent of a quota system.

The district court determined after careful consideration of all of the facts that the "critical mass" concept is functionally equivalent to a quota system. The district court explained:

[O]ver the years, [critical mass] has meant in practice that the law school attempts to enroll an entering class 10% to 17% of which consists of underrepresented minority students. The 10% figure, as a target, has historical roots going back to the late 1960s. Beginning in the 1970s, the law school documents begin referring to 10–12% as the desired percentage. Professor Lempert testified that critical mass lies in the range of 11–17%. Indeed this percentage range appeared in a draft of the 1992 admissions policy, and it was omitted from the final version despite Professor Regan's suggestion that it remain for the sake of "candor."

"Diversity" policies must be described as what they are—means of implementing racial quotas. That such quotas might be informal or hidden under a cloak of rhetoric does not change that essential fact.

C. "Diversity" Is Not a Remedial Interest

Thus far, the only constitutionally compelling interest recognized by this Court as satisfying strict scrutiny for racial classifications is the remediation of the effects of past race discrimination.

Michigan's "diversity" policy is not, and does not purport to be, remedial. The question for this Court then is whether "diversity" should be added as a "compelling," not merely valid or permissible, state interest that can be used to justify direct and intentional racial discrimination.

Because the Court has "strictly" limited the use of racial classifications to the remedial context, respondents must demonstrate that there is something so special, so *compelling*, about marginal differences in the educational experiences of post-secondary students that universities, alone among our government-sponsored institutions, should be allowed to practice what the Constitution prohibit[s]—naked race discrimination. Although the question properly posed seems to answer itself, an examination of the realities of "diversity" in the classroom also leads to the conclusion that this so-called justification for discrimination does not pass constitutional muster.

II. RACIAL "DIVERSITY" IS NOT A COMPELLING INTEREST

Because the pursuit of racial diversity for its own sake is an affront to the Fourteenth Amendment, the defenders of "diversity" ultimately resort to some version of the argument that bringing together persons of different "backgrounds"—as defined by their skin color or national origin—will "enhance" the educational experience of students by creating academic or viewpoint diversity. But Michigan's admissions policy, and other "diversity" policies like it, cannot be defended on the ground that racial diversity promotes academic diversity. The defense of "diversity" programs on the ground that they expose people of different races to one another, thereby facilitating learning, respect and appreciation among the races, does not relate to a true "interest in intellectual diversity—diversity of 'experiences, outlooks and ideas' that would otherwise be left out—but specifically in racial and ethnic diversity as such."

A. Interests in "Diversity" That Assume Stereotyping Cannot Have Compelling Weight

The "diversity" rationale suggests that it is permissible to use race as a proxy for experiences, outlooks or ideas, and that the use of race as a proxy will ensure that different viewpoints are brought to the classroom. But however desirable a diversity of *ideas* may be, there is no basis for categorizing it as "compelling," rather than merely acceptable or substantial for purposes of analyses *other than* strict scrutiny. The abhorrent essential predicate to the interest—governmental stereotyping of different races as to their views—also assures that the interest in racial diversity for its secondary viewpoint effects cannot count as compelling.

Common sense and classroom experiences demonstrate that "viewpoint diversity" and "academic diversity" in the classroom are not affected by the racial composition of a student body. Dean and long-time professor at Michigan, Professor Terrance Sandalow, wrote in the *Michigan Law Review*:

> My own experience and that of colleagues with whom I have discussed the question, experience that concededly is limited to the classroom setting, is that racial diversity is not responsible for generating ideas unfamiliar to some members of the class. Students do, of course, quite frequently express and develop ideas that others in the class have not previously encountered, but even though the subjects I teach deal extensively with racial issues, I cannot recall an instance in which, for example, ideas were expressed by a black student that have not also been expressed by white students. Black students do, at times, call attention to the racial implications of issues that are not facially concerned with race, but white and Asian-American students are in my experience no less likely to do so.

Racial diversity is not required to foster a full discussion of issues and viewpoints in the classroom. If a white applicant and a black applicant each have the same view on an issue, and their respective race is ignored as it must be under the Constitution, there is no true "intellectual" or "academic" reason for admitting one of the students over the other.

Any "diversity" policy that is premised on the notion that people of different races bring particular viewpoints to the classroom solely because of their race should be struck down. If schools truly think that viewpoint diversity enhances education, they can pursue it directly rather than using race as a proxy.

Apparently realizing the difficulty of defending its admissions policy on the ground that race defines viewpoint, Michigan attempts an alternative claim that racial diversity in the classroom is required to *dismantle* stereotypes.

[The University of] Michigan argues in essence that, because it assumes individuals generally believe that members of a "minority" race all share the same viewpoint on all issues, the educational experiences of members of the benighted majority will be "enhanced" by interaction with a "critical mass" of minority students. This argument merely shifts the stereotyped assumptions over to the majority racial group, but is no less offensive therefore.

Moreover, Michigan hardly needs racial preferences to teach the obvious—that not all members of any given minority think alike. If, miraculously, something more were needed to make this point to students, surely a sufficiently diverse *reading list* would suffice. Michigan's self-contradictory treatment of individuals as members of groups, purportedly in order to demonstrate that individuals are *not* members of groups, is closer to being incredible than it is to being compelling.

B. Discrimination Resulting from Racial Stereotyping Results in Stigmatization and Hostility

Even if one were to hypothesize that a compelled increase in racial diversity would increase educationally valuable viewpoint diversity to some degree, it would also generate educationally detrimental stigma and hostility based on precisely the same type of stereotyping regarding race employed by the University. Indeed, policies that seek diversity through race are [according to one scholar] a "statement by government that certain persons identified by race are in fact being placed in positions they may be presumed not likely to hold but for their race."

"Diversity" admissions programs, such as Michigan's, foster rather than minimize the focus on race. The policy treats preferred minorities as a group, rather than as individuals. Although Michigan purports to consider other types of diversity—such as unusual employment experiences and extracurricular activities—race is the most identifiable diversity factor that separates one applicant from another.

Amici's collective experiences support the conclusion that both students who are admitted, and those who are not admitted, recognize that race indisputably plays an important role in admissions. Applicants from races that do not benefit from Michigan's preferences, who have high LSAT scores and GPAs, but who nonetheless are denied admission, will likely conclude that race determined their fate in the admissions process. Similarly, members of all races who gain admission may believe that their minority classmates would not be their classmates but for their race. Because of the lowered expectations that accompany racial preferences in admissions, members of minority groups are and will be stigmatized—sometimes self-stigmatized—as inferior.

The racial hostility and stigmatization that is bred in universities as a result of racial preferences is felt both in our classrooms and throughout all of society. If not stopped now, the hostility and scarring that can result from racial preferences based on "diversity" could take generations to heal. At a minimum, however, such consequences cut against any claimed benefits and render Michigan's asserted interest in the educational benefits of racial diversity necessarily less than compelling.

C. Government-Defined Viewpoint Diversity Is Not a Compelling Interest

Regardless whether racial classifications generate viewpoint diversity and accepting that viewpoint diversity is, in general, a valuable thing in an educational environment, that does not even remotely satisfy the requirement that it must be a "compelling" interest sufficient to justify otherwise unconstitutional conduct. The difficulty in too-easy a transition from merely desirable to constitutionally compelling seems apparent: We would not authorize state universities to violate students' right to free speech or free exercise of religion on the ground that doing so would, in the view of academics, create a better educational environment or a greater "diversity" of views.

But if it is a compelling interest to discriminate on the basis of race in order to promote an educational atmosphere with a supposedly more diverse set of student views, then it is unavoidably a compelling interest for all other constitutional purposes. The notion that the government might impose a myriad of speech restrictions and compulsions in the name of "diversity" demonstrates the absurd premise that marginal differences in educational diversity rise to the level of "compelling" state interests.

D. The "Diversity" Rationale Is Limitless

"Diversity" also fails as a "compelling interest" because it has no logical stopping point. The Court has repeatedly rejected alleged "compelling interests" that extend indefinitely into the future.

By definition, a "diversity" interest supports indefinite discrimination on the basis of race in university admissions because there will always be a need to engage in race-based decisionmaking to ensure a "properly diverse" student body. "Diversity"—with its concomitant quotas and careful monitoring of racial admissions—indeed would *require* unending use of race in admissions.

For this reason, and for all of the other reasons set forth above, "diversity" does not constitute an extraordinary justification sufficient to overcome the presumptive invalidity of government-sponsored race discrimination.

THE CONTINUING DEBATE:
Affirmative Action Admissions

What Is New

In 2003, the Supreme Court upheld the University of Michigan's position in *Grutter v. Bollinger* and rejected it in *Gratz v. Bollinger*. By a 5 to 4 vote in *Grutter*, the Court permitted the law school's use of race as one factor in determining admissions on the grounds that a "compelling state interest" existed in promoting diversity at all levels of society. But by 6 to 3 in *Gratz*, the justices rejected the undergraduate admission process that gave automatic points to minorities on the admissions scale. These decisions reconfirmed *Bakke*, but thereby also left some of that decision's uncertainties in place about how to judge an affirmative action program without resorting to numbers when establishing goals or monitoring progress.

Perhaps reflecting the fine line the Court walked in the two decisions, public opinion about affirmative actions varies with the way the question is asked. For example, consider the wording and results of three polls taken in 2003. The first asked Americans if they "generally favor or oppose affirmative action programs for racial minorities?" A plurality (49%) replied, "favor," 43% said "oppose," and 8% were unsure. The second poll introduced a reason for affirmative action, asking, "In order to overcome past discrimination, do you favor or oppose affirmative action programs…[for minorities]?" With that prompt, support for affirmative action was much higher (63% in favor, 29% opposed, 8% unsure). By contrast, support declined to 38% (with 51% opposed, and 10% unsure) in a poll whose question included the word "preferences" ("Do you favor or oppose affirmative action programs that give preferences to…minorities?").

Where to Find More

For a history of affirmative action, read Terry H. Anderson, *The Pursuit of Fairness: A History of Affirmative Action* (Oxford University Press, 2005). You can read the decisions and the dissents for both *Grutter v. Bollinger* and *Gratz v. Bollinger* by going to the Supreme Court Collection Web page of Cornell University's Legal Information Institute at http://supct.law.cornell.edu/supct/ and entering the case names in the search function. The Web site of the Coalition to Defend Affirmative Action and Integration & Fight for Equality By Any Means Necessary (BAMN), one of the student groups who filed an amicus curiae brief in *Grutter*, is at http://www.bamn.com/. An organization with an opposing point of view is American Civil Rights Institute at http://www.ACRI.org/.

What More to Do

Write an admission policy for your university that addresses the demographic component. Then find out what your school's written policy is (if any) and interview admissions officials to find out how they implement affirmative action. How does the school's policy compare with your views?

FOREIGN POLICY

U.S. MILITARY FORCES IN IRAQ:
Stay the Course *or* Withdraw Quickly?

STAY THE COURSE

ADVOCATE: George W. Bush, President of the United States

SOURCE: Address to the nation, July 28, 2005

WITHDRAW QUICKLY

ADVOCATES: Wesley B. Renfro and Brian Urlacher, doctoral students, Department of Political Science, University of Connecticut

SOURCE: "With Civil War Looming, the United States Must Withdraw from Iraq," article written especially for this volume, October 2005

Since 1990, U.S. foreign policy related to Iraq can be summarized as shifting but unbroken levels of violence and tension. In August, Iraq overran Kuwait. Four months later, President George H. W. Bush sent U.S. troops to war to liberate Iraq and to "defang" Iraq. The United Nations-authorized invasion soon defeated the forces of Iraqi dictator Saddam Hussein and later uncovered huge stocks of Iraqi chemical weapons. The peace terms spelled out by the UN Security Council barred Iraq seeking or having any biological, chemical, or nuclear weapons of mass destruction (WMDs) and required that UN arms inspectors have unrestricted access to ensure compliance.

In the years that followed, tensions between Washington and Baghdad remained high, and President Bill Clinton twice launched bomber and cruise missile attacks against Iraq. The first came in 1993 after a plot by Iraq to assassinate former President Bush was uncovered. The second occurred in December 1998. Iraq had routinely blocked UN inspectors and even expelled them, and it was widely believed in the United States and elsewhere that Saddam Hussein was seeking to develop WMDs. Indeed Clinton indicated his intent was "to attack Iraq's nuclear, chemical and biological weapons programs and its military capacity to threaten its neighbors."

The U.S. posture grew even harder following the 2001 inauguration of President George W. Bush, who believed that the threat from Saddam Hussein could only be eliminated by toppling him from power. Even though UN inspectors, who had gone back to Iraq, found no hard evidence of Iraqi WMD programs, and even though the UN Security Council refused to authorize action, Bush decided to act anyway. In March 2003, U.S. troops, supported by British forces and smaller contingents from several other countries, once again invaded Iraq. Bush offered a number of reasons to justify war. Most prominently, they included Iraq's alleged WMD program and its supposed ties to al-Qaeda and other terrorists groups.

The invading forces quickly routed Iraq's military, and in May the president declared, "Mission accomplished." In a narrow sense, that was true. Iraq's military had been defeated and Saddam had been driven from power. From a broader perspective, though, Bush's declaration missed the mark. The mission to rid Iraq of WMDs could not have been accomplished because none were ever found, and Iraq's alleged connection with terrorist activities remained highly controversial. Moreover, the travails of Americans and Iraqis were not over. Instead they had just begun. Terrorist-style operations soon broke out. Saddam loyalists directed some. Others were the work of outside Muslim extremists such as al-Qaeda operative Abu Musab al-Zarqawi, a Jordanian, who came to Iraq to take advantage of the situation of a largely Christian power occupying a Muslim country. American casualties soon exceeded the number of killed and wounded during invasion, and by October 2005 the number of slain coalition troops reached 2,161, of which 1,965 were Americans. Many thousands of Iraqi also died. Most of them were civilians killed by the terrorists, a much smaller number were insurgents or Iraqi civilians killed by coalition forces.

The mounting casualties were not the only aspects of the occupation of Iraq that many American found discouraging. By October 2005, the cost of the war had surpassed $200 billion. Also, images of American soldiers mistreating Iraqi prisoners at Abu Ghraib shocked and saddened many. Additionally, the work to reconstitute Iraqi security forces to the point where they could take the lead in fighting the insurgency moved slowly. And progress toward democratizing Iraq was problematic. The core issue was the division of Iraq into three competing groups: Shiite Muslims, who are a majority (±60%) of the population, are mostly Arab, and live mostly in the south; Sunni Muslims, who were in control under Saddam, are ± 25% of the population, dominate the central part of the country, and are mostly Arabs; and Kurds, who are non-Arabs (more closely related Persians/Iranians), live in the north, are ±15% of the population, and have aspiration of joining with Kurds in Turkey, Iran, and elsewhere to form an independent Kurdistan. An election to form a provisional government went smoothly in early 2005, but most Sunnis refused to participate. The provisional government's efforts to write a constitution and have elections in December 2005 to choose a regular government proceeded uncertainly amid the ethnic/religious rivalries, with the Sunnis again particularly disaffected.

Most Americans supported the invasion of Iraq in 2003, and that support held for a substantial time. By July 2005, however, public opinion was evenly divided, and to shore up public support, President Bush took to the airwaves and in the first reading explained to Americans why he believed that they should stay the course in Iraq. Others disagree, with some wanting the president to establish a long-term timetable for U.S. withdrawal from Iraq, and others, including Wesley Renfro and Brian Urlacher in the second reading, urging a much more rapid U.S. departure from Iraq.

POINTS TO PONDER

➤ Renfro and Urlacher argue in part for a quick U.S. withdrawal because the war was a mistake to begin with. Consider whether that is a relevant consideration or whether it became a moot point the United States dismantled Iraq existing government.

➤ Ponder President's Bush's argument that withdrawing from Iraq before it is stabilized would "dishonor" those American troops who have died or been wounded there. What does that mean for soldiers who have died and suffered in losing armies throughout history?

➤ Who makes the better case: those who say the occupation of Iraq is fomenting new terrorism or those who argue that democratizing Iraq is an important part of defeating terrorism?

U.S. Military Forces in Iraq:
Stay the Course

GEORGE W. BUSH

My greatest responsibility as president is to protect the American people....[In support of that responsibility, American] troops here [in the United States] and across the world are fighting a global war on terror. The war reached our shores on September the 11th, 2001. The terrorists who attacked us—and the terrorists we face—murder in the name of a totalitarian ideology that hates freedom, rejects tolerance, and despises all dissent. Their aim is to remake the Middle East in their own grim image of tyranny and oppression—by toppling governments, by driving us out of the region, and by exporting terror.

To achieve these aims, they have continued to kill—in Madrid, Istanbul, Jakarta, Casablanca, Riyadh, Bali, and elsewhere. The terrorists believe that free societies are essentially corrupt and decadent, and with a few hard blows they can force us to retreat. They are mistaken. After September the 11th, I made a commitment to the American people: This nation will not wait to be attacked again. We will defend our freedom. We will take the fight to the enemy.

Iraq is the latest battlefield in this war. Many terrorists who kill innocent men, women, and children on the streets of Baghdad are followers of the same murderous ideology that took the lives of our citizens in New York, in Washington, and Pennsylvania. There is only one course of action against them: to defeat them abroad before they attack us at home. The commander in charge of coalition operations in Iraq—who is also senior commander at this base—General John Vines, put it well the other day. He said: "We either deal with

terrorism and this extremism abroad, or we deal with it when it comes to us."

Our mission in Iraq is clear. We're hunting down the terrorists. We're helping Iraqis build a free nation that is an ally in the war on terror. We're advancing freedom in the broader Middle East. We are removing a source of violence and instability, and laying the foundation of peace for our children and our grandchildren.

The work in Iraq is difficult and it is dangerous. Like most Americans, I see the images of violence and bloodshed. Every picture is horrifying, and the suffering is real. Amid all this violence, I know Americans ask the question: Is the sacrifice worth it? It is worth it, and it is vital to the future security of our country. And tonight I will explain the reasons why.

Some of the violence you see in Iraq is being carried out by ruthless killers who are converging on Iraq to fight the advance of peace and freedom. Our military reports that we have killed or captured hundreds of foreign fighters in Iraq who have come from Saudi Arabia and Syria, Iran, Egypt, Sudan, Yemen, Libya and others. They are making common cause with criminal elements, Iraqi insurgents, and remnants of Saddam Hussein's regime who want to restore the old order. They fight because they know that the survival of their hateful ideology is at stake. They know that as freedom takes root in Iraq, it will inspire millions across the Middle East to claim their liberty, as well. And when the Middle East grows in democracy and prosperity and hope, the terrorists will lose their sponsors, lose their recruits, and lose their hopes for turning that region into a base for attacks on America and our allies around the world.

Some wonder whether Iraq is a central front in the war on terror. Among the terrorists, there is no debate. Hear the words of Osama Bin Laden: "This Third World War is raging" in Iraq. "The whole world is watching this war." He says it will end in "victory and glory, or misery and humiliation."

The terrorists know that the outcome will leave them emboldened, or defeated. So they are waging a campaign of murder and destruction. And there is no limit to the innocent lives they are willing to take.

We see the nature of the enemy in terrorists who exploded car bombs along a busy shopping street in Baghdad, including one outside a mosque. We see the nature of the enemy in terrorists who sent a suicide bomber to a teaching hospital in Mosul. We see the nature of the enemy in terrorists who behead civilian hostages and broadcast their atrocities for the world to see.

These are savage acts of violence, but they have not brought the terrorists any closer to achieving their strategic objectives. The terrorists—both foreign and Iraqi—failed to stop the transfer of sovereignty. They failed to break our Coalition and force a mass withdrawal by our allies. They failed to incite an Iraqi civil war. They failed to prevent free elections. They failed to stop the formation of a democratic Iraqi government that represents all of Iraq's diverse population. And they failed to stop Iraqis from signing up in large number with the police forces and the army to defend their new democracy.

The lesson of this experience is clear: The terrorists can kill the innocent, but they cannot stop the advance of freedom. The only way our enemies can succeed is if we forget the lessons of September the 11th, if we abandon the Iraqi people to men like [Jordanian terrorist Abu Musab al-]Zarqawi, and if we yield the future of

the Middle East to men like Bin Laden. For the sake of our nation's security, this will not happen on my watch.

A little over a year ago, I spoke to the nation and described our coalition's goals in Iraq. I said that America's mission in Iraq is to defeat an enemy and give strength to a friend—a free, representative government that is an ally in the war on terror, and a beacon of hope in a part of the world that is desperate for reform. I outlined the steps we would take to achieve this goal: We would hand authority over to a sovereign Iraqi government. We would help Iraqis hold free elections by January 2005. We would continue helping Iraqis rebuild their nation's infrastructure and economy. We would encourage more international support for Iraq's democratic transition, and we would enable Iraqis to take increasing responsibility for their own security and stability.

In the past year, we have made significant progress. One year ago today, we restored sovereignty to the Iraqi people. In January 2005, more than 8 million Iraqi men and women voted in elections that were free and fair, and took time on—and took place on time. We continued our efforts to help them rebuild their country. Rebuilding a country after three decades of tyranny is hard, and rebuilding while at war is even harder. Our progress has been uneven, but progress is being made.

We're improving roads and schools and health clinics. We're working to improve basic services like sanitation, electricity, and water. And together with our allies, we'll help the new Iraqi government deliver a better life for its citizens.

In the past year, the international community has stepped forward with vital assistance. Some 30 nations have troops in Iraq, and many others are contributing non-military assistance. The United Nations is in Iraq to help Iraqis write a constitution and conduct their next elections. Thus far, some 40 countries and three international organizations have pledged about $34 billion in assistance for Iraqi reconstruction. More than 80 countries and international organizations recently came together in Brussels to coordinate their efforts to help Iraqis provide for their security and rebuild their country. And next month, donor countries will meet in Jordan to support Iraqi reconstruction.

Whatever our differences in the past, the world understands that success in Iraq is critical to the security of our nations. As German Chancellor Gerhard Schröder said at the White House yesterday, "There can be no question a stable and democratic Iraq is in the vested interest of not just Germany, but also Europe." Finally, we have continued our efforts to equip and train Iraqi security forces. We made gains in both the number and quality of those forces. Today Iraq has more than 160,000 security forces trained and equipped for a variety of missions. Iraqi forces have fought bravely, helping to capture terrorists and insurgents in Najaf and Samarra, Fallujah and Mosul. And in the past month, Iraqi forces have led a major anti-terrorist campaign in Baghdad called Operation Lightning, which has led to the capture of hundreds of suspected insurgents. Like free people everywhere, Iraqis want to be defended by their own countrymen, and we are helping Iraqis assume those duties.

The progress in the past year has been significant, and we have a clear path forward. To complete the mission, we will continue to hunt down the terrorists and insurgents. To complete the mission, we will prevent al Qaeda and other foreign terrorists from turning Iraq into what Afghanistan was under the Taliban, a safe haven from which they could launch attacks on America and our friends. And the best way to complete the mission is to help Iraqis build a free nation that can govern itself, sustain itself, and defend itself.

So our strategy going forward has both a military track and a political track. The principal task of our military is to find and defeat the terrorists, and that is why we are on the offense. And as we pursue the terrorists, our military is helping to train Iraqi security forces so that they can defend their people and fight the enemy on their own. Our strategy can be summed up this way: As the Iraqis stand up, we will stand down.

We've made progress, but we have a lot of—a lot more work to do. Today Iraqi security forces are at different levels of readiness. Some are capable of taking on the terrorists and insurgents by themselves. A large number can plan and execute anti-terrorist operations with coalition support. The rest are forming and not yet ready to participate fully in security operations. Our task is to make the Iraqi units fully capable and independent. We're building up Iraqi security forces as quickly as possible, so they can assume the lead in defeating the terrorists and insurgents.

Our coalition is devoting considerable resources and manpower to this critical task. Thousands of coalition troops are involved in the training and equipping of Iraqi security forces. NATO is establishing a military academy near Baghdad to train the next generation of Iraqi military leaders, and 17 nations are contributing troops to the NATO training mission. Iraqi army and police are being trained by personnel from Italy, Germany, Ukraine, Turkey, Poland, Romania, Australia, and the United Kingdom. Today, dozens of nations are working toward a common objective: an Iraq that can defend itself, defeat its enemies, and secure its freedom.

To further prepare Iraqi forces to fight the enemy on their own, we are taking three new steps: First, we are partnering coalition units with Iraqi units. These coalition-Iraqi teams are conducting operations together in the field. These combined operations are giving Iraqis a chance to experience how the most professional armed forces in the world operate in combat.

Second, we are embedding coalition "transition teams" inside Iraqi units. These teams are made up of coalition officers and non-commissioned officers who live, work, and fight together with their Iraqi comrades. Under U.S. command, they are providing battlefield advice and assistance to Iraqi forces during combat operations. Between battles, they are assisting the Iraqis with important skills, such as urban combat, and intelligence, surveillance and reconnaissance techniques.

Third, we're working with the Iraqi Ministries of Interior and Defense to improve their capabilities to coordinate anti-terrorist operations. We're helping them develop command and control structures. We're also providing them with civilian and military leadership training, so Iraq's new leaders can effectively manage their forces in the fight against terror.

The new Iraqi security forces are proving their courage every day. More than 2,000 members of Iraqi security forces have given their lives in the line of duty. Thousands more have stepped forward, and are now training to serve their nation. With each engagement, Iraqi soldiers grow more battle-hardened, and their officers grow more experienced. We've learned that Iraqis are courageous and that they need additional skills. And that is why a major part of our mission is to train them so they can do the fighting, and then our troops can come home.

I recognize that Americans want our troops to come home as quickly as possible. So do I. Some contend that we should set a deadline for withdrawing U.S. forces. Let me explain why that would be a serious mistake. Setting an artificial timetable would send the wrong message to the Iraqis, who need to know that America will not leave before the job is done. It would

send the wrong message to our troops, who need to know that we are serious about completing the mission they are risking their lives to achieve. And it would send the wrong message to the enemy, who would know that all they have to do is to wait us out. We will stay in Iraq as long as we are needed, and not a day longer.

Some Americans ask me, if completing the mission is so important, why don't you send more troops? If our commanders on the ground say we need more troops, I will send them. But our commanders tell me they have the number of troops they need to do their job. Sending more Americans would undermine our strategy of encouraging Iraqis to take the lead in this fight. And sending more Americans would suggest that we intend to stay forever, when we are, in fact, working for the day when Iraq can defend itself and we can leave. As we determine the right force level, our troops can know that I will continue to be guided by the advice that matters: the sober judgment of our military leaders.

The other critical element of our strategy is to help ensure that the hopes Iraqis expressed at the polls in January are translated into a secure democracy. The Iraqi people are emerging from decades of tyranny and oppression. Under the regime of Saddam Hussein, the Shia and Kurds were brutally oppressed, and the vast majority of Sunni Arabs were also denied their basic rights, while senior regime officials enjoyed the privileges of unchecked power. The challenge facing Iraqis today is to put this past behind them, and come together to build a new Iraq that includes all of its people.

They're doing that by building the institutions of a free society, a society based on freedom of speech, freedom of assembly, freedom of religion, and equal justice under law. The Iraqis have held free elections and established a Transitional National Assembly. The next step is to write a good constitution that enshrines these freedoms in permanent law. The Assembly plans to expand its constitutional drafting committee to include more Sunni Arabs. Many Sunnis who opposed the January elections are now taking part in the democratic process, and that is essential to Iraq's future.

After a constitution is written, the Iraqi people will have a chance to vote on it. If approved, Iraqis will go to the polls again, to elect a new government under their new, permanent constitution. By taking these critical steps and meeting their deadlines, Iraqis will bind their multiethnic society together in a democracy that respects the will of the majority and protects minority rights.

As Iraqis grow confident that the democratic progress they are making is real and permanent, more will join the political process. And as Iraqis see that their military can protect them, more will step forward with vital intelligence to help defeat the enemies of a free Iraq. The combination of political and military reform will lay a solid foundation for a free and stable Iraq.

As Iraqis make progress toward a free society, the effects are being felt beyond Iraq's borders. Before our coalition liberated Iraq, Libya was secretly pursuing nuclear weapons. Today the leader of Libya has given up his chemical and nuclear weapons programs. Across the broader Middle East, people are claiming their freedom. In the last few months, we've witnessed elections in the Palestinian Territories and Lebanon. These elections are inspiring democratic reformers in places like Egypt and Saudi Arabia. Our strategy to defend ourselves and spread freedom is working. The rise of freedom in this vital region will eliminate the conditions that feed radicalism and ideologies of murder, and make our nation safer.

We have more work to do, and there will be tough moments that test America's resolve. We're fighting against men with blind hatred—and armed with lethal weapons—who are capable of any atrocity. They wear no uniform; they respect no laws of warfare or morality. They take innocent lives to create chaos for the cameras. They are trying to shake our will in Iraq, just as they tried to shake our will on September the 11th, 2001. They will fail. The terrorists do not understand America. The American people do not falter under threat, and we will not allow our future to be determined by car bombers and assassins.

America and our friends are in a conflict that demands much of us. It demands the courage of our fighting men and women, it demands the steadfastness of our allies, and it demands the perseverance of our citizens. We accept these burdens, because we know what is at stake. We fight today because Iraq now carries the hope of freedom in a vital region of the world, and the rise of democracy will be the ultimate triumph over radicalism and terror. And we fight today because terrorists want to attack our country and kill our citizens, and Iraq is where they are making their stand. So we'll fight them there, we'll fight them across the world, and we will stay in the fight until the fight is won.

America has done difficult work before. From our desperate fight for independence to the darkest days of a Civil War, to the hard-fought battles against tyranny in the 20th century, there were many chances to lose our heart, our nerve, or our way. But Americans have always held firm, because we have always believed in certain truths. We know that if evil is not confronted, it gains in strength and audacity, and returns to strike us again. We know that when the work is hard, the proper response is not retreat, it is courage. And we know that this great ideal of human freedom entrusted to us in a special way, and that the ideal of liberty is worth defending....When the history of this period is written, the liberation of Afghanistan and the liberation of Iraq will be remembered as great turning points in the story of freedom.

After September the 11th, 2001, I told the American people that the road ahead would be difficult, and that we would pre-vail. Well, it has been difficult—and we are prevailing. Our enemies are brutal, but they are no match for the United States of America....

U.S. Military Forces in Iraq:
Withdraw Quickly

WESLEY B. RENFRO AND BRIAN R. URLACHER

Since September 11, 2001, President George W. Bush and his advisors have sought to link their Iraq policy with the international terrorism. In March 2003, the United States invaded Iraq because Saddam Hussein's regime was allegedly developing covert nuclear, biological, and chemical weapons programs that posed an imminent threat to the United States. Congress and most Americans approved of the president's preferred policy solution—war—despite international protests and a distinct lack of conclusive evidence. Following the invasion, it became clear that there was little merit behind the original justifications for war. The costs of war and occupation, however, have continued to mount. American credibility is now low among friends and enemies alike; the United States has seriously ruptured long-standing relations with its most important allies, created more terrorists than it has killed, and has brought civil war to Iraq.

This essay aims to rebut the president's justifications for a continued American presence in Iraq. To do this we attempt to demonstrate that much of the reasoning that the president uses to justify the Iraq conflict is as flawed as the reasoning behind the initial invasion of Iraq. Moreover, we argue that a prompt withdrawal, although not an optimum solution, is America's best available option. Based on a review of the president's continuing justifications for the war, the original context of the war, and the implications of the Iraq war on the global security environment, we conclude a quick withdrawal is American's best policy solution.

WINNING THE PEACE? WHAT PEACE?

In his speech to the nation on July 28, 2005, the president provided no solid claim regarding how much progress has actually been made in defeating terrorism in Iraq or worldwide. This is in large part because while the president continues his insistence on winning the War on Terror in Iraq, there remains no credible yardstick to gauge success and failure, winning and losing. President Bush stated, "The principle task of our military is to find and defeat terrorists, and that is why we are on the offense." As long as the United States military remains in Iraq, it will carry out operations against insurgents, and thus will continue to generate intense anti-Americanism throughout the Arab and Muslim world. This anti-Americanism will result in more terrorist attacks, not less as the president suggests.

According to the administration, the number of insurgents killed by the military should measure success in Iraq. This makes sense only if the number of terrorists in the world is fixed. It is not. The American presence in Iraq is itself increasingly responsible for the growing numbers of young men and women willing to participate in the insurgency. Pursuing a policy of killing terrorists and insurgents in Iraq so that the United States does not have to fight terrorism in its own territory is not an effective means for bringing peace to Iraq. Furthermore, the ability of the United States to establish a peaceful Iraq is increasingly in doubt. Iraq is exceedingly fragile, and it is doubtful that anything can be done to avert civil war much less win the peace. Consequently, with success hard to find and the number of terrorists increasing, the only viable policy option is a quick exit.

The U.S. invasion of Iraq, the abuses of Iraqi prisoners by American guards at Abu Ghraib, and the internment camps for suspected terrorists at the U.S. naval base at Guantanamo Bay in Cuba have incensed many in the Arab and Muslim world. Young men, who previously may have regarded the United States as a land of opportunity, now see it as a force of occupation and oppression. Although difficult to measure, we can gauge support for the insurgency by the escalating levels of violence in Iraq. There is little to suggest that support for the insurgency is doing anything but increasing.

Osama bin-Laden has called Iraq the central front in his war against the United States precisely because the American presence in Iraq is a rallying cry for disaffected youth throughout the region. Consequently, foreign fighters continue streaming into Iraq. It is naive to think that these fighters have been lying in wait for years waiting for an opportunity to fight the United States. Foreign fighters in Iraq are responding to the call of bin-Laden, not because they are loyal al-Qaeda members with longstanding ties to the organization, but because they want the United States out of Iraq. They have chosen to participate in the insurgency in Iraq because they believe the U.S. occupation is unjust.

This is precisely why bin-Laden has designated Iraq and not Afghanistan the central front in his fight against the United States. The U.S. campaign against Afghanistan was in response to the 9/11 attacks masterminded by al-Qaeda. During 2001 and 2002, American forces in Afghanistan were reportedly close to capturing Osama bin-Laden. Working with the assistance of local Afghani leaders and neighboring states, many believed that the

United States had created a vice to squeeze al-Qaeda and capture its leaders, including bin-Laden. Instead, the Bush team shifted focus and resources away from Afghanistan in favor of a new confrontation with Iraq.

Bin-Laden has declared Iraq the central front because al-Qaeda can fight and win in Iraq. Iraq's neighbors have made an already bad situation worse. Iran and Syria have, for example, facilitated the passage of foreign fighters into Iraq, specifically with the goal of undermining the U.S. position. The president has attempted to draw the false dichotomy of fighting terrorism in Iraq or in the United States. What President Bush and his advisors neglect to mention is that the United States had the option of fighting terrorism abroad before pursuing regime change in Iraq. Washington continues to fight al-Qaeda and a resurgent Taliban in Afghanistan. However, the United States must now divide its resources, human and material, between Afghanistan and Iraq.

Bin-Laden welcomes the American presence in Iraq because it confirms many Arab's worst suspicions about U.S. motivations, thereby generating increasing numbers of al-Qaeda sympathizers. It seems clear though that bin-Laden prefers Iraq because he is strong there and the United States weak. The United States has killed thousands of insurgents in Iraq, but the Bush administration cannot provide an estimate how many of these insurgents were affiliated with al-Qaeda before the U.S. invasion and how many joined the insurgency because of the invasion. If the United States wants to crush bin-Laden's terrorist organization, it needs to deprive al-Qaeda of its newest and largest recruiting pool— young Muslims who are frustrated by the U.S. presence in Iraq and the abuse of detainees and prisoners at the hands of Americans. It seems unlikely that the United States can deprive the Iraqi insurgency of its most potent weapon, men willing to give their lives for the perceived liberation of their country, while maintaining an occupation force. Unless Washington drafts a clever strategy to win the hearts and minds of Muslim men throughout the region, it seems the only plausible way to diffuse the situation is the withdrawal American troops from Iraq.

The president argued fervently that setting a timetable for leaving Iraq would play into the hands of terrorists in Iraq by emboldening the insurgents to wait out the U.S. withdrawal. Senator Russ Feingold (D-WI) rejects the logic of this assertion. Feingold's rejection of the president's reasoning starts with the premise that there is a sense among Iraqis and across the broader Middle East that the United States has no plans to ever leave Iraq. Furthermore, may Arabs believe that deposing of Saddam Hussein for his alleged weapons of mass destruction (WMDs) was only a cover for a larger policy of colonization that has placed the United States in the heart of the Arab world.

The president is aware of this sentiment. He even uses it as a justification for not sending more troops to Iraq. According to the president, more troops would only send the message that the United States plans on staying in Iraq. Feingold has pointed out that the president's refusal to discuss a tentative timetable "is playing into our enemies hands." Nationalism is a potent force, and the continued presence of the United States has allowed terrorist groups to use patriotism as a recruiting tool. It is also worth noting that the current justification for the continued presence of American troops in Iraq is a highly deceptive bait and switch. When it became clear that Iraq had not harbored WMDs, the president and his advisors began to justify the invasion and continued occupation of Iraq for nobler reasons, including the spread of liberal democracy to a region rife with authoritarian regimes.

FROM ROGUE STATE TO MODEL DEMOCRACY—WISHFUL THINKING BY BUSH

Following September 11, 2001, Bush began asserting that the Iraqi threat was too great to ignore and that America's only option was to invade Iraq and prevent a dictatorial and homicidal Saddam Hussein from acquiring WMDs. In March 2003, the United States did invade and topple the unsavory Hussein regime. The United States has been unable to locate any weapons of mass destruction in Iraq. As weeks turned into months and it became increasingly clear that there were no Iraqi WMDs, the president and his advisors began to justify the Iraqi invasion in other terms, most notably the need to spread peace via democracy in the Middle East and not to allow terrorism a new breeding ground in a failed state. President Bush was correct in his claim that failed states are breeding grounds for terrorism. However, the current Iraq strategy turned a stable, though unsavory, Iraq under Saddam Hussein into a failed state under American supervision. The Bush team now asserts that the United States can remake Iraq into a stable democracy and this will, in turn, encourage other states in the region to democratize. This argument, while perhaps reasonable on the surface, collapses on closer examination and reveals several implicit and questionable assumptions.

The Bush team remains adamant in their claim that the United States can create a stable democracy in Iraq. The president articulates his position when he says, "We're hunting down the terrorists. We're helping Iraqis build a nation that is an ally in the War on Terror. We're advancing freedom in the broader Middle East. We are removing a source of violence and instability, and laying the foundation of peace for our children and grandchildren." This claim seems highly dubious given the ethnic and religious divisions that permeate Iraqi society. The United States was able to foster democracy in Japan and Germany after World War II. However, in each of these situations the United States was dealing with a homogenous country exhausted by war and somewhat receptive to the American state-building enterprise. The situation in Iraq fundamentally differs in several respects. Most Iraqis, contrary to the president's assumptions, do not identify as Iraqi. Rather, they identify themselves on religious and ethnic lines, for example, as Shi'a [Shiites], Sunni, or Kurd.

Iraq, though an overwhelmingly Muslim nation, is not religiously or ethnically homogenous. The Kurds are the predominant ethnic group in the north and are ethnically distinct from most Iraqis, who are Arabs. Differences in history, culture, and language combined with their brutal repression by the Hussein regime have made the Kurds wary of their fellow Iraqis. The Shi'a are Arab Muslims that practice a form of Islam common in Iran but rare in most of the rest of the Middle East. The Shi'a, moreover, comprise about 60% of Iraq's population and like the Kurds they were systematically brutalized by the Sunni dominated Hussein government. Finally, the Sunni's are Arab Muslims who subscribe to the major variant of Islam in the Middle East. Although a minority in Iraq, the Sunni received preferential treatment by Saddam Hussein, a Sunni himself, often at the expense of non-Sunni Iraqis.

These groups have long and acrimonious histories of internecine strife. Nearly two years after the American invasion, the insurgency seems to be growing in strength, and Iraq is in the first stages of a civil war. President Bush has told Americans that, "They [the terrorists/insurgents in Iraq] failed to incite civil war." This conclusion seems incorrect given the rising levels of violence in Iraq. It is likely that without the presence of American troops in the country, civil war would have occurred months ago. U.S. soldiers are providing a temporary bandage to a deeply rooted historical reality, namely that Iraq is unlikely to hold together as a coherent nation state absent massive American military pressure or a forceful dictator.

Second, even if the United States can help establish a democratic Iraq, there is no guarantee that this democratic state will not be radical and opposed to American interests in the region. President Bush would do well to recall the old adage, "be careful what you wish for." The Middle East is increasingly a radicalized region, and U.S. popularity within the Arab and Muslim world is at an all time low. A democratic process in Iraq could yield a government with goals inimical to U.S. preferences for the region, including plentiful access to oil and a peaceful settlement to the Palestinian-Israeli conflict. A democratic Iraq dominated by a pro-Iranian Shi'a majority would likely adopt Iran's strong pro-Palestinian stance in opposition to Washington's pro-Israeli position. Put simply, a reconstituted Iraq that seeks to stymie Washington's regional agenda is not in American's best interest.

THE DUBIOUS LINK BETWEEN IRAQ AND TERRORISM

American losses at the hands of Iraqi insurgents demonstrate that small groups of radical extremists can inflict severe damage, even to the world's most powerful state. This is a lesson that the United States should not have to learn again after the devastating 9/11 attacks illustrated American vulnerability to strikes from terrorists. In one horrific morning, 19 terrorists working on a slim budget managed to take thousands of lives, both American and foreign. In response, President Bush oversaw the most sweeping redesign on U.S. security policy since the end of the Cold War.

Articulated in the *September 2002 National Security Strategy of the United States* (NSS 2002), President Bush claimed, "Enemies in the past needed great armies and great industrial capabilities to endanger America. Now, shadowy networks of individuals can bring great chaos and suffering to our shores for less than it costs to purchase a single tank."

The president's assertion is undoubtedly true. What is less clear, however, is the link between rogue states (such as Iraq, Iran, North Korea, and Libya) and international terrorism. In the NSS 2002, the president repeatedly made the case that rogue states and international terrorists are two facets of one problem facing the international community. His solution to the growing menace, perceived or otherwise, of rogue states and international terrorism is a strategy of preemption and prevention. The argument is simple—in an age of weapons of mass destruction, the United States cannot afford to absorb the first blow. It must attempt to preserve U.S. security by preventing terrorists and their presumed rogue state backers from obtaining the ability to strike the United States. Throughout 2002, the president, his cabinet, and his advisors repeatedly made the case before domestic and international audiences that Iraq was a state on the verge of obtaining nuclear, chemical, or biological weapons. Their argument assumed that once Iraq had these weapons, they would aggressively use them to bring harm to the United States. Although there was ultimately no evidence linking Saddam Hussein to either WMD or al-Qaeda, it stuck many as unusual that the president exercised selective judgment in focusing his efforts on Iraq while refusing to investigate alleged Saudi Arabian links to extremist groups.

If the United States is serious about fighting a "Global War on Terror," it seems strange that the home of Osama bin-Laden and 15 other terrorists whose actions resulted in the death of thousands on September 11, 2001, has remained largely un-scrutinized. The president claims, "Many terrorists who kill innocent men, women, and children on the streets of Baghdad are followers of the same murderous ideology that took the lives of our citizens in New York, in Washington, and Pennsylvania." This argument is less than compelling as there is scant evidence linking Iraq to al-Qaeda before the invasion and occupation. What is clear, however, is that the Bush administration targeted Iraq while ignoring known Saudi links to al-Qaeda.

IRAQ VS. HOMELAND SECURITY

Recent history shows that the world is a dangerous place even for a superpower. The United States may be the wealthiest country in the world, but even the U.S. government must contend with issues of finite resources. Every policy requires hard decisions about what to fund and what not to fund. It is not enough to argue about whether the mushrooming cost of the Iraq war as a necessary expense; rather, Americans should consider what they are not funding by staying in Iraq.

The president has funded the Iraq war through record deficits. This has stripped money from the private sector as surely as a tax would and has been a strain on the U.S. economy. American's appear more than willing to bear this burden to defeat terrorism, yet it is unclear if spending massive sums in Iraq is doing anything but generating more terrorism.

Instead of staying in Iraq and making a dangerous situation even worse, the United States should leave Iraq and concentrate its resources on homeland security. Furthermore, if the president seeks to spread democracy throughout the Middle East, then a national program to reduce dependency on petroleum would force oil-producing nations, which have been able to buy off their populations with petro-dollars, to make reforms to their economies and political systems. The United States likely has to power to affect political and economic change in the Middle East. However, we argue that war and occupation are unlikely to result in positive economic or political change in the region.

The ongoing cost of the Iraq war is not an expense that must be paid. Instead, it is a deliberate choice to use the resources of the American people to open a second, and increasingly dubious, front in the War on Terrorism. Funding and supporting the war in Iraq is an ongoing choice in lieu of dedicating more resources to homeland security, battling terrorism in Afghanistan, the first front, or affecting change in the Middle East through domestic energy independence.

The president says, "And we fight today because terrorists want to attack our country and kill our citizens, and Iraq is where they are making their stand. So we'll fight them there, we'll fight them across the world, and we will stay in the fight until the fight is won." However, is seems increasingly clear that the fight in Iraq cannot be won. The longer we stay the greater the insurgency will become. This will not enhance American security but it will continue to drain resources that could be invested in more fruitful policies, like homeland security. The president is asking the American people to sacrifice much in pursuit of his failing policy in Iraq. The costs, already high, continue to mount and there is little chance of a positive return on this investment.

WITHDRAWAL IS THE FIRST STEP TO REPAIRING FRACTURED ALLIANCES

In addition to diverting American resources from the main effort of destroying al-Qaeda and securing the United States, the war convinced many Europeans that American policies were no longer in sync with European preferences and endangered a stable transatlantic alliance. Since the conclusion of the Second World War in 1945, the United States has remained the single most powerful state in the world. From the ashes of the world's deadliest war, the United States and its European partners established a transatlantic alliance, which has proved one of the most durable and beneficial partnerships in history. American unilateralism, during the Bush administration, now threatens the longevity of the mutually beneficial arrangement.

Continued American leadership to some degree rests on continued European consent. The transatlantic alliance has survived for so long due to the perception that the Americans were willing to work with their allies to achieve the common goals of peace and prosperity. Strong European objections, particularly by the governments of France and Germany, over America's drive to war with Iraq raise serious questions if American and European goals remain compatible.

President Bush's numerous criticisms and subsequent shift away from international forums for multilateral action, most notably the United Nations, have convinced many Europeans that the United States prefers to use its power to bully rather than to lead. The stubborn unwillingness of the Bush administration to admit that Iraq was not the threat the United States claimed that it was, could result in the slow unraveling of the carefully constructed and mutually beneficial transatlantic alliance. This may encourage European states or the European Union to view the United States as a dangerous rival rather than a valuable ally. Repairing this fractured alliance is in America's best interest and the best way for Washington to start is to convince Europe (and others) that the United States is not bent on conquest, empire, or the unilateral use of military force. A withdrawal from Iraq would be the first step in demonstrating to our erstwhile allies that America is serious about pace—not war and occupation.

The Bush administration frequently portrays European criticism as being specific to a few countries and leaders and cites the support of European states including Poland and the United Kingdom to demonstrate that the United States and Europe have no serious rift. Although Poland, the United Kingdom, Italy, and others did support the American invasion of Iraq, these decisions largely do not reflect public opinion within those states. Recent data indicates that America and its war in Iraq are deeply unpopular in Europe as well as in the Muslim and Arab worlds.

Unable to secure the backing of the major European powers other than Great Britain for his war with Iraq, President Bush forged ahead undeterred and created a "coalition of the willing," composed of numerous smaller and weaker states that were willing to support American war in exchange for preferential treatment by the Bush administration. This "coalition of the willing," with the important exception of the United Kingdom, have actually contributed very little to the war other than rhetorical support. In the president's speech he speaks of our allies in the war against Iraq and claims, "Today, dozens of nations are working toward a common objective: and Iraq that can defend itself, defeat its enemies, and secure its freedom." Most of these nations have not contributed substantial numbers of troops or material to the war or occupation. Their support is largely contingent on promises of future American political, economic, and military aid.

By failing to heed our allies calls for restraint and patience in 2002 and early 2003, the Bush administration has alienated our most important allies in Europe while showering less important states with aid in the hopes they will continue to support a war that is unpopular with their citizens. Unless the United States returns to a multilateral foreign policy and ends its unlawful occupation of Iraq, the future of the transatlantic alliance seems uncertain at best and this will make the world a more dangerous place for the United States.

While some supporters of President Bush have questioned the continued utility of the transatlantic alliance, Europe does matter to the United States. European trade and foreign investment, for example, benefit both Europeans and Americans. An acrimonious split may endanger this relationship. Furthermore, Europe and the United States have traditionally cooperated on any number of issues from peacekeeping and nuclear proliferation to attempting to halt the spread of infectious diseases. This cooperation should now be extended to fighting international terrorism. However, the American-European rift caused by war and occupation have thus far precluded the United States and Europe from working together as closely as they should. The quickest and most effective remedy is for the United States to withdraw from Iraq and refocus its energies on working with Europe to make both sides of the Atlantic more secure. Europe too has recently suffered from major attacks at the hands of al-Qaeda, including the Madrid and London attacks. America and Europe should be working together not drifting apart and unless the U.S. abandons its occupation of Iraq it seems unlikely this will happen in the short-term.

CONCLUSION

We have now considered Bush's continuing justification for the war, the original context of the war, and the implications of the Iraq war on the global security environment. We conclude that the United States has two policy options. Washington can either continue to pour resources, both human and material, into a failing project ad infinitum in the hopes the situation will somehow change. Alternatively, the United States can recognize that short of a permanent military occupation Iraq is beyond democratic rehabilitation, at least in its proposed form, and that it is in America's best interest to leave the country as soon as possible.

The president and others claim that an immediate withdrawal would embolden terrorists and insurgents and demonstrate that the United States lacks resolve. Furthermore, the president opines that, "We will stay in Iraq as long as we are needed, and not a day longer." Many argue that although the war may have been unnecessary in the first place, a sudden withdrawal would only make a bad situation worse. They believe that if we simply stay long enough we can help establish a stable Iraq that will be break apart in a civil war. This essay argues that the damage to Iraq is already done and no matter when the United States chooses to leave, civil war will occur. If civil war is inevitable, as most evidence suggests, it does not make sense for the United States to continue to sacrifice resources in an enterprise doomed to failure. Although an unpleasant reality, there is little hope of salvaging Iraq and avoiding civil war.

In recent months, the United States has made a serious commitment to training and equipping an Iraqi army capable of defeating the insurgency without American assistance. The U.S. military is widely recognized as the most professional and efficient in the world. If the world's most capable military is foundering trying to defeat a virulent insurgency, why is there reason to believe that a recently established Iraqi army will be able to do better? Furthermore, train-

ing and arming an Iraqi army seems a poor policy choice given inevitability of a civil war. We argue that today's Iraqi soldiers and officers are likely to become tomorrow's warlords and guerrillas. The United States is not preparing the Iraqi military to defeat the insurgents; it is training and equipping them for a civil war that is sure to come.

While no easy option has presented itself to the Bush administration, withdrawal seems to be more consistent with America's long-term objectives. As argued earlier, the American occupation is not a productive strategy in the "Global War on Terror." The continued occupation is only fostering greater resentment of the United States and creating more potential terrorists. While President Bush remains optimistic about creating a stable Iraq and avoiding a civil war, this seems unwarranted in light of the facts. If civil war will eventually come to Iraq, why stay and waste precious resources fighting a losing battle, while continuing to create enemies at every turn? Moreover, the United States can use a tactical withdrawal as an opportunity to regain the credibility and allies it lost during the past few years. Some argue that if the United States were to leave Iraq, it would be a sign of American weakness and would carry grave consequences for the United States. This, however, is simplistic interpretation. American credibility is not based on its willingness to invade and occupy foreign lands. Rather it is based on economic prowess, practices of mutual respect, and a multilateral approach to foreign policy, based on consent, that helps foster a stable, peaceful, and prosperous international system. America can best start to rectify its recent deviation from these principles by making a strategic withdrawal from its poorly conceived and failing Iraq adventure.

THE CONTINUING DEBATE:
U.S. Military Forces in Iraq

What Is New

American support of the war has sagged even further since President Bush's address. Polls in October 205 found 67% disapproving of the Bush's handling Iraq and 59% believing the war had been a mistake. However, 57% of Americans continued to say they had not "given up on the possibility of the U.S. eventually being able to create a stable government in Iraq." And 51% believed that U.S. troops should remain in Iraq "until the situation has stabilized."

September 2005 saw the largest anti-war protest to that date, with about 100,000 demonstrators gathered in Washington, D.C. Smaller protests took place in other cities across the country. What united the demonstrators was the desire for peace in Iraq; what divided them was the speed of the U.S. withdrawal they all favored. Some wanted to bring the troops home in the near future regardless of the situation in Iraq. Others agreed with one protestor's view, "There has to be a plan to withdraw, we can't stay forever, but we can't pull out now, either. That would make Iraq worse." Yet others, albeit a much smaller number, joined counter-demonstrations in support of the U.S. presence in Iraq.

Where to Find More

A good place to begin is with a understanding of Iraq available in William R. Polk, *Understanding Iraq: The Whole Sweep of Iraqi History, from Genghis Khan's Mongols to the Ottoman Turks to the British Mandate to the American Occupation* (Perennial, 2006). An interesting view of why the United States chose war can be found in Philip Smith, *Why War?: The Cultural Logic of Iraq, the Gulf War, and Suez* (University of Chicago Press, 2005). A detailed account of the thinking inside the Bush administration is in Bob Woodward, *Plan of Attack* (Simon & Schuster, 2004). Current information on the situation in Iraq, including casualties, is available from CNN at www.cnn.com/SPECIALS/2003/iraq/forces/casualties/.

The National Priorities Project has a counter for its up-to-the-minute estimate of the monetary cost of the war is at http://nationalpriorities.org/index.php?option=com_wrapper&Itemid=182.

What More to Do

One key to the future of Iraq is the December 2005 national elections, which will have occurred by the time you read this. Analyze the prospects that Iraq with U.S. support will be able to establish a united, relatively peaceful, democratic country. Also consider the consequences of a rapid U.S. withdrawal. Many predict that would permit a vicious civil war killing countless Iraqis, an even greater destruction to Iraq's oil industry and higher world fuel prices, and even the dismemberment of Iraq and increased Middle East instability. What would be the consequences of a U.S. withdrawal and how to those measure up against the burden of a continued U.S. presence?

20   URBAN POLICY

REBUILDING NEW ORLEANS:
National Imperative *or* Emotional Mistake?

NATIONAL IMPERATIVE

ADVOCATE: James R, Stoner, Jr., professor of political science at Louisiana State University

SOURCE: "Saving a Great City: "Why America Should Rebuild New Orleans," *The Weekly Standard* (Sept 26, 2005)

EMOTIONAL MISTAKE

ADVOCATE: Edward Glaeser, Professor of Economics and Director of the Rappaport Institute for Greater Boston and the Taubman Center for State and Local Government, Harvard University

SOURCE: "Should the Government Rebuild New Orleans, Or Just Give Residents Checks?" *The Economists' Voice*, September, 2005

Hurricane Katrina roared ashore at 7:10 a.m. on August 29, 2005. The category 4 storm (131–155 mph winds) made landfall near Buras, Louisiana, 50 miles south of New Orleans. Southern Louisiana and Mississippi staggered under the onslaught. Most prominently, New Orleans was engulfed. In addition to suffering wind damage, 80% of the low-lying city of 485,000 was flooded when its protecting levees failed in several spots and the waters of Lake Pontchartrain and the Mississippi River rose to as much as 20 feet deep in New Orleans.

The human devastation caused by Katrina was extensive. Over 1,200 people died, with the toll highest in Louisiana (1,003) and Mississippi (219). Of the survivors, most of the people along the coast in those two states became at least temporarily refugees. The economic damage was also vast. Hundreds of thousands of homes and other buildings were destroyed or damaged, thousands of businesses were shut down at least temporarily and their employees left without jobs. Overall, the U.S. Congressional Budget Office estimates that Katrina caused between $70 billion and $130 billion in property damage, and lost tax revenues and other economic factors will add tens of billions more dollars to the cost of the storm.

As horrendous as the impact of Katrina was, the storms impact was initially overstated by some officials and the media in superheated commentary reminiscent of what occurred during the 9/11 terrorists attacks. For example, in that disaster, first reports put the dead at the World Trade Center at about 10,000. The actual number was 2,792. Similarly, after Katrina, New Orleans Mayor Ray Nagin told reporters, "It wouldn't be unreasonable to have 10,000" dead. News reports were also full of horrific stories. Some were accurate, but others were not. New Orleans Police Chief Eddie Compass tool reporters that in the Convention Center where refugees had taken shelter, "We have individuals who are getting raped; we have individuals who are getting beaten." Adding to the image of horror, Mayor Nagin complained on television that other refugees "have been in that frickin' Superdome for five days watching dead bodies, watching hooligans killing people, raping people." All the major news outlets carried such stories, giving them an air of truth. As it turned out, few were, as both officials and the media later conceded. A month later, the New Orleans *Times-Picayune* characterized inflated death estimates and stories about unverified rapes and unconfirmed sniper attacks as examples of the "scores of myths about the dome and Convention Center treated as fact by evacuees, the media and even some of New Orleans' top officials."

Certainly, these exaggerations do not minimize the immense suffering and damage that occurred. Nevertheless, the overly lurid tales helped set the stage for an emotional reaction that in part led to a pledge to rebuild New Orleans by President George Bush. Speaking to the nation in a nationally televised address from the French Quarter of New Orleans, he proclaimed, "There is no way to imagine America without New Orleans, and this great city will rise again."

Arguably another factor that led to Bush's bold assurance was the criticism that had rained down on the administration for its allegedly poor initial response to the crisis. This left Bush with an urgent political need to show he was in both caring and in charge. Congress was also under heavy pressure for such supposed shortcoming as underfunding the U.S. Army Corps of Engineers, which is responsible for building and maintaining the levees. Such political factors helped prompt the president to soon request, and for Congress to immediately approve, $62 billion in aid for the hurricane-damaged Gulf coast. Analysts estimate that another $200 billion in federal aid is necessary to rejuvenate New Orleans and other damaged areas.

Even in the immediate aftermath of the storm, a few questioned rebuilding most of New Orleans. Speaker of the House Dennis Hastert (R-IL) said that spending huge sums to reconstruct a city that mostly lies 7 feet below sea level "doesn't make sense to me" and that, "It looks like a lot of that place could be bulldozed." Louisiana Congressman Charlie Melancon labeled the Speaker's comments "irresponsible." Whether they were or not is the focus of this debate. Does it "make sense" to rebuild New Orleans as a major urban center, rather than just mostly restoring the historic/tourist and commercial parts of the city, most of which escaped with only moderate damage? James R, Stoner, Jr., argues in the first reading that it is imperative to rebuild New Orleans. Edward Glaeser disagrees in the second article, contending that it would be wiser and more cost effective to give displaced New Orleanians a huge financial incentive to relocate permanently to a city less subject to submersion.

POINTS TO PONDER

➢ Americans are steadily migrating toward the coasts. Nearly 60% live there now, and that share is expected to increase to 75% in 2025. Given the obvious risks, should this "liability" be backed by public funds to recover from inevitable natural disasters?

➢ Consider how to pay for the rebuilding. Your options are some combination of higher federal taxes, cuts to existing federal programs, or greater deficit spending.

➢ Ponder how you would allocate the cost of rebuilding among the local, state, and national governments?

Rebuilding New Orleans:
National Imperative

JAMES R. STONER, JR.

It is only by thinking of Walker Percy that I can begin to make sense of what has befallen the city by which I live, where my wife and our four children were born, and that I have come to call home. Percy, the celebrated author of six novels [the last of which was *The Thanatos Syndrome* (Farrar, Straus, 1987)], lived in Covington, Louisiana, just north of Lake Pontchartrain, and set his stories in the orbit of New Orleans and its culture. He wrote of the confrontation of modernity and tradition, of the alienation of the individual, of redemption and apocalypse, of natural disaster and manmade plague. He died in 1990 and was buried with the monks of St. Joseph Abbey near his home.

Percy was a deeply Catholic author, but never alleged to have been a saint. To the Catholic mind, that means his soul was marked for purgatory before admittance to heaven, a place or time of penance or cleansing to prepare to see God. Catholics are bound to believe that purgatory exists, but the precise form of its labors, and the timetable for its completion, have been left to our imagination. Six novels in 30 years suggests an author who did not write quickly or easily, so let us suppose that Percy's purgatory was to write one last novel, a perfect novel about a perfect storm: a monster hurricane headed straight to New Orleans, diverted at the last moment ever so slightly east, weakened in force ever so marginally—no doubt by the prayers of the city's faithful to their Lady of Prompt Succor—but with full disaster doubling back nonetheless as a result of human incompetence, corruption, malice, and neglect. It is a classic Percean plot.

Now, Satan has no purchase on the souls in purgatory—they are destined for salvation—but maybe human error is still possible there, and if so, maybe Percy's novel, like Robert E. Lee's plans for the Battle of Antietam, fell into Satan's hands. Once an angel of light, he knew brilliance when he saw it, and immediately sent a message to God as he had done in the age of Job. "Let me put to the test these Americans," he wagered, "to see which of us they serve, you, as they never tire of professing, or me, as seems to much of the world more likely. Let me stir up the winds of the Atlantic, give them a taste of Florida to distract an unsuspecting nation, then send them right to the port that gathers the grain and coal and other fruits of the heartland, that refines my nectar, oil, and see whether your Americans will do my bidding." A colloquy followed. The Father nodded. And it was done.

II

"Much of what happened in New Orleans this week might have been avoided," Mark Fischetti wrote in the *New York Times* the Friday after Katrina struck. As a matter of civil engineering this is true, but as a matter of political reality, a serious catastrophe was bound to happen. That the sophisticated plan touted by Fischetti was called "Coast 2050" suggests that even those willing to prepare for the future barely expected to see the fruits of their efforts in their lifetimes. Of course all of that changed in 72 hours. New Orleanians are now scattered across America —both those who left of their own accord, and those sent away by bus after harrowing days in the Superdome or the Convention

Center—but one can be sure that most of them will want to come home when they can. It's not a matter of reason; one lives for love in New Orleans, and to most New Orleanians that means for family and home. It's a sentiment that cuts across the many differences of class and race now made visible to the world like an open wound.

But rebuilding New Orleans is not just a dream of the romantic or a demand of those with nowhere else to go. As George Friedman argued in an article that circulated widely on the Internet ["New Orleans: A Geopolitical Prize," September 1, 2005, available at www.stratfor.com] in the days after the storm, it stands to reason as a matter of geopolitics that the United States needs to protect the port at the mouth of the major river that drains the continent. Not software for export nor much by way of consumer goods passes through the city, as they do the ports on the east and west coasts, but coal, grain, and other commodities come down the Mississippi on barges to be loaded for shipping abroad; steel arrives here for manufacturers in the United States; oil from the Gulf (ours and theirs) [that is, the Persian Gulf] is refined and distributed; chemicals are produced along the river above the city, and much more. As Friedman wrote, from the time of the Louisiana Purchase "until last Sunday, New Orleans was, in many ways, the pivot of the American economy." It may not have been its growing point—indeed, part of the inertia in the city and in thinking about it came from the palpable sense that it represented the past rather than the future of American commerce—but New Orleans and the ports of Louisiana and Baton Rouge upriver together handle all the physical commodities still necessary to modern life. (When gasoline prices around the country jumped a dollar or more after the city went under, all America was reminded of that stubborn geographic fact.)

That protection of the city is possible if the political will is there can be seen both in the existing control of the river and in the example of the Dutch. As John McPhee described in his 1989 book *The Control of Nature*, flood-protection along the Mississippi River was once the responsibility of local communities, once even of individual plantations. These did their jobs with various degrees of effectiveness, but the more successful levees put added pressure on the others, for the force of gravity on water is inexorable: High water wants to flood and will find the weakest barrier. Eventually, the only viable solution was to centralize the levee system under the control of the Army Corps of Engineers. This was begun already in the late 19th century; indeed, [Professor] William Graham Sumner complains of it as an example of illegitimate governmental interference in his 1883 classic, *What Social Classes Owe to Each Other*.

The Corps's ambition, according to McPhee, reached a sort of culmination in the building of the Old River dams and locks near the spot where the Red River empties into the Mississippi, designed to keep the great river in its present channel and out of the Atchafalaya basin, where it seems naturally to seek a shorter outlet to the Gulf, while allowing high water from the main river to be released into the basin if necessary to prevent flooding downstream. Though McPhee points to the potential for catastrophe should the dams ever fail, the levee system as a whole has tamed the lower Mississippi. The disastrous flood of 1927 in St. Bernard Parish downriver from New Orleans, memorably described in John Barry's *Rising Tide*, was caused by a deliberate breach in the levee south of New Orleans in order to relieve pressure on the levees through the city itself. (That is why, even today, when a levee is breached, those down water often assume it was deliberate.)

The 1927 flood led to the building of the Bonnet Carre Spillway upriver from the city, permitting the Corps to divert high waters from the river into Lake Pontchartrain, something they have to do every decade or so. When the gates are opened, you can see the brown river water trickle into the lake from Interstate 10 west of the city. It seems so little at any moment, but last time aerial photos showed the whole lake turned brown in barely a week.

Except when the spillway is opened, Lake Pontchartrain is part of a water system that is separate from the river. Fed by slow-moving rivers of its own and by another, smaller lake to its west, Pontchartrain averages only 12 to 14 feet in depth, but is long and wide: 40 miles from east to west, 24 from north to south at its widest point. (The latter span is crossed by a causeway that connects Mandeville and Covington on the North Shore, the city's fastest growing and upscale suburbs, to Metairie, the suburb immediately to the city's west; despite its length, it has become a major commuting route.) On its eastern end, Pontchartrain opens to the Gulf of Mexico just a little way north of the mouth of the Mississippi, through the much smaller Lake Borgne. As the world now knows, not the river but the lake was the cause of the terrible flooding of New Orleans. The lake rose as the storm surged water in from the Gulf and added rains of its own, and it soon broke through a couple of levees, one on the Industrial Canal, which connects the lake and the river on the eastern side of the city, the other on the Seventeenth Street Canal on the city's western edge, into which water is pumped to drain the city into the lake.

Lake Pontchartrain is geologically very similar to the Zuider Zee in the Netherlands. Both are near the mouth of a major river draining the continent—in Holland, of course, it is the Rhine—and

both are naturally fresh water or brackish. And once one does the conversions, even the dimensions are almost identical: four to five meters deep, a little shy of 100 kilometers in length, about 50 in width. Of course the natural history of the Zuider Zee is better known. Called Flevo Lake by the Romans, it was renamed in 1287, after a flood from the North Sea broke dikes and widened its mouth. Fifty thousand people are thought to have died in that flood; some 10,000 died in November 1421, when dikes broke again.

But the Zuider Zee has been tamed by human engineering. A 1918 act initiated the project after flooding two years before, and by 1932 a dam had been completed across its mouth. Some land behind the dam has been reclaimed in polders, some for dwelling, some for farming. What is essential is that the Zuider Zee has never flooded with waters from a North Sea storm since the project was completed, even in 1953, when a winter storm devastated Holland's then-unprotected south. The replacement of individual dikes with a uniform dam and sea wall, imagined since the 17th century, planned by Cornelis Lely as early as 1891, and finally built when he became the Dutch minister of transport and public works, effectively removed vulnerability from the Zuider Zee. A modern series of movable sea walls and dikes has since been built in the southern region, allowing continued tidal flow in fair weather but closable in foul. Modern engineering, with increasing sensitivity to the natural environment so far as is consistent with protecting human life, has restored to the "Low Countries" of Europe the kind of wealth they had known several hundred years before.

What the Dutch could do to the Zuider Zee almost a century ago, and with less disruption to their southern inlets within recent memory, Americans can surely do to the Pontchartrain today and to the other wetlands adjacent to New Orleans. To be sure, our summer hurricanes from the tropics are fiercer than their winter storms off the Arctic, but technology is comparably more advanced. The mouth of the Pontchartrain in Lake Borgne is no wider, indeed a little narrower, than that of the Zuider Zee. If the engineers think it advisable, a second dam might be built in the middle of the Pontchartrain as in the Zuider Zee; in fact, the causeway bridge already spans this route and is slated for expansion. Fully mastered, the water level in the lake could be lowered in hurricane season to compensate for the water that a hurricane would drop as rain and for the height of the waves it could stir. This would limit even the worst surge that could double back from the lake into New Orleans, prevent excessive pressure on the levees once the storm had passed—the cause of the flooding of most of the city—and even keep the city above the lake in case of a breach. And the North Shore, which is largely unleveed, would also be protected from storm surge flooding if the lake were managed, not left to nature's whim.

In short, just as control of the Mississippi took a sort of paradigm shift in thinking—from community levees protecting individual towns and plantations to a long, continuous system maintained by the Corps of Engineers—so the current pattern of individual levees protecting New Orleans and its neighbors from the lake and its canals, each with its own Levee Board staffed by patronage appointments, could be replaced by an integrated system that asserted control over the lake itself, and an analogous system to master the westbank wetlands as well, now also under several jurisdictions. It only requires a change of thinking and federal dollars—though if the estimates in the "Coast 2050" plan are correct, the cost barely exceeds the first emergency relief package passed by Congress in the aftermath of the Katrina flood and is dwarfed by the second. Not even counting the lives lost and the communities destroyed, it would be a bargain.

III

The Zuider Zee system took under 15 years to complete once the Dutch got serious; the more modern system in Holland's south took 30. Even if the plan for New Orleans devised in 1998 had been immediately enacted it would not likely have been finished in time for Katrina, and in fact the scientific analysis of the possible flooding of New Orleans by 15 feet of water from the lake had only been worked out by scientists in the late 1990s and gradually brought to the public's attention in the last few years. The bitter partisan recrimination in the days since the flooding, mostly concerning the relief effort and its various delays, is indicative of the politics that made adoption of an imaginative solution to the threat of a hurricane impossible in recent years. Indeed, as many have rushed to say, the politics of the city and the state are a tangled knot, and when blame eventually gets apportioned, there will be plenty to pass around.

Out-of-state observers are inclined to think the need for massive rebuilding (as some wit noted, one dare not call it "reconstruction") offers planners a clean slate in much of the city, and they must be relieved that the Supreme Court decided the Kelo case as it did [*Kelo v. New London*, 2005; see Debate 15], in favor of the urban planners rather than the private owners. I'm inclined to the view that it will be mostly those who love the city who come back, and they will want to restore as well as rebuild. There will be room enough for both. Leaving to others the matter of sorting out the past, let me point to areas of possible consensus concerning the city's future, first among the locals, then in the nation at large.

Since the oil business pulled out of New Orleans for Houston, company by company over the past decade or so, the city has relied ever more on tourism as its major industry—a dead-end choice for a commercial city that, as Joel Kotkin recently wrote in the *Wall Street Journal*, "lies not in creating its future but selling its past." The city has given in to every weak impulse and temptation, as though they were the cause of its charm. Historically, conventions came to New Orleans as a place to do business, not just a place to play, and its fabled hospitality and charm depended upon a mingling of regular customers and visitors. The world-famous restaurants were gathering places for the well-to-do of the city, not just out-of-towners with expense accounts, and the culinary culture they represented was shared by every level of society, as tourists not on expense accounts discovered to their delight. A clear commitment to master the natural threat to the city ought to send serious commerce, business, and industry the signal they need to return, and this would bring repair of the cultural infrastructure as well as the physical. Moreover, once secure, there is no reason that New Orleans should not find a niche in the growing information economy, which values personality and thrives on human interest as well as technical proficiency. The large housing projects built in the city after World War II had become such shameful dens of misery and criminality that over the past several years some of them have been partially dismantled and others entirely razed. Rebuilding such boondoggles is not the kind of federal project New Orleans needs. But a great public work that at once protects the city, assures its future existence, and brings jobs in construction ought to be public money well spent.

Race is never far from the surface of New Orleans politics—perhaps it is the surface of New Orleans politics—but it operates in a way very different from its depiction in the national press. Blacks have controlled the city government for a generation, and in the election last year the last two whites elected and reelected citywide moved on. The current mayor, Ray Nagin, was no big-city boss but CEO of the local cable company, Cox Communications. He ran as a reformer with the support of the city's business community— "Nagin-Reagan" [A reference to President Ronald W. Reagan] was the taunt in the campaign—and he is representative of a rising class of black professionals and businesspeople in the city. The ancient rivalry of New Orleans and Atlanta—once cast as the Old South versus the New—plays itself out now in black middle-class culture. One has only to drive area highways to see that two major annual events in New Orleans—the Bayou Classic football game between Southern University and Grambling State University over Thanksgiving weekend, and the Essence Festival over the Fourth of July—draw thousands of well-off black Americans back home to New Orleans, even though Atlanta has been more successful in creating modern white-collar jobs.

Except in some of the newer suburbs, but even there to some degree, blacks and whites of every social class encounter one another in New Orleans all the time. This is never more true than at Mardi Gras, when uptown families and the people you saw on TV at the Superdome stand along the same parade route and compare the beads they catch. There is still social separation of the races—different churches (though some mixing between Catholics and evangelicals) and different carnival krewes—but these coexist with physical proximity. The national press still misses this, wanting to tell a story about how white houses stayed dry and black houses flooded. But Lakeview, next to the notorious breach in the Seventeenth Street Canal, is largely white, and so is flooded St. Bernard Parish, while poorer black communities interspersed among the mansions of St. Charles Avenue, over by the river, are dry. It is characteristic of New Orleans that the usual generalizations about race unravel. Many distinctive New Orleanian traits—whether tolerance of corruption on the one hand, or staunch religious faith on the other—cut across racial lines.

No one from the area was surprised by the eruption of violence when the rising waters seemed out of control. Even a week or two later, hints of the extent of the street war are only beginning to trickle out. Those who stayed and have subsequently evacuated tell of the constant sound of gunfire during the moonless nights; others reported seeing armed gangs (though I know of no pictures of such in the major media), and stories of rapes and robberies in the supershelters abound. It quickly became politically incorrect in national circles to express concern about the looting, as though all that was going on was a few desperate people taking what they needed to survive. When and if the full story of the breakdown of order is told, it will be a harrowing tale. What it means for the future of the city—how it will affect crime in an already violent place, how it will affect race relations—is something that only the future knows. One can imagine the criminal bands broken, and one can imagine them resentful and defiant. One cannot imagine the city indifferent about crime and security for a long, long time.

The eruption of partisan rancor almost immediately on the national scene is also not surprising to those observing the tenor of politics in recent years, but it is depressing nonetheless. Most Americans pull together in times of crisis and let go of partisan differences until the danger is past, but bipartisanship in the face of disaster did not seem to be the guiding spirit of the political classes in the first week. It didn't help that prominent northern Republican politicians dropped hints that the city might not be worth saving or rebuilding, as if resentful that the statue of General Lee still stands atop a column at the head of St. Charles Avenue looking serenely yet sternly at the business district and the French Quarter, as if the old sore never quite heals. As modern Republicans readily enough admit among themselves, the party does not always seem equipped ideologically to understand the value and the delicate order of a great city, which is more inegalitarian than the moralists among them wish to admit and more dependent on the character of the community than the libertarians are able to explain. As for the demagoguery of the "angry left," ignoring that both the city and the state are in Democratic hands, it is to my mind beneath contempt.

But the outreach of America to New Orleans and to the surrounding areas of Mississippi and Alabama also affected by the storm has been heartwarming, indeed overwhelming. For all the complaints about the first response, the rescue count by boat and helicopter the first few days now looks as though it will significantly exceed the death toll. Medical teams from around the country arrived with alacrity and worked with quiet competence. The military came when ordered and seems to have gone efficiently about its work. Communities from around the nation have welcomed refugees among them in homes and shelters; schools have generously taken in our students; gifts of money and offers of help abound. Despite the ways in which New Orleanians are different, perhaps because we are different, Americans seem to have a special fondness for the city and its people that goes beyond even the usual generous spirit of a generous people. Maybe it is recognition of the city's importance in the nation's history and economy. Maybe it is the memory that no one leaves a visit to New Orleans unchanged. Maybe it is that, in an age of abstracted materialism, the city's signal trait is human warmth.

IV

The next few months will be the time of decision for the city's future. Already the local spirit is eager to rebuild, and already there has been an outpouring of relief, but the serious decisions are yet to be made: whether New Orleans will be recognized as a strategic asset worth dramatically enhanced federal flood protection, and so whether the rebuilding will be sentimental or substantial. New Orleans will never be another Houston, but it can learn from Houston, and from many another city, even as it recovers a culture that is distinctively its own.

When God gave Satan permission to test Job's faithfulness, it was with one condition: "All that he has is in your power; only the man himself you must not touch." The inundation of New Orleans has tested America and, at least at the outset, exposed more than a couple of our failings. But it has not yet drowned our spirit, not the spirit of the people of the city nor the spirit of the country that has reached out to us as fellow Americans. The taming of the forces of nature has always been a challenge we have welcomed, not a task we have disdained or abandoned. And the fruits of peaceful order and free exchange, amidst commercial plenty shared with family and friends, have never seemed to us ignoble as an end. If this is so, then New Orleans has a place in America's future, not only in her past.

Rebuilding New Orleans:
Emotional Mistake

EDWARD L. GLAESER

In the wake of Hurricane Katrina, President [George W.] Bush declared that a "Great City Will Rise Again." He promised, "Throughout the area hit by the hurricane, we will do what it takes—we will stay as long as it takes—to help citizens rebuild their communities and their lives."

Lawmakers have stumbled over each other to suggest greater and greater public spending to rebuild New Orleans. While details remain to be settled, the current estimates are that federal spending will be close to $200 billion.

Senator Edward Kennedy [D-MA] has proposed a $150 billion agency specifically dedicated to Gulf [of Mexico] area infrastructure. This spending is being justified as federal insurance against disaster.

But the concept of insurance hardly leads inexorably to the conclusion that the government must spend money directly to rebuild New Orleans. To the contrary, if there is disaster insurance, then it is, presumably, the people of New Orleans who are insured, not the place itself. After all, people (or corporations) hold insurance; places don't.

IT SEEMS CLEAR THE GOVERNMENT WILL PAY TO REBUILD. BUT HOW, EXACTLY?

Economists emphasize the moral hazard problems in providing free disaster insurance to high risk areas. [Professor] Gary Becker [of the University of Chicago] has argued, for example, that free insurance creates a "Good Samaritan" problem that encourages bad location decisions.

As a matter of economic principle, Becker is surely right. Going forward, resi-dents of high risk areas should—from an economic efficiency perspective—be charged for the implicit federal insurance that they receive. But politically, given Florida's status as a battleground state, this isn't likely.

Moreover, even if we agree that in the future we should not distort location decisions by providing free insurance, we should presumably still fulfill the current obligations to the residents of New Orleans. And politicians have promised to do just that.

So for the moment, let's accept the principle that the federal government has—wisely or not—insured against disasters. That principle still tells us little about how, exactly, these insurance claims should be paid out.

SHOULD THE GOVERNMENT REBUILD, OR SHOULD RESIDENTS GET CHECKS OR VOUCHERS?

We could try to make good on the idea that the government provides insurance by rebuilding the city. Alternatively, we could provide residents with checks or vouchers, and let them make their own decisions about how to spend that money—including the decision about where to locate, or relocate, themselves. When your car is damaged you can often "cash out" and receive cash to do with as you wish instead of having your car repaired. And, when your car is "totaled," the insurance company generally won't fix your car at all, it will only provide cash compensation, and you decide how to spend it.

In the context of the President's comments, there is a big difference between rebuilding lives and rebuilding communities. Given limited funds, the two objectives may well conflict, and the usual lesson from economics is that people are better off if they are given money and allowed to make their own decisions, much as they are with car insurance.

The case for rebuilding New Orleans, then, depends on whether the residents of New Orleans will be made better off by this spending, than by being given checks or vouchers.

VOUCHERS OR CHECKS WOULD BE LIFE-CHANGING FOR POOR NEW ORLEANS RESIDENTS

To put the numbers in context, imagine that we were to spend $100 billion dollars on infrastructure for the residents of the city. An alternative to this spending is to give each one of the city of New Orleans' residents a check for more than $200,000.

Annual per capita income in that city is less than $20,000, so this check would amount to ten years' income, on average—a hefty, and potentially life-changing sum. That is enough to send several children to college, to buy a modest home, and/or to relocate and start a dreamed-of business.

If this money were spread over the 1.33 million residents in the New Orleans metropolitan area, each resident would still receive $75,000, still enough to pay for a home in many areas of the country.

Can the benefits to the residents' of local infrastructure possibly equal the benefits for receiving three or ten years' income as a lump sum? One has to wonder.

COULD PUBLIC SPENDING POSSIBLY BENEFIT RESIDENTS MORE THAN CHECKS OR VOUCHERS COULD?

Indeed, there are many reasons to suspect that spending vast sums to rebuild the city may not make sense. New Orleans is like many great American cities that were built

during previous eras and have become somewhat obsolete. Before 1900, moving goods by water was much cheaper than moving goods by land. As a result, all of the great American cities were built on rivers, or where an important river meets the sea. From that perspective, the location of New Orleans was unbeatable: it is the port at the mouth of America's greatest river system. New Orleans reached its peak of economic importance relative to the U.S. in 1840. But the Civil War and the relative decline of water-based transportation relative to rail caused the city to lose ground, relative to Northern cities, through much of the Nineteenth century.

In 1840, New Orleans was America's third largest city (after New York and Baltimore); by 1920, it had dropped to being only its *seventeenth* largest city. Still, the city's edge as a port continued to ensure that its population increased until the 1950s.

New Orleans began to decline, in absolute terms, in 1960. The port remains important, but increasing mechanization and containerization, together meant that fewer and fewer people were needed to work in that port. Today, according to the 2003 County Business Patterns [published by the U.S. Census Bureau], less than one-twentieth of the employees in New Orleans are in transportation industries, and more than a quarter of these aren't even working in the port or pipelines.

Even the vaunted energy industry employs a remarkably small number of people. County Business Patterns reports that there are fewer than 2,000 people in New Orleans working in oil and gas extraction, and fewer than 100 people working on pipeline transportation.

While there are fewer than 7,500 people working in the port, there are 32,000 employees in health care and social assistance. New Orleans' biggest industry is tourism, and there are 37,000 employees working in food services and accommodation.

New Orleans remains an important port, but this port doesn't need a large city, and over time, the city has contracted. New Orleans' population has declined steadily—from 627,000 residents in 1960 to 485,000 residents in 2000. If the American Community Survey [published by the U.S. Census Bureau] is to be believed (this is based on a smallish sample), New Orleans has lost another 40,000 inhabitants between 2000 and 2004. The 4.1 percent growth of the New Orleans metropolitan area in the 1990s put it far below the average U.S. population growth. It is hard to find a sunbelt city that is doing as badly as New Orleans.

All of this information cuts strongly against any claim that the rebuilding of New Orleans would be more beneficial for its residents, than their receiving a large check or voucher that would enable them not only to rebuild, but to transform, their lives.

COULD NEW ORLEANS, WITH SPENDING, SOMEHOW RETURN TO ITS LONG-PAST GLORY?

Granted, some previously great ports have managed to rebuild themselves around new industries. New York is now devoted to finance. San Francisco is the center for information technology.

But New Orleans was never able to reinvent itself, perhaps because it lacked the human capital that has been so heavily correlated with urban success over the past 50 years.

Moreover, New Orleans' port locale raises construction costs, relative to, say, the flat, featureless plains of Las Vegas. And New Orleans' climate is problematic relative to California. My own guess is that the city would have declined by more than it has, if it were not for the durability of its housing stock and other infrastructure. And

now, thanks to Hurricane Katrina, that last asset has been decimated.

Nor was New Orleans' housing stock very valuable, in the market, to begin with. The decline in New Orleans' population has been accompanied by economic distress and by low housing prices.

The 2000 Census reported that more than 27 percent of New Orleans residents were in poverty (relative to 12 percent for the U.S. as a whole). Median family income was only 64 percent of the median family income in the U.S. In 2004, according to the American Community Survey, the unemployment rate for the city was over 11 percent. And New Orleans' housing prices, prehurricane, remained far below those of the nation as a whole, providing further evidence of weak pre-existing demand for living in the city.

By most objective measures, the city, pre-hurricane, was not doing a good job of taking care of its poorer residents. For most students of urban distress, New Orleans was a problem, not an ideal. Poverty and continuing economic decline fed upon each other, delivering despair to many of the city's residents.

MORE LIMITED REBUILDING, COMBINED WITH AID TO RESIDENTS, MAY BE WISER

New Orleans' decline suggests that spending huge sums betting on the future of the city makes little sense. Perhaps there are externalities or coordination failures that argue for rebuilding, but they do not immediately come to mind. Most sensible theories about externalities suggest that giving checks to impacted residents, who then will move to Houston or Atlanta or Las Vegas, will actually reduce the negative spillovers from dysfunctional neighborhoods—not increase them.

None of this means, of course, that we shouldn't rebuild New Orleans' port or its pipelines. But rebuilding this basic infrastructure doesn't mean rebuilding the entire city, and it doesn't necessarily require federal funding.

The port and the energy sector are thriving economic entities. Their users can be charged for the costs of this infrastructure. We will all eventually pay those costs in the form of higher prices, but this is surely more efficient than funding reconstruction with tax dollars.

Rebuilding New Orleans requires a cost-benefit analysis that is far behind the scope of this essay. At this point, the only thing that I strongly endorse is having an open-minded national debate about costs and benefits. However, I suspect that for much of the proposed rebuilding, the costs will greatly outweigh the benefits.

One of the biggest problems of urban decline is how to help those residents caught in a declining city. Perhaps, if significant funds are given to New Orleans residents to help them start life anew in some more vibrant city, then there will be a silver lining to Katrina after all.

THE CONTINUING DEBATE:
Rebuilding New Orleans

What Is New

Data available six weeks after Hurricane Katrina struck shows it to have been the greatest natural disaster in American history but less devastating than initial estimates. As noted above, the death toll was much lower than first feared. Additionally, statistics in October indicated some 68,000 increased applications for unemployment assistance in the area, a figure far under some initial estimates of more than 400,000 jobs lost. By mid October the levees were repaired, the neighborhoods pumped dry, and electricity restored to about half the city. Residents were beginning to return in, what to some, were surprisingly large numbers, and many businesses were operating again. It would be a stretch to write that New Orleans was returning to normal, but it was showing signs of life.

As for the future of New Orleans, proposals range from abandoning most of it to creating a model city to replace one that had been plagued by a high unemployment, poverty, and violent crime rates and, reflecting that, had lost 16% of its population between 1980 and 2003. Whether that is possible sociologically or politically, how much it would cost, and who would pay for it and how all remain unclear. As for the public, polls taken soon after Katrina found mixed views on rebuilding New Orleans. One poll found 51% in favor of rebuilding the city where it stands. But another survey at the same time found that 54% supported abandoning the 80% of the city that had been deeply flooded. Paying for the cost was also a public opinion gnarl. Majorities of Americans opposed raising taxes, increasing deficit spending, or cutting domestic programs to pay the bill. A majority favored cutting expenses in Iraq, but that contradicted findings in other polls that a majority of Americans wanted U.S. forces to remain in Iraq until the situation there was stabilized (see Debate 19).

Where to Find More

To monitor New Orleans' recovery from Hurricane Katrina, visit the city's Web site, www.cityofno.com. Also helpful will be Louisiana's site, ww.state.la.us. Use the search function at Thomas, Congress' site at http://thomas.loc.gov/ to follow federal actions regarding hurricane relief and rebuilding. The American Planning Association at www.planning.org/ is one place to look at ideas for the future of New Orleans from an urban planning perspective.

What More to Do

Discuss rebuilding New Orleans in the larger context of national urban policy. New Orleans was a city beset by poverty and its accompanying problems, such as crime. Arguably, it needed a massive rejuvenation program anyway. Would you have favored spending $200 billion to do that prior to Hurricane Katrina? Why should the fact that Katrina was a natural disaster prompt massive federal aid in this case, arguably moving New Orleans to "the front of the line" before other equally or more needy urban areas? Also debate how to reconstitute New Orleans. It should be a model for urban redevelopment. What would that be like?

CREDITS

Amicus Curiae brief to the United States Supreme Court in *Grutter v. Bollinger* (2003).

Amicus Curiae brief to the United States Supreme Court in *Kelo v. New London* (2005).

Beach, William. Testimony during hearings on the "Balanced Budget Amendment" before the U.S. House of Representatives Committee on the Judiciary, Subcommittee on the Constitution, October 10, 2002.

Best, Judith A. Testimony during hearings on "Proposals for Electoral College Reform: H.J. Res. 28 and J.J. Res. 43" before the U.S. House of Representatives Committee on the Judiciary, Subcommittee on the Constitution, September 4, 1997.

Bond, Julian. Testimony during hearings on "Race and the Federal Death Penalty," before the U.S. Senate Committee on the Judiciary, Subcommittee on Constitution, Federalism, and Property Rights, June 13, 2001.

Brief of Petitioners to the U.S. Supreme Court in *Kelo v. New London* (2005).

Bush, George W. From his Address to the nation, July 5, 2005.

Byrd, Harry F. From *Congressional Record*, March 1, 2005.

Cain, Becky. Testimony during hearings on "Proposals for Electoral College Reform: H.J. Res. 28 and J.J. Res. 43" before the U.S. House of Representatives Committee on the Judiciary, Subcommittee on the Constitution, September 4, 1997.

Cannon, Carl. "She Can Win the White House," *Washington Monthly,* July/August 2005.

Charo, R. Alta. Testimony during hearings on "The Consequences of *Roe v. Wade* and *Doe v. Bolton,*" before the U.S. Senate Committee on the Judiciary, Subcommittee on the Constitution, Civil Rights and Property Rights, June 23, 2005.

Collett, Teresa. Testimony during hearings on "The Consequences of *Roe v. Wade* and *Doe v. Bolton,*" before the U.S. Senate Committee on the Judiciary, Subcommittee on the Constitution, Civil Rights and Property Rights, June 23, 2005.

Comey, James B. Testimony during hearings on "Reporters' Shield Legislation: Issues and Implications," before the U.S. Senate Committee on the Judiciary, July 20, 2005.

Farber, Daniel A. From "Disarmed by Time: The Second Amendment and the Failure of Originalism," *Chicago-Kent Law Review*, Vol. 76, No. 1 (2000). Reprinted by permission of the author.

Glaeser, Edward. "Should the Government Rebuild New Orleans, Or Just Give Residents Checks?" *The Economists' Voice*, September, 2005.

Hatch, Orrin G. From *Congressional Record*, May 10, 2005.

Hibbing, John R. Testimony during hearings on "Limiting Terms of Office for Members of the U.S. Senate and U.S. House of Representatives," U.S. House of Representatives, Committee on the Judiciary, Subcommittee on the Constitution, January 22, 1997.

Jacob, Paul. Testimony during hearings on "Limiting Terms of Office for Members of the U.S. Senate and U.S. House of Representatives," U.S. House of Representatives, Committee on the Judiciary, Subcommittee on the Constitution, January 22, 1997.

Kogan, Richard. Testimony during hearings on the "Balanced Budget Amendment" before the U.S. House of Representatives Committee on the Judiciary, Subcommittee on the Constitution, October 10, 2002.

Malcolm, Joyce. "Infringement," *Common-place*, Vol. 2: No. 4, July 2002. http://www.common-place.org/. Copyright © 2002 by Common-place: The Interactive Journal of Early American Life. Reprinted by permission.

McBride, Andrew. Testimony during hearings on "Race and the Federal Death Penalty," before the U.S. Senate Committee on the Judiciary, Subcommittee on Constitution, Federalism, and Property Rights, June 13, 2001.

Munoz, Vincent Phillip. Testimony during hearings on "Beyond the Pledge of Allegiance: Hostility to Religious Expression in the Public Square," before the U.S. Senate Committee on the Judiciary, June 8, 2004.

O'Connor, Sandra Day. Opinion in *Gonzales v. Raich*, U.S. Supreme Court, June 6, 2005.

O'Sullivan John. "Who Are We?" from *The American Conservative*, July 19, 2004. http://www.amconmag.com. All rights reserved. Reprinted with permission of Valeo IP, 800-271-7874.

Pearlstine, Norman. Testimony during hearings on "Reporters' Shield Legislation: Issues and Implications," before the U.S. Senate Committee on the Judiciary, July 20, 2005.

Renfro, Wesley B., and Brian Urlacher. "With Civil War Looming the United States Must Withdraw from Iraq," an essay written for this volume, October 2005.

Rogers, Melissa. Testimony during hearings on "Beyond the Pledge of Allegiance: Hostility to Religious Expression in the Public Square," before the U.S. Senate Committee on the Judiciary, June 8, 2004.

Ross-Edwards, Amanda. "The Department of Education and Title IX: Flawed Interpretation and Implementation," an essay written for this volume, October 2003.

Shain, Yossi. From "For Ethnic Americans, The Old Country Calls," *Foreign Service Journal*, October 2000. Reprinted by permission of Yossi Shain.

Siddique, Asheesh. "The New Nativism," *Campus Progress News*, Spring 2005.

Simcox, Chris. Testimony during hearings on "Securing Our Borders: What We Have Learned From Government Initiatives and Citizen Patrols," before the U.S. House of Representatives Committee on Government Reform, May 12, 2005.

Sleeper, Jim. Review of Samuel Huntington's *Who Are We: The Challenges to America's National Identity*, History News Network, May 3, 2004. Originally appeared in the *Los Angeles Times*. Reprinted by permission of the author.

Spaulding, Matthew. Testimony during hearings on "Maximizing Voter Choice: Opening the Presidency to Naturalized Americans," before the U.S. Senate Judiciary Committee, October 5, 2004.

Stevens, John Paul III. Opinion in *Gonzales v. Raich*, U.S. Supreme Court, June 6, 2005.

Stoner, James R. Jr. "Saving a Great City: Why America should rebuild New Orleans," *The Weekly Standard,* Sept 26, 2005.

Sullivan, Amy. "Not So Fast," *Washington Monthly*, July/August 2005.

Sweet, Judith. U.S. Department of Education, Secretary's Commission on Opportunity in Athletics, Hearings, August 27, 2002.

Wheatcroft, Geoffrey. "Hyphenated Americans," *Guardian Unlimited Online*, April 25, 2000. Reprinted by permission of the author.

Yinger, John. Testimony during hearings on "Maximizing Voter Choice: Opening the Presidency to Naturalized Americans," before the U.S. Senate Judiciary Committee, October 5, 2004.